Customizing Chef

Jon Cowie

Beijing · Cambridge · Farnham · Köln · Sebastopol · Tokyo

Customizing Chef

by Jon Cowie

Printed in the United States of America.

Published by O'Reilly Media, Inc., 1005 Gravenstein Highway North, Sebastopol, CA 95472.

O'Reilly books may be purchased for educational, business, or sales promotional use. Online editions are also available for most titles (*http://safaribooksonline.com*). For more information, contact our corporate/institutional sales department: 800-998-9938 or *corporate@oreilly.com*.

Editors: Courtney Nash and Brian Anderson	**Indexer:** Wendy Catalano
Production Editor: Nicole Shelby	**Cover Designer:** Ellie Volckhausen
Copyeditor: Rachel Head	**Interior Designer:** David Futato
Proofreader: Gillian McGarvey	**Illustrator:** Rebecca Demarest

September 2014:   First Edition

Revision History for the First Edition:

2014-08-26:   First release

See *http://oreilly.com/catalog/errata.csp?isbn=9781491949351* for release details.

ISBN: 978-1-491-94935-1

[LSI]

This book is dedicated to my uncle, David Shrimpton, without whose encouragement and guidance I would likely never have entered this profession. He was a great friend and mentor to all of his students at the University of Kent as well as to myself, and is greatly missed by all who knew and loved him.

Table of Contents

Part I. Chef and Ruby 101

Part II.   Customizing Chef Runs

Part IV. Other Customizations

Foreword

One of the things I most wanted out of Chef was that it be flexible enough to solve problems I couldn't imagine. My experience as a systems administrator told me that no matter how much I learned, there was always something new coming around the corner. I needed a systems automation tool that would be able to help me when I met the unexpected.

Over the lifetime of Chef, I've had the opportunity to witness firsthand what happens when you take Chef's flexibility and pair it with someone who is willing to push it in new directions. The result is almost always the same: that person quickly becomes a satisfied Chef user. It's not actually because of anything Chef did; it's because the user took control of his environment, and crafted with his own hands the perfect solution to his problem. The result is a satisfaction that simply using a tool can never provide.

Jon Cowie has written the ideal book to help you reach that place. He's lived in that space, and his deep understanding of what's possible with Chef combined with practical application of those things in real, messy environments makes him the perfect person to guide you on your journey. I couldn't be prouder to have him in the Chef community, and to have him as the author of this book.

I'm excited to see what you build, and I hope that you find the same joy in solving your problems that I do.

—Adam Jacob
Chief Dev Officer at Chef

Preface

Picture the scene. It's 3 AM. An ops engineer or developer has just been paged. Her brain feels sluggish; simple tasks seem to take just that little bit longer and her body is telling her it's still asleep. This state of tiredness is something that many of us in on-call rotations often deal with as part of our jobs, albeit not a particularly welcome one.

When debugging complex issues in this state, I find myself most grateful for the modern incarnations of configuration management (CM) systems that we as operations professionals are able to make use of today. Although configuration management has been around for a long time, it's only in the last few years that CM systems like Chef, Puppet, CFEngine, Ansible, and SaltStack have come along to evolve these tools from loosely-coupled collections of shell scripts and wiki pages into the rich orchestration frameworks we have today.

When I get paged at 3 AM, I'm quickly able to introspect into any changes that might have been made to the server or system in question and kick-start the late-night troubleshooting process. Imagine if instead of being able to run one command to look at the running config on one of my servers, I instead had to trawl through an internal wiki to find the install document that detailed that specific configuration. This very process might in fact be what some of you are using right now, and to you I say: be strong, brave engineer! There is hope and its name is configuration management!

In this book, we focus on Chef, developed and maintained by Chef, Inc. Chef, Inc. describes Chef as a *server and infrastructure automation tool*, but it could equally be described as a CM system or using any of a number of other definitions.

Chef is an incredibly feature-rich and powerful tool designed to provide a framework for users of any of the major operating systems to automate anything they want. Simply put, Chef is a generic platform that provides a number of built-in tools, resources, and services to facilitate this automation. Typically, the people at Chef, Inc. do not advocate any of these as "the one true way." And how could they? You, dear reader, are one of the greatest experts in the world on your particular infrastructure, if not *the* expert. You understand in detail the servers and operating systems you run; the software stacks that sit on top; and the unique structure, workflows, and processes that keep your business running. The chances are good that out of the box, Chef will allow you to automate a great deal of these systems, especially if you leverage the Chef Supermarket (*http://bit.ly/chef-super*), where Chef users upload cookbooks and recipes for their particular systems and software.

But what do you do when you have a specific requirement for something Chef doesn't provide out of the box? You customize, of course! One of Chef's greatest strengths is that it is nearly infinitely customizable. You can hook Chef into your monitoring systems; you can modify the built-in tooling and processes; you can even add your *own* tooling. But where do you start? You may have a rough idea of what you'd like to achieve, but where in Chef should you add your custom piece? How do you make sure it will work nicely alongside your production environment? That's where this book comes in.

I'm going to take you on a journey through the internals of Chef, exploring how everything fits together, the various places you can hook in custom code, and when it's appropriate to use each one. We'll also look at whether you *should* customize—although this book is very much about helping you to customize Chef, it would be a fallacy for me to tell you that just because you *can* customize something, you automatically *should*. As someone once said, *with great power comes great responsibility.*[1]

Who This Book Is For

This book is designed for Chef users who are already comfortable with the basics of using Chef and writing simple recipes, and are looking to level up their Chef skills to better understand how Chef works and customize it beyond the features it offers out of the box. You might only be interested in customizing specific areas of Chef, such as creating your own resources and providers to use in recipes, or you may be looking for a more comprehensive understanding of how Chef functions under the hood. Either way, if you're interested in customizing Chef, this is the book for you.

Going into this book, you should already be familiar with writing Chef cookbooks using the built-in resource types provided with Chef, and be comfortable using tools such as chef-client to carry out a Chef run on a node. You should have a good grasp of at least the Ruby needed to write cookbooks—you don't need to know any object-oriented programming or any of Ruby's more advanced features, but you should be comfortable with some of the basic techniques, such as variables and `if` statements.

If you're not quite at that stage yet, I recommend you take a look at Learning Chef by Mischa Taylor and Seth Vargo, which covers in detail all of the Chef essentials required to follow the material presented here. By the end of *Customizing Chef*, my hope is that

---

1. Though often attributed to Peter Parker's Uncle Ben, the first literary usage of this phrase appears to have been by François-Marie Arouet, a.k.a. Voltaire.

you will have a solid understanding of how Chef works under the hood, when and where it can be customized, and have the skills needed to dive in and start creating customizations of your own.

How This Book Is Organized

This book is broken down into several parts, each covering different aspects of customizing Chef:

Part I, Chef and Ruby 101
> The first part of the book deals with what you might consider the foundational material needed to customize Chef. In Chapter 1 we take a look at the history and design principles of Chef, moving on to examine the different Chef setups typically used and the prerequisites for the material in this book.
>
> Chapter 2 introduces some Ruby concepts you need to know in order to progress from writing recipe code to writing customizations. Rather than trying to teach the entirety of the Ruby programming language, this chapter focuses on those aspects that will be used throughout the rest of the book.
>
> We close off Part I in Chapter 3 by diving into the internals of Chef to look at how the different components of Chef fit together, the anatomy of a Chef run, and how to make use of the Chef source code to level up your knowledge.
>
> Even if you're only interested in customizing specific aspects of Chef, I recommend reading Part I in its entirety, as the material covered is universally applicable to all types of Chef customizations covered throughout the remainder of the book.

Part II, Customizing Chef Runs
> The second part of the book covers the various customization types Chef supports which allow us to modify and tap into the Chef run process. We start off in Chapter 4 by learning about how we can extend Chef's Ohai tool to enhance the information Chef stores about our nodes.
>
> Chapter 5 looks at the handler model used by Chef, which allows us to add customizable responses to various conditions that occur during the course of our Chef runs (such as the run starting, succeeding, or failing).
>
> We finish off Part II in Chapter 6 by examining the rich and customizable event stream built up by Chef throughout the course of a run, and how we can tap into this event stream to modify the output produced by chef-client and leverage this event data in our own reporting systems.

Part III, Customizing Recipes

The third part of the book focuses on the different sorts of recipe customizations Chef supports to allow us to level up our recipes with custom resource blocks of our own.

We start off in Chapter 7 by learning about definitions, the simplest type of recipe customization, and libraries, which allow us to incorporate custom Ruby helpers to power our recipe code.

Chapter 8 goes on to look at Chef's lightweight resources and providers, which allow us to create more advanced and fully featured resources to use in our recipe code through the use of special domain-specific languages (DSLs), which abstract away much of the more complex Ruby code.

We finish Part III in Chapter 9 by diving into heavyweight resources and providers, which allow us to use native Ruby to create even more powerful resources and providers at the expense of some of the abstractions and simplicity afforded by their lightweight equivalents.

Because many of the customization types in Part III could be used to implement any specific recipe customization, this part of the book also focuses heavily on which customization types might be best to use in different situations.

Part IV, Other Customizations

We close off the book in Part IV by looking at some of the other customization types supported by Chef, and some advice and resources for contributing customizations back to the community.

We start off in Chapter 10 by learning about the `knife` command-line tool supplied with Chef and how we can create our own plugins to implement custom functionality.

In Chapter 11 we dive into the Chef API to learn how we can tap into the data from our own scripts and tools that the Chef server stores, regardless of the programming language we choose to use.

We close off Part IV (and the book) in Chapter 12 by examining some best practices and advice for contributing customizations back to the Chef community, and some of the tools and resources that are typically used for distributing customizations.

Conventions Used in This Book

The following typographical conventions are used in this book:

Italic

Indicates new terms, URLs, email addresses, filenames and file extensions, and directory and pathnames.

`Constant width`

Used for program listings, as well as within paragraphs to refer to program elements such as variable or function names, cookbooks, data types, environment variables, statements, and keywords. Also used for commands and their output.

`Constant width bold`

Shows commands or other text that should be typed literally by the user.

`Constant width italic`

Shows text that should be replaced with user-supplied values or by values determined by context.

 This element signifies a tip or suggestion.

 This element signifies a general note.

 This element indicates a warning or caution.

Using Code Examples

Supplemental material (code examples, exercises, etc.) is available for download at *https://github.com/jonlives/customizing_chef*.

This book is here to help you get your job done. In general, if example code is offered with this book, you may use it in your programs and documentation. You do not need to contact us for permission unless you're reproducing a significant portion of the code. For example, writing a program that uses several chunks of code from this book does not require permission. Selling or distributing a CD-ROM of examples from O'Reilly books does require permission. Answering a question by citing this book and quoting example code does not require permission. Incorporating a significant amount of example code from this book into your product's documentation does require permission.

We appreciate, but do not require, attribution. An attribution usually includes the title, author, publisher, and ISBN. For example: "*Customizing Chef* by Jon Cowie (O'Reilly). Copyright 2014 Jonathan Cowie, 978-1-491-94935-1."

If you feel your use of code examples falls outside fair use or the permission given above, feel free to contact us at *permissions@oreilly.com*.

Safari® Books Online

 *Safari Books Online* is an on-demand digital library that delivers expert content in both book and video form from the world's leading authors in technology and business.

Technology professionals, software developers, web designers, and business and crea- tive professionals use Safari Books Online as their primary resource for research, prob- lem solving, learning, and certification training.

Safari Books Online offers a range of plans and pricing for enterprise, government, education, and individuals.

Members have access to thousands of books, training videos, and prepublication manu- scripts in one fully searchable database from publishers like O'Reilly Media, Prentice Hall Professional, Addison-Wesley Professional, Microsoft Press, Sams, Que, Peachpit Press, Focal Press, Cisco Press, John Wiley & Sons, Syngress, Morgan Kaufmann, IBM Redbooks, Packt, Adobe Press, FT Press, Apress, Manning, New Riders, McGraw-Hill, Jones & Bartlett, Course Technology, and hundreds more. For more information about Safari Books Online, please visit us online.

How to Contact Us

Please address comments and questions concerning this book to the publisher:

O'Reilly Media, Inc.
1005 Gravenstein Highway North
Sebastopol, CA 95472
800-998-9938 (in the United States or Canada)
707-829-0515 (international or local)
707-829-0104 (fax)

We have a web page for this book, where we list errata, examples, and any additional information. You can access this page at *http://bit.ly/customizing-chef*.

To comment or ask technical questions about this book, send email to *bookques tions@oreilly.com*.

For more information about our books, courses, conferences, and news, see our website at *http://www.oreilly.com*.

Find us on Facebook: *http://facebook.com/oreilly*

Follow us on Twitter: *http://twitter.com/oreillymedia*

Watch us on YouTube: *http://www.youtube.com/oreillymedia*

Acknowledgments

Customizing Chef would not have been possible without the help and guidance of many friends, colleagues, and family members.

I'd like to thank the entire team at O'Reilly—Courtney Nash for helping me get this project off the ground, my editor Brian Anderson for his editorial nous and patience, my production editor Nicole Shelby for taking charge of getting the manuscript from first draft to print-ready, and everybody else involved in making this book happen. I'd also like to give special thanks to Mike Rembetsy and John Allspaw at Etsy for their encouragement, support, and tolerance while I spent nine months writing this book.

Many thanks also go to my tech reviewers: Seth Vargo at Chef Inc.; Gergely Hodicska at Ustream; Pete Bellisano, Ben Burry, Laurie Denness, Ryan Frantz, and Daniel Schauenberg at Etsy; and last but not least the Sparkly Devops Princesses Jennifer Davis at Chef, Inc. and Katherine Daniels at GameChanger Media. Thanks also go to Serdar Sutay and Daniel DeLeo at Chef, Inc., and Fletcher Nichol at Heavy Water Operations for their accessibility and sanity checking at various points during this project.

Most importantly, this book would never have been possible without the continual love, support, and infinite patience of my wonderful wife Agne throughout the entire project.

Chef and Ruby 101

The first part of the book focuses on the essential background material you need to begin customizing Chef. We look at:

- An introduction to configuration management, Chef, and the current state of the customization landscape
- How to level up your Ruby knowledge with object-oriented programming techniques
- The internals of Chef's server and client components and how a Chef run functions under the hood

## CHAPTER 1

Introduction

Before we dive into the internals of Chef and look at all the different things we can customize, let's take a step back, remind ourselves what we're dealing with when we talk about configuration management, and look at why you might want or need to customize Chef in the first place and what you need to know to get the most out of this book.

What Is Configuration Management?

> Time stands still for no man.
>
> — Anonymous

The term *configuration management* has been in common usage since the 1950s, when the US Air Force developed an approach to managing the extremely complex manufacturing processes involved in producing military equipment. The USAF needed a way to make sure that its equipment performed as required, while also functioning as expected and complying with the relevant military equipment standards. The term was codified as an actual standard in the early 1960s, and the ideas underpinning CM have since been adopted by a number of other industries, such as civil and industrial engineering and, of course, computing.

What we think of as configuration management in the IT sense has been around in one form or another for as long as people have been running more than one computer, although it was not always recognized as such. Looking back through the mists of time to the era of mainframes and minicomputers, we find system administrators tending single, monolithic systems, every tunable setting and parameter committed to memory or to multivolume technical manuals. Computers of any description were far outside the reach of most companies—only the largest corporations and university labs could afford the asking price. Soon, however, as computing hardware became more common, prices dropped to within the reach of more and more companies, and commoditized "cloud" computing became commonplace. The exploding usage of computers and the corresponding increase in the number of sysadmins that were needed to look after them began to make this model of a single repository of knowledge unsustainable.

The industry quickly recognized this problem, and started to document everything. Thus was born the era of internal configuration guides, document stores, and wikis full of all the information a new hire might need to get up to speed on the employer's infrastructure and systems. This approach, however, also had its limits. As the usage of computers expanded across the globe and more and more companies started developing software systems, manually updated documentation became more and more of a chore to keep relevant and up-to-date. So, people started automating configuration tasks using whatever scripting languages they had on hand. These custom scripts worked perfectly well for a while. They made configuring systems and software much easier because people didn't have to copy and paste from the manual any more.

Eventually, though, progress overtook the industry again. Individuals within the same infrastructure started using different architectures, software versions, and configuration settings. All of a sudden, people found themselves having to maintain an increasing number of very complex scripts to manage all the different permutations they required, cater to all the possible ways these scripted processes could fail, and so on. It was this very problem that led to the development of what we now recognize as CM in the operations sense.

In 1993, a postdoc at Oslo University in Norway named Mark Burgess decided that he'd had quite enough of managing all of these scripts, thank you very much. Mark wrote the very first version of the configuration engine, CFEngine (*http://cfengine.com*), to provide an architecture- and OS-independent way of managing the Unix workstations he was responsible for at the time. This was the first of what we now recognize as configuration management systems.

In the years since CFEngine was first developed, a number of other CM systems were developed to satisfy various requirements that existing tools did not provide for. In 2005 Luke Kanies released Puppet, which was the predominant alternative to CFEngine until Chef came along in 2009. Since then, a number of other CM systems (such as Ansible and SaltStack) have been released, but at the time of this writing, CFEngine, Puppet, and Chef are the dominant players in the space.

So Why Chef?

Why, then, did Chef get written when there were already two well-established and relatively mature CM systems to choose from?

The foundation of Chef can be traced back to a consulting company named HJK Solutions (now better known as Chef, Inc.) that specialized in automating the configuration of infrastructure for startup companies. Through this work, HJK Solutions came to realize that the utopia of fully automated infrastructures was becoming a real possibility, even for companies without a staff of highly experienced operations engineers. But things weren't quite at that stage yet—HJK observed a number of problems with what could be achieved with existing CM systems that needed to be solved first. Here were a few of the main concerns:

Service-oriented architecture

In order for fully automated infrastructure to become a possibility, configuration management systems needed to move toward a service-oriented architecture instead of defining a canonical model of infrastructure. That is, rather than defining the infrastructure configuration in stone, CM systems needed to be able to expose as much data as possible about the state of the infrastructure to allow you to better manage its automation.

Sharable code

For infrastructure as code to work effectively, people needed to be able to *share* the code that built their infrastructure. This is a principle found in traditional software development too—code should be modular, clean, and not repetitive. HJK found that the existing tools didn't provide the sort of generic, reusable building blocks necessary to allow people to effectively share and reuse their infrastructure code.

The folks at HJK didn't think that any other open source CM systems met the requirements they saw as necessary to achieve fully automated infrastructure, so they created Chef. But did they succeed? What makes Chef different from the other CM systems out there, and why might you want to use it? Because you're reading this book, you likely already have an idea of the reasons Chef was chosen by your organization and the key differentiators between Chef and its contemporaries, but I'd like to highlight a few of them anyway:

Chef frees people up where possible

Like other CM systems, Chef aims to help remove people from the process of automating infrastructure whenever possible. This may sound like the classic joke about replacing yourself with a very small shell script, but think about it—the less time you spend having to keep your server configurations in sync, installing the right combinations of packages, and so on, the more time you have to spend doing far more interesting things! You still have to write your infrastructure automation code, of course, but after you've done that Chef takes care of the rest.

Everything is Ruby

Chef uses Ruby as its configuration language, as opposed to a custom DSL. On the surface, the language used to write Chef cookbooks might not always *look* like regular Ruby, but it is.

Chef is infinitely extensible

Chef is infinitely extensible. Right from the outset, Chef was designed to integrate with any system you choose to use, and to allow any system to integrate with it. The people at Chef, Inc. don't see Chef as a carved stone tablet that represents your infrastructure; they see it as a service layer that exposes data about how your infrastructure is behaving and what it looks like. It is this extensibility and data service that allow the sorts of customizations we'll look at in this book.

Chef is modular

Chef was also designed from the ground up to allow you to build your automated infrastructure using modular, reusable components. Chef cookbooks are formed out of discrete "chunks" of automation behavior that can be extended, shared, and reused across your infrastructure.

In Chef, order matters

Chef guarantees that it will run things in the same order, every time. If you define a run list in Chef, no matter how many Chef runs you perform, the resources in that run list will always be applied in the same order. See Chapter 3 for more on how Chef runs are executed.

Thick client, thin server

Chef does as much work as it can on the node being configured rather than the server. The Chef server is responsible for storing, managing, and shipping cookbooks, files, and other data to client nodes, which then run your infrastructure code. Although all of the out-of-the-box client tools supplied with Chef are written in Ruby, the HTTP-based API of the Chef servers means that it can also be accessed using variety of programming languages—some of these client libraries are discussed in Chapter 11.

Chef is a system state service

The *thin server* model allows Chef to store a copy of the "state" of each node on the server, which includes data like the recipes applied to the server, when it last completed a Chef run, its hardware configuration, etc. By capturing this information in a central location, the Chef server is able to provide us with a "system state" service that can tell us the current state of the node, what the state of the node was at the end of the last chef-client run, and what the state of the node should be at the end of the current chef-client run.

Resource signals

Resources in Chef cookbooks are able to "signal" other resources to perform particular actions, allowing you to add conditional logic paths into your infrastructure code while still retaining the modularity and reusability that Chef was designed to provide. You are also able to reuse the same resource several times without redefining it—for example, you can define a "service" resource to control your MySQL server and then use that resource to stop and start your MySQL server by simply instructing the resource to perform different actions.

Chef gives you nearly limitless flexibility to automate your infrastructure as you see fit. It has never been positioned as a panacea to cure all your ills, or magically automate all of the legacy cruft out of that eight-year-old server in the corner. What Chef *is*, however, is a framework designed to give you all of the tools you need to automate your infrastructure however you want.

Think Critically

Ultimately, as technology professionals, our primary function is to add value to our businesses, regardless of how much time we spend writing code or configuring servers. This is just as true for operations engineers and developers as it is for frontline sales and marketing staff. Developers might not be on the front lines shifting product or selling to customers, but we code and configure the infrastructure and platforms that allow our businesses to function in the Internet age. Every business is different, and only that business can make the decisions about what will add value and what won't. As a technical expert in your company, you know better than me, or Chef, Inc., or anyone else for that matter about what adds value to your particular company.

This is worth remembering, as it is the principal reason that Chef, Inc. will not typically advocate particular workflows or tooling combinations as the "canonical" Chef way of doing things, and also the reason that I will not do so in this book. The instant a methodology or technique is declared canonical, anything else is considered to be wrong— even if it might be what makes the most sense for your particular use case. Chef is categorically *not* a system that requires you to do anything in a particular way; rather, it provides you with everything you need to make those decisions for yourself and for the good of your business. As with all systems, however, there *are* some best practices —we'll look at some of those throughout the course of this book.

Simply put, Chef gives you the tools and flexibility to craft infrastructure code that is right for you, your team, and your business. It won't get in the way and it won't try and force you down a particular path. My aim for this book is to help you gain a deeper understanding of how you can make use of this flexibility and extensibility so you can take what you learn and add even more value to your business. To this end, I want you to question everything you read in this book and ask yourself if it's right for you.

I can certainly guarantee that the content of this book will be technically accurate and as comprehensive as I can possibly make it, but just as Chef cannot automate your business needs automatically, I cannot tell you what is best for your company or what will solve your specific infrastructure automation problems. What I *can* do is give you the knowledge and techniques to make you better able to solve those problems for yourself.

In my day job, I work in operations for Etsy, an online marketplace where people around the world connect to buy and sell unique goods. Etsy is fairly well known for its engineering culture, which is rooted in the DevOps movement. We are not particularly driven by procedures or rigid workflows. I usually don't have to deal with committees to get things done, and am given a high degree of autonomy to perform my job. I think it's important to frame the employment background I come from because yours may be very different.

You may work for a small startup where you are the only operations engineer and have very little time for anything but the most crucial work. You may work for a large multinational corporation with a many-layered change control process and ITIL compliance to worry about. You may work for a company that stores credit card data and has to maintain PCI-DSS compliance, with all the procedural and auditing headaches that entails. Every single one of you reading this book comes from a different employment background, and you're all using Chef to solve different problems.

So I propose a pact. I promise to do my best to write an interesting, relevant book that is full of helpful information, useful code snippets, and practical advice for how to approach customizing Chef. And in turn, after I've armed you with all of the knowledge and techniques that I can, you promise to carefully look at the problems you're trying to solve and think critically about the best way to do that. What I'm asking you to consider when looking at customizing your Chef setup is not whether you *can* do something, but whether you *should*. And I have a couple of suggestions to help you do that…

Meet AwesomeInc

To help with the process of critically examining the material covered in this book from the perspective of a business trying to solve real problems, I'd like to introduce AwesomeInc, a fictional company whose operations team and developers will be working through a project to customize various aspects of their Chef infrastructure.

AwesomeInc is a midsize company of around 200 staff based in California that produces and sells custom car parts. It was founded in 2005 by two siblings, Chad and Kate Awesome, who started a small business customizing their friends' cars in their parents' driveway. The business grew rapidly as word spread, and AwesomeInc now ships its own line of custom car parts all across the US and Canada. Business has been so good recently that the executive team decided that this is the year to go international!

AwesomeInc has 3 dedicated operations engineers and 15 full-time development staff, all led by Mike, the straight-shooting, hard-negotiating but secretly lovable Director of Engineering. They've already rolled out Chef across their suite of 150 servers, a mix of both physical hardware and virtualized servers in the cloud. They're using the open source version of Chef server, hosted internally.

Their ops staff and developers are well versed in writing basic cookbooks, and have been through Chef, Inc's "Chef fundamentals" training. But now the word has come down from on high that with the push to go international, AwesomeInc's infrastructure will be moving from a single system to separate geographically diverse systems, linking back to a central stock database in the US.

Spotting a chance to get ahead of the game, Mike instructs his team to do an audit of their servers and make sure that all of their cookbooks are up-to-date prior to commencing the work to support multiple locations. When the team completes its audit, however, it turns out that things aren't quite as rosy as they'd hoped.

Although the majority of AwesomeInc's cookbooks are working perfectly and are up-to-date, there are a few cookbooks that have been modified and not tested properly, and that have been causing Chef runs to fail silently on a number of AwesomeInc's servers. Additionally, AwesomeInc developers are developing a customized stock management tool to distribute to each new location and are struggling with duplicated recipe code to handle the different permutations supported by the tool.

Mike decides to get a grip on the situation and calls a team meeting to ticket up the cleanup work that's needed to bring the cookbooks back up to snuff, and look at ways to avoid the issues they've been seeing. During the meeting, a number of his operations team members express concern about how they'll cope with the increased headcount that will follow AwesomeInc's international expansion. It turns out that operations staff and developers are already beginning to find themselves treading on each other's toes when they make Chef changes, and it's becoming increasingly hard to keep track of what has been changed by whom. The team is worried that with the increased frequency of changes that will likely follow the hiring of more engineering staff, it will become harder and harder to maintain stable systems.

They mull over these issues for a few days, and quickly come to the consensus that things need to change. But then Mike asks the million-dollar question: how do we fix this? The team rapidly realize that out of the box, Chef won't fix these problems for them. Their only option is to customize Chef to give them more visibility into how it's running on their servers, who is making changes and when, and what those changes are doing.

As we work through the material in this book, we'll follow the team at AwesomeInc as they learn about the possibilities for customizing Chef, and what they can do to solve the specific problems they've encountered in the past. We'll focus on what solutions they can make use of as well as why each might be a good or bad idea. In addition, we'll look at what members of the Chef community have done to solve the same problems in the real world—these techniques are no use, after all, if they don't transfer to real life.

Criteria for Customization

With great power comes great responsibility.

— Voltaire (François-Marie Arouet)

You could be forgiven for thinking that having written a book called *Customizing Chef*, my advice to you would always be to customize Chef. It isn't. I'd much rather you carefully consider each customization you're thinking about making, possibly deciding that maybe it's not the best idea, than make a whole bunch of customizations that don't really help you.

One of the recurring problems that our industry as a whole suffers from is a terminal case of the "new shinies." We're all of us somewhat prone to taking a new methodology or tool and trying to make it do *everything*, regardless of whether or not it is actually well-suited to those things.

With a system as flexible and customizable as Chef, you're more limited by your imagination than by anything technical, and that carries with it the risk of new-shiny overtaking a rational decision-making process. So how do you make sure that when you customize Chef, you're doing it for well-thought-out reasons that will ultimately add value to your business? We've met AwesomeInc and begun to explore the challenges they're dealing with, but what happens when your specific challenges don't mesh nicely with my carefully selected examples?

Let's look at some more general criteria you can use to vet proposed customizations. When you're thinking about developing or implementing customizations to your Chef setup, I want you to come back to this list and mentally check off how many criteria are satisfied. If the answer is none, it's probably time to take a really careful look at why you're considering the customization—you might be doing it because you can, rather than because you should. If you're like me and enjoy symmetry and easy-to-remember acronyms, remember SMVMS:

Simplicity

Will the customization you're considering make something simpler? This could range from simplifying your deployment process by automating cookbook upload and testing, through cleaning up an old legacy recipe full of labyrinthine control statements, all the way to making it easier for a new hire to work with your Apache configurations.

Modularity

Will the customization you're considering make your infrastructure code more modular and reusable? Are you taking multiple slightly modified chunks of "copy-pasta" code and refining them into a more generic modular resource that can be defined once and then called from the various places that need it?

Visibility

Will the customization you're considering increase your visibility into your Chef infrastructure? Will it let you introspect deeper into your Chef runs than you've ever been able to before? Will it generate metrics for you so you can tell at a glance whether your Chef runs are getting slower or faster? Will people be able to gain greater awareness of when Chef changes have gone live and what exactly they did?

Maintainability

Will the customization you're considering make it easier for your Chef users to maintain your infrastructure codebase? Will it make people less afraid to change the one cookbook that runs on all of your servers? When a new hire starts, will she be able to tear up the manual of voodoo incantations previously required to work with this code?

Scalability

Will the customization you're considering help your infrastructure scale to meet your business's growth needs? Have you hit the point where you need to diversify your infrastructure from a single data center, and all of a sudden the assumptions you made in your recipes about server naming conventions break down? Are you building out a small software stack into a much larger n-tier cluster?

Let's look in a little more detail at some questions the folks at AwesomeInc asked themselves when looking at how to solve the problems they identified and how they map to the "Criteria for Customization" just discussed—all are excellent candidates for a sound decision to customize, but for different reasons.

How Do We Find Out When Our Chef Runs Are Failing, and Why?

The folks at AwesomeInc are looking to improve the visibility they have into Chef and how it's performing. Out of the box, Chef will expose some information to you through both the web UI and the command line on when a particular node last checked in with the Chef server and what its current run list is, but it won't tell you whether or not the last Chef run failed or the causes of any failures. This might sound like somewhat of an omission, but look at it this way: bearing in mind the wide variety of notification and alerting systems out there, how should Chef expose this information to a Windows user? A Linux user? Should it *always* alert on every failed run?

Rather than trying to solve all possible use cases, Chef, Inc. has made it extremely easy to capture this information in Chef so that you can handle it in a way that works well with your particular choice of monitoring and alerting software. We'll look in more detail at how you can capture and make use of this information in Chapter 5.

Some Chef setups, such as chef-solo, do not use a centralized Chef server and will not support some types of customization, such as those making use of persistent node attributes. Please see "Chef Installation Types and Limitations" on page 18 for more details.

How Do We Simplify Our Recipes to Reduce the Amount of Replicated Code?

The team at AwesomeInc are looking to improve both the modularity and the simplicity of their infrastructure code. As we've already seen, Chef provides building blocks and tools to let you automate your infrastructure however you want. Out of the box it provides resources for a number of operations, from configuring users through downloading remote files to managing packages and services. But like Chef itself, these resources are designed to be as simple and generic as possible. Chef doesn't provide a built-in resource for configuring a virtual host in Apache, for example, although this can still be done with a combination of out-of-the-box resources.

Again, though, this is where the extensibility and flexibility of Chef really come in handy. There is nothing to stop you from writing your own resource to configure Apache virtual hosts, or set up Ruby Version Manager (RVM) on your development workstations, or configure access to your MySQL databases. The sky is the limit here—Chef gives you the framework and lets you decide for yourself. We'll look at how to write your own resources and recipe logic in Part III.

How Do We Stop Our Developers and Ops Staff from Treading All over Each Other's Changes?

The people at AwesomeInc are looking to improve the visibility they have into Chef changes and the scalability of their engineering organization so that they can increase their headcount without compromising the stability of their infrastructure with a sudden increase in the volume of Chef changes. Out of the box, Chef comes with Knife, a command-line tool that lets you perform a number of operations such as uploading cookbooks, configuring node run lists, running commands across a group of servers, and running search queries against your infrastructure. The team at AwesomeInc have been using these built-in Knife commands to work with Chef.

Knife ships with a powerful set of features, but once again, it is specifically designed to be as generic as possible. Knife does not ship with built-in functionality to spin up nodes on Amazon EC2. It does not ship with functionality to stop teams with large numbers of Chef users from treading on each other's toes (although it does have a flag to stop you from uploading the same cookbook version twice). What Knife *does* ship with is a design that allows it to be customized easily and extensively. We'll look at how to customize Knife in Chapter 10.

Some Chef setups, such as chef-solo, do not use a centralized Chef server and will not work with some Knife commands or plugins. Please see "Chef Installation Types and Limitations" on page 18 for more details.

State of the Customization Nation

Now that we've examined the example scenarios we'll be working through in this book and looked at some general criteria to weigh your customization ideas against, let's get those creative juices flowing and have a brief look at some of the customizations the Chef community have already produced and the problems they were trying to solve. This is by no means an exhaustive list, and my inclusion (or exclusion) of a tool by no means implies that I'm passing judgment on it or recommending it—my aim is simply to take you on a whistle-stop tour of some of the Chef customizations to be found in the wild today to get you thinking about what is possible. The discussion may also help you identify particular chapters of this book to read first.

Chef Supermarket

One of the most comprehensive and extensive Chef resources available today is the Chef Supermarket (*http://bit.ly/chef-super*) (formerly "Community Cookbooks") site. It is a publicly accessible website hosted by Chef, Inc. where Chef users can upload their cookbooks and share them with the wider community. You'll find cookbooks for a decent proportion of the software package systems you're likely to want to use, varying from simple cookbooks containing one or two recipes all the way through to more advanced cookbooks containing custom providers and resources for a wide range of tasks (see Part III for more details on how to write resources and providers).

It's important to remember that the majority of the cookbooks are open source code uploaded by members of the Chef community. They are not supported or warrantied by Chef, Inc., and their presence on the Chef Supermarket site is not an indication of quality or correctness—as we've already discussed, as with all solutions it's very important that you make sure these cookbooks are right for your infrastructure. For example, some cookbooks may only support a particular Linux distribution, or make certain assumptions about how you configure your software. Community members are able to review and comment on cookbooks, however, which can be a good starting point for evaluating suitability.

Development Tooling

Although more strictly tooling built *around* Chef than direct customizations, a number of tools have been written to help support the Chef development process. One of the benefits of "infrastructure as code" is that we get to benefit from the expertise and experience of the wider development community, and adopt software engineering best practices to write awesome infrastructure code. The following tools are some of the fruits of this way of thinking:

Foodcritic

Foodcritic (*http://bit.ly/food-critic*) is a lint checker that checks your cookbooks against a set of "best practice" rules as well as letting you define your own rules. Foodcritic can check for coding style as well as the actual correctness of your cookbooks.

Test Kitchen

Test Kitchen (*http://bit.ly/t-kitchen*) is a tool created by Fletcher Nichol that lets you write integration tests for your Chef cookbooks. It uses the Vagrant virtualization software to spin up "test" nodes that run your integration tests and produce a report after.

ChefSpec

ChefSpec (*http://bit.ly/chefspec*) is a unit testing framework that allows you to write RSpec-style tests for testing Chef cookbooks and verifying that they behave as expected.

Leibniz

Leibniz (*http://bit.ly/a-leibniz*) is an acceptance testing tool that leverages the provisioning features of Test Kitchen to allow you to run acceptance tests against your infrastructure using Cucumber/Gherkin features.

Jenkins chef-plugin

chef-plugin (*http://bit.ly/chef-plugin*) is a plugin for the Jenkins continuous integration (CI) tool that allows you to initiate a Chef run on a remote host with the specified configuration and report its status.

Workflow Tooling

Cookbooks aside, some of the most popular tooling written for Chef has been to support different workflows for working with Chef. As we've already seen, Chef, Inc. intends Chef to be as generic as possible and correspondingly will not generally advocate a particular workflow or methodology—if it did, as soon as your requirements fell outside of that "one true way," you'd be doing it wrong. The workflow tools described in this section are good examples of members of the Chef community producing tools to fulfill business requirements that were not satisfied by Chef out of the box. In the three particular cases mentioned here, it turns out that a decent chunk of the community had the same requirements and adopted one or the other of these tools, so they've become relatively well known as a result:

Berkshelf

Berkshelf (*http://bit.ly/berkshelf*) was initially developed by the engineering team at Riot Games to solve some of the issues they were experiencing around managing cookbook dependencies. Berkshelf is essentially a bundler for Chef—it allows you to quickly and simply install all the cookbook dependencies your own cookbook has, and stores them in a special "berkshelf" in a similar way to how Ruby installs gems. Berkshelf treats cookbook dependencies as libraries to be utilized and extended by your cookbooks, rather than adding them into your main cookbook repository to be customized themselves.

Librarian-Chef

Librarian-Chef (*http://bit.ly/lib-chef*) is based on a similar idea to Berkshelf: that of managing cookbook dependencies. Rather than storing cookbook dependencies in a separate area, however, Librarian-Chef effectively takes control of the */cookbooks* directory in your Chef repository and uses a special "Cheffile" to specify what cookbooks should be installed and from where. Librarian-Chef is designed to work with cookbooks that are each separate projects (like those on the Chef Supermarket (*https://supermarket.getchef.com/cookbooks*) site) rather than cookbooks that are solely stored in your Chef repository.

knife-spork

knife-spork (*http://bit.ly/knife-spork*) (disclosure: written by me) was developed at Etsy to support the unusually large number of developers and operations staff who were regularly making Chef changes. At Etsy, we found that having 30 or 40 Chef users regularly changing and uploading the same environment files resulted in uncertainty over whether or not changes had gone "live," been overwritten by subsequent changes, or just flat out been lost in the noise. Since its initial release, knife-spork has been extended to include plugins for various tasks, such as automatically running Foodcritic prior to uploading cookbooks and broadcasting Chef changes to a number of different systems, including IRC, HipChat, Campfire, and Graphite.

Knife Plugins

 Some Chef setups, such as chef-solo, do not use a centralized Chef server and will not work with some Knife commands or plugins. Please see "Chef Installation Types and Limitations" on page 18 for more details.

Knife is one of the most versatile tools provided with Chef, and the community has been quick to take advantage of this. Out of the box, it supports a number of built-in commands for uploading, editing, and deleting a variety of Chef objects such as cookbooks, roles, users, and clients. But Knife's main strength is its flexibility and customizability. Knife provides an extremely powerful interface to Chef and its underlying functionality that can be leveraged in any number of ways. We'll look in much greater detail at how you can write your own Knife plugins in Chapter 10.

One of the categories of Knife plugin that has seen the most development activity is that surrounding working with cloud providers. Plugins already exist for provisioning nodes on a number of different cloud providers (Amazon EC2 (*http://bit.ly/knife-ec2*), Rackspace (*http://bit.ly/knife-rack*), and Joyent (*http://bit.ly/knife-joyent*), to mention but a few). Knife ships with the "bootstrap" command, which is used to install and configure Chef on nodes that are already running an OS, and as more and more people started to use cloud infrastructure, it was a logical progression that Knife plugins be written to handle the provisioning of cloud instances prior to setting up Chef.

Here's a quick sampling of some of the other Knife plugins that have been created by the Chef community, and what they're for (the *knife-* prefix is a naming convention rather than a functional requirement):

knife-elb
> The knife-elb (*http://bit.ly/knife-elb*) plugin automates the adding and removing of nodes to and from Elastic Load Balancers on Amazon's EC2 service.

knife-kvm
> knife-kvm (*http://bit.ly/knife-kvm*) gives you the ability to provision, manage, and bootstrap Chef on virtual machines using the open source KVM virtualization platform.

knife-rhn
> knife-rhn (*http://bit.ly/knife-rhn*) is a Knife plugin for managing your nodes within the Red Hat Satellite systems management platform. The plugin lets you add nodes to and remove them from Red Hat Network, as well as manage system groups.

knife-block
> knife-block (*http://bit.ly/knife-block*) allows you to configure and manage multiple Knife configuration files, if you're using multiple Chef servers.

knife-crawl
> knife-crawl (*http://bit.ly/knife-crawl*) is a Knife plugin to display role hierarchies. It will show you all the roles that are included within the specified role, and optionally all roles that in turn include the specified role.

knife-community
> knife-community (*http://bit.ly/knife-comm*) is a Knife plugin that assists with deploying Chef cookbooks to the Chef Supermarket (*http://bit.ly/chef-super*) site. This plugin aims to help users comply with a number of best practices for submitting community cookbooks, such as correct cookbook version numbering and Git-tagging new cookbook releases.

Handlers

Handlers in Chef are extensions that can be triggered in response to specific situations to carry out a variety of tasks. Handlers are typically integrated with the chef-client run process and are called depending on whether or not errors occurred during the Chef run, as shown in Figure 1-1.

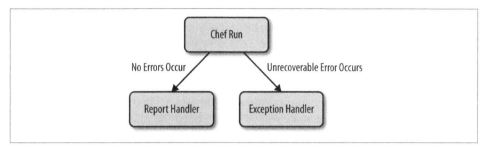

Figure 1-1. Chef handler flow

There are two main types of handler:

Report handlers
> As shown in Figure 1-1, report handlers are used to carry out actions when the chef-client run has succeeded without error.

Exception handlers
> As shown in Figure 1-1, exception handlers are used to carry out actions when an error has occurred during the chef-client run that cannot be recovered from.

Handlers allow you to capture all sorts of data about how Chef runs are behaving. We will look at these further in Chapter 5, but in the meantime let's look at some of the ways that the members of the Chef community have made use of this information:

chef-graphite_handler
> chef-graphite_handler (*http://bit.ly/chef-graphite*) is a report handler (provided as a cookbook) for sending Chef run results to the open source Graphite graphing system.

chef-handler-splunkstorm
> chef-handler-splunkstorm (*http://bit.ly/splunkstorm*) is a combination report and exception handler that reports Chef run statuses to Splunk. It will also log full stack traces in the event of a run failure.

chef-irc-snitch
> chef-irc-snitch (*http://bit.ly/chef-snitch*) is an exception handler that sends notifications of Chef run failures to an IRC channel, complete with a GitHub gist con-

taining node information, the exception message itself, and the backtrace to assist in debugging.

Recipes and Resources

In addition to publishing cookbooks on Chef Supermarket (*http://bit.ly/chef-super*), a number of community members have created open source libraries and providers that are more generally useful to the community than to users of a specific cookbook. We'll look at how to write providers in Chapters 8 and 9, but until then here's a taste of what's currently available:

chef-whitelist
> chef-whitelist (*http://bit.ly/chef-wl*) is a library developed at Etsy to allow host-based rollouts of changes. It allows you to define a whitelist (containing hostnames, roles, or wildcard pattern matches) in a data bag, and then add simple control statements to your cookbooks to apply different logic to roles that match an entry in the whitelist.

chef-deploy
> chef-deploy (*http://bit.ly/chef-deploy*) is a Ruby gem that provides Chef resources and providers to allow you to deploy Ruby web applications without using Capistrano. It maintains forward and backward compatibility with Capistrano by using the same directory structure and deployment strategy.

Chef Installation Types and Limitations

Before we move on to the technical portion of the book, it's worth noting that not all of the material covered will work on all types of Chef setup. Throughout the book, when I list examples of techniques I'll note whether or not there are any compatibility issues with different types of Chef install; here, I list each type of install along with details on how they differ and which features are not supported.

 Although both variants of Enterprise Chef listed here are commercial products, all of the material in this book is fully compatible with the open source version of Chef server. You do not need a paid-for version of Chef to work through this book.

chef-solo

chef-solo is the simplest Chef setup you can run. It is a function-limited version of chef-client, and you have no central Chef server. chef-solo requires a copy of all your cookbooks on each node (including all cookbook dependencies); it reads each cookbook from the local disk and applies it to your server.

You would typically use chef-solo if for some reason you didn't want to use a central Chef server—say, when initially evaluating Chef, or when configuring appliance-type systems that may not have network access.

As there is no central Chef server in a chef-solo setup, the following features are not supported:

Node data
> Nodes do not save state when they finish a run.

Persistent attributes
> Attributes do not persist across Chef runs. Any attributes needed by a chef-solo run should be set either in cookbooks, or in a JSON configuration file passed to chef-solo.

Search
> chef-solo does not allow you to use search in your recipes (or by using Knife), as there is no central server to store node state or attributes in search indexes.

Centralized cookbooks
> chef-solo doesn't support centralized cookbook storage and distribution. You must have a separate copy of each of your cookbooks, roles, environments, etc. on each node. This also means that you need to make sure you keep all of the copies in sync to ensure your changes are applied consistently across your infrastructure.

Centralized API
> The lack of a centralized Chef server in chef-solo means that you don't have access to the Chef Server API, which is the interface used to access the "system state" service that Chef provides.

Authentication
> Because chef-solo runs entirely self-contained on the node, you don't have the authentication controls that the Chef server provides to determine whether or not a client on a node is authorized to download and run cookbooks, roles, and environments, etc. Any node with a copy of your cookbook data can run those cookbooks; all you need is access to log onto the node itself to initiate a Chef run.

Open Source Chef

Chef, Inc. provides a free and open source version of Chef server that stores cookbooks, node run lists, and attributes, and provides a centralized API. Each node runs chef-client and queries the server to obtain information about the configuration to be applied during the run. chef-client then performs the run on the node, using locally cached copies of the cookbooks (which are synced with the copies stored on the server at the start of the run). When the run concludes, chef-client saves the node state and updated attributes back to the central server.

The open source version of Chef server has to be configured, installed, and updated locally by the user and will not automatically scale. It is entirely possible to scale out components, but the user must do this manually. Chef, Inc. can provide optional paid support for open source Chef servers, but the Chef community is the more usual source of technical advice. Open source Chef is recommended for advanced users, or at the very least those comfortable with manually maintaining the respective components.

All material covered in this book is fully compatible with the open source version of Chef server.

Local Mode

Introduced in Chef version 11.8, *local mode* is an extension to chef-client designed to fill the gap between chef-solo and running with a full Chef server. chef-solo is ideal for quickly testing cookbooks, or situations where Chef needs to run in total isolation without access to a Chef server (embedded appliances, for example). Sometimes, however, you might find yourself wishing to test out features usually provided by the Chef server (like search) without the hassle of having to set up a full Chef server, or to test in a sandbox environment isolated from your production Chef server. This is where local mode comes in!

Local mode makes use of an open source tool created by Chef, Inc. called *chef-zero* *(http://bit.ly/chef-zero)*. chef-zero provides an extremely simple memory-resident Chef server that supports many of the commands and features that can be run against a full Chef server. It's very lightweight and easy to use, but it does not perform any input validation or authorization checking, and it does not save any "state" data in the way a full Chef server would. Every time chef-zero starts up, it is completely empty and contains no cookbooks or saved node data. Provided that you bear these limitations in mind, it can be an extremely useful tool for testing more advanced cookbook features. It's important to remember that chef-zero is *not* intended to be used as a production replacement for the open source Chef server or any of the Enterprise Chef servers.

To run chef-client under local mode, you simply run it with the -z option. This will start up a chef-zero server, and your Chef run will communicate with chef-zero instead of any Chef server specified in the *client.rb* configuration file. We'll look more at how this functionality is implemented in "Tracing a chef-client Run" on page 77, and you can find out more about how to use chef-zero in your cookbook testing workflow on the Chef blog *(http://bit.ly/zerotochef)*.

chef-zero provides a lightweight implementation of a Chef server, and supports all of the same commands and operations as the open source Chef server.

Private Enterprise Chef

Enterprise Chef is the commercial version of the open source Chef server. The private version of Enterprise Chef is hosted inside your firewall on your own hardware and provides clustering support out of the box. After hosted Enterprise Chef (discussed next), private Enterprise Chef is the next-easiest option to get up and running with, and is particularly recommended for those new to Chef or looking to evaluate it in a setting with the budget to accommodate the hardware and licensing costs of running a private Chef appliance. Along with the features provided in the open source version, Enterprise Chef provides a number of additional features, some of which are touched on elsewhere in this book. These include:

Role-based access control
> Enterprise Chef provides more fine-grained access control than the open source version. Whereas open source Chef will give access to all objects (cookbooks, nodes, users, roles, etc.) to any properly authenticated user, Enterprise Chef allows you to refine this permissions model to grant different permission levels (for example, create, read, update) to different users or groups of users.

Multitenancy
> Enterprise Chef allows a user to maintain totally distinct Chef setups for different "tenants." For example, if you were running a Chef server that served a number of companies, Enterprise Chef would allow you to keep functionally separate Chef "environments" for each client—cookbooks, node data, attributes, search indexes, etc. would all be separated per client.

Push client runs
> Under the open source version of Chef server, chef-client runs on a "pull" model. This means that chef-client typically runs in daemonized mode, and queries the server for details on what it should run on the node at a configurable interval. When you make a change, unless you script a manual Chef run on all of your nodes, you have to wait until the next Chef run for the changes to go out. Enterprise Chef allows you to push runs out to your nodes, which means that if you so desire you can kick off chef-client runs as soon as a change has gone out without the need for any manual scripting.

 All material covered in this book is fully compatible with private Enterprise Chef.

Hosted Enterprise Chef

The hosted version of Enterprise Chef provides all of the same features as the private version, with the addition that it is not hosted inside your organization but rather managed by Chef, Inc. This means that Chef, Inc. hosts the systems that power hosted Chef and handles all updating, scaling, and support.

Hosted Enterprise Chef is the easiest option to get up and running with, and is particularly recommended for those new to Chef or looking to evaluate it.

 All material covered in this book is fully compatible with hosted Enterprise Chef.

Prerequisites

The last thing I'd like to cover in this chapter is a quick note on the prerequisite tooling and knowledge I'm assuming in my readers. This book is aimed at people who are already comfortable using Chef and want to level up their skills; it assumes that if you're not using hosted Enterprise Chef, you already have a Chef server installed and configured, or are using chef-solo.

Although advanced Chef knowledge is not a prerequisite for this material, you should ideally have read or be familiar with the concepts covered in Mischa Taylor and Seth Vargo's book *Learning Chef*, and be familiar with most of the topics mentioned in this section.

Knife

Although you don't have to be familiar with every supported Knife command, you should be comfortable with how to configure and install Knife and run basic commands for tasks such as:

- Uploading cookbooks
- Creating clients
- Uploading and editing roles and environments

Nodes and Clients

You should understand how to register nodes with Chef, how to configure the run list of a node, and how to run chef-client. You should be at least roughly familiar with the anatomy of a Chef run and be able to interpret basic errors when a run fails.

Cookbooks, Attributes, Roles, Environments, and Data Bags

You should be comfortable writing recipes using the resources provided by out-of-the-box Chef, using `notifies` to initiate actions on other resources, and combining those recipes into a cookbook. You should have a basic understanding of the concept of attributes in Chef and how to set and read them.

You should at least roughly understand how to edit and use roles, environments, and data bags. Advanced knowledge isn't necessary, but you should be aware of the concepts and how they integrate with the rest of Chef.

Chef Search

You should understand how to perform simple searches in Chef, either in recipes or using Knife, such as finding a list of all nodes containing "foo" in their names.

Ruby

You don't need to be a Ruby expert to work through the material in this book, but you should be comfortable with the level of Ruby covered in *Learning Chef* or on Chef, Inc.'s "Just Enough Ruby for Chef" (*http://bit.ly/jer4c*) page. We'll cover all of the Ruby concepts you'll need for this book in Chapter 2, but if you'd like a more comprehensive Ruby reference to help you along I'd recommend either *The Ruby Programming Language* by David Flanagan and Yukihiro Matsumoto, or *Learning Ruby* by Michael Fitzgerald (both from O'Reilly). Both are excellent and extremely comprehensive books, and although they contain far more Ruby than is necessary to follow the material in this book, they cover a lot more about writing "correct" Ruby and how to stick to Ruby best practices than we do here.

Assumptions

As Chef is supported on a number of different platforms, throughout this book I've had to make several assumptions about the environment in which you're running Chef in order to keep the examples as readable and simple as possible. I assume that:

- You're running on a Linux/Unix-based operating system (this includes Mac OS X).
- You installed Chef via the omnibus installer documented on the Chef, Inc. "Install Chef" (*http://bit.ly/install-chef*) page.

- You're running at least chef-client version 11.10.0.

- You have at least version 1.9.2 of Ruby installed—many of the examples in this book will not work with Ruby 1.8.

- You have the Git source code management system (*http://git-scm.com/*) installed.

- You're familiar with the use of a programmer's text editor such as Vim, Emacs, or TextMate.

If any of these assumptions do not apply to you (for example, if you're running Windows or installed Chef from RubyGems), you may find that some of the directory paths and commands used throughout the book require a little tweaking to work in your environment. I've done my best to indicate when this is likely to be the case.

## CHAPTER 2

Just Enough Ruby to Customize Chef

 If you're already familiar with object-oriented programming with Ruby, including inheritance, namespaces, exceptions, and the Ruby scoping model, then you may wish to skip this chapter.

As you'll most likely already have realized while writing cookbooks and recipes, the amount of actual Ruby knowledge needed to write Chef recipes is relatively light. The out-of-the-box resources provided with Chef do an excellent job of abstracting away many of the common tasks required, and a smattering of Ruby basics such as assigning values to variables and writing if statements fill in the gaps. But there's a lot more going on under the hood to provide those Chef resources, Knife plugins, and libraries, and before we can customize them, it is necessary to understand them.

This chapter will teach you some fundamental Ruby concepts that are essential knowledge for customizing Chef. I've tried to make the material in this chapter as accessible as possible to those new to Ruby, but as I only have a limited space in which to present some sizable concepts, don't worry if it feels like a little too much to take in all at once.

Needless to say, this chapter will not cover everything there is to know about the Ruby programming language, and throughout the course of the book I'll be introducing some additional Ruby concepts and expanding on those covered here—the aim of this chapter is simply to give you a good foundation to build on as we work through the material in this book.

With that out of the way (hopefully I haven't scared you off yet!), let's get started by taking a look at what sort of programming language Ruby actually is. If you've worked with other languages in the past, such as Java, C, or Perl, this will help frame the material in this chapter. To give it its proper technical classification, Ruby is an object-oriented, dynamically typed language. But what does this actually mean? We'll get to dynamic typing later in this chapter, but first let's look at what it means for a language to be object-oriented.

 The material in this chapter is compatible with Ruby 1.9 and up. If you're using Ruby 1.8, some of the material and examples in this chapter will not work.

To run any of the example code in this book yourself, copy and paste the program listing into a text file named as indicated in the example title, and execute it using:

```
$> ruby [name_of_example_file]
```

Ruby Is Object-Oriented

If you have previous experience with other programming languages, you may already be used to the concept of *primitive values*. If you haven't encountered the term before, a primitive value is simply a value such as text string or number that has been assigned to a variable. We can't do anything fancy with it; it's just a value. In Ruby, however, all values are actually *objects*.

An object is a special kind of structure that can possess both *attributes* that describe particular parts of it, and *methods* that can be used to control it and manipulate its attributes. In Ruby, objects are actually instances of a *class*, which can be thought of as the template for the object. Don't worry too much about this terminology for now; we'll look at how classes are defined in more detail in "Classes" on page 30. For now, it's enough to remember that all values in Ruby are really objects under the hood. Consider the following simple example of assigning a primitive value to a variable:

```
foo = 'Chef Rocks!'
```

In this example, what we're actually doing is creating a new object of class String with the value "Chef Rocks!" and assigning a *reference* to that object to the variable foo. Note that foo does not hold the actual object, just a reference to it. This may seem like a trivial distinction, but as we'll see later in this chapter, it is a rather important one. Don't worry if some of that terminology was unfamiliar to you; we'll examine each part in due course.

For certain object types, such as String, Ruby performs this object creation under the hood, allowing us to use the simple code seen above. Let's try writing the full version of this code now to demonstrate this:

```
foo = String.new('Chef Rocks!')
```

As far as the Ruby interpreter is concerned, this long-form example above is identical to the first simple example we looked at. Let's prove this with the code in Example 2-1, which we'll paste into a file called *example.rb*.

Example 2-1. example.rb

```
foo = 'Chef Rocks!'
bar = String.new('Chef Rocks!')
puts "foo class: #{foo.class}"
puts "bar class: #{bar.class}"
puts foo == bar
```

In this code, when we say `foo.class` this means that we're calling the `class` method of the variable `foo`, which is a `String` object. In Ruby, a call to a method of an object is always indicated by the `.` character using the `<object>.<method>` syntax seen here.

When we run *example.rb*, we see the following output:

```
$> ruby example.rb
foo class: String
bar class: String
true
```

When this code is run, the Ruby interpreter creates two variables, foo and bar, which hold references to `String` objects. It `puts` a string containing some interpolated Ruby that calls the `class` method of the `String` object (all object types in Ruby have this method, and it does exactly what you might expect: returns the object's class), then `puts` whether or not foo and bar have equal values. In this case this returns `true`, as we'd expect.

 puts is a Ruby function that prints a `String` to the console followed by a newline, unless the specified string already ends with a newline. If the object passed to `puts` is not a `String`, it will be converted to one. For example, in Example 2-1, `puts "foo class: #{foo.class}"` will print `foo class: String` to the console.

The idea that variables only store references to objects holds true for the majority of object types you'll encounter in Ruby—we'll touch on one exception to this rule further on in the chapter.

Ruby Is Dynamically Typed

So now we know what is meant when we say that Ruby is an "object-oriented" programming language. But what does "dynamically typed" mean? Consider again that first example we looked at:

```
foo = 'Chef Rocks!'
```

Note that here we didn't tell Ruby that the variable `foo` was going to contain a `String`; we just assigned a value to it and let the Ruby interpreter figure out what it was. Compare this with the equivalent code in Java, which is a *statically typed* language:

```
String foo = new String("Chef Rocks!");
```

In the Java example, we had to tell the Java compiler specifically that we wanted to create a `String` variable, and then assign an actual `String` value to it. Because Java is statically typed, once a variable has been declared as of a particular type, it can never be any other type unless you redeclare it all over again. If you attempt to assign an `Integer` to a variable previously declared as a `String`, you'll get an error.

In dynamically typed languages such as Ruby, you don't need to declare exactly what type of object your variable is going to reference; you just assign values to it. You can even assign values of different types to the same variable, as seen here:

```
foo = 'Chef Rocks!' # Here we're assigning a String to foo

foo = 1 # Here we're assigning an Integer to foo
```

In Ruby, a # followed by text indicates a *comment* rather than actual Ruby code. We'll use this syntax extensively throughout the book as a way of documenting code examples.

In the first line, we're assigning a `String` value to `foo`, which Ruby detects because the value is surrounded by quotation marks. However, in the last line, we're assigning an `Integer` value to `foo`, which Ruby also detects because the `1` is not enclosed in quotes like a `String` would have been. This is a simple but effective demonstration of both the power and danger of dynamic typing. "What danger?" you may be thinking. "Doesn't it just make things simpler and your code more compact?"

Well, dynamic typing does indeed do these things, but there are also some pitfalls to be aware of. Dynamic typing make our lives easier insofar as it means we don't have to worry about specifically telling our code the type of every single object every time we want to use it. But it also means that we can't always tell what type a variable is when we want to use it (without checking its `.class` method, of course). When we start looking at creating classes and passing variables around this danger will become more apparent, but for now let's look at another simple example. Consider the code in Example 2-2.

Example 2-2. example2.rb

```
foo = 'Chef Rocks!'
bar = 1

if foo = bar
```

```
  puts "Something's wrong, #{foo} shouldn't equal #{bar}"
else
  puts "All is well with the world, #{foo} does not equal #{bar}"
end
```

Simple enough, right? We should always hit the `puts` statement that tells us `foo` does not equal `bar`. Let's put the code into a file called *example2.rb*, run it, and see what happens:

```
$> ruby example2.rb
Something's wrong, 1 shouldn't equal 1
```

Huh, that's not what we expected at all—how did that happen? The more observant of you might have spotted the typo in *example2.rb*:instead of my `if` statement testing for equality, which would have been `if foo == bar`, what I *actually* did was test whether assigning `bar` to `foo` was successful with `if foo = bar`.

Not All Equality Checks Are Created Equal

If you're used to the way checking for equality works in Java-like languages, where `foo == bar` tests whether the two objects are the same object and `foo.equals(bar)` tests whether the two objects have identical values, then right about now you might be a little confused. In Ruby, equality checking actually works the other way around: `foo == bar` tests whether the two objects have the same value, and `foo.equal?(bar)` tests whether `foo` and `bar` are the same object.

Now, in a statically typed language, the code in Example 2-2 would have caused an error at compile time even before it was run. `foo` is clearly a `String`, and bar is clearly an `Integer`. You just can't run around assigning `Integers` to `String` variables in statically typed languages. In Ruby, however, with its dynamic typing, the code did not produce an error, and we hit the part of the `if` statement that should be logically unreachable, all because of a misplaced equals sign.

Of course, this was a contrived example designed to check specifically for this gotcha, but imagine if that typo had occurred in a complex method containing tens of lines of code. All of a sudden, something you took for granted as being a `String` is an `Integer`. Tracking down this sort of issue in dynamically typed languages can be extremely tricky, and it's important to make you aware of this scenario so that you know to be careful. Dynamic typing *does* make things simpler than in statically typed languages, but it also means we as programmers have to be extra careful that our variables refer to objects of the type we think they do.

So now that we've got a good handle on what "object-oriented" and "dynamically typed" actually mean, it's time to start learning how to create our own objects—after all, Ruby would be quite a limited language if you could only make use of the built-in objects. Like Chef, Ruby is nearly infinitely customizable, but it would take another book entirely to explore this topic in depth, so let's just focus on the bits that will be useful when customizing Chef.

Classes

All objects in Ruby are instances of a class. As we've already seen earlier in this chapter, an object in Ruby is a special structure that can contain both attributes to describe it and methods to control it. A class definition is the blueprint for an object, which defines these attributes and methods. For example, whenever you assign a `String` to a variable in Ruby, what you're actually doing is creating an instance (a `String` object) of the `String` class.

Classes are not always standalone templates, either—classes can inherit methods from other classes and override methods defined in classes from which they inherit. In fact, all classes in Ruby inherit from a class called `BaseObject`, which can be thought of as a "master blueprint" that defines the methods like `.class` that we've been using in our examples. But let's not get too far ahead of ourselves. Let's start at the very beginning, with how you define a class in the first place:

```
class Awesome
end
```

That's it—pretty simple, huh? Now, let's use our new class definition and create an instance of it. We'll put the code in Example 2-3 in a file called *example3.rb*.

Example 2-3. example3.rb

```
class Awesome
end

awesome_sauce = Awesome.new
puts "awesome_sauce class: #{awesome_sauce.class}"
```

When we run *example3.rb*, we see the following output:

```
$> ruby example3.rb
awesome_sauce class: Awesome
```

When we create an *instance* of a class, we're essentially creating a new copy of the template contained in the class definition. The methods and variables inside each instance of a class are unique to that instance. This means that we could create two completely separate instances of our `Awesome` class by replacing the code in *example3.rb* with the following:

```
class Awesome
end
```

```
awesome_sauce = Awesome.new
awesome_sauce2 = Awesome.new
puts "awesome_sauce class: #{awesome_sauce.class}"
puts "awesome_sauce2 class: #{awesome_sauce2.class}"
```

Now when we run *example3.rb*, we'll see the following output:

```
$> ruby example3.rb
awesome_sauce class: Awesome
awesome_sauce2 class: Awesome
```

Unfortunately, our Awesome class isn't so awesome yet—we can create as many instances of our class as we want, but we can't really do anything with it because it has no methods. Let's define a method that lets us initialize our Awesome object with a parameter:

```
class Awesome
  def initialize(awesome_level)
    @awesome_level = awesome_level
  end
end
```

The initialize method in Ruby is a special method that is called when you instantiate your object with .new. In this case, our initialize method takes one parameter, awesome_level. Inside the body of the method, we're assigning the value of this parameter to a *class instance* variable named @awesome_level (that's what the @ means). We'll go into more detail about the different sorts of variable scopes you can use in "Variable Scoping" on page 33, but for now it's sufficient to say that the parameter is only accessible ("in scope," to use the correct terminology) inside the method it was passed to, whereas the class instance variable is in scope to any methods in an instances of that class. So now, when we create our new Awesome method, we can do this:

```
awesome_sauce = Awesome.new(100) # We're now passing in the parameter our
# initialize method expects
```

We're getting there, but our class still isn't as awesome as its name implies. We've defined an initialize method to let us set an initial awesome_level, but how do we get that value out again later? And what if we want to change the awesome_level?

Getter and Setter Methods

To retrieve the awesome_level from our new class, we could add a new method that returns the class instance variable like this:

```
class Awesome
  def initialize(awesome_level)
    @awesome_level = awesome_level
  end

  def awesome_level # getter method for awesome_level
    @awesome_level
```

```
    end
  end
```

This new method is what's known as an *accessor* method—it lets you access the value of your class instance variable. Now that we've defined our accessor method, we can do this with our object:

```
awesome_sauce = Awesome.new(99)
puts "Awesome level is #{awesome_sauce.awesome_level}"
```

Now that's more like it; we can create our object with an initial awesome_value, and we can get that value back out again. But what if we want to change the awesome_level after we've already created the object? Well, we could add a new method like this:

```
class Awesome
  def initialize(awesome_level)
    @awesome_level = awesome_level
  end

  def awesome_level # getter method for awesome_level
    @awesome_level
  end

  def awesome_level=(new_awesome_level) # setter method for awesome_level
    @awesome_level = new_awesome_level
  end
end
```

This new type of method is called a *setter* method. Note that we've used the same name as we did for the accessor method, but with an equals sign (=) after it. This is a special method-naming convention used in Ruby to define setter methods. If your setter method is named awesome_level=, when you actually use it in code you are able to do the following:

```
awesome_sauce.awesome_level = 99
```

Tying this all together in *example4.rb* (Example 2-4), we are now able to both set and get the value of Awesome.awesome_level:

Example 2-4. example4.rb

```
class Awesome
  def initialize(awesome_level)
    @awesome_level = awesome_level
  end

  def awesome_level # getter method for awesome_level
    @awesome_level
  end

  def awesome_level=(new_awesome_level) # setter method for awesome_level
    @awesome_level = new_awesome_level
```

```
    end
end

awesome_sauce = Awesome.new(100)
puts "awesome_sauce has an awesome_level of  #{awesome_sauce.awesome_level}"

awesome_sauce.awesome_level = 99
puts "awesome_sauce has an awesome_level of  #{awesome_sauce.awesome_level}"
```

When we run *example4.rb*, we'll see the following output:

```
$> ruby example4.rb
awesome_sauce has an awesome_level of  100
awesome_sauce has an awesome_level of  99
```

This combination of *getter* and *setter* methods in Ruby is extremely common. In the majority of cases, if you declared a class instance variable inside your class, you will want to define accessor and setter methods to go along with it. Because this usage pattern is so common, Ruby provides a special method called `attr_accessor` that automates the creation of getter and setter methods. Using this method, we can reduce our Awesome class down to the following:

```
class Awesome

  attr_accessor :awesome_level

  def initialize(awesome_level)
    @awesome_level = awesome_level
  end
end
```

This class is functionally identical to the earlier long-form version—the : character before the name `awesome_level` indicates that `awesome_level` is a *symbol* being passed as a parameter to the `attr_accessor` method. Symbols in Ruby are the closest it has to the concept of *primitive values* that we looked at in "Ruby Is Object-Oriented" on page 26. For the purposes of this example it's sufficient to treat them as *immutable* variables —that is, their values cannot be changed once set. So in this case, we're passing the immutable variable `awesome_level` to the method `attr_accessor` because we need to ensure the name of the method can't be changed after it's defined.

Try replacing the class definition in *example4.rb* with the condensed definition and see for yourself!

Variable Scoping

In the preceding examples, we took a normal variable passed as a parameter to our `initialize` method and assigned it to a class instance variable. Why was that necessary?

Why couldn't we just use the method parameter everywhere inside our class? The answer lies in something called *variable scoping*.

Although you will find far more complex definitions of the term elsewhere, the definition of variable scoping I'm going to use here is "the thing that determines how much of your program can see the variable in question." We're going to look at two different levels of variable scopes here: *local* and *class instance*.

Local Variables

Local variables are variables that are only visible to the method or block in which they are defined. Unless you add the prefix necessary to indicate that they're class instance variables, your variables will be locally scoped by default. Consider the code in Example 2-5.

Example 2-5. example5.rb

```
def mymethod(awesome_level)
  puts awesome_level # This will work
end

awesome_level = 50
puts awesome_level # This will print 50
mymethod(100)
puts awesome_level # This will still print 50
```

When we run *example5.rb*, we'll see the following output:

```
$> ruby example5.rb
50
100
50
```

In this example, we set the value of awesome_level to 50, and then the following puts statement prints it out. Next, we make a call to the mymethod method, passing it a value of 100. Inside the body of mymethod, we also have a parameter called awesome_level, which we then print using another puts statement. It's important to note here that although we have two variables named awesome_level, Ruby treats them as if they were totally separate. The awesome_level variable used inside the body of mymethod is only visible (*in scope*) inside that method; outside of the method body, it's as if it doesn't exist, so our first awesome_level variable still has a value of 50. We demonstrate this by printing the value of awesome_level again using another puts statement.

Example 2-6 further illustrates the restrictions placed on locally scoped variables.

Example 2-6. example6.rb

```ruby
awesome_level = 99

5.times do
  puts "Awesome level is #{awesome_level}" # this will work
  how_much_awesome = "so much awesome!"
end

puts how_much_awesome # this won't work
```

When we run *example6.rb*, we see the following output:

```
$> ruby example6.rb
Awesome level is 99
Awesome level is 99
Awesome level is 99
Awesome level is 99
Awesome level is 99
example6.rb:8:in 'main': undefined local variable or method
  `how_much_awesome' for main:Object (NameError)
```

The puts statement inside our 5.times block will work perfectly, because awesome_lev
el was declared outside of the block. However, the last line where we try to put
how_much_awesome will fail because the variable how_much_awesome is only in scope
inside the block.

Class Instance Variables

In contrast to local variables, class instance variables are visible to everything inside the
specific instance of the class in which they are defined. To indicate a variable as a class
instance variable, we prefix it with the @ symbol. We've already seen how class instance
variables behave in the Awesome class we created earlier in the chapter:

```ruby
module AwesomeInc
  class Awesome

    attr_accessor :awesome_level

    def initialize(awesome_level)
      @awesome_level = awesome_level
    end
  end
end
```

The @awesome_level variable is defined in our initialize method, and is then also
visible inside our getter and setter methods. It's important to note, though, that @awe
some_level is only visible *inside* the class; this is why we had to create our accessor
method earlier to expose this value to code outside of our class definition.

Because class instance variables are only visible inside a specific instance of the class that defines them, we can quite happily have two `Awesome` objects created side by side without altering each other's `awesome_level`. To verify that this works, copy the code in Example 2-7 into a file called *example7.rb*.

Example 2-7. example7.rb

```
module AwesomeInc
  class Awesome

    attr_accessor :awesome_level

    def initialize(awesome_level)
      @awesome_level = awesome_level
    end
  end
end

foo = AwesomeInc::Awesome.new(10)
bar = AwesomeInc::Awesome.new(20)

puts foo.awesome_level
puts bar.awesome_level
```

When we run *example7.rb*, we'll see the following output:

```
$> ruby example7.rb
10
20
```

Inheritance

As we've talked about already in this chapter, classes don't just have to be standalone chunks of code. Ruby, in common with most other object-oriented languages, allows you to base your classes on already existing classes, modifying their behavior as you please. Before we look at how exactly to do this, there are a couple of definitions to get out of the way:

Superclass
> When your class extends the behavior of another class, the class whose methods it inherits is known as the superclass.

Subclass
> Conversely, the class that is modifying the behavior of a class it inherits from is known as the subclass.

Those definitions can sometimes be a little confusing, so let's look at an example using the `Awesome` class we defined before. Let's say we want to have another class, called

ReallyAwesome, that *inherits* the method we defined in our Awesome class. This would make Awesome the *superclass* and ReallyAwesome the *subclass*, as shown in Figure 2-1.

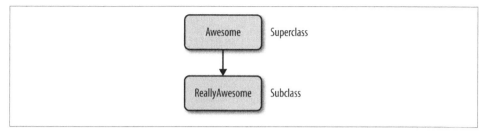

Figure 2-1. Inheritance

Here's how we define that inheritance in our code:

```
class ReallyAwesome < Awesome
end
```

In this example, we're declaring that the class ReallyAwesome inherits from Awesome. So in this case, ReallyAwesome is the subclass and Awesome is the superclass (it's worth noting that once defined, this superclass/subclass relationship cannot be changed while the program is running). We can demonstrate how method inheritance works by creating a new instance of the ReallyAwesome class:

```
really_awesome_sauce = ReallyAwesome.new(1000)
```

In this example, you can see that we called the initialize method of our ReallyAwesome object. But wait, in the ReallyAwesome class we didn't define any methods, did we? That's where inheritance comes in. The initialize method and the attr_accessor method from the Awesome class were inherited by the ReallyAwesome class. When we look at creating Knife plugins and handlers in later chapters, we'll see how inheritance allows us to extend the powerful object classes provided with Chef to avoid having to reimplement them from scratch.

Modules

Much like a class, a *module* in Ruby is a collection of methods, class variables, and constants. Unlike with classes, however, you can't create instances of modules and you can't declare classes to be subclasses of a module (this means that you cannot inherit module methods). Modules stand alone and have no concept of inheriting from a base object in the way that all classes inherit from BaseObject. So what are modules useful for? Modules in Ruby are typically used for two specific purposes: namespaces and mixins.

Modules as Namespaces

Namespaces in programming terminology are essentially "containers" that help you organize things like methods and classes. The usefulness of namespaces becomes more apparent as the programs you write become more and more complex and you start to make use of libraries and classes provided by other programmers—it becomes a useful tool to have objects and methods use descriptive and helpful naming schemes.

By way of an example, let's look at the Awesome class we created earlier:

```
class Awesome

  attr_accessor :awesome_level

  def initialize(awesome_level)
    @awesome_level = awesome_level
  end
end
```

Now that we've defined a class called Awesome, what happens if we want to make use of another library in our code that *also* defines a class called Awesome? Do we change the name of our class? Do we ask the library's creators to change the name of their class? Fear not, brave programmer, this is where module namespaces come in! We can wrap our existing class in a module definition like this:

```
module AwesomeInc
  class Awesome

    attr_accessor :awesome_level

    def initialize(awesome_level)
      @awesome_level = awesome_level
    end
  end
end
```

This now means that we can easily keep our Awesome class separate from any others that happen to use that name. One important thing to note, though, is that now that we've wrapped our class in a namespace, the code we used for creating new instances of our object before won't work:

```
awesome_sauce = Awesome.new # This will now produce an error
```

The reason for this is actually very simple. When we're asking Ruby to create a new instance of the Awesome class, what we're actually doing is asking it to look in the *global* namespace for a class called Awesome, and create an instance of that. The global namespace is where Ruby keeps classes that have not been given a specific namespace of their own. But we just added our class to its namespace with a module definition, so how do we create instances of it now? Again, the answer is simple. We just have to tell Ruby which namespace to look in for the object, like this:

```
awesome_sauce = AwesomeInc::Awesome.new # Yay, it works again!
```

Our code now works again, and our Awesome class is now nicely organized under the AwesomeInc namespace, where it won't clash with any other classes. Although we've just used one module definition here, it's actually possible to have namespaces that are multiple levels deep. As we progress through the book, you might see objects being created with a statement like this:

```
query = Chef::Search::Query.new
```

All this means is that in the definition for that class, you'll find it declared like this:

```
module Chef
  module Search
    class Query
      ...
    end
  end
end
```

A useful feature of namespaces is that a class in a particular module is able to address other classes in that module without specifying the full namespace—Ruby figures that part out for you by searching the inheritance chain. For example:

```
module Chef
    class AwesomeSearch
        # Here we're able to create a Chef::Search::Query object
        # without specifying the Chef part because our class is also
        # in that module
        query = Search::Query.new
    end
  end
end
```

For large, complex systems like Chef, module namespaces are an excellent way to keep things neat and tidy, and also to keep programmers from going insane like they would if everything were declared in the global namespace. Imagine hundreds or thousands of classes' definitions, all having to be uniquely named—this is why module namespaces are an essential tool to keep in your Ruby toolbox!

Modules as Mixins

Modules in Ruby are able to hold methods as well as classes. Imagine for a moment that you're implementing several classes in Ruby that will make use of a shared set of methods to provide common functionality.

One approach to this problem might be to create a "helper" class, which is instantiated inside each of your classes to provide access to these methods. Rather than creating objects that we don't strictly need, a more elegant approach is to store these common methods inside a module and include this module in each class that needs them. This technique of including methods from a module inside a class is called a *mixin*, because we're literally "mixing in" the methods to our class.

But let's not get too far ahead of ourselves—let's look at an example of a mixin in action. Put the code in Example 2-8 into a file called *mixin_example1.rb*:

Example 2-8. mixin_example1.rb

```ruby
# Define our module called 'Awesome'
module AwesomeModule
  # Define a method called add
  def add(a,b) ❶
    # Return parameter a added to parameter b
    a+b
  end
end

# Now define our class called 'AwesomeClass'
class AwesomeClass ❷
  # Include methods defined in the module Awesome in this class
  include AwesomeModule ❸

  attr_accessor :a, :b

  def initialize(a,b)
    @a = a
    @b = b
  end

  def add_numbers
    # Call the add method from the Awesome module
    add(@a,@b) ❹
  end
end

awesome_class = AwesomeClass.new(1,2)
puts "Result is #{awesome_class.add_numbers}"
```

❶ Here we're creating a method called add inside a module called AwesomeModule. Note that this method doesn't live inside a class definition—if it did, we couldn't use it in a mixin.

❷ Here we're defining our AwesomeClass class. Note that this class is not defined inside the AwesomeModule namespace—it could be if we wished, but it's not necessary for mixins to function.

❸ Here we're using the include directive to tell Ruby that all methods defined in AwesomeModule should be available to this class.

❹ Here we're calling the add method. This method isn't defined inside the `Aweso`
`meClass` class, but rather in `AwesomeModule`. The `include` statement allowed us
to make use of this method.

When we run *mixin_example1.rb*, we'll see the following output:

```
$> ruby mixin_example1.rb
Result is 3
```

As this example demonstrates, Ruby allows us to define methods in a module, and then
make use of those methods in our classes through the use of the `include` directive. This
"mixin" technique is a powerful way of avoiding repetition of shared code throughout
our classes, while avoiding the creation of hordes of objects used just to share methods
between classes.

Using Other Classes and Modules

So far we've looked at how to write our own classes and modules, but of course at some
point we're probably going to want to incorporate classes and modules written by third
parties—in the case of the material covered in this book, we're going to want to use the
classes that Chef, Inc. provides for interfacing with your Chef setup. In this section, we'll
look at the different ways to incorporate third-party modules and classes into our code
and make use of them.

Including other classes and modules in your Ruby program is done using a special
function called `require`. Adding `require` followed by a string will add the specified
classes to the list your program knows about. There are several different types of classes
you can require, including local classes, Ruby gems, and built-in classes.

Local Classes

The simplest use of the `require` function is to include a class defined in another file you
want to require by name. Suppose we have the file in Example 2-9 declared.

Example 2-9. awesomeclass.rb

```
module AwesomeInc
  class Awesome

    attr_accessor :awesome_level

    def initialize(awesome_level)
      @awesome_level = awesome_level
    end
  end
end
```

And we want to make use of this class in a new file. We can `require` and use it as shown in Example 2-10.

Example 2-10. really_awesomeclass.rb

```ruby
require '/path/to/awesomeclass'

module AwesomeInc  # Awesome class is declared in the file we're requiring
  class ReallyAwesome < Awesome
  end
end
```

Note that here we've had to tell Ruby the full path to *awesomeclass.rb* (as you'll see in the next section, including the *.rb* file extension is not necessary). This is because by default, Ruby looks for included Ruby files in a special list of directories known as the `LOAD_PATH`. When you specify a full file path like we've done here, the `LOAD_PATH` is bypassed. This is somewhat inconvenient when you're only including files that are in the same directory as your new file or a subdirectory, though, so Ruby 1.9 introduced a function called `require_relative` that looks for files *relative* to the location of the current file. This allows us to replace our full file path in the preceding example as shown in Example 2-11.

Example 2-11. really_awesomeclass.rb (relative paths)

```ruby
require_relative './awesomeclass'

module AwesomeInc
  class ReallyAwesome < Awesome
  end
end
```

RubyGems

When you want to make use of classes and modules written by third parties, you will most likely find that they've been distributed as *gems*. This is the format in which Ruby's package management system, *RubyGems*, distributes classes and modules. RubyGems not only handles the installation of these third-party modules and classes, but also handles installing any other classes and modules depended on by the gem you're installing. Most gems are distributed through the RubyGems (*https://rubygems.org/*) website.

To install a RubyGem, we use the `gem install` command bundled with Ruby, followed by the name of the gem to be installed, like this:

```
$> gem install diffy

Fetching: diffy-3.0.2.gem (100%)
Successfully installed diffy-3.0.2
Installing ri documentation for diffy-3.0.2
Done installing documentation for diffy after 0 seconds
```

Because RubyGems takes care of installing the classes and modules from gems under the LOAD_PATH expected by Ruby, we can include the newly installed gem in our code like this:

```ruby
require 'diffy' # Our newly installed diffy gem
require_relative './awesomeclass'

module AwesomeInc
  class ReallyAwesome < Awesome
  end
end
```

It's important to note that what we're actually requiring here is not the name of the gem itself, but a file under the LOAD_PATH called *diffy.rb*, which was installed as part of the diffy gem by RubyGems. You might also note that we referred to the file as diffy, not diffy.rb—Ruby allows you to optionally skip the *.rb* extension when requiring files. We could equally have written require "diffy.rb", but the convention when requiring files from gems is to omit the *.rb* extension. Another convention is to name the "main" file from the gem that you need to require after the name of the gem itself, but this is not always done.

Because we're able to specify which files provided by a gem we wish to include, it's common to only require those classes installed by a gem that are actually needed. For example, further on in this book, you might see something like:

```ruby
require 'chef/knife'
```

All this means is that we're requiring the *knife.rb* class file under the *chef* directory installed by the chef gem—you'll see this technique throughout the material presented in this book, as it makes our programs more efficient if we avoid requiring classes that we don't plan to use. To illustrate this point, Table 2-1 illustrates the difference in load time between requiring the entire chef gem versus just requiring the chef/knife class.

Table 2-1. Class load time comparison

Load statement	Load time
require "chef"	1.955s
require "chef/knife"	0.982s

Built-in Classes

Ruby also ships with a number of classes that are installed by default but not explicitly included in your program by default. These classes collectively form what's known as the *standard library*, or *stdlib*, and are available under the LOAD_PATH just like classes installed by RubyGems. You can make use of these classes by adding a require statement, just as you would when including local files or RubyGems. For example, we can include the `FileUtils` class from the standard library in the example we looked at earlier as follows:

```
require 'fileutils' # A standard library class
require 'diffy' # A class installed by the diffy gem
require_relative './awesomeclass.rb' # A local class file

module AwesomeInc
  class ReallyAwesome < Awesome
  end
end
```

In this example, you can see that we're now making use of classes from all three categories: a local class file, a stdlib class, and a class installed by a gem.

When Things Go Wrong

Now that we've discussed several Ruby concepts that you may not have previously encountered when writing Chef code, let's take a moment to examine what happens when your code goes wrong and what you can do to manage this. Code errors can be caused by a wide variety of factors, from attempting to call a nonexistent method of an object through trying to divide a number by zero, to more complex errors like a Chef run failing. To make its error mechanism as convenient and easy to use as possible, Ruby implements a standard method of telling you about errors—it throws an exception.

Exceptions

The `Exception` class is specially designed to provide an error-handling mechanism in Ruby. Exceptions in your code can either be raised by Ruby (including by any gems or other classes you're including), or raised directly from your code. To illustrate the latter, copy the code in Example 2-12 into a file called *example12.rb*.

Example 2-12. example12.rb

```
foo = "Hello"
raise "This is an error!"
bar = Goodbye
```

The raise Method

The `raise` method used in Example 2-12 is a method provided by the `Kernel` module that is in turn included by all instances of the `Object` class. Essentially, this means that any object in Ruby has access to the `raise` method and can throw exceptions.

When we run *example12.rb*, we'll see the following output:

```
$> ruby example12.rb
example12.rb:2:in `<main>': This is an error! (RuntimeError)
```

What we see here is known as a *stack trace*. Along with the actual error thrown by the code This is an error! (RuntimeError:), Ruby highlights the file in which the error occurred (example12.rb) and even the exact line number (:2), and then stops the code from executing further.

This behavior is the main difference between printing an error message and raising an exception. When you print an error message, your code can continue executing as normal, but when you throw an exception, you're telling Ruby to stop executing further code immediately because something has gone wrong. Perhaps more importantly, you're also letting code that might be using instances of your object know that an error has happened, like in Example 2-13.

Example 2-13. example13.rb

```
class Awesome
  def break_stuff
    raise "Whoa, this is broken!"
  end
end

foo = Awesome.new
foo.break_stuff # This will throw a RuntimeError
```

When we run *example13.rb*, we'll see the following output:

```
$> ruby example13.rb
example13.rb:3:in `break_stuff': Whoa, this is broken! (RuntimeError)
        from example13.rb:8:in `<main>'
```

In this output, the usefulness of the stack trace that Ruby gives us when exceptions are raised becomes even more obvious—it doesn't just tell us that the exception was caused at example13.rb:3 in the break_stuff method, but also that the break_stuff method was called by example13.rb:8:in *<main>*. As your code begins to make use of more libraries and method calls, the *depth* of the stack traces shown when exceptions are thrown can increase dramatically. This sometimes makes them a little challenging to interpret, but also gives an invaluable level of detail about exactly what went wrong with your program.

RuntimeError, the exception class that was thrown in the preceding examples, is the default type of Exception that Ruby will raise if you don't specify the exception type. It is actually a subclass of StandardError, which is in turn a subclass of Exception, and both of these superclasses have a number of other exception subclasses that you can use. It's largely left up to you to decide what exception type to use depending on the type of error being responded to, but here are a few of the more commonly encountered Exception classes:

RuntimeError
> A generic error class that is raised when an invalid operation is attempted.

ArgumentError
> Raised when the number of arguments passed to a method is incorrect.

IOError
> Raised when an input/output operation fails.

TypeError
> Raised when an object is encountered that is not of the type expected by the code.

ZeroDivisionError
> Raised when attempting to divide an integer by 0.

When you've identified the exception class you want to use, you can throw an exception of a specific type in your code like this:

```
foo = AwesomeInc::Awesome.new(10)
raise IOError.new("This is an IO error!")
```

This example outputs `This is an IO error! (IOError)`.

Handling Exceptions

As we've already seen, when your Ruby code raises an `Exception`, code execution stops immediately. But what happens if, for example, you're using a third-party RubyGem to access a web service and it throws an exception when a user specifies incorrect login credentials? It doesn't seem very user-friendly for the program to stop dead in its tracks at this point. Let's take another look at the code from *example13.rb*:

```
class Awesome
  def break_stuff
    raise "Whoa, this is broken!"
  end
end

foo = Awesome.new
foo.break_stuff # This will throw a RuntimeError
```

Wouldn't it be nice if the code calling the `break_stuff` method of our `Awesome` class was able to gracefully handle this error and carry on? Fortunately, Ruby gives us a way to do just this with a special keyword called `rescue`. The `rescue` keyword is used within a block defined by a `begin` statement to indicate the parts of our code for which we want to capture exceptions. Let's try replacing the last two lines of *example13.rb* with the following:

```
foo = Awesome.new
begin
  foo.break_stuff # This will throw an exception
```

```
rescue
  puts "Looks like there was an exception!" # But this will handle it!
end
```

Try running our revised *example13.rb* again and see what happens. You should see the following output:

```
$> ruby example13.rb
Looks like there was an exception!
```

This time when the code throws an exception we'll see the friendly error message defined inside the rescue block rather than the Exception error we saw before. If any code executed inside the begin block throws an exception, the code inside the rescue section will be run, allowing the error to be gracefully handled and program execution to continue.

Ruby also allows us to access methods of the Exception object being thrown by naming it in the rescue statement like this:

```
foo = Awesome.new
begin
  foo.break_stuff # This will throw an exception
rescue => ex # Let's name our exception object and use it
  puts "Exception of class #{ex.class} thrown with message #{ex.message}"
end
```

If we alter the rescue block in *example13.rb* to the above, when we run it we will get the following output:

```
$> ruby example13.rb
Exception of class RuntimeError thrown with message Whoa, this is broken!
```

Rescuing exceptions is a powerful method of ensuring that your code can continue executing when errors occur, but it would make our programs rather unwieldy if we had to include code for every possible exception type in the same rescue section. To make handling different exception types easier to manage, Ruby also lets us specify exactly which classes of Exception we want our rescue statement to apply to. We can even specify multiple different rescue statements for different exception types, like this:

```
foo = Awesome.new
begin
  foo.break_stuff # This will throw an exception
rescue RuntimeError => ex
    # Code to handle RuntimeErrors
rescue IOError => ex
    # Code to handle IOErrors
end
```

The judicious combination of begin blocks with rescue statements that capture specific types of Exception allow you to gracefully handle errors in your code while presenting the user with meaningful feedback. Of course, it's totally possible to capture all exceptions with a single `rescue` block and return a generic error message, but as is the case with much of the material in this book, something you *can* do is not necessarily something you *should* do. In general, you want to focus your error handling as tightly as possible and be sure to make your error messages as descriptive and helpful as you can.

Defining Custom Exception Types

Sometimes the relatively limited number of standard `Exception` types provided in Ruby is not sufficient to allow us to properly manage our exception handling, and we find ourselves needing to declare a new class of exception. The object-oriented nature of Ruby makes this extremely easy to do by allowing us to create a class that inherits from one of the built-in Ruby `Exception` classes, such as `StandardError`, as shown here:

```
class SuperSeriousProblem < StandardError
end
```

Note that this `SuperSeriousProblem` class is simply an empty class definition. Although you can add extra methods and attributes if you want, the `Exception` class that is its eventual superclass already provides all of the methods like `.class` and `.message` that we used in our earlier examples.

Custom exception classes are an excellent way of giving additional context to error messages that might not be possible with the built-in exception types. Let's now combine all the techniques discussed in this section to augment our example class with a custom `Exception` class, and code to handle that specific exception type. Copy the code in Example 2-14 into a file called *example14.rb*.

Example 2-14. example14.rb

```
class SuperSeriousProblem < Exception # Our new custom exception class
end

class Awesome
  def break_stuff
    # Raise our new exception type
    raise SuperSeriousProblem.new("Whoa, this is broken!")
  end
end

foo = Awesome.new
begin
  foo.break_stuff # This will throw a SuperSecretProblem exception
rescue SuperSeriousProblem => ex # Which we're now handling
    puts "SuperSeriousProblem: Something went really, really wrong."
end
```

When we run *example14.rb*, we'll see the following output:

```
$> ruby example14.rb
SuperSeriousProblem: Something went really, really wrong.
```

By defining meaningful and descriptive exception classes in your code and making sure that your error-handling code deals with all the errors it can, you improve both the readability of your code and the overall usability of your application. Most people don't like having to try to interpret a Ruby stack trace; it's much more useful to present the user with a helpful error message, or, even better, have your code handle the error transparently, recover from it, and move on.

Tying It All Together

We've covered a number of Ruby concepts that are essential to understand when working through the material in this book. Thus far I've demonstrated these ideas in small, standalone chunks. To help tie everything together, we're now going to look at some more realistic code examples that will demonstrate these concepts working in concert, in addition to introducing you to some useful stdlib classes.

We'll look at two short example programs:

file_operations.rb

> This example will show you how to perform various operations on local files in Ruby by creating and using a class for writing data to log files. It will demonstrate opening, writing to, and clearing files and also introduce you to the Ruby stdlib class `File`.

http_requests.rb

> This example will introduce you to two of the stdlib classes Ruby provides for talking to HTTP services (`Net::HTTP`) and working with URLs (`URI`), and also how to work with the response object returned by the request.

 All of the examples in this section are compatible with Ruby 1.9 and forward, and only make use of standard library classes. No third-party gems or classes are required.

To run the example code yourself, copy and paste the program listing into a text file named as indicated in the sample title, and execute it using:

```
$> ruby [name_of_example_file]
```

File Operations

This example defines a module called `Examples` that contains a custom exception class called `FileCreationError`, and our main class called `FileLogger`. It introduces you to several methods provided by the `File` stdlib class.

The `FileLogger` class contains an `attr_accessor` method for our single class instance variable and defines the following additional methods:

`initialize`
> This method takes a single parameter for the log file path.

`file_writeable?`
> This method returns `true` or `false` depending on whether or not the user running the example has permissions to write to the file.

`write_to_log`
> This method takes a string as a parameter, and writes it to the file.

`clear_log`
> This method clears the contents of the log file.

The code for this example (*file_operations.rb*) is given in Example 2-15.

Example 2-15. file_operations.rb

```
# The module namespace our classes will live in
module Examples
  # Custom exception class
  class FileCreationError < StandardError
  end

  # Our main class definition
  class FileLogger
    # attr_accessor method for log_file class instance variable
    attr_accessor :log_file

    # initialize method
    def initialize(log_file)
      # Set @logfile class instance variable to value of parameter
      @log_file = log_file
      # Wrap initial file creation in a begin block
      begin
        # Try creating the file in "write" mode
        File.new(@log_file, "w")
      # Rescue Errno::EACCES exception that occurs
      # when file can't be created due to insufficient permissions
      rescue Errno::EACCES
        # Raise a custom exception with a more friendly message
        # (split over two lines below because of space constraints)
        raise FileCreationError.new("#{@log_file} could not be created. "+
```

```
          "Please check the specified directory is writeable by your user.")
      end
    end

    # methods of our FileLogger object

    def file_writeable?
      # Return true if our created file is writeable, false if not
      File.writeable?(@log_file)
    end

    def write_to_log(message)
      # Open our file in "append" mode and write the message string to it
      # This {} syntax in Ruby allows a do...end block to be written on
      # one line
      File.open(@log_file, 'a') {|f| f.write(message) }
    end

    def clear_log
      # Clear the contents of the file
      File.truncate(@log_file, 0)
    end
  end
end

# Try creating and writing to a file we should have permissions to

# Initialize our object; note that we're specifying Module::Class
puts "Creating log file /tmp/testfile"
file_logger = Examples::FileLogger.new("/tmp/testfile")
puts "file writeable: #{file_logger.file_writeable?}"
puts "Writing to log file"
file_logger.write_to_log ("Test log message")
puts "Clearing log file"
file_logger.clear_log

# puts a blank line for spacing
puts ""

# Try creating and writing to a file we should *not* have permissions to

# Initialize our object; note that we're specifying Module::Class
puts "Creating log file /usr/testfile"
file_logger = Examples::FileLogger.new("/usr/testfile")
puts "file writeable: #{file_logger.file_writeable?}"
puts "Writing to log file"
file_logger.write_to_log ("Test log message")
puts "Clearing log file"
file_logger.clear_log
```

When you run the example code, you should see the following output:

```
$> ruby file_operations.rb
Creating log file /tmp/testfile
file writeable: true
Writing to log file
Clearing log file

Creating log file /usr/testfile
file_operations.rb:25:in 'rescue in initialize': /usr/testfile could not
    be created. Please check the specified directory is writeable
    by your user. (Examples::FileCreationError)
        from file_operations.rb:17:in 'initialize'
        from file_operations.rb:65:in 'new'
        from file_operations.rb:65:in '<main>'
```

As the output shows, our attempt to create, log to, and clear */tmp/testfile* succeeded because we have permissions to write to that file.

However, our attempt to create, log to, and clear */usr/testfile* failed, because we don't have permissions to write to that file. The `initialize` method of our `FileUtils` object caught the exception that was thrown when this happened because the initial file creation was wrapped in a `begin` block, and the `rescue` block in turn raises our custom `FileCreationError` exception with a more friendly error message.

As we progress through the book and interact with different Ruby classes and components of Chef that may throw a wide variety of errors, the ability to handle these errors and display clear and informative output becomes more and more useful and allows us to greatly enhance the user-friendliness and stability of our customizations.

HTTP Requests

This example defines a module called `Examples` that contains a custom exception class called `InvalidURLError`, and our main class called `HTTPRequester`. It will introduce you to two stdlib classes, called `net/http` (the HTTP class of the Net module) and `uri`. Note that in this example we have to explicitly require both classes because, unlike the `File` class, they are not included for us by default.

Unlike in the previous example, the `HTTPRequester` class doesn't use an `attr_acces sor` method for the class instance variable `@url`, because we want to define custom behavior when setting a new value for `@url`. The `HTTPRequester` class defines the following methods:

`initialize`
> The `initialize` method takes a single parameter for the URL we want to work with.

url, url=

> These are the getter and setter methods for the @url class instance variable. We're specifying getter and setter methods instead of an `attr_accessor` method here because we're doing more than just assigning a value to the @url variable.

get_request

> This method performs a GET request on the parsed URL in the @url variable and returns a `Net::HTTP::Response` object.

The code for this example (*http_requests.rb*) is given in Example 2-16.

Example 2-16. http_requests.rb

```ruby
# Require the two stdlib classes we need,
# which aren't included by default
require "net/http"
require "uri"

# The module namespace our classes will live in
module Examples
  # Custom exception class
  class InvalidURLError < StandardError
  end

  # Our main class definition
  class HTTPRequester

    # Custom getter method for @url class instance variable
    def url
      # The to_s method returns the String representation
      # of the @url variable
      @url.to_s
    end

    # Custom setter method for @url class instance variable
    # because we're parsing the url parameter before assigning
    # to @url
    def url=(url)
      begin
        @url = URI.parse(url)
      # rescue URI::InvalidURIError exception that occurs
      # when we try to parse an invalid URL
      rescue URI::InvalidURIError
        # Raise a custom exception with a more friendly message
        raise InvalidURLError.new("#{url} was not a valid URL.")
      end
    end

    # initialize method
    def initialize(url)
```

```
      # Call the setter method for the url attribute to set it
      # to the value passed to this method
      @self.url = url

      # When we're sure our URL is valid, create a Net::HTTP object
      # and assign it to the @http_object class instance variable
      @http_object = Net::HTTP.new(@url.host, @url.port)
    end

    # Class method to make a GET request
    def get_request
      # Use our @http_object object's request method to call the
      # Net::HTTP::Get class and return the resulting response object
      @http_object.request(Net::HTTP::Get.new(@url.request_uri))
    end
  end
end

# Let's try out our class with a valid URL

# Initialize our object; note that we're specifying Module::Class
puts "Initializing Example::HTTPRequester for http://www.oreilly.com"
http_requestor = Examples::HTTPRequester.new("http://www.oreilly.com")
puts "Performing GET request"
# Here we're calling the .code method of the Net::HTTP::Request
# object that is returned by the get_request method
puts "Response code was #{http_requestor.get_request.code}"

# puts a blank line for spacing
puts ""

# Let's try out our class with an *invalid* URL

# Initialize our object; note that we're specifying Module::Class
puts "Initializing Examples::HTTPRequester for 123"
http_requestor = Examples::HTTPRequester.new(123)
puts "Performing GET request"
# Here we're calling the .code method of the Net::HTTP::Request
# object that is returned by the get_request method
puts "Response code was #{http_requestor.get_request.code}"
```

When you run the example code, you should see the following output:

```
$> ruby http_requests.rb
Initializing HTTPRequester for http://www.oreilly.com
Performing GET request
Response code was 200

Initializing HTTPRequester for 123
http_requests.rb:36:in `rescue in initialize': 123 was not a valid URL.
    (Examples::InvalidURLError)
        from http_requests.rb:29:in `initialize'
```

```
        from http_requests.rb:68:in `new'
        from http_requests.rb:68:in `<main>'
```

As the output shows, our first attempt to make a GET request to `http://www.oreil`
`ly.com` succeeded because we passed a valid URL to our object. Our second attempt to
attempt to make a GET request to 123 failed because the URL we passed was not valid.
The `initialize` method of our `HTTPRequester` object caught the exception that was
thrown when this happened because the initial object creation was wrapped in a `be`
`gin` block, and the `rescue` block in turn raises our custom `InvalidURLError` exception
with a more friendly error message.

Although the example we've looked at in this section was somewhat contrived, the
techniques we've used here to communicate with an external HTTP resource are widely
applicable to writing Chef customizations. As we'll see in later chapters, the ability to
integrate Chef with third-party software such as monitoring, metrics collection, and
communication systems is a valuable tool in our customization toolbox, and many of
these systems will use HTTP to allow our code to communicate with their APIs.

Summary

In this chapter, we've covered a large number of quite complex Ruby concepts in a
relatively condensed format. If you'd like to dive a little deeper into the topics covered
here before moving on, I recommend picking up *Learning Ruby* or *The Ruby Programming Language*. Both are excellent books, and explain the Ruby programming language
in far more comprehensive detail than I've been able to in this single chapter. As its title
suggests, this chapter has covered just enough of Ruby to allow you to customize Chef,
but the more you learn about the features and functionality of Ruby, the greater your
understanding of the behavior and underlying code of Chef and its tools will become
—you might even end up submitting patches or pull requests to the Chef source code
yourself!

## CHAPTER 3

Chef Internals

In Chapter 1, we examined *why* we might want to customize our Chef setup. Before we can dive into the meat of the book and start actually creating our own Chef customizations, it's important to ensure that we are able to make an informed decision about *what* to customize. Chef is designed to be extensible in a wide variety of ways, each suited to different types of tasks.

One of the most powerful tools in your toolbox to help you make this sort of decision is a comprehensive understanding of how Chef works under the hood and how the different components interact. To use an analogy from AwesomeInc's line of work, before we can customize a particular component of a car we need to have an overall picture of how the car functions, and the effects that a change to one component will have on other components.

In this chapter, we'll look at:

- An overview of the architecture behind a Chef server—we won't be customizing the Chef server in this book, but it's useful to be aware of its components and structure nonetheless.

- The anatomy of a Chef run.

- How Chef's design methodology allows us to examine what a run would do to a node if executed.

- A quick tour of Chef's source code to become familiar you with how the classes that make up Chef are organized.

- Tracing the execution path of a chef-client run through the Chef codebase, using our Ruby knowledge from Chapter 2.

The material in this chapter is based on (and compatible with) the latest stable release of Chef at the time of writing, version 11.10.0. If you're using an older version of Chef, some of the features or behavior mentioned in this chapter may differ slightly—I'll note when this is the case.

Chef Architecture

Under the hood, a number of different components interact to form a Chef server and client, along with the supporting tooling. These components are illustrated in Figure 3-1, in which I've split Chef into two sections:

Chef client tools
> This section describes the Chef client programs that run on your nodes, and the other tooling that is used to interface with Chef.

Chef server
> This section describes the components and interfaces that make up a Chef server, and applies to all forms of Chef that make use of a centralized Chef server. In the case of an open source Chef setup, all of the server components might be on the same physical or virtual machine while in a hosted Enterprise Chef, each component is likely to be powered by multiple machines behind the scenes, but the basic architecture is the same.

After the diagram, I'll go on to explain each component in more detail.

If you're a chef-solo user, Figure 3-1 won't apply to you because chef-solo does not make use of a central server. If you're using hosted Enterprise Chef, the diagram represents a simplified form of the platform. Hosted Enterprise Chef users cannot access this infrastructure other than via the Chef API.

Now that we have a top-level view of how the components that make up Chef link together, let's examine each of them in more detail.

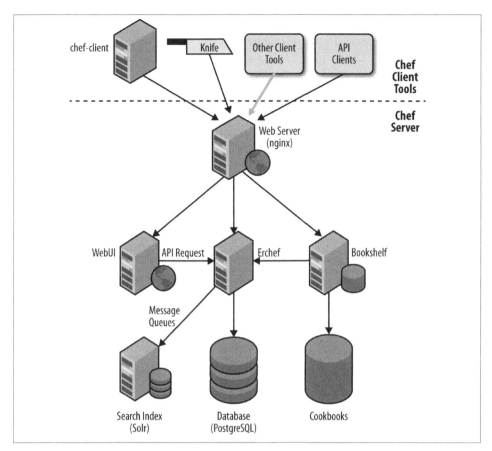

Figure 3-1. Chef architecture

Chef Client Tools

Chef client tools include the following:

chef-client
> *chef-client* is the client program that runs on all of your nodes and actually executes
> cookbook code during Chef runs. As we saw in "So Why Chef?" on page 4, Chef
> uses a "thin server, thick client" design, and as much work as possible is done on
> the client side by chef-client. The chef-client can be run as a *daemonized* process
> on Unix/Linux-based systems, or it can run in a continuous loop controlled by the
> `interval` and `splay` configuration options. If run with the `--once` command-line
> option, chef-client can also perform a single run and terminate.

Knife

Knife is the primary command-line tool for interfacing with Chef. It's used for a number of tasks, from uploading cookbooks through running search queries to editing roles. Knife is also extremely extensible, as we'll see in Chapter 10.

Other client tools

Chef also provides a number of other client tools out of the box, such as *chef-shell* (a Chef-specific version of ruby's *irb* interactive ruby shell, which was called *shef* in earlier Chef versions) and *chef-apply* (a tool that allows you to run a single recipe from the command line). Some of these tools (such as chef-shell) can also communicate with the Chef server, whereas others (like chef-apply) do not, and run solely on the client node—this is why the "Other Client Tools" bubble in Figure 3-1 is joined to the server with a lighter colored arrow.

API clients

Chef's API is accessible to anybody who is authorized to use it, not just out-of-the box Chef tooling. This makes it possible to write scripts and programs that talk directly to the Chef API to perform any number of tasks around the data that the API exposes. We'll look more at interfacing with the Chef API in Chapter 11.

Chef Server

The Chef server is made up of a variety of components and interfaces, including:

Web server

The nginx web server is the first "port of call" when communicating with the Chef server. It allows everything that interfaces with Chef to communicate with it on a single port—Chef's API is entirely HTTP-based, so this is port 443 because HTTPS is used by default. Depending on the route specified in the URL sent to the nginx server, it will proxy each request to the appropriate backend component. For example, requests to nginx containing /bookshelf will be passed straight through to the Bookshelf, whereas other requests by default will be passed on to Erchef.

Web UI

The Chef web UI gives you a graphical interface for working with Chef. The exact UI and features vary depending on whether you're using open source Chef or Enterprise Chef, but all versions allow you to perform tasks such as editing nodes run lists, monitoring the status of your nodes, and managing users. See "Chef Installation Types and Limitations" on page 18 for more details on the different features supported by each version.

Erchef

Erchef is the core API component of the Chef server. It got the name Erchef after the original Ruby version of the Chef server was rewritten in Erlang in 2013 (the API interface remains unchanged between both versions, however). Erchef is the component of the Chef server that exposes the "system state" service we discussed in "So Why Chef?" on page 4 via its HTTP-based API. Whether you're creating a client or uploading a cookbook, your code is talking to Erchef.

 Even though Erchef is written in Erlang, you do not need to use Erlang to interface with the Chef API. All of the examples and techniques in this book are written in Ruby.

Search index

The Chef search index is powered by the open source Solr search platform. When you run Chef search queries like `node_platform:centos`, the Chef API is actually sending the queries to these search indexes. Under the hood, Chef stores a number of different search indexes for nodes, environments, clients, roles, and data bags. This is why we specify Chef searches like `knife search node node_platform:cen tos`. What we're actually doing here is querying the `node` search index. Chef wraps Solr with a service called *chef-solr*, which provides a REST API for indexing and searching.

Message queues

Chef uses message queues to send items to be added to the search indexes. Each item to be indexed is added to a message queue; these are powered by the open source RabbitMQ messaging queue. Queued items are pulled from the queue by a process called *chef-expander*, which processes the items into the correct format for indexing. The processed items are then passed to chef-solr for indexing.

Database

The backend data storage repository behind the Chef server is powered by the open source PostgreSQL database server. This repository stores data such as saved node attributes, client configuration, roles, data bags, and environments.

Bookshelf

This is where Chef stores the files and content uploaded with a version of a specific cookbook. All content in the Bookshelf is stored alongside a checksum so that if different cookbooks (or two different versions of the same cookbook) upload the same file, it is only stored once in the Bookshelf.

Cookbooks

The cookbook content managed by the Bookshelf service is stored in flat files in a dedicated data repository. The file naming structure and format used here isn't especially "human-friendly," and is only used by the Bookshelf service.

Because of Chef's "thin server, thick client" design, the vast majority of the time your Chef customizations expend will be on one of the Chef client tools, simply because that is where most of Chef's logic lives. The Chef server can mainly be thought of as the "system state" service we learned about in "So Why Chef?" on page 4, but just because we won't be directly customizing the server doesn't mean we won't be using it.

As we work through the material in this book, we'll need to communicate with the Chef server for a variety of different tasks—particularly when we come to write knife plugins in Chapter 10 and interface with the Chef API in Chapter 11—so a good understanding of the different components that make up a chef server will make working through the material in these chapters much easier.

Anatomy of a Chef Run

When we initiate a Chef run on one of our nodes, we expect the eventual state of the node to be that which we described in our recipes. This concept is known as *convergence*.

To give the term its proper definition, in infrastructure automation *convergence* is the act of bringing a system closer to a *correct* state with each action taken. In Chef, *correctness* means bringing the node to the state defined by the recipes to be run on that node. In an ideal world, the initial Chef run performed on a node will result in full convergence, with the node ending up in exactly the state defined by its recipes, and this is what you should aim for when writing cookbooks. In the event that this is not the case, however, performing a second run will bring the node closer to the state defined in its recipes. Essentially, even if a node cannot become fully converged with one Chef run, subsequent Chef runs will always bring the node closer to the state defined in its recipes, and not further from it.

nother key concept to remember when writing Chef cookbooks and performing Chef runs is that we also expect our recipes to be applied to the node with only required actions being performed—this is known as *idempotence*.

Idempotence in the configuration management sense refers to the idea that no matter how many times you run a recipe or resource on a node, you will get the same result. A good example of an idempotent recipe is one that uses the built-in `package` resource to install a specific version of a package. Once the package has been installed, running the recipe over and over again will never result in the package being reinstalled, as the resource will always detect that the specified version has already been installed. Although it is possible to write *non*-idempotent recipes in Chef, this is not recommended —idempotence is always something you should strive for, especially when creating your own resources, providers, and definitions. We'll look at how to do this in Part III.

Under the hood, a number of distinct steps take place to form a complete run and provide this convergent behavior. Much in the same way that modifying the engine of a car requires an understanding of how the different components function, when customizing Chef it's very important to understand the "anatomy" of Chef runs and how the different stages interact.

The first stage of a Chef run is to execute chef-client or chef-solo, either manually or via a scheduled task. After this has been done, the run will proceed through a number of different stages, illustrated in Figure 3-2.

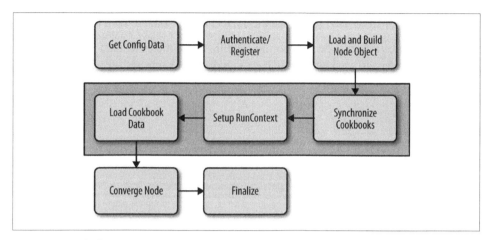

Figure 3-2. Chef run process

Some stages of the Chef run process differ depending on whether you're using chef-solo or chef-client with a Chef server. These differences will be clearly indicated in tip boxes like this one.

Let's examine these stages in a little more detail.

Get Configuration Data

The first step performed when a Chef run is initiated is for chef-client to load its configuration from the *client.rb* file. This file contains a number of configuration settings, such as the URL of the Chef server, the authentication credentials to use, and where to store local copies of cookbooks, etc.

A full list of options supported by *client.rb* can be found on the Chef Documents site (*http://bit.ly/client-rb*).

Ohai

After the configuration has been loaded from the configuration file, chef-client runs an included tool called ohai to build up an initial collection of data about the node (operating system, hardware platform, etc.). This data also includes the node's fully qualified hostname, which will be used to ensure the correct data is loaded from the Chef server.

You can run ohai yourself from the command line to see the exact data it produces (in JSON format) and passes to chef-client. Here's a sample of some of the output you might see:

```
$> ohai

{
  "languages": {
    "php": {
      "version": "5.4.20",
      "builddate": "Sep 27 2013"
    },
    "lua": {
      "version": "5.1.4"
    },
    "nodejs": {
      "version": "0.10.16"
    },
    "perl": {
      "version": "5.10.1",
      "archname": "x86_64-linux-thread-multi"
    }
  }
}

<snip>
```

We'll look at how ohai collects attributes and how you can implement your own attributes in Chapter 4. You can also find more ohai documentation on the Chef Documents site (*http://bit.ly/about-ohai*).

 When you're using chef-solo, the configuration file is called *solo.rb*. It contains a number of solo-specific settings documented on the Chef Documents site (*http://bit.ly/solo-rb*).

Authenticate/Register

After the node's hostname has been obtained, chef-client uses the authentication key and server URL specified in *client.rb* to attempt to authenticate to the Chef server. If a node with that particular hostname doesn't exist on the server yet, chef-client attempts to register the node using a special chef_validator key also specified in *client.rb*. If the server does not verify that the server is authenticated or if registration fails, the run does not continue and jumps straight to the last step (see "Finalize" on page 69).

When using chef-solo, the authentication/registration step is bypassed as there is no central Chef server to communicate with.

Load and Build Node Object

chef-client will now download from the Chef server a *node* object representing the current node, which contains the attributes saved during its last Chef run. If this is the first time the node has executed a run, however, there will be no object to download. Chef combines this historical data with the ohai data obtained in the "Get Configuration Data" on page 63 step of the run process and any other attribute or run list changes to be applied on this run.

The node data downloaded from the server includes the run list that has been specified for this node. Chef-client then *expands* the run list to produce an ordered list of roles and recipes to be applied to the node. This is how Chef provides its guarantee that run lists will always be applied in the same order—each expanded copy of a run list will always be identically ordered, provided the user has not made any changes to the run list.

When using chef-solo, the lack of a Chef server means that no saved node object data exists. During the load stage, chef-solo builds a new node object from the supplied node configuration data. Optionally, attributes can also be passed to chef-solo as a JSON file, using the -j option.

The next part of this step is the creation of a run status object. The *run status* object keeps track of the overall status of the Chef run, and contains a number of different attributes that are populated over the course of the run, depending on whether or not the run is successful. Among other things, it contains a reference to the node object created in this step, along with the run context object created later (see "SetUp Run-Context" on page 66); if an exception occurs during the course of the chef-client run this will also be stored. We'll look at the run status object in more detail in "The Run Status Object" on page 119.

The final part of this step is to run any start handlers that have been defined. Handlers come in a variety of forms that we'll see throughout this chapter, and are designed to trigger certain actions in response to specific situations encountered by the Chef run. Start handlers run before the Chef run has fully begun and are typically used to initialize reporting systems and the like that will be used throughout the rest of the run, or to notify external systems about the start of a Chef run. We'll look at how to define and implement start handlers in detail in Chapter 5.

Synchronize Cookbooks

After the expanded run list has been calculated (see "Load and Build Node Object" on page 65), chef-client asks the Chef server for a list of all cookbook files, which will allow the client to complete all actions specified by the run list. Requesting only those files needed to complete the run allows chef-client to avoid maintaining a complete copy of all of your cookbooks on each node. For example, templates and files not used within the requested recipes are not downloaded. After the server provides the list, chef-client compares it against the local copies of those files stored in its file cache. It then downloads copies of any files that are missing (as they would be on the first chef-client run) or different from those stored on the server.

This *cookbook collection*, to use Chef's terminology, is eventually stored in the RunCon text object created in the next step.

> When using chef-solo, this step is bypassed because a complete copy of all cookbooks is stored on each node—there is no central server from which to download files.

SetUp RunContext

The next stage in the run process is for Chef to create a *run context* object, which is used to track a variety of data about the state of the current Chef run. The data stored in the run context object is built up over the course of the remaining stages of the chef-client run; by the time Chef actually executes recipe code on the node itself, the run context object will contain a complete list of cookbook files required for the run and an ordered list of all resources to be applied to the node.

Note that the run context object is distinct from the run status object created in step 3 of the Chef run process (see "Load and Build Node Object" on page 65). Whereas the run status object contains data on the Chef run as a whole, the run context object only stores data to be used during the "Converge Node" on page 69 step in the process, as we'll see later in this section.

We'll be interacting with the run context object more directly in Chapter 5, but I'll give a quick summary of the data it stores here. As previously mentioned, it's important to note that some of this data is populated during later stages of the Chef run—I've noted this where applicable. The run context object stores all of the following:

The cookbook collection

This collection contains the cookbook files needed to perform the Chef run. This is populated in the "Synchronize Cookbooks" on page 66 step of the run process.

The definitions list

This is a list of all resource definitions to be used during this run. Resource definitions are populated by the "Load Cookbook Data" on page 68 step, when the */definitions* folder of each cookbook is loaded. We'll look at how to create definitions in Chapter 7.

Events

chef-client keeps track of a large number of events that occur during the course of the Chef run, such as when `ohai` has finished running, when a recipe file has been loaded, or when the run has completed. These events are used in combination with an *event dispatcher* publish/subscribe system to provide the chef-client we're all used to seeing, but also to allow the customization of the formatting and verbosity of chef-client's output or the implementation of our own client-side data collection and reporting. We'll see some examples of how Chef adds events to this collection in "Tracing a chef-client Run" on page 77. We'll look in detail at how to interact with the event dispatcher system in Chapter 6.

The delayed notifications collection

During the Chef run, the run context object has to keep track of notifications triggered by the resource's delayed notifications collection. For example, when a `file` resource notifies a `service` resource to restart. By default, notifications are processed at the end of the Chef run. These notifications are stored in the delayed notifications collection.

The immediate notifications collection

It is also possible to tell Chef that a notification must be processed immediately (by adding `:immediately` to your `notifies` statement). As the name suggests, these notifications are processed as soon as they are triggered, rather than at the end of the Chef run. The immediate notifications collection is where the run context object keeps track of these.

The node object

This is the node object created in step 3 of the run process (see "Load and Build Node Object" on page 65), which represents the current state of the node being updated and contains all of the data fetched by `ohai`. Storing a reference to the node object in the run context object is useful for later stages of the run, such as when we save new attributes to the Chef server.

The resource collection

This is where Chef stores its ordered list of all the resources to be applied to the node during the Chef run. This list is populated during the next step of the process.

Load Cookbook Data

Now that chef-client has up-to-date copies of all the cookbook files it needs, it loads all of the cookbook data into memory to build an up-to-date version of the attributes to be used by the node, along with a resource collection containing all of the resources to be applied to the node. As we saw in the previous step, the resource collection is stored inside the run context object for this run. Cookbook data is loaded in a very specific order during this step, as shown in Figure 3-3.

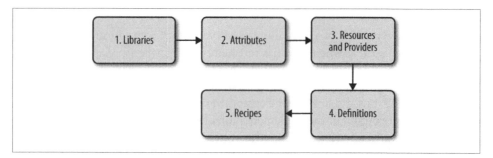

Figure 3-3. Cookbook load order

This strict load order exists to ensure that certain cookbook components are loaded prior to other components that might need to use them. Let's examine this ordering in a little more detail:

1. **Libraries**. Located in the cookbook's */libraries* directory, libraries are loaded before any other cookbook files as they typically extend Chef classes or define custom Ruby classes that you have created. These will usually be included in recipes, definitions, etc. so need to be loaded first. We'll look more at creating libraries in Chapter 7.

2. **Attributes**. Located in the cookbook's */attributes* directory, attribute files are loaded next. Attributes are loaded at this stage as they need to be accessible to recipes, definitions, resources, and providers.

3. **Resources and Providers**. Located in the cookbook's *resources* and *providers* directories, resources and providers are loaded next. These must be loaded prior to recipes as they declare new resource types that can be used in recipe code. We'll look more at creating resources and providers in Chapters 8 and 9.

4. **Definitions**. Located in the cookbook's */definitions* directory, definitions are loaded at this stage as they declare new "pseudo-resources" that can be used within recipes, but may also in turn make use of resources and providers. We'll look more at creating definitions in Chapter 7.

5. **Recipes**. Located in the cookbook's */recipes* directory, recipe files are only loaded after all other cookbook components have been loaded. Recipes are loaded last as

they can make use of all of the cookbook components listed in the previous load steps.

Converge Node

In this stage of the run process, the information collected throughout all of the previous stages is used to apply configurations to the node itself. Until now, the node itself has not actually been changed.

It's also during the converge step that the run context object created in step 5 of the process (see "SetUp RunContext" on page 66) really demonstrates its usefulness. chef-client (or chef-solo) now has access to a single object that contains all of the cookbook files it needs for the run, alongside an ordered list of all of the resources to be applied to the node. chef-client (or chef-solo) steps through this resource collection, carrying out the actions requested by each resource (such as installing software packages, writing template files, restarting services, etc.) to bring the node to convergence.

If any resources raise exceptions during this stage for any reason, Chef will jump straight to the "Finalize" step and execute any exception handlers that have been defined. If no exceptions are raised, it will carry on until all resources in the resource collection have been applied before continuing to the "Finalize" step and executing any report handlers that have been defined.

Finalize

The behavior of chef-client during this last step depends on the outcome of the previous step, or whether an exception earlier in the run caused this stage to be started early. Both possible outcomes result in the execution of *handlers*.

Put simply, handlers trigger certain actions in response to specific situations encountered by the Chef run. We'll cover creating and using handlers in more detail in Chapter 5, but for now let's look at what happens when the converge step in the run process succeeds or fails and what type of handlers are executed:

Successful run
> If the "Converge Node" step completed without any errors, chef-client saves the new node object containing any run list changes and updated attributes back to the Chef server. It also executes any report handlers that have been defined. Report handlers can be created to perform a wide variety of tasks, such as sending metrics to a graphing system to produce a graph of successful Chef runs and their durations.

Failed run
> If an exception occurred during the "Converge Node" step, chef-client does *not* save the updated node object back to the server, and executes any exception handlers that have been defined. It's important to note, however, that if the Chef run failed

before loading handler definitions, exception handlers will not be run as chef-client doesn't know about them yet. Exception handlers can be created to perform tasks such as broadcasting chef run failures to IRC channels or other chat systems.

 When using chef-solo, there is no central server to send updated node data to, but both types of handler are still executed.

At this stage, whether successful or failed, our Chef run is complete.

As we've seen in this section, although a Chef run is initiated with a single command and outputs a single unified view of run progress to our screen, behind the scenes a Chef run is actually broken down into a number of discrete, modular steps. This modularity makes it much easier for us to identify possible customization types that might be of use to us than if we had to deal with a single monolithic step.

For example, if we want to customize the actions Chef performs on run success or failure, we now know that we need to focus on the behavior of the "Finalize" stage. Likewise, if we want to customize the attributes collected by ohai, we know that we need to focus on the behavior of the "Get Configuration Data" stage. As we cover these different types of customizations in later chapters, this section will provide a handy reference point if you need a reminder of which exact stage of the Chef run we're working with, and how it might affect subsequent stages.

But wouldn't it be nice if we could verify exactly what actions a Chef run would perform on a node without actually having to perform a real Chef run?

Dry-Run and Why-Run

When writing infrastructure code (or, for that matter, any code) that involves as many complex steps and stages as Chef runs, it's extremely useful to be able to model what exactly happens when the code is executed without actually executing it. Many tools we use as operations engineers and developers come with a "dry-run" mode to provide this facility. For example, the *rake* task management tool commonly used in the Ruby world allows you to specify `--dry-run` on the command line to print out the steps to be performed by the *rake* task instead of executing them. The *rsync* file transfer utility also provides a `--dry-run` option that causes it to print the list of files to be transferred without actually transferring them.

The Problem with Dry-Run

For tools such as *rake* and *rsync* that build up a list of commands and execute them, a dry-run mode is relatively easy to implement. With configuration management systems such as Chef, however, things become a little more complex. At first glance, the reason for this might not be entirely obvious—after all, Chef builds up an ordered collection of resources and then executes them.

This is indeed the case, but each of those resources does not actually represent a single standalone task like, say, transferring a file with *rsync*. As we saw in "Anatomy of a Chef Run" on page 62, Chef resources are *convergent*, which means they bring the system closer to a *correct* state. For a resource to implement this convergent behavior, it actually requires two separate sets of instructions: the first set determines whether or not the object in question is already in the correct state, and the second defines the actions to take to correct the object if it is not already in a converged state.

Take the example of the `package` resource in Chef, used to install software packages on a wide variety of operating systems. This resource does not simply wrap `yum` or `apt` to run an "install" command every time Chef runs, but rather checks to see if the required package has already been installed at the right version, and then attempts to install the package if it is not found. Similarly, the "start" action of the `service` resource does not simply call the service management layer of the OS to start a service every time Chef runs, but rather checks to see if the required service is already running, only starting it if this is not the case.

To implement traditional dry-run behavior in Chef, it would be necessary to examine each convergent resource and have it describe the actions, if any, it would perform based on the current state of the system. However, in configuration management systems such as Chef, the behavior of a resource can be affected by that of previously executed resources, which potentially means the node state may change between the execution of each resource.

For example, sticking with the `package` and `service` resources, it might be the case that the package installed by the `package` resource adds the service subsequently used by the `service` resource. But without actually installing the package and observing the change to the node (which would defeat the point of dry-run mode entirely), this interdependency is impossible to reflect in dry-run mode. So how can we make dry-run functionality work in Chef?

Why-Run Mode

In order to mitigate these issues somewhat, chef-client (and chef-solo) can be run in a mode called *why-run* (by using the `--why-run` option). Why-run mode provides the functionality we want from the dry-run model we looked at, but makes a number of assumptions to allow it to work with the convergent model of Chef. When using why-run mode, it's extremely important to understand these assumptions as they can cause a run executed in why-run mode to behave differently than one executed in "normal" mode.

When running in why-run mode, chef-client (or chef-solo) makes the following assumptions:

Services
> If Chef in why-run mode is unable to find the command required to configure a service—for instance, in our earlier example, if the service would normally be installed by a `package` resource earlier in the same run—it will *assume* that this service command has been installed by a previous resource, and that the service is not running.
>
> Of course, it's important to ensure that the required service management command (e.g., the *init.d* or *upstart* script) actually *is* installed by a previous resource. Otherwise, you might discover that a run in why-run mode completes without error, while a "normal" run fails when it tries to start a service that is not yet installed or defined.

Resource conditionals
> When Chef in why-run mode encounters `not_if` or `only_if` conditionals declared in resources, it will assume that the conditional is a command or a Ruby block that is safe to run in why-run mode—resource conditionals in Chef are intended to help make resources idempotent, and they should not normally alter the state of the underlying node.
>
> However, it is theoretically possible to define an `only_if` or `not_if` conditional that tests the output of running a `yum install` command, for example. In this case, why-run mode assumes that it is safe to run the conditional block, which could potentially result in a run executed in why-run mode modifying the system. If you find yourself in this situation, I strongly recommend rewriting the relevant portion of your recipe—using conditionals in a non-idempotent fashion is very much an anti-pattern and something to be avoided.

Usefulness of Why-Run

As we've seen, why-run mode makes some assumptions to allow it to approximate the functionality of dry-run mode in the convergent world of Chef runs, which can result in a why-run potentially behaving differently than a "normal" Chef run. So how useful is why-run, given that we can't be absolutely sure that it's telling us exactly how our run will behave in reality?

Simply put, the usefulness of why-run increases the closer the node is to the *correct* state at the start of the Chef run. If you're running the first ever Chef run on a node in why-run mode, you will probably find that a large number of resources are not in the "correct" state, and hence your Chef run will be making a large number of changes to the underlying system to *converge* it. The greater the number of resources requiring corrective action to bring them to convergence is, the greater the chance is for the assumptions made under why-run mode to show different results than a normal run. On the other hand, if your why-run run is checking what will happen when you execute your changes to a single recipe, it's much more likely that the results will mirror those seen in a normal Chef run.

Helpfully, why-run mode specifically informs you of the assumptions it has made during a run to help you identify potential issues that may crop up when performing a normal run. For example, consider the following `service` resource:

```
service "chef-client" do
    action :enable
end
```

When a Chef run in why-run mode reaches this resource, we see the following output:

```
* service[chef-client] action enable
    * Service status not available. Assuming a prior action would have
        installed the service.
    * Assuming status of not running. (up to date)
```

Providing you understand the assumptions being made, why-run mode can be an extremely helpful development tool when writing Chef recipes and particularly when writing your own providers and resources, as we'll be doing in Chapters 8 and 9. As with many operations and development tools, why-run's usefulness depends on what functionality you expect from it versus what it was designed to provide.

If you expect why-run to provide you a 100% accurate list of every single step performed by a Chef run that will be mirrored exactly by a normal run, you may not find it especially useful—it is not designed to provide a replacement for properly validating your cookbooks in a test environment using the tools we looked at in "Development Tooling" on page 13, and will not behave in the same way. On the other hand, if you treat why-run as an addition to your cookbook development toolbox that helps you check the probable behavior of your cookbooks, the combination of why-run's explicitly stated assumptions with your own intuition and skill as a cookbook developer can make it an extremely useful tool. When we come to develop our own recipe resources, providers, and libraries in Part III of this book, we'll be making extensive use of why-run to help us identify whether or not our recipe customizations are behaving correctly.

 For a more detailed analysis of dry-run, why-run, and the difficulties that arise when applying these concepts to configuration management systems such as Chef, I highly recommend taking a look at Sean O'Meara's excellent article on the subject at his blog *A Fistful of Servers* (*http://bit.ly/fistful-servers*).

Using the Source

When we want to dive even deeper into the internals of Chef, an extremely powerful tool that we have available to us is the Chef source code itself. Although the code for the server side of Chef varies between the open source and enterprise variants, all versions of Chef use the same open source client code, which is freely available on GitHub (*http://bit.ly/chef-gh*). This repository contains code for chef-client, chef-solo, Knife, and all of the other client tools we looked at in "Chef Client Tools" on page 59. Chef, Inc. actively encourages community contributions to this code, and new Chef releases usually combine a mix of features and patches added by the people at Chef, Inc. and features and patches added by the Chef community.

The chef-client codebase is an invaluable reference guide when analyzing exactly how Chef implements particular functionality, and it allows us to benefit from the experience and expertise of the developers who work on Chef day in, day out. Often when implementing customizations in Chef, a good starting point can be looking at how the team at Chef, Inc. implemented similar functionality.

In this section, we'll start with how to get a copy of the Chef source code and find your way around the repository, along with where to find the code that controls some of the Chef behavior we've seen already. We'll then combine the Ruby knowledge we gained in Chapter 2 with the Chef internals knowledge gained so far in this chapter to trace the execution of an actual Chef run through the Chef codebase.

 We're taking a whistle-stop tour around the Chef codebase here, aimed to familiarize you with how Chef's code is organized and the classes that make up an actual Chef run. Don't worry if you aren't able to fully understand the code in some of Chef's class definitions—in parts of the book where a more comprehensive understanding is required as we extend or inherit from Chef classes, we'll cover the code in much greater detail.

Getting the Chef Source Code

You might find it useful to download your own copy of the Chef source code from GitHub when working through this chapter and the rest of the material in the book. To download a copy of the Chef repository, run the following command (which requires that git be installed):

```
$> git clone https://github.com/opscode/chef.git
```

This places a copy of the Chef codebase in a directory called *chef* under the directory where you ran the command.

This command actually gives us a copy of the master branch of the Chef repository. It's important to note that the *master* branch may contain code not yet released to the public, so if you're writing code that inherits from Chef code, please check to ensure that code is deployed in the latest stable release.

If you want to switch your local copy of Chef to the latest stable release (11.10.0 at the time of writing), you can use the following command, run from the directory produced above:

```
$> git checkout --track -b 11-stable origin/11-stable
```

Chef Source Structure

Let's take a moment to look at how the Chef source code repository is structured, to give you the lay of the land, so to speak. Please note that the directory structure shown here is somewhat abbreviated to remove directories that aren't of immediate interest to us here. It's worth exploring the full directory structure at your leisure, but for now we'll focus on the areas we explore throughout this book.

 Where directories in the following repository directory listing have been removed for brevity, this is indicated by an ellipsis (...).

The Chef source code repository is structured as follows:

```
.
├── bin ❶
├── ...
├── lib
│   └── chef ❷
│       ├── ...
│       ├── application ❸
│       ├── ...
│       ├── cookbook ❹
│       ├── ...
│       ├── event_dispatch ❺
│       ├── ...
│       ├── formatters ❻
│       │   └── error_inspectors
│       ├── ...
│       ├── knife ❼
│       │   ├── bootstrap
│       │   └── core
│       ├── ...
│       ├── provider ❽
│       │   ├── cookbook_file
│       │   ├── cron
```

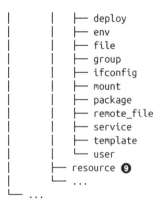

```
|         |    ├── deploy
|         |    ├── env
|         |    ├── file
|         |    ├── group
|         |    ├── ifconfig
|         |    ├── mount
|         |    ├── package
|         |    ├── remote_file
|         |    ├── service
|         |    ├── template
|         |    └── user
|         ├── resource ❾
|         └── ...
└── ...
```

❶   The *bin* directory contains the executable scripts for Chef client tools such as chef-client, chef-solo, and Knife.

❷   The *lib/chef* directory is where the majority of the classes used by the Chef client tools are stored. This directory contains a number of subdirectories covered in more detail below, as well as class definitions for core Chef objects such as cookbooks, nodes, and roles. You can typically find these definitions in files called *<object>.rb*, as in *node.rb* or *cookbook.rb*.

❸   The *lib/chef/application* directory contains a number of class definitions for objects that are used by the Chef client tools. We'll look in more detail at some of these classes in "Tracing a chef-client Run" on page 77.

❹   The *lib/chef/cookbook* directory contains a number of class definitions for objects associated with cookbooks. This directory contains class files such as *synchronizer.rb* (used during the "Synchronize Cookbooks" on page 66 stage of the Chef run process) and *cookbook_collection.rb* (the object that contains the cookbook collection produced during that step).

❺   The *lib/chef/event_dispatch* directory contains the classes used for the event dispatcher touched on this briefly in "SetUp RunContext" on page 66, and we'll look at the event dispatcher in much more detail, including how to extend and interact with it, in Chapter 6.

❻   The *lib/chef/formatters* directory contains the formatter classes used to display the output of chef-client and chef-solo to the user when these commands are run in an interactive terminal—these also make use of the event dispatcher system. Inside this directory, *doc.rb* is the default formatter used by chef-client; if you have a peek inside this file you'll probably recognize a number of the output messages it contains. We'll look at formatters and the overall event dispatcher system in more detail in Chapter 6.

❼ The *lib/chef/knife* directory contains class definitions for all of the default Knife commands provided with Chef, along with classes used to power Knife itself. Class files for Knife commands are named similarly to the commands that make use of them—the code for `knife node list`, for example, is contained in *node_list.rb*. We'll be using and extending some of these classes in Chapter 10 when we look at creating our own Knife plugins.

❽ The `lib/chef/provider` directory contains the class definitions for providers, which contain the code to carry out the actions defined in cookbook resources. Provider class definitions are named according to the resources they support, so for example you'll find the class for the `execute` provider inside *execute.rb*. Some more complex providers declare several classes inside their own directories; for example, `package` providers have to be implemented for a variety of packaging systems, and all of the relevant classes are included in the package directory. We'll explore providers in greater detail in Part III.

❾ The *lib/chef/resource* directory contains class definitions for all of the cookbook resources that come with Chef out of the box—you've likely already used many of them in your recipes. Resource class definitions are named according to the resources they define, so for example you'll find the class for the `execute` resource inside *execute.rb*. We'll create our own resources in Part III.

Tracing a chef-client Run

Now that we've leveled up our Ruby skills and explored the structure of Chef's source code, let's put this knowledge to use and dive headfirst into a real example. When the `chef-client` command runs, what happens behind the scenes to actually drive the process we've looked at?

We're going to trace the execution of the `chef-client` command down through the Chef codebase to help demonstrate that the concepts we learned in Chapter 2 (such as inheritance, dynamic typing, and modules) work in practice as well as in theory. Chef contains some complex Ruby code, but the basic principles are no different to those we covered in Chapter 2.

 A number of the methods utilized by the classes in this example contain fairly complex Ruby code. To avoid making this example too overwhelming, I've summarized the behavior of these methods in plain English or listed excerpts of the code. For the interested reader or more confident Ruby programmers, I'll link to the source code of the files involved so you can take a look at the full code.

Execute the chef-client Command

The first step in tracing the execution of the `chef-client` command is, of course, to run it. When the `chef-client` command is run, your operating system scans a list of directories to search for an executable program by that name. This directory list is stored in the PATH environment variable, which is used by your operating system in much the same way that Ruby uses the LOAD_PATH variable to locate Ruby files.

By default, executable scripts used by RubyGems are not installed under directories listed in PATH, so when Chef is installed, the omnibus installer (or RubyGems, if you did a manual install) drops a *chef-client* script into a directory listed in PATH. This is typically */usr/bin/* on Linux systems—I've used that path for the script in this section, but it will vary for users of Windows and other operating systems.

This *chef-client* script is actually just a wrapper file that locates and executes the *real chef-client* script under the *bin* directory of the *chef* gem installed in the omnibus install directory. Inside this *chef* gem, the code is structured exactly as we saw in "Chef Source Structure" on page 75.

> The first line of the wrapper script specifies that the code should be run using the Ruby binary located in */opt/chef/embedded/bin/ruby*. If you're running on a non-Linux/Unix-based system or you installed Chef from RubyGems, you will need to alter this to the correct path to your Ruby binary.

Inside this wrapper script, we find the Ruby code listed in Example 3-1.

Example 3-1. /usr/bin/chef-client

```
#!/opt/chef/embedded/bin/ruby

# Comments added for clarity

# Require the 'rubygems' gem, so we can use its classes and methods
require 'rubygems'

# Specify what version of the chef gem we require (>=0 means "any version")
version = ">= 0"

# Code to handle running a specific version of a command
# removed for brevity
<snip>

# Check that the required version of the chef gem is installed at the right version
# using the gem method provided by the rubygems gem
gem 'chef', version ❶

# Find the bin_path of the installed chef gem,
```

```
# locate the binary called chef-client and load it
load Gem.bin_path('chef', 'chef-client', version) ❷
```

❶   This line verifies that the required version of the chef gem is actually installed. If a version of the chef gem that matches the version requirement >= 0 (this means "any version is installed") is not found, then an exception will be thrown and execution will stop. There's no point in trying to continue when the gem we need isn't present!

❷   We then locate the bin_path of the chef gem (where its executable scripts are located), find the exact path to the chef-client gem, and then run it using the built-in load keyword. The load keyword (defined under the Kernel module we encountered in Chapter 2) simply takes a string containing the path to the file to be executed, and then loads and runs that file.

Run the Real chef-client Script

Now that the load statement in the previous example has located and executed the real chef-client script, we need to take a look at that script. Although the wrapper script in Example 3-1 did not print out the actual location of the real chef-client script, you can check the location of the script for yourself by pasting the Ruby code in Example 3-2 into a file called *chef_client_path.rb* and running it.

Example 3-2. chef_client_path.rb

```
#!/opt/chef/embedded/bin/ruby
puts Gem.bin_path('chef', 'chef-client')
```

When you run *chef_client_path.rb*, you should see output similar to the following, with the full path to the real *chef-client* script printed:

```
$> ./chef_client_path.rb
/opt/chef/embedded/lib/ruby/gems/1.9.1/gems/chef-11.8.2/bin/chef-client
```

We've identified and located the script that powers the next stage in our Chef run, so let's have a look at what this script actually does. Like the wrapper script, the actual *chef-client* script (Example 3-3) is extremely short—in fact, it's only four lines of code. Nonetheless, it demonstrates a number of the concepts we looked at in Chapter 2.

Example 3-3. /opt/chef/embedded/lib/ruby/gems/1.9.1/gems/chef-11.8.2/bin/chef-client

```
require 'rubygems' ❶
$:.unshift(File.join(File.dirname(__FILE__), "..", "lib")) ❷
require 'chef' ❸
require 'chef/application/client' ❹

Chef::Application::Client.new.run ❺
```

❶ Here we're requiring the rubygems gem (as explained in "RubyGems" on page 42), so that the methods and classes it provides are available to our Ruby program.

❷ The $: syntax used here is a shortcut to the LOAD_PATH variable we looked at in "Local Classes" on page 41. What we're actually doing here is adding the *lib* directory located one directory level up from the *knife* script to our LOAD_PATH. Because LOAD_PATH is an array, here we're doing that with the Array class's .unshift method, which adds an element to the start of an array.

❸❹ Now that our LOAD_PATH is correct, we require a gem called chef and a class called chef/application/client.

❺ Finally, we create a new instance of the Chef::Application::Client class (which we can now use thanks to the previous require line) and call its run method.

The Chef::Application::Client Class

The class definition for the Chef::Application::Client object created in the previous step can be found, as its name might suggest, in *lib/chef/application/client.rb* (*http://bit.ly/gh-clientrb*). If we look inside this class, we'll see that it's defined as shown in Example 3-4.

Example 3-4. Excerpt of lib/chef/application/client.rb

```
class Chef::Application::Client < Chef::Application
 # Lots of code
end
```

The Chef::Application::Client class inherits from the superclass Chef::Application, located at *lib/chef/application.rb* (*http://bit.ly/gh-apprb*). The Chef::Application class is shared between all of the Chef client tools, including chef-client and knife, and declares a number of methods common to all these tools.

The run method called in the last line of the *chef-client* script (Example 3-3) is actually defined by the Chef::Application class, but because Chef::Application::Client is a subclass of this, it has that method available to it as well. Example 3-5 shows what's inside the run method in Chef::Application.

Example 3-5. Excerpt of lib/chef/application.rb

```
class Chef::Application
  ...
  def run
    reconfigure
    setup_application
    run_application
```

```
  end
  ...
end
```

The `run` method is also extremely short and straightforward. It calls three methods, one after the other—but this is where some cleverness starts to creep in. Although there are method definitions for all three of these methods inside `Chef::Application`, they are *overridden* by `Chef::Application::Client` to provide logic specific to chef-client.

 Overriding a method in Ruby essentially means a subclass changing the implementation of a method that was already defined by the superclass. This demonstrates some of the power of object-oriented programming—without the subclass and superclass concept, the Chef client tools would have to contain separate copies of common methods. With object-oriented languages like Ruby, the superclass is able to define methods common to all subclasses, while still allowing the subclasses to override methods that implement specific behavior.

To demonstrate overriding in action, if we look at the definition of the `run_applica tion` method in `Chef::Application`, we see:

```
class Chef::Application

  # Other code removed for clarity, comments added

  def run_application
    # Raise an exception printing the name of the class that has called
    # this method and tell it to override
    raise Chef::Exceptions::Application, "#{self.to_s}: you must
      override run_application"
  end

end
```

But if we look in `Chef::Application::Client`, we see:

```
class Chef::Application::Client < Chef::Application

  # Other code removed for clarity

  def run_application
    # Lots of code
  end

end
```

Note here that the method names are identical. When an object of the `Chef::Applica tion::Client` class is created, it contains all the methods defined by `Chef::Applica tion` as well as any methods it defines itself, including those that override methods from

Chef::Application. This somewhat subtle behavior allows all subclasses of Chef::Application to share a common run method while implementing their own versions of the setup_application, reconfigure, and run_application methods.

Now let's take a closer look at the three methods of Chef::Application::Client being run by the run method. To keep things simple, I'll summarize the behavior of each method in plain text rather than listing the full code, but interested readers can explore the actual code on GitHub (*http://bit.ly/gh-clientrb*) or in their local copies of the repository. The methods are:

reconfigure

The reconfigure method carries out two steps. First, it validates and parses the command-line options given to chef-client. Next, it loads the configuration contained in the *client.rb* configuration file and stores it in a Chef::Config object for use by later steps in the run process. As a side exercise for the interested reader, why not see if you can locate the class definition for Chef::Config in the Chef repository and explore its methods?

setup_application

The setup_application method sets the *user* and *group* who own the chef-client process, if these have been specified in the configuration loaded from *client.rb*. This is particularly important when chef-client is running in daemonized mode, as typically occurs in this case because we want it to always run under a particular user or group.

run_application

The run_application method is the one we're most interested in here, as it's the method that carries out the next step in executing the Chef run. This method contains logic to either run chef-client in daemonized mode, or run it in a continuous loop if the --once option was not passed to chef-client. Incidentally, it's here that the splay and interval options that we can specify in *client.rb* come into play—when running in a loop, this method ensures that chef-client will only initiate a run every interval seconds, with an added delay of up to splay seconds at the start of the run. An excerpt of the run_application method is shown in Example 3-6 (comments added for clarity).

Example 3-6. Excerpt of run_application method from Chef::Application::Client

```
# If a splay has been specified
if Chef::Config[:splay]
  # Pick a random number between 0 and 'splay'
  splay = rand Chef::Config[:splay]

  # Log how long 'splay' will be
  Chef::Log.debug("Splay sleep #{splay} seconds")
```

```
  # Sleep for 'splay' seconds
  sleep splay
end

# Run 'run_chef_client' method
run_chef_client
```

As we can see here, after program execution (using the built-in Ruby sleep method) for splay seconds, we're now calling a method called run_chef_client.

The Chef::Application::Client run_chef_client Method

The run_chef_client method is defined in the superclass Chef::Application, as its implementation is common to any Chef client tool (such as chef-client or chef-solo) that is going to initiate a Chef. This method is the last "preparatory" step before the actual Chef run is initiated, and it contains the code in Example 3-7.

Example 3-7. run_chef_client method from Chef::Application

```
# Initializes Chef::Client instance and runs it
def run_chef_client
  Chef::Application.setup_server_connectivity ❶

  @chef_client = Chef::Client.new(
    @chef_client_json,
    :override_runlist => config[:override_runlist]
  ) ❷
  @chef_client_json = nil ❸

  @chef_client.run ❹
  @chef_client = nil ❺

  Chef::Application.destroy_server_connectivity ❻
end
```

❶ The setup_server_connectivity method of the Chef::Application class starts up the chef-zero server we saw in "Local Mode" on page 20, if the -z option was passed to chef-client to run it in local mode. This step also updates configuration parameters such as chef_server_url to point to chef-zero instead of the server specified in *client.rb*. If the -z parameter was not passed to chef-client, this step does nothing and chef-client will connect to the server specified by the chef_server_url configuration option as normal.

❷ Next, we create a new instance of the Chef::Client class, passing as parameters the JSON representation of the configuration loaded from *config.rb*, and an optional overridden run list passed to chef-client with the --override-runlist option. We'll look at the Chef::Client class in more detail in "The Chef::Client Class" on page 84.

❸   Now that we've created our `Chef::Client` object, we can delete the JSON version of the loaded configuration because we don't need it any more.

❹   Next, we call the `run` method of the `Chef::Client` object we created in step 2 to actually carry out the Chef run. We'll look at this step in more detail in the next section.

❺   When the Chef run has completed, we delete the `Chef::Client` object we created.

❻   If we were using chef-zero to run chef-client in local mode, here we kill the chef-zero instance we created in step 1.

The Chef::Client Class

The `Chef::Client` class is the final crucial component needed to carry out a Chef run, and is located in *lib/chef/client.rb* (*http://bit.ly/gh-apprb*). This class handles all of the run stages shown in Figure 3-2, aside from the "Get Config Data" step, which, as we saw in "The Chef::Application::Client Class" on page 80, was handled by the `reconfigure` method of the `Chef::Application::Client class`.

When this object is created by the `run chef_client` method we looked at in the previous section, the `initialize` method (shown in Example 3-8) creates a number of the objects that will be used during the Chef run, including placeholders for the node object, run status object, and events collection (see "SetUp RunContext" on page 66).

The `run` method of the `Chef::Client` class that we called in the previous section is a "wrapper" method for the actual method that carries out a Chef run. Before going ahead with the run, the `run` method contains code to handle forking the run itself off as a new process if the `--fork` option was passed to chef-client. The code also makes sure that if chef-client is running on Windows (which does not support process forking), we don't try to fork the process.

The code is shown in Example 3-8.

Example 3-8. Excerpt of lib/chef/client.rb

```
class Chef
  class Client

    # Other methods, etc. removed for simplicity

    # Create a new Chef::Client
    def initialize(json_attribs=nil, args={})

        # Create objects needed during the Chef run
        @json_attribs = json_attribs
        @node = nil
        @run_status = nil
```

```ruby
    @runner = nil
    @ohai = Ohai::System.new

    # Load event handler and formatter classes
    event_handlers = configure_formatters
    event_handlers += Array(Chef::Config[:event_handlers])

    # Create new events collection
    @events = EventDispatch::Dispatcher.new(*event_handlers)

    # Load overridden run list, if one was passed in as a parameter
    @override_runlist = args.delete(:override_runlist)
    runlist_override_sanity_check!
  end

  def run

    # If the chef-client run should be forked...
    if(Chef::Config[:client_fork] && Process.respond_to?(:fork) &&
       !Chef::Platform.windows?)

      Chef::Log.info "Forking chef instance to converge..."
      # Start a "fork" block
      pid = fork do

        # Fork configuration code removed for simplicity

        # Code is wrapped in a begin/rescue block to trap errors
        begin
          # Call the 'do_run' method
          do_run
        rescue Exception => e
          Chef::Log.error(e.to_s)
          # Terminate the program with the status code "1",
          # which indicates that an error occurred
          exit 1
        else
          # Terminate the program with the status code "0",
          # which indicates that the program finished successfully
          exit 0
        end
      end

      # Code to handle cleaning up after forked process has finished
      # removed for simplicity

    # If forking is not needed, just call 'do_run' straight away
    else
    # Call the 'do_run' method
      do_run
    end
  end
end
```

As we can see in this example, regardless of whether the Chef run is forked or not, both branches of the code end up calling the do_run method, which is also defined in Chef::Application::Client. We'll look at this method next.

The Chef::Client Class do_run Method

After working our way through a number of class definitions and methods in the Chef codebase, we've finally reached our destination—the method that actually carries out the majority of the steps of our chef-client run (see "Anatomy of a Chef Run" on page 62).

Unlike with many of the examples so far in this section, I've listed the code of the do_run method in full in Example 3-9; however, I haven't listed the code for the methods it calls. We'll look in detail at the methods called by do_run after the code listing, and I've added descriptive comments throughout the method body. For additional clarity, I've also included an expanded version of the Chef run stage diagram we saw earlier in the chapter with each method call aligned with the run stage it represents (Figure 3-4).

 If you're interested in diving even deeper into the Chef source code, the full code for each method called by do_run can be found in */lib/ chef/client.rb (http://bit.ly/gh-apprb)*.

Example 3-9. do_run method of the Chef::Client class

```
def do_run

  # Create a lock so we can't perform multiple Chef
  # runs at once
  runlock = RunLock.new(Chef::Config.lockfile)
  runlock.acquire

  # Don't add code that may fail before entering this section to be sure
  # to release lock

  begin

    # Save the process ID of the chef-client process into our run lock
    runlock.save_pid

    # The variable we will use to store our RunContext object
    run_context = nil

    # Add an event to our events collection to indicate run_start
    @events.run_start(Chef::VERSION)

    # Log that the run has started, and log its PID
    Chef::Log.info("*** Chef #{Chef::VERSION} ***")
```

```
Chef::Log.info "Chef-client pid: #{Process.pid}"

# Call enforce_path_sanity method
# Ensures PATH variable is set correctly for chef-client
enforce_path_sanity

# Call run_ohai method
run_ohai ❶

# Add an event to our events collection to indicate ohai_completed
@events.ohai_completed(node)

# Call register method unless running chef-solo
# Registers/authenticates chef-client with the server
register unless Chef::Config[:solo] ❷

# Call load_node method
# Loads existing node object from the server
load_node ❸

# Calls build_node method
# Build node object from ohai data
build_node ❹

# Call start_clock method of run_status object
# This is a Chef::RunStatus object created by the build_node method
run_status.start_clock
Chef::Log.info("Starting Chef Run for #{node.name}")

# Run any start handlers that have been defined
# and add an event to the events collection to indicate run started
run_started ❺

# Call do_windows_admin_check method
# If we're running on Windows, this checks Chef is running as
# an administrative user
do_windows_admin_check

# Call the setup_run_context object and assign it to
# a variable called run_context
run_context = setup_run_context ❻

# Call the converge method, passing the run_context variable
# as a parameter
converge(run_context) ❼

# Call save_updated_note method
# Saves node changes to the server
save_updated_node ❽

# Call the stop_clock method of the run_status object
run_status.stop_clock
```

```ruby
    Chef::Log.info("Chef Run complete in #{run_status.elapsed_time} seconds")
    # Call run_completed method
    # Runs any report handlers that have been defined
    run_completed_successfully ❾

    # Add an event to our events collection to indicate run_completed
    @events.run_completed(node)

    # We're all done! Return "true".
    true

  # Code to handle any exceptions that occur during the run
  # Here we're catching *all* exceptions
  rescue Exception => e
    # Log error message before doing anything else
    Chef::Log.debug("Re-raising exception: #{e.class} - \
      #{e.message}\n#{e.backtrace.join("\n  ")}")
    # Check if we failed after creating the run_status object
    # If we didn't, our error handlers won't be of much use
    if run_status
      run_status.stop_clock
      # Store the exception in the run_status object
      run_status.exception = e
      # Call the run_failed method
      # Runs any exception handlers that have been defined
      run_failed ❿
    end
    Chef::Application.debug_stacktrace(e)
    # Add an event to our events collection to indicate run_failed
    @events.run_failed(e)
    # Now that we've run our error handlers, reraise the exception
    # and let Ruby stop program execution as normal
    raise
  # Code to clean up after exception handling:
  # delete all of our objects, release the run lock, and
  # start garbage collection to clean up memory
  ensure
    @run_status = nil
    run_context = nil
    runlock.release
    GC.start
  end
  true
end
```

Before diving into what each method does, let's take a moment to remind ourselves of the different stages of a Chef run and match the method calls here with each step. Figure 3-4 shows the same diagram we saw earlier in the chapter, expanded to show which stage of the run each method call relates to.

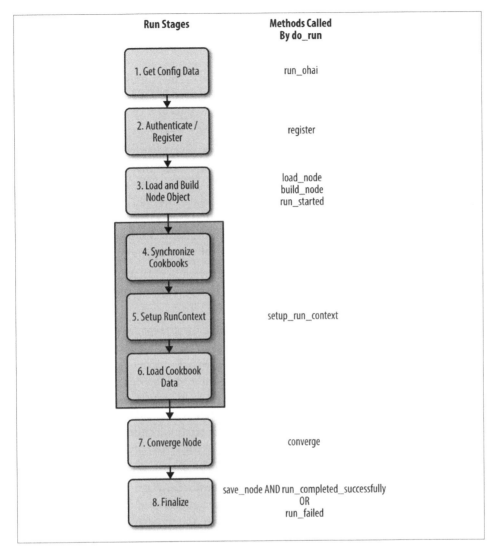

Run Stages	Methods Called By do_run
1. Get Config Data	run_ohai
2. Authenticate / Register	register
3. Load and Build Node Object	load_node build_node run_started
4. Synchronize Cookbooks	
5. Setup RunContext	setup_run_context
6. Load Cookbook Data	
7. Converge Node	converge
8. Finalize	save_node AND run_completed_successfully OR run_failed

Figure 3-4. Chef run process with method calls

Now let's take a closer look at the method calls in Example 3-9 and examine exactly what each does. I've included references to the explanations of each run stage we covered earlier in the chapter:

❶   run_ohai method runs the included ohai tool to gather updated information about the nodes for step 1 of the Chef run process (see "Get Configuration Data" on page 63).

❷   The `register` method registers the node with the configured Chef server, or authenticates it if it already exists. This drives step 2 of the run process (see "Authenticate/Register" on page 64).

❸   The `load_node` method loads the existing `Chef::Node` object (defined in */lib/ chef/node.rb*) from the Chef server. If running in chef-solo mode, this method creates a new blank node object. This is the first part of step 3 of the run process (see "Load and Build Node Object" on page 65).

❹   The `build_node` method takes the `Chef::Node` object loaded in the first part of step 3 and adds in the `ohai` data gathered in step 1, together with any additional attributes or run list overrides, before finally expanding the run list into a list of roles and recipes to apply to the node. It also creates the `Chef::RunStatus` object (defined in */lib/chef/run_status.rb*), which will be used to keep track of the run status throughout the rest of the run. This forms the second part of step 3 of the run process (see "Load and Build Node Object" on page 65).

❺   The `run_started` method executes any start handlers that have been defined and forms the final part of the third step of the Chef run process ("Load and Build Node Object" on page 65).

❻   The `setup_run_context` method performs the three steps in Figure 3-4 that are enclosed in a separate box. First, cookbook data is synchronized with the server (step 4 in the Chef run process, described in "Synchronize Cookbooks" on page 66). Then, a `Chef::RunContext` object (defined in */lib/chef/run_context.rb*) is created and initialized (step 5, covered in "SetUp RunContext" on page 66). Lastly, the sixth step in the process is performed (see "Load Cookbook Data" on page 68): the data from each cookbook in the cookbook collection is loaded into memory and stored in the run context object as the *resource collection* we looked at in "SetUp RunContext" on page 66.

❼   The call to the `converge` method triggers the entire convergence step ("Converge Node" on page 69), which applies the resource collection to the node. This is the first point during the entire run process where the underlying node is actually changed to bring it to convergence.

❽   The `save_node` method saves the updated node object back to the server, provided the run was successful. This takes care of the first part of what's done for a successful run, as described in "Finalize" on page 69.

❾   The `run_completed_successfully` method executes any report handlers that have been defined, provided the run was successful. This is the second part of what's done for a successful run, as described in "Finalize" on page 69.

❿   If the run failed, the `run_failed` method will execute any exception handlers that have been defined, in the event that the run fails (see "Finalize" on page 69).

In this section, we've taken our existing knowledge of the different stages of a Chef run from "Anatomy of a Chef Run" on page 62 and augmented it by looking under the hood at the actual code that makes the entire process happen. The Chef source code is not "magic" in any way, nor is it something to be afraid of—although complex in places, it is still fundamentally a collection of modules, classes, and methods just like the examples we looked at in Chapter 2. Every single operation you carry out with Chef's client tools, from Knife commands to converging cookbooks, can be traced through the code as we did here with Chef runs.

Throughout the rest of the book, we'll build on this introduction to some of Chef's classes and methods to develop a wide variety of customizations—my hope is that the foundations I've laid in this chapter will enable you to gain a fuller understanding of where and how these customizations fit into your Chef setup.

Summary

Over the course of this chapter we've dived deep into the internals of Chef, from an initial top-level overview of the components that make up Chef's server and client tools, through the anatomy of how a Chef run is carried out, and into the Chef codebase itself to examine some of the actual classes and methods that power this behavior. I strongly believe that an in-depth understanding of how Chef functions under the hood is an invaluable tool when looking to customize and extend its behavior, and it's my hope that this chapter has assisted you in that regard.

Before moving on to the rest of the chapters in this book, if a lot of the material we've covered so far was new to you I'd encourage you to skim through Chapters 2 and 3 one more time. A good understanding of object-oriented programming with Ruby and the internals of Chef is essential to make the most of Chef's incredible flexibility and extensibility, so it's worth taking a little extra time to let everything sink in.

With that out of the way, let's get customizing! Most of the remainder of the book is broken down into chapters focusing on customizing specific aspects of Chef. Although it's my hope that you'll read through all of the book, Chapters 4 through 12 are written so that they can be treated as self-contained units if you choose to skip ahead.

## PART II

Customizing Chef Runs

Now that we've seen an overview of the Ruby concepts necessary for customizing Chef and examined in detail how Chef runs work under the hood, we're ready to start looking at how to create our own customizations. The upcoming chapters focus in detail on how to customize different aspects of Chef, and explore the tasks to which each type of customization is best suited.

In Part II, we focus specifically on customizing various components of the Chef run process that we looked at in Chapter 3, and the Chef classes we'll be making use of along the way:

- In Chapter 4, we learn how to write plugins for ohai that let you store your own attributes in your Chef nodes.

- In Chapter 5, we learn how to implement our own customizations to leverage the run status information that Chef exposes to create our own start, report, and exception handlers.

- In Chapter 6, we learn how to make use of the events collection that Chef builds up during the course of a run to create our own customized views into the *progress* of Chef runs through the use of the Chef event dispatcher.

We then finish by using the concepts learned throughout these chapters to revisit one of the problems AwesomeInc has been experiencing, which we explored in "Criteria for Customization" on page 10.

## CHAPTER 4

Extending Ohai

As we saw in Chapter 3, during the initial stage of the Chef run process (described in "Get Configuration Data" on page 63) Chef runs the Ohai tool to build up a collection of data about the node, which is saved on the Chef server as part of the node object. Ohai is installed as part of the Chef installation process and must be present on a node for chef-client or chef-solo to function correctly.

The core Ohai tool is driven by its flexible and powerful plugin interface. Out of the box, Ohai ships with a number of useful plugins that collect data on various generic aspects of the underlying system, such as the hardware, operating system, and networking configuration.

The power of Ohai's plugin framework, however, comes from the fact that it allows us to define our own plugins to augment the information stored about our nodes on the Chef server. Say, for example, we want our nodes to define an attribute stating whether they are virtual machines (VMs) or physical servers, so that our recipes only install VM-specific packages on nodes that need them. Perhaps we want to add a node attribute that fetches the physical location of a node from an asset management system so that we can make use of this logic in our recipe code. Out of the box, Ohai does not collect any of this data—but we can easily create our own plugins that do.

Much in the same way as the Chef Recipe domain-specific language (DSL) provides us with a number of useful resource blocks to abstract away the complexities of the underlying Ruby code, Ohai defines its own Ruby-based DSL to simplify the process of writing plugins. In this chapter, we'll explore this DSL by analyzing the "skeleton code" necessary to create a working plugin, and how to test your plugins and integrate them into Chef runs. We'll then add functionality to our plugin skeleton to explore some of the different features provided by the Ohai DSL before looking at some of the actual plugins that ship with Ohai.

This chapter assumes that you are using Ohai version 7.0 or greater, which was released in April 2014 and included with Chef version 11.20.0 forward. Version 7 of Ohai introduced a new DSL for defining plugins, which supersedes the DSL used in previous Ohai versions.

Introduction

Before we start to look at Ohai's DSL, let's take a moment to examine the way in which Chef treats attributes gathered by Ohai and how they are given precedence over attributes defined in recipes, roles, and environments.

Ohai Attribute Collection

When ohai runs, it iterates through all of the plugins it knows about to build up a collection of attributes describing the underlying node, which it then passes to the chef-client process. Because these attributes represent information about the node itself rather than the recipes being executed, Chef needs to ensure that they do not get altered during the course of the Chef run—when we use attributes collected by ohai like node[:fqdn] and node[:platform_version] in our recipes, it wouldn't be particularly desirable to be able to accidentally switch our node's platform from centos to debian in the middle of a run. To provide this guarantee that ohai attributes will not be changed during the run, Chef assigns them *automatic* precedence.

> # Chef Attribute Precedence
>
> In Chef, where an attribute is defined and what level it is defined at determines whether or not it takes precedence over other attributes defined with the same name in recipes, roles, environments, etc. This system of attribute precedence can often be somewhat confusing to new Chef users. Here's a handy list of the order in which attributes take precedence (from lowest to highest):
>
> 1. A default attribute located in a cookbook attribute file (*lowest precedence level*)
> 2. A default attribute located in a recipe
> 3. A default attribute located in an environment
> 4. A default attribute located in a role
> 5. A force_default attribute located in a cookbook attribute file
> 6. A force_default attribute located in a recipe
> 7. A normal attribute located in a cookbook attribute file
> 8. A normal attribute located in a recipe

9. An `override` attribute located in a cookbook attribute file

10. An `override` attribute located in a recipe

11. An `override` attribute located in a role

12. An `override` attribute located in an environment

13. A `force_override` attribute located in a cookbook attribute file

14. A `force_override` attribute located in a recipe

15. An `automatic` attribute identified by Ohai at the start of the chef-client run (*highest precedence level*)

As shown in the previous sidebar, *automatic* attributes take the absolute highest level of precedence. This means that even if we were to try and override an attribute collected by `ohai` in our recipe, the `ohai` version would always "win" because it is at a higher precedence level. This enables `ohai` to guarantee that the attributes it gives us are immutable during the course of a Chef run, and that (providing the Chef run is successful) they will be saved to the node object on the Chef server exactly as collected by `ohai` at the start of the run.

The Ohai Source Code

Just as the Chef source code is an extremely useful tool for examining the behavior of Chef, the source code of Ohai—particularly its plugins—is a useful (but optional) aid when working through the material in this chapter.

The Ohai source code is located in a separate repository from that of Chef, and is available on GitHub (*http://bit.ly/gh-ohai*). To clone a copy of the Ohai source code, run the following command (which requires `git` to be installed):

```
$> git clone https://github.com/opscode/ohai.git
```

We won't be examining the under-the-hood implementation of Ohai in as much detail as we did that of chef-client in "Tracing a chef-client Run" on page 77, although interested readers may wish to dive a little deeper into its inner workings. We will, however, be looking at the implementation of Ohai plugins, and the source code of the plugins shipped with Ohai can be a useful reference to augment the examples shown in this chapter. These are located in the *lib/ohai/plugins* directory in the repository.

Now, on to the code!

Ohai Example 1: Plugin Skeleton

Throughout this chapter we'll actually be running the example plugin code we create, so at this point I'd recommend creating a directory to place your example plugins in.

I've used */tmp/ohai_plugins* in all of the examples: if you're on Windows or want to use a different directory path, you'll need to amend the path used in the examples as appropriate.

Let's start off by looking at an example of the absolute minimum code necessary to produce a functioning Ohai plugin—it won't actually add any attributes to our node yet, but it will demonstrate the framework with which we'll create more functional plugins as the chapter progresses. Paste the code in Example 4-1 into */tmp/ohai_plugins/example1.rb*.

Example 4-1. /tmp/ohai_plugins/example1.rb

```
Ohai.plugin(:Example1) do ❶
  provides "awesome_level" ❷

  collect_data do ❸
    awesome_level 100 ❹
  end
end
```

❶ This first line tells Ohai what the name of the plugin class will be—under the hood, all Ohai plugins are actually treated as classes that live under the `Ohai::NamedPlugin` namespace, and Ohai needs to know what the class will be called. The name passed to the `Ohai.plugin` method (a symbol, because it must be immutable) must be a valid Ruby class name and start with a capital letter. Here we've used `Example1`.

❷ Next, we call the `provides` method with a comma-separated list of all the attributes our plugin will provide. In this example, we're just creating one attribute called `awesome_level`.

❸ The `collect_data` block is called by Ohai when it executes each plugin to ask it to collect its data. This block is mandatory: if a `collect_data` block is not defined in the plugin code, the plugin will not do anything.

❹ Inside the `collect data` block, we're stating that the value of our `awesome_lev el` attribute should be `100`. Note that the Ohai DSL does not require us to use the = sign when assigning a value to an attribute—in fact, if you *do* use an equals sign, the plugin will not work correctly. This variance from normal Ruby behavior is worth remembering because although it makes for shorter plugin code, it can sometimes be confusing when debugging.

This is a nice, simple example of an Ohai plugin, but examples are much more meaningful if they can be observed working in real life. Let's take a look at the ways in which we can test and run our own Ohai plugins.

Testing and Running Ohai Plugins

There are two ways in which we can try out our custom Ohai plugins. The first is to use Ruby's *irb* interactive shell, and the second is to include the plugin during a chef-client run. We'll look at both of these methods in this section, and when you might want to use them.

Testing Using irb

While Ohai plugins are being developed, running them in the *irb* Ruby shell is by far the most convenient method. *irb* allows us to paste lines of Ruby code into a shell prompt, and immediately see the results of each line as it is executed. This functionality allows us to repeatedly run our plugins without the need to perform full Chef runs or alter our node's Chef configuration.

The *irb* shell is started by running the `irb` command in a terminal, and will give you a prompt looking something like this:

```
irb(main):001:0>
```

 The exact text shown before the > symbol vary depending on your operating system and Ruby version; in the examples shown in this section I've used >> to represent a standard *irb* prompt.

Let's look at how we can test our example plugin from "Ohai Example 1: Plugin Skeleton" on page 97 using `irb`. Note that I've assumed that you have the example code saved in a file called */tmp/ohai_plugins/example1.rb*; if you chose to store your example plugins in a different location, you'll need to substitute */tmp/ohai_plugins* with the path you are using.

In the interactions shown here, each time you see the >> prompt followed by text, this indicates a line of Ruby code that you should paste into your *irb* shell (don't copy the >>). The results you should see are shown below each >> line on lines beginning with =>. Where the output of a command is particularly long, I've replaced it with `<snip>`.

Now, let's try out *example1.rb*:

```
$> irb

>> require 'ohai' ❶
=> true

>> Ohai::Config[:plugin_path] << '/tmp/ohai_plugins' ❷
=> ["/usr/lib64/ruby/gems/1.9.1/gems/ohai-7.0.0/lib/ohai/plugins",
        "/tmp/ohai_plugins"]
```

```
>> o = Ohai::System.new ❸
=< #<Ohai::System:0x000000045d3028 @plugin_path="", @data={}, <snip>>

>> o.all_plugins ❹
=> <snip>

>>  o.attributes_print("awesome_level") ❺
 => "100"
```

❶   The first thing we need to do is require the ohai gem so we can make use of
     its objects and methods.

❷   Next, we append the path where we stored our example plugins (/tmp/
     ohai_plugins) to the [:plugin_path] array stored under the Ohai::Config
     class. Just as Ruby uses the LOAD_PATH variable to tell it where to locate class
     definition files, this line tells ohai to look for plugins in our examples directory
     in addition to the default location. The exact directory paths output by this
     command may vary depending on the versions of Ruby and ohai you have
     installed, but the important part is that we see /tmp/ohai_plugins at the end of
     the array.

❸   Now we need to create a new instance of the Ohai::System object, and assign
     it to a variable called o.

❹   Next, we call the all_plugins method of o (our Ohai::System object). This
     method loads all plugins that it finds under the plugin_path that we set in step
     2, and executes their collect_data block. I've abbreviated the output of this
     command as it is extremely verbose, but the eventual result of the command is
     to populate a class instance variable called @data inside our Ohai::System object
     with the attributes collected and returned by all the plugins. You can run this
     step repeatedly (without repeating steps 1–3) to re-execute all Ohai plugins,
     which is handy when making small tweaks to your plugin code.

❺   Finally, we call the attributes_print method of our Ohai::System object,
     passing the name of the attribute we're interested in—in this case, it's the awe
     some_level attribute we created in our *example1.rb* plugin. This method
     searches the @data class instance variable mentioned in step 4 to find the method
     name we're looking for, and if everything worked correctly we should see the
     value "100" returned, just as we set it in our plugin. As with step 4, this step can
     be run repeatedly to verify correct output when tweaking your plugin code.

The code we pasted into *irb* here is part of the actual code used by ohai when it's running
as part of a Chef client run. Executing this code in *irb* allows us to quickly and easily
test our plugin code to verify that it works correctly, but how do we use it as part of a
real Chef run.

Running Using Chef

Once you're actually ready to run your plugin for real, you need to tell chef-client (or chef-solo) where your plugins are located so that ohai is able to find them when it runs. This is done by adding the `Ohai::Config[:plugin_path]` << */location/of/ plugins* line to your *client.rb* or *solo.rb* configuration file— the same variable we modified when testing our plugin example with *irb*.

When chef-client or chef-solo runs, this configuration will be passed to ohai and your plugin will be executed when ohai calls the `all_plugins` method we saw in the previous section, as ohai will automatically load any plugins it finds under `Ohai::Config[:plu gin_path]`. You also need to make sure that your Ohai plugins are Cheffed out to the correct location on all of your nodes—to make this process easier, Chef, Inc. provides the ohai cookbook (*http://bit.ly/ohai-ckbk*), which will automatically Chef out plugins from the configured locations to your nodes, and dynamically update the chef-client configuration to load and run these plugins.

We've looked at a very simple example Ohai plugin and seen how to test it and run it on our nodes, but what happens if we want the attributes provided by our plugin to contain more complex data or behave differently on other operating systems? Let's look at a slightly more advanced example plugin.

Ohai Example 2: Adding More to the Plugin

In "Ohai Example 1: Plugin Skeleton" on page 97, we looked at a very simple plugin that assigned a string value to an attribute. As with many examples, it served well to demonstrate the concepts involved, but in the real world you're likely to need to write plugins that work across multiple operating systems, and to store more complex and structured attribute data. So how do we do that? Fortunately for us, the Ohai plugin DSL provides convenient functionality to support both of these cases. Consider the code in Example 4-2, which we'll paste into */tmp/ohai_plugins/example2.rb*.

Example 4-2. /tmp/ohai_plugins/example2.rb

```
Ohai.plugin(:Example2) do
  provides "awesome" ❶

  # Method to initialize object for our attribute
  def create_objects
    # Create a new "Mash" object and assign it to "awesome"
    awesome Mash.new
  end

  # Collect data block with symbol :default
  collect_data(:default) do

    # Call the create_objects method to initialize our "awesome" attribute
```

```
  create_objects
  # Assign the value 100 to the :level key of awesome
  awesome[:level] = 100
  # Assign the value "Sriracha" to the :sauce key of awesome
  awesome[:sauce] = "Sriracha"

end

# Collect data block with symbol :windows
collect_data(:windows) do

  # Call the create_objects method to initialize our "awesome" attribute
  create_objects
  # Assign the value 101 to the :level key of awesome
  awesome[:level] = 101
  # Assign the value "Cholula" to the :sauce key of awesome
  awesome[:sauce] = "Cholula"

end

end
```

❶   This line states that this plugin provides the `awesome` attribute. This also means that when `ohai` runs this plugin, the `awesome` object is in scope for all plugin methods—this is how the `collect_data` method is able to access an object created in the `create_objects` method.

I've introduced two key new concepts in this plugin example: the `Mash` object that we're now using to store our `awesome` attribute, and the fact that we now have two `collect_data` blocks, each with a different *symbol* as its parameter. Let's examine these one at a time.

The Mash Object

The `Mash` class, defined in *lib/ohai/mash.rb* in the repository (*http://bit.ly/gh-mashrb*), is a subclass of Ruby's built-in `Hash` class. In our example, we're using our `Mash` object `awesome` to store two related subattributes, `level` and `sauce`. This multilevel organizational structure is what allows us to use nested attributes like `node[:languages][:ruby][:version]` in our recipes—under the hood, `ohai` collects those attributes into a `Mash` object.

`Mash` can mostly be used just as if it were a regular `Hash`, but there is one important distinction between these classes, which is in fact the reason `Mash` is used in Chef in the first place. With a standard `Hash` in Ruby, `foo[:bar]` and `foo["bar"]` are actually treated as two different items in the `Hash`. Try running the following code in *irb*:

```
$> irb

>> foo = Hash.new
=> {}

>>foo[:bar] = "hello"
=> "hello"

>>foo["bar"] = "goodbye"
=> "goodbye"

>>foo
=> {:bar=>"hello", "bar"=>"goodbye"}
```

In this code sample, foo[:bar] has the *symbol* :bar as its key while foo["bar"] has the *string* "bar" as its key. To avoid this potentially confusing behavior, the Mash class will treat foo["bar"] and foo[:bar] as the *same* item by always converting the hash key to a string behind the scenes. Let's repeat the preceding example in *irb* using a Mash:

```
$> irb

>> require 'ohai'

>> foo = Mash.new
=> {}

>>foo[:bar] = "hello"
=> "hello"

>>foo["bar"] = "goodbye"
=> "goodbye"

>>foo
=> {"bar"=>"goodbye"}
```

As we can see, this time foo[:bar] and foo["bar"] were treated as the same item. In practical terms, you can often treat Mash objects just as if they were standard Hash objects, but it's useful to be aware of the difference.

Now, let's move on to the other new concept introduced in Example 4-2: that of having multiple collect_data blocks in our plugin.

Multiple collect_data Methods

As I mentioned in the preamble to this example, in the real world we often want to create Ohai plugins that work on different operating systems. Many of the default Ohai plugins also follow this pattern—for example, the plugin that provides the hostname attribute has to be able to retrieve the hostname from Windows systems as well as Linux systems, and it would not be ideal to have to implement separate plugins for every possible operating system that can run Chef.

Being clever, the folks at Chef, Inc. have provided a neat piece of functionality in ohai to remove the need for this replication of code. Let's look again at the method definitions we used in our plugin code (Example 4-3).

Example 4-3. Excerpt of /tmp/ohai_plugins/example2.rb

```
Ohai.plugin(:Example2) do

  ...

  collect_data(:default) do
    ...
  end

  collect_data(:windows) do
    ...
  end

end
```

We're actually defining *two* collect_data blocks here, each with a different symbol as its parameter. This is because ohai allows us to define a collect_data block for each operating system for which we require specific behavior.

The first block with the :default key will be used if no other collect_data block can be found with a more specific symbol for the operating system running the plugin. You may remember that the collect_data block we used in Example 4-1 had no :default symbol—this is because collect_data blocks are *implicitly* treated as :default if no other symbol has been specified. I've added the :default symbol in the this example for clarity, but the plugin will work just as well if the first :default block has no symbol at all.

The second block has the :windows symbol as its parameter. When ohai detects that it is being run on a Windows system, this collect_data method will be executed instead of the :default block. It's important to remember that within a plugin you can only define one collect_data block for each operating system—ohai will throw an error if you try to define two blocks with the :windows symbol, for example.

 Currently, ohai allows you to specify the following symbols (hence supported operating systems) as parameters to collect_data blocks:

```
:aix, :darwin, :hpux, :linux, :freebsd, :openbsd, :netbsd,
:solaris2, :windows
```

Running example2.rb

Now that we've examined the new concepts introduced in Example 4-2, let's run our new plugin in *irb* on both Linux (Example 4-4) and Windows (Example 4-5) to see it in action.

Example 4-4. Running example2.rb on Linux

```
$> irb

>> require 'ohai'
=> true

>> Ohai::Config[:plugin_path] << '/tmp/ohai_plugins'
=> ["/usr/lib64/ruby/gems/1.9.1/gems/ohai-7.0.0/lib/ohai/plugins",
      "/tmp/ohai_plugins"]

>> o = Ohai::System.new
=> <snip>

>> o.all_plugins
=> <snip>

>>  o.attributes_print("awesome")
=> "{\n  \"level\": 100,\n  \"sauce\": \"Sriracha\"\n}"

>>  o.attributes_print("awesome/sauce") ❶
 => "[\n  \"Sriracha\"\n]"
```

❶   When calling the attributes_print method on a Mash, we use the / character to indicate when we want to "descend" through the Mash. For example, here we're asking for awesome/sauce, which is the equivalent of awesome[:sauce] if we were referring to this attribute inside our plugin. Note that the attributes_print method includes \n newline characters, as this method is typically used to output "pretty printed" formatted output to a terminal.

Those results were exactly what we expected. Since no collect_data block was defined with the :linux symbol, the collect_data block with the :default symbol was executed, giving us an awesome Mash containing two attributes: level, with the value 100, and sauce, with the value Sriracha. Now let's try running the same plugin in *irb* on a Windows machine, as shown in Example 4-5, and see what happens.

Example 4-5. Running example2.rb on Windows

```
C:\> irb

>> require 'ohai'
=> true
```

```
>> Ohai::Config[:plugin_path] << 'C:\tmp\ohai_plugins'
=> ["C:\ruby\gems\1.9.1\gems\ohai-7.0.0\lib\ohai\plugins", "C:\tmp\ohai_plugins"]

>> o = Ohai::System.new
=> <snip>

>> o.all_plugins
=> <snip>

>>  o.attributes_print("awesome")
=> "{\n  \"level\": 101,\n  \"sauce\": \"Cholula\"\n}"

>>  o.attributes_print("awesome/sauce")
 => "[\n  \"Cholula\"\n]"
```

As we see here, when the plugin is run on a Windows machine, the `collect_data` block with the `:windows` symbol is used instead of the `:default` block. We again get an `awesome` Mash containing our two attributes, but this time `level` has the value `101` and `sauce` has the value `Cholula`. If you have both Windows and another operating system available for testing, why not try running this plugin on both systems to replicate these results?

With the addition of `Mash` objects and multiple operating system–specific `collect_da ta` methods to our toolbox, we're now getting to the stage where we can start to write more useful Ohai plugins—but what if you don't just want to write a single plugin, but rather a family of plugins that provide different "branches" of the same attribute structure? Let's look at some real examples from the plugins that actually ship with Ohai.

Ohai Example 3: Multilevel Plugins

As we worked through "Ohai Example 1: Plugin Skeleton" on page 97 and "Ohai Example 2: Adding More to the Plugin" on page 101, we progressed from a bare-bones Ohai plugin with minimal functionality to a more advanced plugin that implements OS-specific behavior and a nested attribute structure. But how far does that leave us from the functionality contained in the real plugins that Ohai ships with? To finish off this chapter we're going to look at one final feature of Ohai, its dependency system, to learn how to create a single attribute structure that contains information collected from a variety of related but functionally different tools.

Rather than looking at another canned example to illustrate Ohai plugin dependency, we're going to look at three plugins that ship with Ohai and provide various attributes that live under the `languages` attribute, which stores information about any installed programming language tools. You can see an example of the attributes stored under `languages` in "Get Configuration Data" on page 63.

The first of these plugins is the *languages.rb* plugin, shown in Example 4-6.

Example 4-6. lib/ohai/plugins/languages.rb

```
Ohai.plugin(:Languages) do
  provides "languages"

  collect_data do
    languages Mash.new
  end
end
```

This plugin is actually fairly close to the code we saw in "Ohai Example 1: Plugin Skeleton" on page 97. It defines a single `collect_data` method, and initializes the top-level `languages` attribute with a new `Mash` object. Note that it does not itself set any attributes beyond initializing `languages`—this is a commonly used pattern in Ohai when defining a plugin that will sit at the "top" of a dependency tree. But how does the `languages` `Mash` get populated with attributes that store information on a number of different programming languages? That's where Ohai's dependency system comes in.

Let's now look at the code of the *php.rb* plugin (shown in Example 4-7, with comments added), which provides attributes related to the PHP programming language.

Example 4-7. lib/ohai/plugins/php.rb

```
Ohai.plugin(:PHP) do
  provides "languages/php" ❶

  depends "languages" ❷

  collect_data do

    # Set the output variable to nil
    output = nil

    # Create a new Mash object called php
    php = Mash.new

    # Execute the shell command "php -v" and store the results in
    # the variable so
    so = shell_out("php -v")

    # If the exit code of the command was 0 (i.e., successful)...
    if so.exitstatus == 0

      # Parse the php version command's output to extract the data we care about
      output = /PHP (\S+).+built: ([^)]+)/.match(so.stdout)

      # If the above step produced any results
      if output
        # Set the :version and :builddate keys of our php Mash
```

```
        php[:version] = output[1]
        php[:builddate] = output[2]
      end
      # If the php Mash has a :version key, assign the php Mash to the :php key
      # of the languages Mash
      languages[:php] = php if php[:version] ❸
    end
  end
end
```

❶ This line tells ohai that this plugin is only providing the php key of the languag
    es Mash. As we saw when requesting a nested ohai attribute in "Running
    example2.rb" on page 105, the / character is used to indicate different levels of
    the languages Mash. Essentially, this plugin is stating that it does not provide
    the entire languages attribute, just a single element of it called php.

❷ This line states that this plugin depends on the languages plugin. When Ohai
    evaluates this line, it looks for a plugin named *languages.rb* to satisfy the
    dependency. Any attributes defined in the languages plugin are available to all
    plugins that depend on it. In this case, this means that the languages Mash we
    declared in *languages.rb* is available to *php.rb*—this allows *php.rb* to add PHP-
    specific attributes to the languages Mash, as we'll see later in the plugin.

❸ This line sets the value of the :php key of the languages Mash to the php Mash if
    there is a non-nil php[:version] key. Note that the languages Mash is actually
    defined in *languages.rb*, rather than in this plugin—this is where the Ohai plugin
    dependency model comes in handy. We can declare separate plugins to provide
    different elements of the same top-level ohai attribute.

Now let's look at the code of the *perl.rb* plugin (shown in Example 4-8, again with
comments added), which provides attributes related to the Perl programming language.

Example 4-8. lib/ohai/plugins/perl.rb

```
Ohai.plugin(:Perl) do
  provides "languages/perl" ❶

  depends "languages" ❷

  collect_data do

    # Set the output variable to nil
    output = nil

    # Create a new Mash object called perl
    perl = Mash.new

    # Execute the shell command "perl -V:version -V:archname" and store the results in
    # the variable so
```

```
so = shell_out("perl -V:version -V:archname")

# If the exit code of the command was 0 (i.e., successful)
if so.exitstatus == 0

  # Parse the perl version command's output to extract the data we care about
  so.stdout.split(/\r?\n/).each do |line|
    case line
    when /^version=\'(.+)\';$/
      perl[:version] = $1
    when /^archname=\'(.+)\';$/
      perl[:archname] = $1
    end
  end
end

# If the exit code of the command was 0 (i.e., successful)
if so.exitstatus == 0
  # Assign the perl Mash to the :perl key of the languages Mash
  languages[:perl] = perl ❸
end
  end
end
```

❶   This line tells ohai that this plugin is only providing the perl key of the lan
    guages Mash.

❷   This line states that, like *php.rb*, this plugin depends on the languages plugin.

❸   This line sets the value of the :perl key of the languages Mash to the perl Mash.
    Again, the languages Mash is actually defined in *languages.rb* rather than in this
    plugin.

In this example, we see another plugin that also provides part of the languages attribute,
but implements entirely different behavior to fetch the data needed to provide the perl
key.

These three plugins combine to provide a useful demonstration of the power and flexibility of Ohai's plugin interface. We see a top-level *languages.rb* plugin that defines the
parent attribute, named languages, and two "dependent" plugins (php.rb and
perl.rb) that implement totally separate behavior specific to the programming language tools they describe, and set specific and separate elements of the parent languag
es attribute.

When we actually run ohai and look at the results, this hierarchical plugin dependency
is hidden from us—what we see is a single languages attribute containing all of the
information set by the various plugins that depend on languages.

To see this behavior in action, let's run ohai in *irb* again, as illustrated in Example 4-9, and look at the languages attribute in the output.

 Note that because this time we're only running plugins that ship with Ohai by default, we don't need to add our example plugin path to Ohai::Config[:plugin_path]. It you do not have the same programming languages I do installed on your machine, the output you see when running this example locally might vary.

Example 4-9. Exploring the language attribute

```
$> irb

>> require 'ohai'
=> true

>> o = Ohai::System.new
=> <snip>

>> o.all_plugins
=> <snip>

>> o.attributes_print("languages")
 => "{\n  \"lua\": {\n     \"version\": \"5.1.4\"\n   },\n
        \"nodejs\": {\n     \"version\": \"0.10.21\"\n   },\n
        \"perl\": {\n     \"version\": \"5.16.2\",\n
         \"archname\": \"darwin-thread-multi-2level\"\n   },\n
        \"php\": {\n     \"version\": \"5.4.17\",\n
         \"builddate\": \"Aug 25 2013\"\n   },\n   }\n}"
          <<snip>>

>> o.attributes_print("languages/php")
 => "{\n  \"version\": \"5.4.17\",\n  \"builddate\": \"Aug 25 2013\"\n}"

>> o.attributes_print("languages/perl")
 => "{\n  \"version\": \"5.16.2\",\n
         \"archname\": \"darwin-thread-multi-2level\"\n}"
```

We can see here that the languages attribute contains data on a number of different programming languages—although the output of ohai doesn't show us this, as we saw earlier, this output is provided by a number of different plugins. In our sample output, for example, we see the specific attributes set by the PHP and Perl plugins we explored in this section, in the same languages attribute as attributes describing the Lua and Node.js programming languages.

Summary

Ohai's flexible and extensible plugin interface allows us to leverage any information source we choose to store information about our Chef nodes. If we want to store information about a new programming language, for example, we can extend one of the existing Ohai plugins to make use of its existing data structures, or we can define entirely new attributes of our own choosing.

In this chapter we worked through a number of examples, starting with the minimal code necessary for a functioning Ohai plugin, then moving on to a plugin that implemented operating-system-specific behavior and nested data structures, before finally looking at some of the plugins that actually ship with Ohai to explore its dependency model. It's my hope that these examples have served to give you an idea of the flexibility and power that Ohai plugins give you to store information about your nodes in Chef, as well as some ideas about the kinds of information you might be able to store about your nodes to enhance your Chef recipes.

In the next chapter, we'll examine how Chef allows us to specify custom behavior on the success or failure of our Chef runs through the use of *handlers*.

## CHAPTER 5

Creating Handlers

As we learned when exploring the different stages of a Chef run in "Anatomy of a Chef Run" on page 62, Chef executes *handlers* as specific situations arise during the run to allow us to respond to these events. As we'll see in this chapter, handlers are special Ruby classes that we incorporate into our Chef runs. Three types of handler are supported:

Start handlers

These run before the Chef run has fully begun, during stage 3 (see "Load and Build Node Object" on page 65) and are typically used to notify monitoring systems and the like about the start of a Chef run or to initialize reporting systems that will be used throughout the rest of the run.

Report handlers

These run during the last stage of the run (see "Finalize" on page 69) and are triggered when the Chef run has been successful. Report handlers can be created for a variety of tasks, and are typically used to report statistics and data on the successful Chef run to monitoring systems.

Exception handlers

These also run during the last stage of the run, but are triggered when the Chef run has failed. Exception handlers are typically used to generate alerts or notifications to inform people that Chef has failed, and provide data on the nature of the failure.

In this chapter, we'll create a test environment to allow us to safely run code examples before examining the three handler types and how to implement and run each one. We'll also look at the various Chef classes we'll make use of to power and enhance the usefulness of our handlers, and some best practices to keep in mind when implementing them.

Preparing a Test Environment

Before we move on to the other types of run customization that we'll examine in the remainder of the chapters in Part II, we need to pause for a moment to prepare a test environment to allow us to run our example code. Unlike Ohai plugins, which we were able to test using the *irb* interactive shell, the other customization types we'll cover in these chapters need to be tested as part of an actual Chef run as they make use of objects and methods that are created during the run process.

In this section, we're going to create a test environment that enables us to safely and repeatedly simulate a full chef-client run to test each of our customizations.

Our test environment will run chef-client in *local mode* (which we learned about in "Local Mode" on page 20) with the why-run feature enabled (which we saw in "Why-Run Mode" on page 71). The use of local mode allows us to simulate a full Chef run against a mock Chef server, while the use of why-run mode ensures that the underlying node will not change at any point. We'll also create a simple test cookbook to use as our run list for these tests.

> To run the examples in this section, you'll need to make sure you have Chef (at least version 11.10.0) installed on a machine suitable for running development code—please don't run example code on one of your production servers! As with other examples in this book, I've assumed that you're using a Linux/Unix-based OS. If this is not the case, you'll need to adjust the directory paths used as appropriate.

To set up the test environment, complete the following steps.

Create the Test chef-client Configuration

The first step in creating our test environment is to create a new *client.rb* file to use with chef-client—we don't want to pick up any settings from default configuration files like */etc/chef/client.rb*.

> The customizations we cover in this chapter are also fully compatible with chef-solo; however, I've chosen to use chef-client for our test environment so that we can use local mode to replicate communicating with an actual Chef server. To use our customizations with chef-solo, the same configuration directives that we use here can also be used with *solo.rb*.

First, we're going to create a directory file called */tmp/part2_examples*:

```
$> mkdir /tmp/part2_examples
```

Next, we're going to create an extremely minimal *client.rb* configuration file. Paste the line of code in Example 5-1 into */tmp/part2_examples/client.rb*.

Example 5-1. /tmp/part2_examples/client.rb

```
verify_api_cert true
```

This line instructs chef-client to verify the Chef server's SSL certificate if we're accessing it over HTTPS; without this line, chef-client will warn us that SSL certificates are not being verified.

We'll flesh out this configuration file more fully as we come to test our customization examples later in the chapter. Since chef-client will be running in local mode, we don't need any configuration details in our *client.rb* file at this stage, other than the line we just added; local mode will create the configuration options it needs to run.

 If you're using a non-Linux/Unix-based operating system, you might need to alter the */tmp/part2_examples* directory path we're using for our examples to one that's appropriate for your operating system.

Create a Test Cookbook

Now that we have our blank *client.rb* file to use with our test Chef run, our next step is to create a simple cookbook to use during our tests. First, we'll need to create a directory called */tmp/part2_examples/cookbooks*:

```
$> mkdir /tmp/part2_examples/cookbooks
```

Next, we'll use Knife's cookbook create command to create a cookbook skeleton in */tmp/part2_examples/cookbooks*. When you run this command, you should see output similar to that shown here:

```
$> knife cookbook create testcookbook -o /tmp/part2_examples/cookbooks
WARNING: No knife configuration file found
** Creating cookbook testcookbook
** Creating README for cookbook: testcookbook
** Creating CHANGELOG for cookbook: testcookbook
** Creating metadata for cookbook: testcookbook
```

Next, we're going to add two simple resources into the *default.rb* recipe created with our cookbook so that our test Chef run will actually have some resources to run. Replace the contents of */tmp/part2_examples/cookbooks/testcookbook/recipes/default.rb* with the code in Example 5-2.

Example 5-2. /tmp/part2_examples/cookbooks/testcookbook/recipes/default.rb

```
# This directory already exists, so this resource
# should always do nothing
```

```
directory "/tmp/part2_examples"

# This file will not exist, so this resource
# should create it
file "/tmp/part2_examples/testfile"
```

As I mentioned earlier, we'll be running this recipe in why-run mode. When we kick off a Chef run, the `directory` resource will of course not create */tmp/part2_examples*, as this directory already exists. However, the `file` resource should tell us that a normal Chef run would create the file */tmp/part2_examples/testfile*, as it does not yet exist. Note that why-run mode will not actually *create* the file, which means that we can reliably reproduce the behavior of this test run when running our example customization code.

When we want to test our customizations, this recipe will give us a base run list that we can run repeatedly with identical results—this will make observing the effect of our customizations much easier!

Verify That the Test Environment Works Correctly

With our blank *client.rb* file and our test cookbook created, we have all the components we require for our test environment—but now we need to make sure that it works correctly! To do this, we're going to perform a Chef run using the following command from */tmp/part2_examples*:

```
$> sudo chef-client --once --why-run --local-mode \
  --config /tmp/part2_examples/client.rb --override-runlist testcookbook::default
```

In this command, we've passed the following options to chef-client (note that we're running the command as `sudo` to avoid any permission issues with log files, etc.):

`--once`
    This option tells chef-client to only run once instead of in a continuous loop, as it would by default.

`--why-run`
    This option tells chef-client to run in why-run mode, as we saw in "Why-Run Mode" on page 71.

`--local-mode`
    This option tells chef-client to run in local mode, starting up a local chef-zero server as we saw in "Local Mode" on page 20.

`--config /tmp/part2_examples/client.rb`
    This option tells chef-client to use the blank *client.rb* configuration file we created, instead of looking for the default configuration file at */etc/chef/client.rb*.

```
--override-runlist testcookbook::default
```
This option tells chef-client to override the run list to be executed on our node, and set it to `testcookbook::default`.

Now let's actually run this command. If you followed all of the instructions in the previous steps, you should see similar output to that shown here:

```
$> sudo chef-client --once --why-run --local-mode\
--config /tmp/part2_examples/client.rb --override-runlist testcookbook::default

Starting Chef Client, version 11.10.4
[Sat, 22 Feb 2014 13:48:32 +0000] WARN: Run List override has been provided.
[Sat, 22 Feb 2014 13:48:32 +0000] WARN: Original Run List: []
[Sat, 22 Feb 2014 13:48:32 +0000] WARN: Overridden Run List:
  [recipe[testcookbook::default]]
resolving cookbooks for run list: ["testcookbook::default"]
Synchronizing Cookbooks:
  - testcookbook
Compiling Cookbooks...
Converging 2 resources
Recipe: testcookbook::default
  * directory[/tmp/part2_examples] action create (up to date)
  * file[/tmp/part2_examples/testfile] action create
    - Would create new file /tmp/part2_examples/testfile

[Sat, 22 Feb 2014 13:48:32 +0000] WARN: Skipping final node save
  because override_runlist was given

Running handlers:
Running handlers complete
```

Note that as we're running in why-run mode, Chef does not actually create the file */tmp/part2_examples/testfile* but instead tells us that this is what *would* happen if Chef were not being run in why-run mode. Chef also reminds us that as we're running in why-run mode, it will not save node attributes to the server.

Although we gave chef-client a blank *client.rb* configuration file, running in local mode means that chef-client started up chef-zero at the beginning of the run and set its configuration parameters to the chef-zero server (as opposed to a remote Chef server), just as we saw in "The Chef::Application::Client run_chef_client Method" on page 83.

Now that we've validated that our test environment works correctly, it's time to look at how to implement some more customizations.

Introduction to Handlers

Although triggered by very different situations during a Chef run, under the hood all handlers build on the same underlying framework. Understanding this common structure and how it integrates with Chef runs is crucial when implementing your own handlers, so we're going to examine these areas in detail before moving on to more specific implementation examples.

Regardless of their type, all handlers share the same skeleton code structure:

```
require "chef/handler"

class Chef
  class Handler
    class HandlerName < Chef::Handler ❶
      def report ❷
        # Ruby code goes here
      def
    end
  end
end
```

❶ The handler skeleton inherits from the superclass `Chef::Handler`, which lives at *lib/chef/handler.rb* (*http://bit.ly/gh-handler*).

❷ Here, we're overriding a single method from `Chef::Handler` called `report`. Whenever Chef needs to activate handlers of a particular type during the run, it calls their `report` method.

Given this common code structure and `report` method, what distinguishes each handler type? How does Chef know which handlers are exception handlers and which are report or start handlers, so it can call the `report` methods of the right handlers at the right times?

Part of the answer lies in the chef-client (or chef-solo) configuration file. For each supported handler type, Chef defines a list to which we can append our handler classes, as seen in Example 5-3.

Example 5-3. Declaring handlers in client.rb

```
verify_api_cert true

require "/var/chef/handlers/mystarthandler.rb"
require "/var/chef/handlers/myhandler.rb"

my_start_handler = MyStartHandler.new
my_handler = MyHandler.new

start_handlers << my_start_handler        # List of start handler classes
report_handlers << my_handler             # List of report handler classes
exception_handlers << my_handler          # List of exception handler classes
```

Don't worry too much about exactly what's going on here for now—we'll examine each handler type and how to run them in much more detail later in this chapter. For now it's sufficient to understand that we create instances of our handlers and add them to the appropriate lists, which Chef then uses to decide which handlers to call at the appropriate times during the run.

For example, when Chef calls any start handlers during stage 3 of the run process (see "Load and Build Node Object" on page 65), it does this by calling the *report* method of all handlers contained in the `start_handlers` list in the Chef configuration file. Likewise, when exception or report handlers are called during the "Finalize" stage (see "Finalize" on page 69), Chef calls the `report` method of any handlers contained in the `report_handlers` or `exception_handlers` list.

You may also have noticed that in this example we're defining a separate object to use as a start handler, but are using the *same* object as both a report and exception handler. This isn't a mistake; because Chef calls the `report` method of all handler objects added to each list, as we just saw, there's nothing to stop us from defining a handler with a `report` method that can cater to both failed and successful runs.

But enough theory—how do our handler classes tell whether the Chef run they are responding to has succeeded or failed if the `report` method is called in both cases? Chef exposes this Chef run information to handler classes through an object we already met in "Load and Build Node Object" on page 65 step: the run status object.

The Run Status Object

As we saw in Chapter 3, the run status object is created during the "Load and Build Node Object" stage of the Chef run and contains a number of different attributes that are populated throughout the course of the Chef run and hold information on different aspects of the Chef run's status. Chef exposes the run status object to all handlers to allow them to introspect into the run that triggered them and react accordingly.

The run status object is an instance of the `Chef::RunStatus` class, which lives at *lib/chef/run_status.rb* (*http://bit.ly/gh-runstatus*), and provides us with a number of methods to access the attributes it stores on the status of the current Chef run. In this section we'll briefly examine some of these methods and look at how they might be of use when implementing the example handler code later in this chapter.

Run Status Methods

The run status object provides two methods for querying the status of the Chef run that triggered the handler. These methods are especially useful when implementing report and exception handlers in the same class, as it allows you to control the logic of the `report` method as appropriate for successful or failed runs. These methods are:

success?
> The `success?` method returns `true` when the Chef run succeeded. *Success* in this context means that no unhandled exceptions were thrown during the progress of

the Chef run. When this method returns `true`, logic for a report handler should be executed.

failed?

> The `failed?` method returns `true` when the Chef run failed. *Failure* in this context means that an unhandled exception was thrown during the progress of the Chef run. When this method returns `true`, logic for an exception handler should be executed.

 As start handlers run at a very earliest stage of the run, before much of the data in the run status object has been populated, there is no `started?` method to indicate that the run has just started—after all, the fact that the handler has been executed in the first place means that the run *must* have started. For this reason, start handlers are typically implemented as separate classes from report or exception handlers and controlled by making sure that they are only added to the `start_handlers` list in the Chef configuration file.

Run Information Methods

After we've identified the status of the Chef run that triggered our handler class, there are a number of methods provided by the run status object that allow us to introspect deeper into the run to identify exactly what was happening at the time the handler was triggered. These include:

exception

> If an unhandled exception occurred during the Chef run, the `exception` method returns the exception object that was thrown. It's worth noting that this method returns the actual `Exception` object, just as we would get in a `rescue` block if catching the exception ourselves. If no unhandled exceptions occurred during the Chef run, this method will return `nil`.

backtrace

> If an unhandled exception occurred during the Chef run, the `backtrace` method returns an array containing the *backtrace* of the exception that was thrown. The backtrace is the text we see when an exception has been thrown that tells us in which lines of what class files the exception occurred. If no unhandled exceptions occurred during the Chef run, this method will return `nil`.

start_time

> The `start_time` method returns a `Time` object containing the time that the Chef run started.

end_time

The end_time method returns a Time object containing the time that the Chef run ended.

elapsed_time

The elapsed_time method returns the difference between start_time and end_time as a Float object, if both methods have values. If start_time, end_time, or both have not been set, elapsed_time returns nil.

Run Object Methods

The remainder of the methods provided by the run status object provide access to a number of other objects used during the Chef run that can be used to add extra context or information to your handler code. These include:

node

The node method returns the Chef::Node object produced during step 3 of the Chef run process (see "Load and Build Node Object" on page 65). This object contains the saved node data loaded from the Chef server (if applicable), which includes useful data like the run list to be applied to the node, attributes loaded by ohai, etc. See "The Chef::Client Class do_run Method" on page 86 for details of exactly where in the Chef code this object is created.

events

The events method returns the EventDispatcher::Dispatcher object that forms the *publisher* component of the event dispatcher. We'll look at the event dispatcher in more detail in Chapter 6.

run_context

The run_context method returns the Chef::RunContext object produced during step 5 of the Chef run process (see "SetUp RunContext" on page 66). This object contains a variety of useful data about the overall Chef run, such as the cookbook files needed to perform the run, the list of all resources to be applied during the run, and the list of all notifications triggered by resources during the run.

all_resources

The all_resources method provides a list of all resources stored in the resource collection of the run context object. As we saw in "SetUp RunContext" on page 66, this is the expanded list of resources that will be applied to the node during the Chef run.

updated_resources

The updated_resources method provides a list of resources that were marked as *updated* during the Chef run; i.e., resources that were not already converged.

As start handlers are executed at the very beginning of the Chef run, the only run status attributes that will have been populated at the point when start handlers run are `start_time` and `node`. All other run status attributes are populated at later stages of the run and will return `nil` if called in a start handler. Please see "The Chef::Client Class do_run Method" on page 86 for a reminder of how the different Chef run stages fit together in code.

So far in this chapter, we've looked at the common code skeleton shared by all Chef handlers, how Chef keeps track of handlers of each type, and the data exposed by the run status object to help us implement our handlers. Let's put that knowledge to use now and look at some examples of implementing each handler type.

Handler Example 1: Start Handler

Since start handlers are the first handlers to be executed during a Chef run, we'll begin with these for our first handler example. As we touched on briefly in "Load and Build Node Object" on page 65, start handlers are most typically used for two specific purposes:

- Producing a notification that a Chef run has started on the node, which can be useful for analyzing the duration of Chef runs or how long it's been since a node last started a Chef run

- Initializing reporting systems used throughout the rest of the run—we'll look at an example of this in Chapter 6

In this example, we'll look at the first of these use cases, generating a notification that a Chef run has started on the node. Usually, such a start handler would be used to send notifications to a metrics or monitoring system such as Graphite (*http://graphite.read thedocs.org*) or StatsD (*http://bit.ly/gh-statsd*); however, because in this case as I want readers to be able to easily try these examples out for themselves, our example start handler will simply write to a text file.

I'll list handlers that interact with a number of common monitoring systems in "Handlers: Summary and Further Reading" on page 136, and we'll learn how to write a start handler to initialize reporting systems in "Creating Custom Subscribers" on page 151.

Start by pasting the code in Example 5-4 into */tmp/part2_examples/ awesome_start_handler.rb*.

Example 5-4. /tmp/part2_examples/awesome_start_handler.rb

```ruby
require "chef/handler"

class Chef
  class Handler
    class AwesomeStartHandler < Chef::Handler ❶

      # Override report method from Chef::Handler
      def report

          # Print a log message when our handler is executed
          Chef::Log.warn("Handler #{self.class} executed") ❷

          # Grab data from the @run_status object
          # and assign to local variables for clarity
          run_start_time = @run_status.start_time ❸
          node_name = @run_status.node.name ❹

          # Open output file in append mode and write handler output to it
          File.open("/tmp/handler_output", 'a') do |file|
              file.write("\n#{self.class}: Run started on #{node_name} at " +
              "#{run_start_time}\n") ❺
          end
      end
    end
  end
end
```

❶ Just as we saw in "Introduction to Handlers" on page 117, our start handler makes use of the common handler skeleton that forms the basis of all handlers —it inherits from the superclass Chef::Handler and overrides a method called report.

❷ Here we're logging a warning-level message to show the handler being executed in the run output. By default, only report and exception handler executions are logged.

❸ Here we're making use of the run status object we learned about in the previous section to capture the start_time of the Chef run on this node. Note that the run status object is accessed using the @run_status class instance variable— this is declared in the Chef::Handler superclass, and hence is available to all handler subclasses.

❹ Here we're calling the name method of the Chef::Node object returned by the @run_status.node method—this gives us the name of the object representing our node, usually the node's fully qualified domain name (FQDN).

❺ Finally, we use Ruby's `File` class to open the file */tmp/handler_output* and append our handler output message to it—the `self.class` method call on this line simply adds the name of the current handler class to the start of the output string. I've also broken the `file.write` line here over two lines for formatting purposes; this is not a functional requirement.

We've created our example start handler, but before we can run it using the test environment we prepared in "Preparing a Test Environment" on page 114 we need to tell our *client.rb* configuration file that we want our handler to be added to the `start_han dlers` list. To do this, we need to add the lines in Example 5-5 to */tmp/part2_examples/ client.rb*.

Example 5-5. /tmp/part2_examples/client.rb

```
verify_api_cert true

require "/tmp/part2_examples/awesome_start_handler.rb" ❶

example_start_handler = Chef::Handler::AwesomeStartHandler.new ❷

start_handlers << example_start_handler ❸
```

❶ Here, we're telling *client.rb* to `require` the *awesome_start_handler.rb* file we created earlier.

❷ Next, we create an instance of our `Chef::Handler::AwesomeStartHandler` class. Note that because we specified in our class definition that our handler class lives in the `Chef::Handler` namespace, we need to refer to our handler by its full name here rather than just `AwesomeStartHandler`.

❸ Finally, we add our `example_start_handler` object to the `start_handlers` list.

With our *client.rb* file configured to use our start handler, we can now perform a Chef run on our test environment using the same command we saw in "Preparing a Test Environment" on page 114:

```
$> chef-client --once --why-run \ --local-mode \
  --config /tmp/part2_examples/client.rb \
  --override-runlist testcookbook::default

Starting Chef Client, version 11.10.4
[Sat, 22 Feb 2014 13:48:32 +0000] WARN: Run List override has been provided.
[Sat, 22 Feb 2014 13:48:32 +0000] WARN: Original Run List: []
[Sat, 22 Feb 2014 13:48:32 +0000] WARN: Overridden Run List:
  [recipe[testcookbook::default]]
[Sat, 22 Feb 2014 13:48:32 +0000] WARN: Start Handler
  Chef::Handler::AwesomeStartHandler executed
resolving cookbooks for run list: ["testcookbook::default"]
Synchronizing Cookbooks:
```

```
    - testcookbook
Compiling Cookbooks...
Converging 2 resources
Recipe: testcookbook::default
  * directory[/tmp/part2_examples] action create (up to date)
  * file[/tmp/part2_examples/testfile] action create
    - Would create new file /tmp/part2_examples/testfile

[Sat, 22 Feb 2014 13:48:32 +0000] WARN: Skipping final node save
  because override_runlist was given

Running handlers:
Running handlers complete
```

If everything was correctly configured, you should see output from your Chef run similar to that shown here. Note the log message telling us when our start handler has been executed. If we take a look in the */tmp/handler_output* file we specified in our handler class, we should now see output similar to the following:

```
$> cat /tmp/handler_output
```

```
Chef::Handler::AwesomeStartHandler: Run started on mynode.mydomain.com at
  2014-02-13 11:36:06 +0000
```

This tells us that when our test run reached step 3 of the process (see "Load and Build Node Object" on page 65), Chef executed our `AwesomeStartHandler` by calling its `report` method, which resulted in the preceding output being printed to */tmp/ handler_output*. Now every time we kick off a Chef run, our start handler will output a notification line to */tmp/handler_output* with the exact time that the run started—try running a few more example Chef runs and see for yourself!

As I mentioned before, this type of start handler would usually send this notification to a monitoring system such as Graphite or StatsD to allow the collection of metrics such as run duration and when a node last started a Chef run. The flexibility of start handlers, however, means that you can send notifications to any destination you desire, in any format you can implement in Ruby.

It's also important to remember that because the `start_handlers` list in *client.rb* is an array, you can add as many start handlers as you want and they will all be executed at the beginning of the run—Chef doesn't limit the number of handlers we can run at once. Check out "Handlers: Summary and Further Reading" on page 136 for some examples of handlers that interact with real-world monitoring systems.

Now that we've implemented a start handler to notify us that our run has started, it's time to move to the latter stages of the Chef run and examine how to implement a report handler to provide us with information on successful Chef runs.

Handler Example 2: Report Handler

As we saw in "Finalize" on page 69, report handlers run at the very end of a Chef run if the run succeeded. This means that unlike start handlers, report handlers are able to access the full range of data exposed through the run status object as by the end of the run it has been fully populated the attributes accessed by the methods we examined in "The Run Status Object" on page 119.

The information provided by report handlers, although technically relating to successful runs only, can often be extremely useful in identifying performance bottlenecks and inefficiencies in infrastructure automation code. This is because these handlers can feed monitoring and metrics systems with information about our Chef runs, such as:

- The number of resources updated during each run (useful for tracking how idempotent your recipes are.)
- The average duration of Chef runs across your infrastructure (useful for a global overview of how your Chef runs are performing.)
- More detailed profiling of the performance of individual resources and recipes during Chef runs (useful for tracking down performance bottlenecks.)

Consider for example a recipe that contains a `bash` resource that, as part of compiling a piece of software from source, uses the `wget` command to download a large file from the Internet on every Chef run, instead of using a `remote_file` resource to download it once.

This recipe is not technically broken in the strictest sense, as it does not cause the run to fail, but it is behaving in a decidedly suboptimal manner that could seriously impact network performance if run on a large number of nodes. Report handlers are able to feed our metrics and monitoring systems with data on our Chef runs that makes it much easier for us to capture this type of event, as we'll see in this example.

As with our start handler example, to keep our example implementation as simple and easy to test as possible we're going to have our report handler write various details about the successful Chef run to the */tmp/handler_output* file. Start by pasting the code in Example 5-6 into */tmp/part2_examples/awesome_report_handler.rb*.

Example 5-6. /tmp/part2_examples/awesome_report_handler.rb

```
require "chef/handler"

class Chef
  class Handler
    class AwesomeReportHandler < Chef::Handler  ❶

      # Override report method from Chef::Handler
      def report
```

```
    # If the run was successful, run this code
    if @run_status.success? ❷

        # Grab data from the @run_status object
        # and assign to local variables for clarity
        run_elapsed_time = @run_status.elapsed_time ❸
        node_name = @run_status.node.name
        resource_count = @run_status.all_resources.length ❹
        updated_resources = @run_status.updated_resources ❺
        updated_resource_count = updated_resources.length ❻

        # Open output file in append mode and write handler output to it
        File.open("/tmp/handler_output", 'a') do |file| ❼
            file.write("\n#{self.class}: Run successfully completed on " +
              "#{node_name} and took " +
              "#{run_elapsed_time} seconds:\n")
            file.write("  #{resource_count} resources in total, " +
              "#{updated_resource_count} updated:\n")

            # Write each resource in the updated_resources list to our
            # output file
            updated_resources.each do |resource|
              m = "recipe[#{resource.cookbook_name}::" +
                  "#{resource.recipe_name}]" +
                " ran '#{resource.action}' on #{resource.resource_name}" +
                " '#{resource.name}'"
              file.write("     #{m}\n")
            end
          end
        end
      end
    end
  end
end
```

❶   As we saw in "Introduction to Handlers" on page 117, our report handler makes use of the common handler skeleton that forms the basis of all handlers—it inherits from the superclass Chef::Handler and overrides a method called report.

❷   We're making use of the @run_success.success? method here to run our report handler code only if the run succeeded. If it failed, our handler does nothing.

❸   Here we're using the elapsed_time method of the @run_status object to get the duration of the Chef run.

❹   Next, we fetch the total number of resources executed in this Chef run by getting the length of @run_status.all_resources. As we learned in "Run Status Methods" on page 119, the all_resources method returns the resource collection array from the run context object.

❺ Then we fetch the list of resources updated in this Chef run by calling the `updated_resources` method of the `@run_status` object.

❻ Here, we get the total number of updated resources executed in this Chef run by getting the `length` of `@run_status.updated_resources`.

❼ As with our start handler example earlier in this chapter, here we open the */tmp/handler_output* file and append our handler output to it.

Now that we've created our report handler class, we need to tell our *client.rb* configuration file that we want our handler to be added to the `report_handlers` list—this is done in a very similar fashion to how we added the start handler to the `start_han dlers` list in the previous example. To add our report handler to the configuration, as we're going to leave our start handler example in place, we need to add the lines in Example 5-7 ending with the comment `# ADD` to our *client.rb* file.

Example 5-7. /tmp/part2_examples/client.rb

```
verify_api_cert true

require "/tmp/part2_examples/awesome_start_handler.rb"

require "/tmp/part2_examples/awesome_report_handler.rb" # ADD ❶

example_start_handler = Chef::Handler::AwesomeStartHandler.new

example_report_handler = Chef::Handler::AwesomeReportHandler.new # ADD ❷

start_handlers << example_start_handler

report_handlers << example_report_handler # ADD ❸
```

❶ Here, we're telling *client.rb* to `require` the *awesome_report_handler.rb* file we created earlier.

❷ Next, we create an instance of our `Chef::Handler::AwesomeReportHandler` class.

❸ Finally, we add our `awesome_report_handler` object to the `report_handlers` list.

With that done, we can now perform a Chef run on our test environment using the same command we saw in "Preparing a Test Environment" on page 114 to see the output produced by our report handler:

```
$> chef-client --once --why-run --local-mode \
  --config /tmp/part2_examples/client.rb --override-runlist testcookbook::default

Starting Chef Client, version 11.10.4
[Sat, 22 Feb 2014 13:59:16 +0000] WARN: Run List override has been provided.
```

```
[Sat, 22 Feb 2014 13:59:16 +0000] WARN: Original Run List: []
[Sat, 22 Feb 2014 13:59:16 +0000] WARN: Overridden Run List:
  [recipe[testcookbook::default]]
[Sat, 22 Feb 2014 13:59:16 +0000] WARN: Start Handler
  Chef::Handler::AwesomeStartHandler executed
resolving cookbooks for run list: ["testcookbook::default"]
Synchronizing Cookbooks:
  - testcookbook
Compiling Cookbooks...
Converging 2 resources
Recipe: testcookbook::default
  * directory[/tmp/part2_examples] action create (up to date)
  * file[/tmp/part2_examples/testfile] action create
    - Would create new file /tmp/part2_examples/testfile

[Sat, 22 Feb 2014 13:59:16 +0000] WARN: Skipping final node save
  because override_runlist was given

Running handlers:
  - Chef::Handler::AwesomeReportHandler
```

As we can see above, at the end of the run Chef shows our Chef::Handler::AwesomeR
eportHandler class being executed. If we look in the *tmp/handler_output* file we specified in our handler class, we should now also see output similar to the following:

```
$> cat /tmp/handler_output

Chef::Handler::AwesomeStartHandler: Run started on mynode.mydomain.com at
  2014-02-13 14:46:12 +0000

Chef::Handler::AwesomeReportHandler: Run successfully completed on
  mynode.mydomain.com and took 0.110945093 seconds:
    2 resources in total, 1 updated:
    recipe[testcookbook::default] ran 'create' on file
    '/tmp/part2_examples/testfile'
```

This tells us that when our test run reached the "Finalize" step without any exceptions
being thrown, Chef executed our AwesomeReportHandler by calling its report method,
which resulted in the preceding output being printed to *tmp/handler_output*. Now
every time we kick off a Chef run that does not throw any exceptions, our report handler
will output a notification line to *tmp/handler_output* with the output we saw here—
try running a few more example Chef runs and see for yourself!

We've examined the implementation of two out of the three handler types supported
by Chef now, to notify us when our runs have *started* and *succeeded*. To finish off our
examples, we need to look at exception handlers, which allow us to respond to *failed*
Chef runs.

Handler Example 3: Exception Handler

The final type of handlers that Chef supports are exception handlers, which are executed if an unhandled exception is thrown at any point during the Chef run. As we saw in "Handling Exceptions" on page 46, an *unhandled* exception is one that is not caught by a `rescue` block. In the context of our Chef run, this means that something has gone wrong during the run and it cannot continue.

Unsuccessful Chef runs generally indicate a situation that requires active remediation. This means that exception handlers, which alert us to those failures, are by far the most commonly used handler variety, as failing Chef runs are often of more immediate interest than successful ones. Correspondingly, a good number of the open source handlers provided by the Chef community are exception handlers that can be used to send data on failed runs to a wide variety of monitoring and notification systems.

As with the other handler examples we've looked at, to keep things simple our example exception handler will write its output to the */tmp/handler_output* file. Rather than implementing an entirely separate class, as we did for our start and report handler examples, however, we're going to leverage the information exposed by the run status object to let us combine exception handling logic with the report handler logic from our previous example into a single multipurpose handler class.

We could, of course, implement our exception handler as a separate class if we wished, but a combined report and exception handler provides a useful illustration of the flexibility and power of handlers in Chef. Let's add the exception and report handling code for our new combined handler, shown in Example 5-8, to */tmp/part2_examples/awesome_handler.rb*.

Example 5-8. /tmp/part2_examples/awesome_handler.rb

```
require "chef/handler"

class Chef
  class Handler
    class AwesomeHandler < Chef::Handler ❶
      def report

        # Existing logic from our report handler
        # If the run was successful, run this code
        if @run_status.success? ❷

          # Grab data from the @run_status object
          # and assign to local variables for clarity
          run_elapsed_time = @run_status.elapsed_time
          node_name = @run_status.node.name
          resource_count = @run_status.all_resources.length
          updated_resources = @run_status.updated_resources
          updated_resource_count = updated_resources.length
```

```
          # Open output file in append mode and write handler output to it
          File.open("/tmp/handler_output", 'a') do |file|
              file.write("\n#{self.class}: Run successfully completed on " +
                "#{node_name} and took " +
                "#{run_elapsed_time} seconds:\n")
              file.write("  #{resource_count} resources in total, " +
                "#{updated_resource_count} updated:\n")

              # Write each resource in the updated_resources list to our
              # output file
              updated_resources.each do |resource|
                m = "recipe[#{resource.cookbook_name}::" +
                    "#{resource.recipe_name}]" +
                  " ran '#{resource.action}' on #{resource.resource_name}" +
                  " '#{resource.name}'"
                file.write("      #{m}\n")
              end
          end

        # New logic to implement exception handler behavior
        # If the run failed, run this code
        elsif @run_status.failed? ❸

            # Grab data from the @run_status object
            # and assign to local variables for clarity
            run_elapsed_time = @run_status.elapsed_time ❹
            node_name = @run_status.node.name
            exception = @run_status.exception ❺
            backtrace = @run_status.backtrace ❻

            # Open output file in append mode and write handler output to it
            File.open("/tmp/handler_output", 'a') do |file| ❼
                file.write("\n#{self.class}: Run failed on " +
                  "#{node_name} after #{run_elapsed_time} seconds:\n")
                file.write("  Exception: #{exception}\n")
                file.write("  Backtrace: \n")
                backtrace.each do |b|
                  file.write("      #{b} \n")
                end
            end
          end
        end
      end
    end
  end
end
```

❶   As with all of the previous handler examples, our new combined handler class makes use of the common handler skeleton that forms the basis of all handlers. It inherits from the superclass Chef::Handler and overrides a method called report.

❷ We're making use of the `@run_success.success?` method here to run our *report* handler code only if the run succeeded. The code in this part of the `if` statement is directly copied from the report handler we implemented in "Handler Example 2: Report Handler" on page 126.

❸ We're making use of the `@run_success.failed?` method here to run our *exception* handler code only if the run failed.

❹ Here we're using the `elapsed_time` method of the `@run_status` object to get the duration of the Chef run.

❺ Next, we call the `exception` method of the `@run_status` object to get the `Exception` object that was thrown during the run.

❻ Here we call the `backtrace` method of the `@run_status` object to get the full backtrace, which tells us exactly where our exception occurred.

❼ As in our other examples earlier in this chapter, here we open the */tmp/handler_output* file and append our handler output to it.

Before we can run our new multipurpose handler, we need to modify our *client.rb* file. We'll use our separate start handler as before, but instead of keeping the report handler we used in Example 5-7 in the `report_handlers` list, we're going to add our new combined handler class to both the `exception_handlers` *and* `report_handlers` lists. Replace the contents of */tmp/part2_examples/client.rb* with the code in Example 5-9:

Example 5-9. /tmp/part2_examples/client.rb

```
verify_api_cert true

require "/tmp/part2_examples/awesome_start_handler.rb"
require "/tmp/part2_examples/awesome_handler.rb"

example_start_handler = Chef::Handler::AwesomeStartHandler.new
example_handler = Chef::Handler::AwesomeHandler.new

start_handlers << example_start_handler
report_handlers << example_handler ❶
exception_handlers << example_handler ❷
```

❶ ❷ Note that here, we're adding our `example_handler` object (which is an instance of `Chef::Handler::AwesomeHandler`) to both the `report_handlers` and `exception_handlers` lists.

Now we're ready to try out our combined report and exception handler and see how it behaves on successful and failed Chef runs. First, let's test the report handler portion of our `AwesomeHandler` class by performing the same Chef run as we used in the previous section:

```
$> chef-client --once --why-run --local-mode \
  --config /tmp/part2_examples/client.rb --override-runlist testcookbook::default

Starting Chef Client, version 11.10.4
[Sat, 22 Feb 2014 14:22:49 +0000] WARN: Run List override has been provided.
[Sat, 22 Feb 2014 14:22:49 +0000] WARN: Original Run List: []
[Sat, 22 Feb 2014 14:22:49 +0000] WARN: Overridden Run List:
  [recipe[testcookbook::default]]
[Sat, 22 Feb 2014 14:22:49 +0000] WARN: Start Handler
  Chef::Handler::AwesomeStartHandler executed
resolving cookbooks for run list: ["testcookbook::default"]
Synchronizing Cookbooks:
  - testcookbook
Compiling Cookbooks...
Converging 2 resources
Recipe: testcookbook::default
  * directory[/tmp/part2_examples] action create (up to date)
  * file[/tmp/part2_examples/testfile] action create
    - Would create new file /tmp/part2_examples/testfile

[Sat, 22 Feb 2014 14:22:49 +0000] WARN: Skipping final node save
  because override_runlist was given

Running handlers:
  - Chef::Handler::AwesomeReportHandler
```

As expected, the run completed successfully. Let's check the contents of */tmp/ handler_output* to verify that the output of our handler was as we expected, too:

```
$> cat /tmp/handler_output

Chef::Handler::AwesomeStartHandler: Run started on mynode.mydomain.com at
  2014-02-22 14:22:49 +0000

Chef::Handler::AwesomeHandler: Run successfully completed on
  mynode.mydomain.com and took 0.168382415 seconds:
  2 resources in total, 1 updated:
    recipe[testcookbook::default] ran 'create' on file
      '/tmp/part2_examples/testfile'
```

Just as in previous Chef runs, we see our AwesomeStartHandler being executed at the start of the run. But when the run finishes, we now see our combined AwesomeHandler class writing its report handler output, triggered by checking @run_status.success? and having it return true, indicating a successful Chef run. This output is exactly as we saw in our separate report handler class, and exactly what we wanted to see.

Now that we've verified that the report handler portion of our AwesomeHandler class still works, we need to test the exception handler part. This means that we need to deliberately break our Chef run in such a way that it throws an exception. There are a number of ways that we could do this, but the simplest is to make use of Chef's built-in safety mechanisms and tell our test run to execute a run_list containing a recipe that does not exist. Let's change the value passed to the -o parameter of our run command from `testcookbook::default` to `testcookbook::shrubbery`, which is a nonexistent recipe:

```
$> chef-client --once --why-run --local-mode \
   --config /tmp/part2_examples/client.rb \
   --override-runlist testcookbook::shrubbery

Starting Chef Client, version 11.10.4
[Sat, 22 Feb 2014 14:05:06 +0000] WARN: Run List override has been provided.
[Sat, 22 Feb 2014 14:05:06 +0000] WARN: Original Run List: []
[Sat, 22 Feb 2014 14:05:06 +0000] WARN: Overridden Run List:
  [recipe[testcookbook::defaults]]
[Sat, 22 Feb 2014 14:05:06 +0000] WARN: Start Handler
  Chef::Handler::AwesomeStartHandler executed
resolving cookbooks for run list: ["testcookbook::defaults"]
Synchronizing Cookbooks:
  - testcookbook
Compiling Cookbooks...


================================================================================
Recipe Compile Error
================================================================================


Chef::Exceptions::RecipeNotFound
================================
could not find recipe defaults for cookbook testcookbook

Running handlers:
[Sat, 22 Feb 2014 14:05:06 +0000] ERROR: Running exception handlers
  - Chef::Handler::AwesomeHandler
Running handlers complete

[Sat, 22 Feb 2014 14:05:06 +0000] ERROR: Exception handlers complete
[Sat, 22 Feb 2014 14:05:06 +0000] FATAL: Stacktrace dumped to
  /home/jcowie/.chef/local-mode-cache/cache/chef-stacktrace.out
Chef Client failed. 0 resources would have been updated
[Sat, 22 Feb 2014 14:05:06 +0000] ERROR: could not find recipe
  defaults for cookbook testcookbook
[Sat, 22 Feb 2014 14:05:06 +0000] FATAL: Chef::Exceptions::ChildConvergeError:
  Chef run process exited unsuccessfully (exit code 1)
```

As we see here, this time our Chef run failed, and our `Chef::Handler::AwesomeHan dler` was executed as an exception handler. The output of the run told us about the failure and wrote the exception's stack trace to disk, but of course, if Chef had been running in daemonized mode here instead of in an interactive terminal, we'd never have known that the run failed unless we were looking for it. Let's look at */tmp/ handler_output* now and see what output was written by our exception handler (I've abbreviated directory paths with ellipses because of space constraints):

```
$> cat /tmp/handler_output

Chef::Handler::AwesomeStartHandler: Run started on mynode.mydomain.com
  at 2014-02-22 14:05:06 +0000

Chef::Handler::AwesomeHandler: Run failed on
  mynode.mydomain.com after 0.034007263 seconds:

  Exception: could not find recipe shrubbery for cookbook testcookbook
  Backtrace:
    /usr/.../lib/chef/cookbook_version.rb:226:in `load_recipe'
    /usr/.../lib/chef/run_context.rb:151:in `load_recipe'
    /usr/.../lib/chef/run_context/cookbook_compiler.rb:139:in
      `block in compile_recipes'
    /usr/.../lib/chef/run_context/cookbook_compiler.rb:137:in `each'
    /usr/.../lib/chef/run_context/cookbook_compiler.rb:137:in `compile_recipes'
    /usr/.../lib/chef/run_context/cookbook_compiler.rb:74:in `compile'
    /usr/.../lib/chef/run_context.rb:86:in `load'
    /usr/.../lib/chef/client.rb:250:in `setup_run_context'
    /usr/.../lib/chef/client.rb:498:in `do_run'
    /usr/.../lib/chef/client.rb:199:in `block in run'
    /usr/.../lib/chef/client.rb:193:in `fork'
    /usr/.../lib/chef/client.rb:193:in `run'
    /usr/.../lib/chef/application.rb:208:in `run_chef_client'
    /usr/.../lib/chef/application/client.rb:312:in `block in run_application'
    /usr/.../lib/chef/application/client.rb:304:in `loop'
    /usr/.../lib/chef/application/client.rb:304:in `run_application'
    /usr/.../lib/chef/application.rb:66:in `run'
    /usr/.../bin/chef-client:26:in `<top (required)>'
    /usr/bin/chef-client:19:in `load'
    /usr/bin/chef-client:19:in `<main>'
```

Here we see that, as expected, the AwesomeStartHandler was executed at the start of the run. This time, however, when the run failed, our combined AwesomeHandler class wrote its exception handler output, triggered by checking @run_status.failed? and having it return true, indicating a failed Chef run.

In this case, our exception handler outputs the string representation of the Exception object that was thrown during the run and then prints the backtrace to tell us exactly where in the codebase the exception was triggered. However, it could equally have posted a notification to a chat system like IRC or Campfire—exception handlers make it extremely simple for us to capture and utilize detailed information on any errors that occur during our Chef runs.

Handlers: Summary and Further Reading

In this chapter we've looked at the underlying `Chef::Handler` superclass shared by all handlers and the run status object it provides that can be used to extract incredibly detailed information about what happened during our Chef run. We've also looked at example implementations of each type of handler, but the flexibility of handlers combined with the huge variety of available monitoring and notification systems means that we can't possibly cover all possible handler implementations in this limited space.

For readers interested in deploying or implementing their own Chef handlers, or those just interested in exploring more example code, here I've listed some of the open source Chef handlers implemented by the Chef community:

Sensu
> The Sensu (*http://bit.ly/gh-sensu*) handler provides start and report handlers for silencing checks on a node in the Sensu (*http://sensuapp.org/*) monitoring system while Chef is running.

Datadog
> The Datadog (*http://bit.ly/gh-datadog*) handler provides exception and report handlers for feeding detailed information on your Chef runs to the Datadog (*https://www.datadoghq.com/*) monitoring service.

Graphite
> The Graphite (*http://bit.ly/gh-graphite*) handler provides exception and report handlers for feeding the Graphite (*http://graphite.readthedocs.org/en/latest/*) monitoring system with a number of metrics on Chef runs, including successful and failed runs, average elapsed run time, and number of resources updated.

IRCSnitch
> The IRCSnitch (*http://bit.ly/chef-snitch*) handler provides an exception handler for sending an IRC notification when a Chef run fails. The plugin also creates a private GitHub gist (*https://gist.github.com/*) containing information on the node, the exception that was thrown, and the backtrace of the exception.

Nagios NSCA handler
> The Nagios NSCA (*http://bit.ly/gh-nscahandler*) handler provides exception and report handlers to send notifications to the Nagios (*http://www.nagios.org/*) monitoring system when Chef runs fail or take an unusually long time to run.

To make deploying handlers easier without the need to modify the *client.rb* file, Chef, Inc. has also developed the `chef_handler` cookbook (*http://bit.ly/chefhandler*). This cookbook provides a resource to allow handlers to be configured in recipe code instead of hardcoding them in *client.rb*, which can be particularly useful for open sourcing handlers as it allows you to distribute your handler with a recipe to enable or disable it.

Hopefully, this chapter has served to give you a good understanding of how handlers integrate with the Chef run process to allow you to mine the behavior of Chef runs for useful information. Deployed effectively, handlers are able to give us detailed insight into exactly how our Chef runs are performing, and make sure that we find out when they fail (and why) without us having to visually observe the output of every Chef run.

In the next chapter, we'll examine how Chef tracks the individual events that occur during runs, and how we can tap into this information to give us even deeper insight into how our infrastructure automation code is behaving under the hood.

CHAPTER 6
Extending Chef Run Events

As we touched on briefly in Chapter 3 (see "SetUp RunContext" on page 66), Chef builds up a comprehensive collection of the events that occur during the course of a run that it exposes through a system called the *event dispatcher*. The event dispatcher works on what's known as a *publish/subscribe* model. This means that classes that wish to be notified of events that occur during a Chef run can *subscribe* to the event dispatcher, and each time the event dispatcher receives an event it *publishes* it to all registered subscribers. In fact, the output you see displayed on your terminal when running chef-client or chef-solo manually is generated by a type of subscriber called a *formatter*, which we'll be looking at later in this chapter.

Introduction to the Event Dispatcher

Out of the box, Chef leverages the event dispatcher system to power the terminal output produced by chef-client and send reporting data to Enterprise Chef (if it's being used), but the detailed information it exposes to us about our Chef runs can be used for a variety of purposes. Say you want to augment or alter the output of chef-client to structure the information it presents in a different way. Or perhaps you'd like to integrate Chef run data into an internal event tracking system so that you can collect information on when a recipe change has been processed by all of your nodes. The event dispatcher allows us to quickly and easily tap into its event stream to access all of the information we need to do these things.

In this chapter we'll look at how exactly the Chef event dispatcher works and the different types of subscribers we can create to tap into the event dispatcher to make use of the event notifications it publishes. We'll then look at examples of actually implementing these subscriber types to add custom behavior to our Chef run, such as altering the format and content of the output chef-client prints to the screen during a Chef run and sending data about our Chef run to an external reporting system.

Before running the example code contained in this chapter, please ensure that you've followed the steps covered in "Preparing a Test Environment" on page 114 to prepare the test environment we'll use to run our examples. If you've already completed these steps and worked through the examples in Chapter 5, you can reuse the same test environment for this chapter.

Event Dispatcher Initialization

As we saw in "The Chef::Client Class" on page 84, the event dispatcher is created in the `initialize` method of the `Chef::Client` class with this line:

```
@events = EventDispatch::Dispatcher.new(*event_handlers)
```

Here we're creating a new instance of the `EventDispatch::Dispatcher` class that lives at *lib/chef/event_dispatch/dispatch.rb* (*http://bit.ly/gh-dispatcher*) and passing in `*event_handlers` as a parameter to this object. The `*` character used before `event_han dlers` is known as the "splat operator" and turns the `event_handlers` array into a list of parameters to be passed to the method.

The `event_handlers` parameter contains a list of subscribers to automatically register with the event dispatcher. The only subscriber to be automatically registered at this stage of the run is usually Chef's default formatter which will be used to write the run output to the screen if Chef is being run in an interactive terminal by the user (we'll look at formatters in more detail in "Creating Formatters" on page 142).

Now that we've seen how the event dispatcher is initialized, let's lift the hood and look at how it actually works. We'll first examine how the publish side of the event dispatcher works, before going on to look at an overview of how classes can subscribe to the event dispatcher to receive event notifications.

Publish Overview

To implement the publish side of the publish/subscribe system, the `EventDis patch::Dispatcher` class we met in the previous section inherits from a class called `EventDispatch::Base` which lives at *lib/chef/event_dispatch/base.rb* (*http://bit.ly/gh-baserb*). This class defines a number of empty methods representing all of the event types that can occur during the Chef run, as seen in Example 6-1.

Example 6-1. Excerpt of lib/chef/event_dispatch/base.rb

```
def run_start(version)
end

def run_started(run_status)
end
```

```
# Called at the end a successful Chef run.
def run_completed(node)
end

# Called at the end of a failed Chef run.
def run_failed(exception)
end
```

As we can see, these event method definitions also specify the number and expected content of parameters required for each event type. When Chef adds events to the event collection during a run, as described in "The Chef::Client Class do_run Method" on page 86, it does so with lines like these:

```
@events.run_start(Chef::VERSION)
@events.ohai_completed(node)
@events.run_completed(node)
@events.run_failed(e)
```

What we're actually doing here is calling methods like `run_start` and `ohai_comple ted` on the `EventDispatch::Dispatcher` object that was created earlier in the run. Each of these method calls tells the event dispatcher that an event has occurred and should be published to its subscribers.

To publish these events to its subscribers, the event dispatcher does something rather clever. All subscribers to the event dispatcher must also inherit from `EventDis patch::Base`. This shared superclass means that both publisher and subscriber define methods for all possible events. If a subscriber wants to define specific behavior for a particular event, it can override the method inherited from `EventDispatch::Base`; if it doesn't, it will still inherit the empty methods defined in `EventDispatch::Base`.

This means that, for example, when the `run_start` method of the `EventDispatch::Dis patcher` object is called, it in turn is able to call the `run_start` method of any objects that have registered as subscribers. Interested readers may wish to explore the code of the `EventDispatch::Dispatcher` (*http://bit.ly/gh-dispatcher*) class to look at exactly how this behavior is implemented; the entire class definition is only 41 lines of Ruby code.

Subscribe Overview

The simple yet effective strategy of subscribers inheriting from `EventDispatch::Base` means that if a subscriber wants to implement specific behavior when notified about a particular event, it simply needs to *override* the method for that event inherited from `EventDispatch::Base`. If no specific action needs to be taken, the empty method from `EventDispatch::Base` will be used instead. This approach gives us the flexibility to implement subscribers that are able to respond to any number of events, while also ensuring that the subscriber only has to implement code for the events it cares about.

Understanding the theory behind how subscribers to the event dispatcher work is one thing, but how do we actually implement them? I've divided the types of subscriber we'll be implementing in this chapter into two categories. Both behave in similar ways—they are, after all, both subclasses of `EventDispatch::Base`—but there are also enough differences to warrant each having its own section. The categories we'll be looking at are:

Formatters
> Formatters format the output of Chef run events and display it on the screen when running in an interactive terminal. Only one formatter can be active at a time, and it is specified by passing the `-F` option to `chef-client`. In the event that the `-F` option is omitted, Chef will automatically use its default formatter, `doc`. As we saw in "Event Dispatcher Initialization" on page 140, the active formatter is automatically subscribed to the event dispatcher. We'll look at how to create and use our own formatters in "Creating Formatters" on page 142.

Other subscribers
> To create a subscriber to the event dispatcher system that is *not* a formatter, we must manually register the subscribing class with the event dispatcher using a start handler. We'll look at how to create a custom subscriber and a start handler to register it in "Creating Custom Subscribers" on page 151.

Creating Formatters

In this section, we'll explore the various classes Chef provides for implementing formatters, and see how to create our own formatter classes. We'll cover the following topics:

- The "skeleton code" necessary to create a working formatter using Chef's built-in formatter classes
- Adding functionality to our formatter skeleton to handle Chef run events
- Creating a more complex plugin to completely customize the output of a Chef run

 Before running the example code contained in this section, please ensure that you've followed the steps covered in "Preparing a Test Environment" on page 114 to prepare the test environment we'll use to run our examples. If you've already completed these steps and worked through the examples in Chapter 5, you can reuse the same test environment for this chapter.

Formatter Example 1: Skeleton Formatter

Just as we did when looking at how to implement Ohai plugins, let's start off by looking at the absolute minimum code needed to implement a functional formatter (we're not going to customize the output it produces yet). Paste the code in Example 6-2 into */tmp/part2_examples/awesome.rb*.

Example 6-2. /tmp/part2_examples/awesome.rb

```ruby
require 'chef/formatters/base' ❶

class Chef
  module Formatters ❷
    class Awesome < Formatters::Base ❸
      cli_name(:awesome) ❹
    end
  end
end
```

❶ We begin by telling our formatter class to require the `Chef::Format` `ters::Base` class, which lives at *lib/chef/formatters/base.rb* (*http://bit.ly/base-rb*). This is the base class that all formatters must inherit from; it inherits from `EventDispatch::Base`, as any event dispatcher subscriber must.

❷ Here we're stating that our formatter class will live under the `Formatters` module in the `Chef` class—this makes its full namespace `Chef::Formatters::Awesome`. This is purely for organizational reasons; there is no functional reason why our formatter class needs to live inside this namespace, but it does help make the purpose of our class clearer.

❸ Here we're stating that our `Awesome` class inherits from `Format` `ters::Base`;because our class also lives under the `Chef` class, we're able to use `Formatters::Base` instead of the full `Chef::Formatters::Base` name.

❹ This line calls the `cli_name` method inherited from `Chef::Formatters::Base`. This method tells Chef what name we'll use to request our formatter on the command line with the `-F` option. Without this method call, our formatter will not work.

Before we can test our skeleton formatter, we need to add a line to our *client.rb* file to tell it to `require` our new formatter class. Add the line shown in Example 6-3 to */tmp/part2_examples/client.rb*.

Example 6-3. /tmp/part2_examples/client.rb

```ruby
verify_api_cert true

require "/tmp/part2_examples/awesome.rb"
```

Now that we've examined our skeleton formatter code and added a `require` statement to our *client.rb*, we can perform a Chef run on our test environment using the same command we saw in "Preparing a Test Environment" on page 114, but this time adding the `-F awesome` option to specify that we want to use our new `awesome` formatter:

```
$> chef-client --once --why-run --local-mode \
  --config /tmp/part2_examples/client.rb \
  --override-runlist testcookbook::default -F awesome
[Sat, 22 Feb 2014 14:08:49 +0000] WARN: Run List override has been provided.
[Sat, 22 Feb 2014 14:08:49 +0000] WARN: Original Run List: []
[Sat, 22 Feb 2014 14:08:49 +0000] WARN: Overridden Run List:
  [recipe[testcookbook]]
[Sat, 22 Feb 2014 14:08:49 +0000] WARN: In whyrun mode, so NOT performing node
save.
```

As we can see, our Chef run worked perfectly—it just didn't show much output. This is because the `Chef::Formatters::Base` class doesn't define any methods to handle events generated by the event dispatcher, so of course nothing is printed to the screen when each event is fired. That's left up to us, and we'll look at how to do that in "Formatter Example 3: Custom Event Methods" on page 146.

Formatter Example 2: Slightly Less Skeletal

If you intend to implement a formatter that handles the formatting and output of *all* events produced during a Chef run, then `Chef::Formatters::Base` is a good place to start. However, for many use cases we might only want to customize output for selected events—for example, when resources are updated or skipped.

In these cases, a more useful formatter class to inherit from is `Chef::Formatters::Minimal`, which lives at *lib/chef/formatters/minimal.rb* (*http://bit.ly/gh-minimal*). `Chef::Formatters::Minimal` defines methods that will display very simplistic output for each event. If we only want to define custom output for a few event methods, this lets us avoid having to implement unnecessary methods to handle events that we aren't directly interested in.

Let's change our *awesome.rb* class so that it inherits from `Chef::Formatters::Minimal` instead, as shown in Example 6-4.

Example 6-4. /tmp/part2_examples/awesome.rb

```
require 'chef/formatters/minimal' ❶

class Chef
  module Formatters
    class Awesome < Formatters::Minimal ❷
      cli_name(:awesome)
    end
  end
end
```

❶ We're now requiring `chef/formatters/minimal` instead of `chef/formatters/base`.

❷ Our class now inherits from `Chef::Formatters::Minimal` instead of `Chef::Formatters::Base`.

The only thing that we've changed in our `Awesome` formatter class is that it now inherits from `Chef::Formatters::Minimal` instead of `Chef::Formatters::Base`; we're still not defining any of our own methods to generate custom output for events. Let's try running our test Chef run again to see how the output of the run has changed:

```
$> chef-client --once --why-run --local-mode \
  --config /tmp/part2_examples/client.rb \
  --override-runlist testcookbook::default -F awesome
Starting Chef Client, version 11.10.4
[Sat, 22 Feb 2014 14:24:55 +0000] WARN: Run List override has been provided.
[Sat, 22 Feb 2014 14:24:55 +0000] WARN: Original Run List: []
[Sat, 22 Feb 2014 14:24:55 +0000] WARN: Overridden Run List:
  [recipe[testcookbook::default]]
resolving cookbooks for run list: ["testcookbook::default"]
Synchronizing cookbooks
.done.
Compiling cookbooks
done.
Converging 2 resources
.U

System converged.


resources updated this run:
* file[/tmp/part2_examples/testfile]
  - create new file /tmp/part2_examples/testfile

[Sat, 22 Feb 2014 14:24:55 +0000] WARN: Skipping final node save
  because override_runlist was given
chef client finished, 1 resources updated
```

As we can see, simply changing the superclass of the formatter defined in *awesome.rb* results in much more output from our Chef run. `Chef::Formatters::Minimal` defines some useful methods to output when cookbook synchronization and compilation have taken place, and also to display a list at the end of the run of all resources updated during the run. During the "Converge Node" stage of the run, it prints extremely simple output to tell us when resources have been skipped (`S`), are up-to-date (`.`), or have been updated (`U`).

Now that we've looked at two possible superclasses for our custom formatters, it's time to actually start defining our own methods to format event output!

Formatter Example 3: Custom Event Methods

In this example, we're going to extend our Awesome formatter class with our own methods to handle the output from three specific events:

synchronized_cookbook

> This event method is called when a cookbook has been synchronized (see "Synchronize Cookbooks" on page 66).

resource_up_to_date

> This event method is called when a resource is to be found already up-to-date (i.e.,fully converged).

resource_updated

> This event method is called when a resource has been updated (i.e., was not already converged).

As we learned in "Subscribe Overview" on page 141, all formatters are subclasses of the EventDispatch::Base class, which defines a specific method for each event that can occur during a Chef run. This means that for each of the events just listed, we need to identify the method names from EventDispatch::Base that we'll need to override in our formatter—why not have a look at *lib/chef/event_dispatch/base.rb* (*http://bit.ly/gh-baserb*) and see if you can identify the methods we'll need to define for these events before I list them?

Example 6-5 shows the methods from EventDispatch::Base that we will be overriding.

Example 6-5. Excerpt of lib/chef/event_dispatcher/base.rb

```
class Chef
  module EventDispatch
    class Base

      # Other methods removed

      # Called when cookbook, cookbook_name, has been synced
      def synchronized_cookbook(cookbook_name)
      end

      # Called when a resource has no converge actions (i.e., was already correct)
      def resource_up_to_date(resource, action)
      end

      # Called after a resource has been completely converged, but only if
      # modifications were made
      def resource_updated(resource, action)
      end
    end
  end
end
```

We can see here that each of the methods from `EventDispatch::Base` that we'll be overriding takes a number of parameters. We'll be able to make use of these in our methods to add context to the output of our formatter class.

As we saw in our first two formatter examples, the superclass we choose to build our formatter on will dictate how much output is shown by our Chef run, in addition to that which we explicitly define in our formatter class. To keep the output of our test runs as easy to read as possible, I've used `Chef::Formatters::Base` as the superclass of our example formatter here to ensure that the only output printed is that defined by the methods we're overriding.

Modify *awesome.rb* with our new overridden methods, as shown in Example 6-6.

Example 6-6. /tmp/part2_examples/awesome.rb

```
require 'chef/formatters/base'

class Chef
  module Formatters
    class Awesome < Formatters::Base
      cli_name(:awesome)

      def synchronized_cookbook(cookbook_name) ❶
        puts "\nCookbook #{cookbook_name} synchronized.\n"
      end

      def resource_up_to_date(resource, action) ❷
        puts "#{resource.cookbook_name}::#{resource.recipe_name}"
        puts "  #{resource}:\n    Up to date, skipped action #{action}\n"
      end

      def resource_updated(resource, action) ❸
        puts "#{resource.cookbook_name}::#{resource.recipe_name}"
        puts "  #{resource}:\n    Updated, performed action #{action}\n"
      end
    end
  end
end
```

❶ In this method, we're simply using `puts` to display the name of the cookbook that has been synchronized—this is passed to the method via the `cookbook_name` parameter.

❷ In this method, we're printing several attributes of `resource`, which is passed to the method as a parameter, and also the value of the `action` parameter.

❸ In this method, we're printing the same attributes of `resource` and `action` that we used in `resource_up_to_date`, but the explanatory text we're outputting has been changed to reflect that the resource has been updated this time.

EventDispatch::Base Method Parameters

Although in Example 6-6 we're mainly using the parameters of our methods as strings injected into a `puts` statement, in the `resource_up_to_date` and `resource_skipped` methods we're also calling several methods of the `resource` parameter, like `cook book_name` and `recipe_name`.

Under the hood, the `resource` parameter is an instance of `Chef::Resource`, which lives in *lib/chef/resource.rb* (*http://bit.ly/gh-resourcerb*). While it can certainly be treated like a string, it also defines a number of additional methods that can be used to give more context to our output.

As a general rule, it's safe to assume that parameters passed to methods in `EventDis patch::Base` can be treated as strings (and hence included in `puts` statements); however, examining the code of existing formatters such as `Chef::Formatters::Minimal` can offer insight into when additional context can be extracted from parameters via method calls.

Interested readers may also wish to examine the object types passed as parameters to method calls on the `@events` object we met in "The Chef::Client Class" on page 84. These will be passed through to all subscribers as the same type that they were sent to the publisher.

Let's try a Chef run with our expanded `awesome` formatter to see our new methods in action:

```
$> chef-client --once --why-run --local-mode \
  --config /tmp/part2_examples/client.rb \
  --override-runlist testcookbook::default -F awesome
[Sat, 22 Feb 2014 14:25:56 +0000] WARN: Run List override has been provided.
[Sat, 22 Feb 2014 14:25:56 +0000] WARN: Original Run List: []
[Sat, 22 Feb 2014 14:25:56 +0000] WARN: Overridden Run List:
  [recipe[testcookbook::default]]

Cookbook testcookbook synchronized.

testcookbook::default
  directory[/tmp/part2_examples]:
    Up to date, skipped action create

testcookbook::default
  file[/tmp/part2_examples/testfile]:
    Updated, performed action create

[Sat, 22 Feb 2014 14:25:57 +0000] WARN: Skipping final node
  save because override_runlist was given
```

As we can see, when the event dispatcher calls the three event methods we've defined in our `awesome` formatter, our custom output now appears in the output of the Chef run.

Setting the Default Formatter

Out of the box, the default formatter used by Chef when no `-F` option is passed to `chef-client` is the doc formatter, which lives at *lib/chef/formatters/doc.rb* (*http://bit.ly/gh-docrb*). It is this formatter that produces the onscreen output we've all seen when performing Chef runs. In all of the examples we've seen so far, we've specified our `awesome` formatter by passing the `-F` option to `chef-client`. But what do we do if we want to use our new formatter as the default instead of doc?

Chef allows us to choose the default formatter by adding a single line to our *client.rb* file. To make `awesome` the default formatter, we can modify that file to look like Example 6-7.

Example 6-7. /tmp/part2_examples/client.rb

```
verify_api_cert true

require "/tmp/part2_examples/awesome.rb"
formatters [:awesome]  ❶
```

❶ In this line, we're overriding the array of formatters that chef-client knows about. The formatter name given here must match the one we passed to the `cli_name` method in our formatter class definition. If you specify more than one formatter in this array, they will all be used—this can produce duplicate results for events, but this technique can also be used to augment an existing formatter without having to re-implement it.

Now let's try one more Chef run, this time without passing the `-F` option to `chef-client`:

```
$> chef-client --once --why-run --local-mode \
   --config /tmp/part2_examples/client.rb \
   --override-runlist testcookbook::default
[Sat, 22 Feb 2014 14:27:56 +0000] WARN: Run List override has been provided.
[Sat, 22 Feb 2014 14:27:56 +0000] WARN: Original Run List: []
[Sat, 22 Feb 2014 14:27:56 +0000] WARN: Overridden Run List:
  [recipe[testcookbook::default]]

Cookbook testcookbook synchronized.

testcookbook::default
  directory[/tmp/part2_examples]:
    Up to date, skipped action create

testcookbook::default
```

```
file[/tmp/part2_examples/testfile]:
  Updated, performed action create

[Sat, 22 Feb 2014 14:27:57 +0000] WARN: Skipping final node save
  because override_runlist was given
```

As we see, our one-line change to *client.rb* means that our `awesome` formatter is now being used as the default for chef-client runs instead of doc, and we no longer need to specify it using the `-F` option.

Formatters: Summary and Further Reading

In this section, we've covered the foundations of creating your own formatters and the various formatter base classes you can inherit from. However, there are simply too many event methods and implementation possibilities for us to comprehensively cover everything here.

Readers interested in diving deeper into implementing formatters may wish to take a look at the following:

The `EventDispatcher::Base` *class*
> As we've seen throughout this chapter, the `EventDispatch::Base` class, which lives at *lib/chef/event_dispatch/base.rb* (*http://bit.ly/gh-baserb*), is the definitive source for the list of event methods supported by formatters and other event dispatcher subscribers.

The `Doc` *formatter class*
> The doc formatter, which lives at *lib/chef/formatters/doc.rb* (*http://bit.ly/gh-docrb*), is the default formatter used by Chef when no `-F` option is passed to `chef-client`. The doc formatter implements methods for a sizable proportion of the events defined in `EventDispatch::Base`, and is also an excellent reference guide to extracting information from the parameters passed to event methods.

Nyan formatter
> For a slightly more fun formatter example, have a look at Andrea Campi's Nyan Cat formatter (*http://bit.ly/nyan-chef*). Andrea's formatter returns *rspec*-type output for Chef runs in the style of the Nyan Cat meme and implements some clever behavior to assemble and correctly color the "rainbow" while still correctly indicating updated and skipped resources, etc.

ChefSpec formatter
> A more minimal formatter example is included with the ChefSpec unit testing framework, which you can find on GitHub (*http://bit.ly/gh-format*). As it forms part of a unit testing framework, this formatter suppresses the output of nearly all events generated during a Chef run, except for errors. It's an excellent reference guide to best practices for implementing customized handling of events that indi-

cate errors in your Chef run—it's also an easy class to read through, as the non-error event methods are entirely empty.

Hopefully this section has given you a taste of the flexibility and power that formatters provide to customize the output of our Chef runs. Because they can be optionally specified on the command line and do not affect the Chef server or the recipes run on your node, formatters are one of the safest Chef customizations to experiment with. But formatters are only half of the story when it comes to event dispatcher subscribers.

As we saw earlier in this chapter, Chef also allows us to register our own custom subscribers to provide functionality such as reporting or event streaming of our Chef runs. In the next section, we're going to take the knowledge we've gained in this section about working with Chef events and expand it to look at how to create our own subscriber classes and register them with the event dispatcher.

Creating Custom Subscribers

As we touched on briefly in "Subscribe Overview" on page 141, the Chef event dispatcher system also allows us to implement our own custom subscribers to receive event notifications. These subscriber classes work in a similar fashion to the formatters we examined in the last section, as they share the `EventDispatch::Base` superclass and define behavior for specific events by overriding methods from this class. These subscriber classes are typically used to send data on Chef run events to external monitoring or metrics systems, but can be used in any scenario where you want to receive notifications of specific events occurring during a run, and trigger specific behavior with those notifications.

Although functionally similar to formatters, custom event dispatcher classes have two key differences:

- They must be manually registered with the event dispatcher, unlike formatters, which are registered automatically when loaded by Chef.

- They inherit directly from `EventDispatch::Base` rather than a class under the `Formatters` namespace, like `Formatters::Base` or `Formatters::Minimal`, as formatters do.

In this section, we'll look at how to create a start handler to register our event dispatcher subscriber with the publisher, and how to create and run our own class to handle Chef event notifications.

Before running the example code contained in this section, please ensure that you've followed the steps covered in "Preparing a Test Environment" on page 114 to prepare the test environment we'll use to run our examples. If you've already completed these steps and worked through the examples in Chapter 5, you can reuse the same test environment for this chapter.

Subscriber Example 1: Skeleton Subscriber

Before we define any custom event behaviors as we did with the previous examples, let's look at the absolute minimum code necessary to implement our own event dispatcher subscriber. As with our skeleton formatter example, our custom subscriber class won't actually do anything yet—we're just putting the framework in place to customize it further in later examples in this chapter. We'll put the code for this class, shown in Example 6-8, into */tmp/part2_examples/awesome_subscriber.rb*.

Example 6-8. /tmp/part2_examples/awesome_subscriber.rb

```
require 'chef/event_dispatch/base' ❶

class AwesomeSubscriber < Chef::EventDispatch::Base ❷
end
```

❶   Here, we're telling our subscriber class to require the `Chef::EventDis patch::Base` class which lives at *lib/chef/event_dispatch/base.rb* (*http://bit.ly/gh-baserb*).

❷   Next, we declare that our subscriber class is a subclass of `Chef::EventDis patch::Base`. As we saw in "Publish Overview" on page 140, both the event dispatcher publisher and all subscribers must inherit from this superclass.

Although we have not yet declared any custom event methods, the `AwesomeSubscrib er` class now contains all of the code necessary to function as an event dispatcher subscriber. As with the formatters we looked at earlier in the chapter, the empty method definitions inherited from `EventDispatcher::Base` mean that our class has all of the method definitions that it needs to function—it won't actually *do* anything, but it also won't throw any errors.

Before we can kick off a test run to try out our custom subscriber class, however, we need to register it with the event dispatcher. For this, we're going to create a special start handler.

Subscriber Example 2: Registration with Start Handlers

To register our custom subscriber class with the event dispatcher, we're going to create a start handler using exactly the same techniques we examined in "Handler Example 1:

Start Handler" on page 122. The main difference between this handler and the examples we saw earlier is that it will only register our subscriber class, rather than sending notifications itself. Paste the code for our start handler shown in Example 6-9 into */tmp/part2_examples/awesome_subscriber_start_handler.rb*.

Example 6-9. /tmp/part2_examples/awesome_subscriber_start_handler.rb

```
require "chef/handler"
require "/tmp/part2_examples/awesome_subscriber.rb" ❶

class Chef
  class Handler
    class AwesomeSubscriberStartHandler < Chef::Handler ❷
      def report ❸
          event_dispatcher_subscriber = AwesomeSubscriber.new ❹
          @run_status.events.register(event_dispatcher_subscriber) ❺
      end
    end
  end
end
```

❶ In addition to requiring the `chef/handler` class we'll inherit from, we also need to require the class we defined in */tmp/part2_examples/awesome_subscriber.rb*.

❷ Just as in the handler examples we looked at in Chapter 5, our start handler inherits from the `Chef::Handler` superclass.

❸ Next, again as in our previous handler examples, we override the `report` method defined in the `Chef::Handler` class to define our own behavior.

❹ Now we need to create a new instance of our `AwesomeSubscriber` class so we can register it with the event dispatcher.

❺ As we saw in "The Run Status Object" on page 119, the `events` method of the run status object returns the `EventDispatcher::Dispatch` object, which forms the publish side of the event dispatcher. Here, we're calling the `register` method on this object and passing as a parameter the `AwesomeSubscriber` object we created on the previous line—our subscriber is now registered with the event dispatcher.

Now that we've created both our subscriber class and a start handler to register it with the event dispatcher, we're ready to test it out and make sure that the run still works as we expect—but first, we need to add our start handler to the *client.rb* configuration file. Paste the contents of Example 6-10 into */tmp/part2_examples/client.rb*, replacing any lines contained in that file from previous examples.

Example 6-10. /tmp/part2_examples/client.rb

```
verify_api_cert true

require "/tmp/part2_examples/awesome_subscriber_start_handler.rb"

awesome_subscriber_start_handler = Chef::Handler::AwesomeSubscriberStartHandler.new

start_handlers << awesome_subscriber_start_handler
```

Exactly as we did for the example handler we created in "Handler Example 1: Start Handler" on page 122, in our *client.rb* configuration file we first create an instance of our Chef::Handler::AwesomeSubscriberStartHandler class and then add it to the start_handlers array. Note that we're not requiring or instantiating our AwesomeSub scriber class here; our start handler takes care of that.

Although our AwesomeSubscriber class does not define any event methods (and hence will not do anything), let's kick off a test Chef run to verify that everything still works as it should. We'll use the same command that we've used for our other examples:

```
$> chef-client --once --why-run --local-mode \
  --config /tmp/part2_examples/client.rb \
  --override-runlist testcookbook::default
Starting Chef Client, version 11.10.4
[Sat, 22 Feb 2014 14:50:41 +0000] WARN: Run List override has been provided.
[Sat, 22 Feb 2014 14:50:41 +0000] WARN: Original Run List: []
[Sat, 22 Feb 2014 14:50:41 +0000] WARN: Overridden Run List:
  [recipe[testcookbook::default]]
resolving cookbooks for run list: ["testcookbook::default"]
Synchronizing Cookbooks:
  - testcookbook
Compiling Cookbooks...
Converging 2 resources
Recipe: testcookbook::default
  * directory[/tmp/part2_examples] action create (up to date)
  * file[/tmp/part2_examples/testfile] action create
    - Would create new file /tmp/part2_examples/testfile

[Sat, 22 Feb 2014 14:50:41 +0000] WARN: Skipping final node save
  because override_runlist was given

Running handlers:
Running handlers complete

Chef Client finished, 1/2 resources would have been updated
```

Nothing in this output visibly indicates that our event dispatcher subscriber has been initialized or received notifications, but that's what we'd expect at this stage, as the AwesomeSubscriber class is still using the empty method bodies inherited from Even tDispatcher::Base. At this stage, we just wanted to check that our subscriber didn't

---

cause any errors during the run. Now that we've validated that our subscriber class works, let's add some event methods to it so that we can see it in action.

Subscriber Example 3: Custom Event Methods

To have our subscriber class respond to events published by the event dispatcher, as with the formatter example we looked at in "Formatter Example 3: Custom Event Methods" on page 146, we need to override some of the methods defined in `EventDispatch`
`er::Base`. A full listing of all supported event methods can be found in *lib/chef/
event_dispatch/base.rb* (*http://bit.ly/gh-baserb*), but for this example we're going to override the following methods:

run_started
> This event method is called when the Chef run has started, after stage 3 (see "Load and Build Node Object" on page 65) has been completed.

resource_up_to_date
> This event method is called when a resource is found to be already up-to-date, (i.e., fully converged).

resource_updated
> This event method is called when a resource has been updated (i.e., was not already converged).

run_completed
> This event method is called when the Chef run has successfully completed.

run_failed
> This event method is called when the Chef run has failed.

As with the other examples in this chapter, I want to keep the behavior of our example subscriber as simple as possible so that you can try it out for yourselves without the need to set up third-party monitoring systems, etc. For this reason, our custom subscriber class will stick to the technique I've used throughout this chapter and write its output to a local file, */tmp/subscriber_output*. Paste the expanded class definition in Example 6-11 into */tmp/part2_examples/awesome_subscriber.rb* (note that some lines have been split over two lines here for formatting purposes).

Example 6-11. /tmp/part2_examples/awesome_subscriber.rb

```
require "chef/event_dispatch/base"

class AwesomeSubscriber < Chef::EventDispatch::Base

  # Method to write a message string to our output file
  def write_to_file(message) ❶
    File.open('/tmp/subscriber_output', 'a') do |f|
      f.write("#{self.class} #{Time.now}: #{message}\n")
```

```
      end
    end

    # Methods overridden from Chef::EventDispatch::Base

    def run_started(run_status)
      write_to_file("run_started: Run started")
    end

    def converge_start(run_context)
      write_to_file("converge_start: Coo")
    end

    def converge_complete
    end

    def resource_up_to_date(new_resource, action)
      write_to_file("resource_up_to_date: Resource #{new_resource} " +
      "action #{action} already up to date")
    end

    def resource_updated(new_resource, action)
      write_to_file("resource_updated: Resource #{new_resource} was " +
      "updated with action #{action}")
    end

    def run_completed(node)
      write_to_file("run_completed: Run completed")
    end

    def run_failed(exception)
      write_to_file("run_failed: Run failed with #{exception}")
    end

  end
```

❶ The `write_to_file` method is the only method defined in our `AwesomeSub`
`scriber` class that is not overriding an event method defined in `Chef::Even`
`tDispatch::Base`. It is used to provide a simple, reusable method for writing a
string to the */tmp/subscriber_output* file, prefixed with the name of the class and
a timestamp.

The example code here is very similar to that used in our formatter examples earlier in
the chapter—after all, both subscriber types override the same methods from `EventDis`
`patcher::Base` and take the same parameters. Let's try one more test Chef run and see
how our `AwesomeSubscriber` class behaves now that we've overridden some event
methods:

```
$> chef-client --once --why-run --local-mode \
  --config /tmp/part2_examples/client.rb \
```

```
--override-runlist testcookbook::default
Starting Chef Client, version 11.10.4
[Sat, 22 Feb 2014 14:51:34 +0000] WARN: Run List override has been provided.
[Sat, 22 Feb 2014 14:51:34 +0000] WARN: Original Run List: []
[Sat, 22 Feb 2014 14:51:34 +0000] WARN: Overridden Run List:
  [recipe[testcookbook::default]]
resolving cookbooks for run list: ["testcookbook::default"]
Synchronizing Cookbooks:
  - testcookbook
Compiling Cookbooks...
Converging 2 resources
Recipe: testcookbook::default
  * directory[/tmp/part2_examples] action create (up to date)
  * file[/tmp/part2_examples/testfile] action create
    - Would create new file /tmp/part2_examples/testfile

[Sat, 22 Feb 2014 14:51:34 +0000] WARN: Skipping final node save
  because override_runlist was given

Running handlers:
Running handlers complete

Chef Client finished, 1/2 resources would have been updated
```

Just as we saw with our skeleton subscriber class, nothing in this output visibly indicates that our event dispatcher subscriber has been initialized or received notifications. But let's take a look in the */tmp/subscriber_output* file, whose contents are reproduced in Example 6-12.

Example 6-12. /tmp/subscriber_output

```
AwesomeSubscriber 2014-02-22 14:51:34 +0000: run_started: Run started
AwesomeSubscriber 2014-02-22 14:51:34 +0000: resource_up_to_date:
  Resource directory[/tmp/part2_examples] action create already up to date
AwesomeSubscriber 2014-02-22 14:51:34 +0000: resource_updated:
  Resource file[/tmp/part2_examples/testfile] was updated with action create
AwesomeSubscriber 2014-02-22 14:51:34 +0000: run_completed: Run completed
```

As we see here, when the event dispatcher publishes each method, the corresponding method of our AwesomeSubscriber subscriber class is called, and a line is output to the */tmp/subscriber_output* file.

Custom Subscribers: Summary

As mentioned in previous sections, the custom subscriber examples we've looked at here have been kept intentionally simple, but the techniques used can easily be adapted to create more complex subscriber classes. The comprehensive list of event methods defined in EventDispatch::Base means that custom subscriber classes can be utilized to provide metrics on your Chef runs that aren't exposed to more typically used methods, such as handlers. These metrics can help you answer questions like:

- How long does it take your nodes to register with the Chef server at the start of the run?

- Exactly how long does it take Chef to get a list of cookbook versions from the server?

- Once the client has that list, how long does the cookbook synchronization process take?

> Most of the existing uses of Chef's event dispatcher system relate to altering the format of chef-client's output or sending data to monitoring and metrics systems, as we've seen here. Why not see if you can think of some new uses for this data? Answers on a postcard!

Readers interested in looking at a real-world example of a custom subscriber class may wish to dive into the chef-reporting (*http://bit.ly/chef-reporting*) gem created by Chef, Inc. to allow older chef-client versions to send reporting data to Enterprise Chef for use with its reporting feature (this feature is not provided with the open source Chef server). The code is, of course, fairly specific to Chef's reporting system, but it gives a good idea of how to implement a more complex event dispatcher subscriber that sends event data to an external system.

Revisiting AwesomeInc—Which Customization?

Throughout the course of Part II, we've looked at a number of possibilities for customizing different aspects of the Chef run process. But when you're trying to solve a problem that could be solved by several of these customizations, which do you pick? To try and assist with that decision-making process, let's revisit one of the problems that AwesomeInc identified in "Criteria for Customization" on page 10:

> How do we find out when our Chef runs are failing and why?

As we've explored throughout these chapters, Chef exposes data on failing runs to nearly all of the customization types we've looked at here (Ohai plugins are an exception). So should AwesomeInc pick an exception handler? A formatter? A custom event dispatcher subscriber? At this stage, without knowing more about exactly what the people at AwesomeInc want to get from Chef and how they want to expose it, the best answer we could give them is *it depends*.

If you cast your minds back to "Think Critically" on page 7, I said that a large part of effectively customizing your infrastructure code is choosing the best solution to add value to your business—this may be the same solution that almost everybody else uses, or it may be a bespoke solution specific to your infrastructure and business needs. I could simply say, "Clearly, AwesomeInc should use an exception handler," but that's not going to help you understand *why* that is or is not the best solution for them. To figure that out, we need a little more information about Mike's team at AwesomeInc and how they operate. Here are a few more details:

- The team at AwesomeInc mainly utilizes Nagios and Graphite to monitor their systems. They have checks and graphs for most of the critical services and components of their infrastructure, but there are some known monitoring blind spots—they're not looking to implement anything too complex at the moment, until they finish their ongoing project to eliminate these blind spots.

- Because the AwesomeInc staff are currently all located in the same office, they mainly communicate face to face or via email. They've started to experiment with chat systems, though, as they expect to need to hire international ops engineers and developers as the business expands.

- The team at AwesomeInc are not looking for an extremely granular view of their Chef runs—at the moment all they want is to easily and quickly identify when runs fail and what caused the failure.

With this new information, we're now better able to look at making a recommendation to AwesomeInc. In theory, it would be possible for them to extract information on failing runs from three of the customization types we've looked at in this and the previous chapter: formatters, custom event dispatcher subscribers, and handlers. Let's look at each of these possible solutions in turn and explore which might fit AwesomeInc's needs most effectively:

Formatters

Although it would be possible to create a formatter to both print output to the screen *and* create a separate alert when a run failed, this is not really the purpose for which formatters were intended—as we saw earlier in this chapter, formatters are designed to format the event notifications published by the event dispatcher and display them to the screen when Chef is being run in an interactive terminal.

Solving this problem with a formatter would definitely be possible, but there are more suitable methods we could make use of—remember the SMVMS criteria we looked at in "Criteria for Customization" on page 10. To use a formatter to solve this problem, Mike's team at AwesomeInc would have to create an entirely new formatter class and add their custom alerting behavior alongside the existing formatter behavior for printing text to the screen. This would mean that they could no longer use Chef's default formatter, and would have to maintain their own. When we consider this alongside the fact that they are only really interested in a single run event—that of a failed run—a formatter really doesn't seem like the best solution to this problem.

Custom event dispatcher subscriber

A custom event dispatcher subscriber class could be a much more attractive option for AwesomeInc—as we saw earlier in this chapter, event dispatcher subscribers are intended for tasks such as sending information on Chef events to reporting and monitoring systems. Although subscriber classes and formatters share the same superclass, subscribers are intended specifically for the sort of thing the people at AwesomeInc are looking to do, and can co-exist perfectly happily alongside formatters and any other subscribers to the event dispatcher.

Although certainly more suitable than formatters, an event dispatcher subscriber is still in my opinion not the best solution to AwesomeInc's problem. Remember, as we saw above, the team at AwesomeInc are not currently looking to analyze their Chef runs in fine detail; they just want to know when runs have failed and why. This means using just one of the event methods that can be defined in a custom subscriber class. With this approach, AwesomeInc would have to create an event dispatcher subscriber class that generated a notification when the single `run_failed` event they're interested in was published, and a start handler to initialize and register the subscriber class. Given that a simpler and more lightweight solution exists to capture the specific information they're interested in, in this instance I would not recommend a custom subscriber class as the best solution either.

Handlers

Based on the information we know about AwesomeInc's infrastructure and requirements, I would recommend that they explore using an exception handler to solve the problem they're experiencing. An exception handler would provide AwesomeInc with a *modular* solution to the problem that integrates with Chef and does not affect the functioning of any other components.

Creating a handler is also the *simplest* option in this case, as once the handler class has been created, it can be added to the `exception_handlers` list in the Chef configuration file and will work straight away. No start handlers are needed, and no existing Chef functionality is being reimplemented to provide notifications. Exception handlers are also a more lightweight solution for this purpose than the other options we've considered—the single function of exception handlers is, after all, to respond to run failures.

In addition, an important consideration is that a number of open source handler implementations already exist, as we saw in "Handlers: Summary and Further Reading" on page 136. The team at AwesomeInc will be able to implement or modify community-created handlers that support both email and a number of common chat systems, increasing the likelihood that they will not have to write a new handler class from scratch themselves. Although using community customizations is not always possible, it's a valuable time-saving option worth considering.

In this example scenario, creating a handler emerged as the customization that is best suited to solving AwesomeInc's problem, given their specific use case and situation. If AwesomeInc's requirements had been different, however, our recommendation may well have been different, too. If, for example, AwesomeInc had been looking to create a full suite of metrics analyzing the performance and behavior of the Chef runs rather than only capturing run failures, we may have recommended that they create an event dispatcher subscriber class. As we progress through the material in this book, we'll carry out this exercise again to evaluate possible solutions to some more of AwesomeInc's problems.

Summary

In Part II, we've explored a number of ways to customize different aspects of our Chef runs. We looked at how to inject additional node attributes with Ohai plugins, how to create handlers to respond to particular situations during the Chef run, and how to leverage the event dispatcher to create our own formatters and subscriber classes before revisiting AwesomeInc to evaluate solutions for how they might gain more visibility into the behavior of their Chef runs.

In Part III, we're going to look at the different ways that Chef provides for us to customize our cookbooks. As we've already seen, Chef is extremely extensible and provides a number of ways in which to define new resources and providers to use in our cookbooks, and libraries to support them.

PART III
Customizing Recipes

In Part III of this book, we're going to learn about the different ways Chef provides for us to customize our cookbooks and recipes by creating our own resource definitions and the code to support them. We'll learn:

- How to create definitions
- How to create libraries to support our resources
- How to create lightweight resources and providers
- How to create heavyweight resources and providers
- The pros and cons of each customization type

Up to this point, the majority of the customization types we've looked at have been largely "monotasked"; that is, they have a clear function or use case that guides when they are likely to be used and which dictates your likely customization choice.

Recipe customizations, on the other hand, are not so easily separated. The chances are good that for any scenario in which you wish to create a custom resource, you could implement more than one of the customization types covered in this part of the book. Choosing the best customization type to use is extremely important, especially when considering the criteria we looked at in "Criteria for Customization" on page 10, so we'll cover this in much more detail than we have for the customization types discussed in the first two parts of this book.

Throughout the following chapters, we'll be working through a series of examples to solve problems for AwesomeInc, and exploring the decision-making process that must be worked through when considering each solution.

## CHAPTER 7

Definitions and Libraries

Possibly the most customizable aspect of Chef is the recipe code we run on our nodes, and the resources that comprise them. Because our recipes form the backbone of our infrastructure code, here more than ever it's important that Chef provides us with the flexibility and power to write infrastructure code to fit our requirements. Part of this flexibility involves making sure that cookbook authors who want to create a simple cookbook resource are able to do so without having to become an expert in Chef's internal classes, while making sure that more experienced users are able to do just that should they wish.

In this chapter, we're going to revisit the underlying structure of cookbooks in Chef before looking at two of the simpler customization types, *definitions* and *libraries*. Don't make the mistake of assuming that *simple* means that these customization types aren't powerful, however—it just means that their fundamentals are quite straightforward to explain. As with many aspects of customizing Chef, the real power comes from what you use that fundamental knowledge to implement.

In this chapter, we're going to learn:

- How cookbooks in Chef are structured and where each component part sits in this structure
- How to prepare a test environment to safely run our recipe customizations
- What definitions are and how to create and use them
- What libraries are and how to create and use them

As always, we'll work through a number of code examples for each customization type to enable us to see them in action.

Cookbook Structure Revisited

Before we dive into creating the various different types of recipe customizations we'll be looking at in this part of the book, let's revisit the structure of Chef cookbooks and how the different components we'll learn about fit together.

Let's start off by taking a look at the typical structure of a Chef cookbook and its component parts. The following directory listing shows the default directories created when running the `knife cookbook create` command. I've removed README files and the like for clarity:

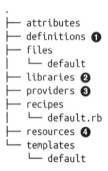

```
.
├── attributes
├── definitions ❶
├── files
│   └── default
├── libraries ❷
├── providers ❸
├── recipes
│   └── default.rb
├── resources ❹
└── templates
    └── default
```

❶ The *definitions* folder contains the simplest type of resources Chef allows us to create: definitions. These are typically used as wrappers around frequently used resource combinations, or when passing data from multiple recipes into the same resource. We'll look at definitions in more detail in "Definitions" on page 168.

❷ The *libraries* folder contains native Ruby classes and modules that allow us to add additional functionality to our recipes and other cookbook components. We'll learn about libraries in more detail in "Libraries" on page 179, and see how they help us implement heavyweight resources and providers in Chapter 9.

❸ The *providers* folder is where we put our own lightweight provider classes, used to drive the behavior that backs custom resource types. We'll learn how to create our own lightweight resources and providers in Chapter 8.

❹ The *resources* folder is where we define our own resource types to be used in our recipes to implement our own custom functionality, backed by supporting lightweight or heavyweight providers. We'll learn about creating our own resources in Chapters 8 and 9.

In each of these chapters, along with how to actually create these customizations, we'll examine the typical use cases for each and how to decide which customization type might be best for a particular use case. Before we dive into customizing our recipe code, however, we need to create a test environment so that we can safely try our customizations out.

Creating a Test Environment

To enable us to test our cookbook customizations, we're going to reuse the test environment we created for Part II of the book in "Preparing a Test Environment" on page 114. If you haven't already created this test environment and would like to run the examples in this part of the book, please follow the steps in that section before moving on.

Next, we're going to make a copy of the test environment from Part II so that we can test our cookbook changes in isolation from our earlier customization examples. Run the following command to make a new copy of the test environment:

```
$> cp -R /tmp/part2_examples /tmp/part3_examples
```

Next, we need to check our newly copied test environment and update all directory paths to ensure that they refer to /tmp/part3_examples instead of /tmp/part2_examples. This can either be done manually by checking the files yourself, or automatically by running the following command:

```
$> find /tmp/part3_examples -type f -
   print0 | \
   xargs -0 sed -i \'s/part2_examples/part3_examples/g'
```

Now let's double-check that our newly copied test environment still works correctly. Run the following command from /tmp/part3_examples:

```
$> chef-client --once --why-run --local-mode \
   --config /tmp/part3_examples/client.rb \
   --override-runlist testcookbook::default

Starting Chef Client, version 11.10.4
[Sat, 22 Feb 2014 13:48:32 +0000] WARN: Run List override has been provided.
[Sat, 22 Feb 2014 13:48:32 +0000] WARN: Original Run List: []
[Sat, 22 Feb 2014 13:48:32 +0000] WARN: Overridden Run List:
   [recipe[testcookbook::default]]
resolving cookbooks for run list: ["testcookbook::default"]
Synchronizing Cookbooks:
  - testcookbook
Compiling Cookbooks...
Converging 2 resources
Recipe: testcookbook::default
   * directory[/tmp/part3_examples] action create (up to date)
   * file[/tmp/part3_examples/testfile] action create
     - Would create new file /tmp/part3_examples/testfile

[Sat, 22 Feb 2014 13:48:32 +0000] WARN: Skipping final node save
   because override_runlist was given
```

```
Running handlers:
Running handlers complete
```

If everything's working correctly, you should see the output shown here, which lets us know that our Chef run successfully executed the `testcookbook::default` cookbook in why-run mode.

As with the test environments we used in previous chapters, we're using why-run mode here to ensure that we don't actually execute any experimental code on our node, and local mode to ensure that we can safely run experimental code against a mock Chef server without touching the production Chef setup.

Now that we've refreshed our knowledge of the cookbook structure and prepared a test environment, we're ready to start learning about the first recipe customization type we're going to cover in this chapter, *definitions*.

Definitions

In "Cookbook Structure Revisited" on page 166, we looked at an overview of how Chef cookbooks are structured and where the various cookbook customization types live. Now it's time to dive into how to actually create them. In this part of the chapter, we're going to learn about the simplest type of recipe customization, definitions. We'll examine:

- What definitions are
- The code structure shared by all definitions
- The strengths and weaknesses of definitions, and when you may or may not want to use them

We'll also look at a number of examples demonstrating the functionality and features of definitions.

What Is a Definition?

Before we learn how to create our own definitions, let's pause for a moment to examine in a little more detail exactly what a definition is and how it differs from the default resource blocks we're already familiar with, such as `package` and `cookbook_file`.

In Chef, a recipe resource such as `package` comprises two components: a resource definition, which describes the characteristics of that resource, and one or more providers to provide its underlying functionality. These resources and providers can be implemented using a lightweight DSL, or as fully fledged Ruby code. These are the *lightweight* and *heavyweight* resources and providers we will be learning about in later chapters.

A *definition*, on the other hand, is a wrapper around an existing resource or group of resources that allows us to treat those resources as a single whole. Imagine taking a chunk of recipe code that you find yourself repeating throughout your cookbooks and assigning that code chunk a name that you can use to represent that code each time you want to use it. This is exactly the functionality provided by definitions.

In programing parlance, this is what we might think of as a recipe *macro*. Rather than defining an entirely new set of behaviors with a new resource type, we're simply creating a wrapper around already existing resources to group them together into a single macro for convenience and reuse.

Definitions in Chef are marked by several characteristics:

- Definitions are always stored in the cookbook's */definitions* folder.
- A definition will create a "wrapper" that groups one or more other resources together.
- A definition can not receive notifications, but the resources it contains can notify other resources.

Let's take a look at these characteristics in a little more detail:

Definitions are always stored in the cookbook's /definitions folder
As we saw in "Load Cookbook Data" on page 68, definitions are the last part of a cookbook to be loaded into memory, other than recipes themselves. They live in the cookbook's */definitions* folder, and unlike fully fledged resources and classes, they are treated as single blocks of code when executed by Chef, rather than as Ruby classes. Definitions are loaded at the end of stage 6 of the run process (described in "Load Cookbook Data" on page 68), because they might wrap other resources created during the earlier steps of this stage.

A definition will create a wrapper that groups one or more other resources together.
Definitions in Chef are designed to fulfill a very specific purpose, which is to allow us to create a wrapper around a resource or resources to allow us to treat them as a single reusable block of code. Definitions should only contain code that would work equally well if it lived in the actual recipe.

During the Chef run, a definition will be shown in the output of the run in fully expanded form—that is, its component resources will be shown in the output of the run, but the name of the definition itself will not. We'll see an example of this in "Definition Example 3: Using Resources" on page 176.

A definition cannot receive notifications, but the resources it contains can notify other resources.
Because definitions are intended to be used as recipe macros rather than as fully fledged new resources, they incur one very specific limitation—they cannot be no-

tified or subscribed to by other resources. If we consider a notification example like this:

```
notifies :restart, resources(:service => "httpd")
```

what is actually happening here is that the `service` resource called `httpd` is being notified that it should carry out its `restart` action. Because definitions simply serve as wrappers around other resources, they don't actually define any actions, and hence cannot themselves be notified.

These characteristics serve to give a particularly clear indication as to when creating a definition might or might not be appropriate. If you find yourself using a definition to define behavior that cannot be easily constructed using existing resources or that you might later want other resources to notify, you should probably be looking at implementing lightweight or heavyweight resources and providers (LWRPs and HWRPs), which will be covered in subsequent chapters.

If you're looking to construct a reusable wrapper around a frequently used collection of resources and recipe code, however, definitions may be a good option. We'll look at some more detailed case studies to demonstrate this sort of decision-making process with the aid of our friends at AwesomeInc at the end of this part of the book, after we've learned about each customization type.

Definition Example 1: Skeleton

Now that we've examined the characteristics of a definition in Chef, let's dive into the code. Throughout this chapter, we'll use a series of examples to construct a definition that will solve a fictional problem. Our friends at AwesomeInc have created a bespoke stock management tool called "awesomeator" and are creating a cookbook to install and configure the various permutations of the tool that their global locations require.

Before installing the tool, it is necessary to create a configuration file and directory structure for the tool to store its data in. Rather than having the tool use a default directory, the folks at AwesomeInc have decided to make this configurable at install time, as it may vary from site to site. They want to create a definition to allow them to treat these preparatory steps as a single resource.

Throughout this chapter, we're going to incrementally build up a definition to solve AwesomeInc's problem, which we'll call `awesomeator_prepare`.

 Before continuing with this example, you should ensure that you followed the steps in "Creating a Test Environment" on page 167 to create a test environment in which to run our example code.

We'll start by looking at the minimum code needed to create our `awesomeator_pre`
`pare` definition. As we saw earlier in the chapter, all definitions need to live under the /
definitions folder of a cookbook. The name of the definition file itself doesn't matter,
but it's good practice to name the file the same as the definition it contains, so we're
going to paste the code for our `awesomeator_prepare` definition, shown in
Example 7-1, into */tmp/part3_examples/cookbooks/testcookbook/definitions/aweso-
meator_prepare.rb*.

*Example 7-1. /tmp/part3_examples/cookbooks/testcookbook/definitions/awesomea-
tor_prepare.rb*

```
define :awesomeator_prepare do
end
```

As you can see in this code listing, the code needed to create a definition is actually
extremely minimal—we simply create a `define` block, with the name of our definition
as its symbol. We haven't actually made our definition do anything yet, but let's try using
it in a recipe now to prove that this code does in fact work.

We'll create a new recipe for running the examples in this chapter under our `testcook`
book, cookbook called *awesomeator.rb*. Paste the line of code in Example 7-2 into */tmp/
part3_examples/cookbooks/testcookbook/recipes/awesomeator.rb*

Example 7-2. /tmp/part3_examples/cookbooks/testcookbook/recipes/awesomeator.rb

```
awesomeator_prepare "foo"
```

Here, we've simply added a single `awesomeator_prepare` resource to our recipe, with
the name `foo`.

 Don't worry too much about the fact that we've given our `awesomea`
`tor_prepare` resource the meaningless name `foo`—we'll look at resource naming and attributes in greater detail in the next section.

Now let's try performing a Chef run with our `testcookbook::awesomeator` recipe and
see what happens:

```
$> chef-client --once --why-run --local-mode \
  --config /tmp/part3_examples/client.rb \
  --override-runlist testcookbook::awesomeator
Starting Chef Client, version 11.10.4
[Thu, 24 Apr 2014 10:04:11 +0000] WARN: Run List override has been provided.
[Thu, 24 Apr 2014 10:04:11 +0000] WARN: Original Run List: []
[Thu, 24 Apr 2014 10:04:11 +0000] WARN: Overridden Run List:
  [recipe[testcookbook::awesomeator]]
resolving cookbooks for run list: ["testcookbook::awesomeator"]
```

```
Synchronizing Cookbooks:
  - testcookbook
Compiling Cookbooks...
Converging 0 resources
[Thu, 24 Apr 2014 10:04:11 +0000] WARN: Skipping final node save because
  override_runlist was given

Running handlers:
Running handlers complete

Chef Client finished, 0/0 resources would have been updated
```

As we can see, our Chef run completed successfully. No resources were updated because our definition does not itself contain any resources yet, but the run also didn't throw any errors. We've just created and executed our first custom definition! Next, let's look at how we actually make our definition do something a little more useful.

Because we want our `awesomeator_prepare` definition to configure a directory structure and configuration file for the `awesome` tool, it would be useful to be able to instruct our definition about where we want these files and directories to live. We do that by adding parameters.

Adding Parameters

As with the default resources provided with Chef, definitions wouldn't be especially useful if we couldn't pass them necessary configuration information as parameters—the whole point of a reusable pattern, after all, is that we're able to use it more than once! In this section, we'll look at how to make use of parameters in our definitions to provide them with the information they need in order to execute the resources they contain.

Definitions in Chef support parameters through the use of a built-in `Hash` called `params`. Although we didn't do so explicitly, we've actually already used this hash. Cast your mind back to "Definition Example 1: Skeleton" on page 170—when we used the `awesomeator_prepare` resource in our recipe, we gave it the name `production`:

```
awesomeator_prepare "production"
```

The name we give to a definition when we use it in recipes is automatically made available to the code for that definition as `params[:name]`. Assigning a name to our definition is optional, however, and can be omitted. We can also easily add any other parameters we wish to the definition when we use it in recipe code:

```
awesomeator_prepare "production" do
  working_dir "/tmp/awesomeator"
  config_file "/etc/awesomeator.conf"
end
```

These parameters will automatically be available to the code of our definition as `params[:working_dir]` and `params[:config_file]`. We don't need to explicitly define the parameters we wish to use in our definitions, because Chef automatically adds any parameters it finds to the params hash when our definitions are executed.

Chef also allows us to specify default values for specific parameters when we define our definitions, which will be used if no value is given to that parameter in the recipe. Let's look at another example to allow our awesomeator_prepare definition to make use of these working_dir and config_file parameters.

Definition Example 2: Using Parameters

As we've seen, definitions wouldn't be of much use when creating reusable and modular recipe macros if we weren't able to configure them with parameters. Let's extend the definition we created in "Definition Example 1: Skeleton" on page 170 to allow it to make use of two parameters: working_dir and config_file.

We'll also set default values for both parameters to make sure that our definition can behave sensibly if no values are given for those parameters. Paste the code in Example 7-3 into */tmp/part3_examples/cookbooks/testcookbook/definitions/awesomeator_prepare.rb*.

Example 7-3. /tmp/part3_examples/cookbooks/testcookbook/definitions/awesomeator_prepare.rb

```
define :awesomeator_prepare,
       :working_dir => '/tmp/awesomeator',
       :config_file => '/etc/awesomeator.conf' do ❶
 puts "working_dir = #{params[:working_dir]}" ❷
 puts "config_file = #{params[:config_file]}"
end
```

❶ In addition to naming our definition :awesomeator_prepare, here we're setting default values for the :working_dir and :config_file parameters. We can still set values for these parameters in our recipes, but if we don't, the defaults will be used. Note that if we're not setting a default value for a parameter, we can omit the parameter from our define line; Chef will automatically add it to the params hash.

❷ Here we're simply using puts to write the value of params[:working_dir] to the screen. We do the same on the following line with params[:config_file].

Now that we've added some parameters with default values and output statements to our definition, let's try performing our Chef run again. Note here that we're not changing anything in the testcookbook::awesomeator recipe—only the definition code itself has been altered:

```
$> chef-client --once --why-run --local-mode \
  --config /tmp/part3_examples/client.rb \
```

```
--override-runlist testcookbook::awesomeator
Starting Chef Client, version 11.10.4
[Thu, 24 Apr 2014 12:41:18 +0000] WARN: Run List override has been provided.
[Thu, 24 Apr 2014 12:41:18 +0000] WARN: Original Run List: []
[Thu, 24 Apr 2014 12:41:18 +0000] WARN: Overridden Run List:
  [recipe[testcookbook::awesomeator]]
resolving cookbooks for run list: ["testcookbook::awesomeator"]
Synchronizing Cookbooks:
  - testcookbook
Compiling Cookbooks...
working_dir = /tmp/awesomeator
config_file = /etc/awesomeator.conf
Converging 0 resources
[Thu, 24 Apr 2014 12:41:18 +0000] WARN: Skipping final node save because
  override_runlist was given

Running handlers:
Running handlers complete

Chef Client finished, 0/0 resources would have been updated
```

In this output, immediately after the "Compiling Cookbooks" log line, we see that the
two puts statements we added to our definition have been executed, printing the default
values for the working_dir and config_file parameters that we specified in our definition code.

Let's now set a different value for the working_dir parameter when we call the aweso
meator_prepare resource in our awesomeator recipe to see how the output changes.
Paste the code in Example 7-4 into */tmp/part3_examples/cookbooks/testcookbook/
recipes/awesomeator.rb*

Example 7-4. /tmp/part3_examples/cookbooks/testcookbook/recipes/awesomeator.rb

```
awesomeator_prepare "production" do
  working_dir "/tmp/awesomeator/working_dir"
end
```

We're still using the awesomeator_prepare resource in the same way as we would any
other built-in resource, but this time we're adding a value for the working_dir parameter. Let's perform the same Chef run again and see how the output changes this time:

```
$> chef-client --once --why-run --local-mode \
  --config /tmp/part3_examples/client.rb \
  --override-runlist testcookbook::awesomeator
Starting Chef Client, version 11.10.4
[Thu, 24 Apr 2014 12:50:30 +0000] WARN: Run List override has been provided.
[Thu, 24 Apr 2014 12:50:30 +0000] WARN: Original Run List: []
[Thu, 24 Apr 2014 12:50:30 +0000] WARN: Overridden Run List:
  [recipe[testcookbook::awesomeator]]
resolving cookbooks for run list: ["testcookbook::awesomeator"]
Synchronizing Cookbooks:
```

```
      - testcookbook
    Compiling Cookbooks...
    working_dir = /tmp/awesomeator/working_dir
    config_file = /etc/awesomeator.conf
    Converging 0 resources
    [Thu, 24 Apr 2014 12:50:30 +0000] WARN: Skipping final node save because
      override_runlist was given

    Running handlers:
    Running handlers complete

    Chef Client finished, 0/0 resources would have been updated
```

This time we see that the value of working_dir has been taken from the parameter we passed in our recipe (*/tmp/awesomeator/working_dir*), but the value of config_file is still the default set in the definition code (*/etc/awesomeator.conf*) as we didn't pass in an explicit value for this parameter in the recipe code.

Our definition is starting to resemble a solution to AwesomeInc's problem now. We've learned how to define a definition and use it in our cookbooks, and how to pass it parameters and make use of default values, but we haven't actually added any resources to our definition yet. We'll see how to do that next, to build up the recipe macro concept that we discussed earlier in this chapter.

Adding Resources

So far in this chapter we've looked at the skeleton code needed to create a definition and how to supply configuration parameters to it. But for our definition to be of much practical use, we need to actually add some resources to it. Because definitions are essentially recipe macros, as we discussed earlier in the chapter, the code we add to our definitions will be nearly identical to the code we would use to carry out the same tasks in our recipes.

If, for example, we wanted to add a directory resource to our awesomeator_prepare definition, we could do so like this:

```
define :awesomeator_prepare,
       :working_dir => '/tmp/awesomeator',
       :config_file => '/etc/awesomeator.conf' do

  directory params[:working_dir] do ❶
    action :create
    recursive true
  end
end
```

❶ Here we're using the value of params[:working_dir] as the name of the directory to be created by our directory resource.

It's also possible to use arbitrary Ruby code and resources inside the body of a definition, just as we would in a recipe; however, definitions are intended to be wrappers around simple and reusable chunks of recipe code. If you find yourself adding significant amounts of native Ruby code to a definition or too many complex cookbook resources, this may be an indication that you should consider creating an LWRP or HWRP instead (we'll learn about these in Chapters 9 and 10).

It's worth noting again at this point that definitions cannot be notified by other resources —if you find yourself wanting to do so, this is a clear indication that a definition is not the best solution (see Chapter 8 for how to create your own notifiable resources). Although the `awesomeator_prepare` definition we created here cannot itself be notified, however, resources defined inside it can of course notify *other* resources, just as they would in recipes. Let's say that we wanted the `directory` resource we just added to send a `restart` notification to a fictional `awesomeator` service. We could do something like this:

```
define :awesomeator_prepare,
        :working_dir => '/tmp/awesomeator',
        :config_file => '/etc/awesomeator.conf' do

  directory params[:working_dir] do
    action :create
    recursive true
    notifies :restart, resources(:service => "awesomeator")
  end
end
```

Now that we've learned how to add resources to our definitions and the restrictions imposed by the recipe macro model, it's time to look at a final example to extend our definition with the resources needed to carry out the preparatory steps for the installation of AwesomeInc's tool.

Definition Example 3: Using Resources

Before we can add resources to our definition, we need to define what exactly we want our definition to do. AwesomeInc has identified the following steps that should be completed to prepare the tool's working environment:

1. The working directory needs to be created.
2. The specified configuration file should be created, and populated with the chosen working directory.

As both of these steps can be performed with the default resources supplied with Chef, let's paste the code shown in Example 7-5 into */tmp/part3_examples/cookbooks/test-cookbook/definitions/awesomeator_prepare.rb*:

Example 7-5. /tmp/part3_examples/cookbooks/testcookbook/definitions/awesomeator_prepare.rb

```
define :awesomeator_prepare,
       :working_dir => '/tmp/awesomeator',
       :config_file => '/etc/awesomeator.conf' do

  directory params[:working_dir] do
    action :create
    recursive true
  end

  template params[:config_file] do
    source 'awesomeator.conf.erb'
    variables({
      :working_dir => params[:working_dir]
    })
  end
end
```

As we see here, we're using a `directory` resource to create the working directory specified by the `params[:working_dir]` parameter, then using a template that takes the `params[:working_dir]` as a variable to write a configuration file to `params[:config_file]`, which contains the working directory.

Before we can actually try out this new definition, we need to add the *awesomeator.conf.erb* template that our `template` resource will be using to our cookbook. Paste the line of code in Example 7-6 into */tmp/part3_examples/cookbooks/testcookbook/templates/default/awesomeator.conf.erb*.

Example 7-6. /tmp/part3_examples/cookbooks/testcookbook/templates/default/awesomeator.conf.erb

```
working_directory = <%= @working_dir %>
```

The code we're using for our template here is very simple. We're simply taking the template variable `@working_dir`, which is passed into our template resource when we call it in a recipe, and printing the value into the desired place in our configuration file.

Now that we've added some resources to our definition code and created the supporting template file that we need, let's try running our expanded definition and see what happens:

```
$> chef-client --once --why-run --local-mode \
   --config /tmp/part3_examples/client.rb \
   --override-runlist testcookbook::awesomeator
```

```
Starting Chef Client, version 11.10.4
[Thu, 24 Apr 2014 14:58:30 +0000] WARN: Run List override has been provided.
[Thu, 24 Apr 2014 14:58:30 +0000] WARN: Original Run List: []
[Thu, 24 Apr 2014 14:58:30 +0000] WARN: Overridden Run List:
  [recipe[testcookbook::awesomeator]]
resolving cookbooks for run list: ["testcookbook::awesomeator"]
Synchronizing Cookbooks:
  - testcookbook
Compiling Cookbooks...
Converging 2 resources
Recipe: testcookbook::awesomeator
  * directory[/tmp/awesomeator/working_dir] action create
    - Would create new directory /tmp/awesomeator/working_dir

  * template[/etc/awesomeator.conf] action create
    - Would create new file /etc/awesomeator.conf

[Thu, 24 Apr 2014 14:58:30 +0000] WARN: Skipping final node save because
  override_runlist was given

Running handlers:
Running handlers complete

Chef Client finished, 2/2 resources would have been updated
```

As we saw in "What Is a Definition?" on page 168, in the output when our definition is executed it is expanded into its constituent resources—this means that we see our `directory` and `template` resources show up directly in the run output, rather than the `awesomeator_prepare` definition that we defined to wrap them. It's worth bearing in mind that as the definition name itself does not show up in the default run output, if you have to debug any run issues you might find the resource in question located in definition files in addition to recipes.

 As we saw in "SetUp RunContext" on page 66, the RunContext object stores a list of all recipe *definitions* separately from the list of resources in the resource collection. This is because, rather than defining new resource types, definitions will contain one or more already existing resource types.

In this part of the chapter, we've seen that definitions provide us with a quick and easy way to create reusable, parameterized macros in our recipes that can contain frequently used resource combinations. We've also explored when definitions can be useful, and some of their limitations—namely, that they are not able to be notified by other resources and cannot define multiple actions. Next, we're going to learn about libraries and how they can help us level up our cookbooks with additional functionality, along with how they help to power the resources and providers we'll create in later chapters.

Libraries

So far in this chapter, we've looked at where the various customization components of our cookbooks fit into Chef's overall cookbook structure, and explored definitions. In this part of the chapter, we're going to learn about a type of customization that is both very simple to explain and massively powerful: the *library*. We'll examine:

- What exactly a library is
- The typical use cases of libraries in Chef

We'll also look at a number of examples demonstrating the functionality and features of libraries.

What Is a Library?

So what exactly is a library in Chef? Put perfectly simply, a library allows us to include arbitrary Ruby code in our cookbooks to do anything from defining useful helper methods, to implementing database functionality to be used in our resources, to extending the core classes of Chef itself. Libraries in Chef have two defining characteristics:

- They always live in the cookbook's */libraries* folder.
- They are the first part of the cookbook to be loaded.

As we saw in "Cookbook Structure Revisited" on page 166, our cookbook libraries always live in the */libraries* folder. This structure enables Chef to easily distinguish Ruby files that are intended to be libraries from Ruby files that are intended to be recipes, definitions, or any other recipe component—remember, everything in Chef is Ruby!

In "Load Cookbook Data" on page 68, we saw that libraries are the very first part of our cookbooks to be loaded into memory when Chef loads our cookbook data. Let's take a peek at the exact method in Chef that loads library files to see exactly how this is done. The method that is responsible for loading libraries is called `load_libra ries_from_cookbook` and lives in the `Chef::RunContext::CookbookCompiler` class, which lives at *lib/chef/run_context/cookbook_compiler.rb* (*http://bit.ly/ckbk-compile*). Its code can be seen in Example 7-7.

Example 7-7. Excerpt of lib/chef/run_context/cookbook_compiler.rb

```
class Chef
  class RunContext
    class CookbookCompiler

      ...

      def load_libraries_from_cookbook(cookbook_name)
        files_in_cookbook_by_segment(cookbook_name, :libraries).each do |filename|
```

```
        begin
          Chef::Log.debug("Loading cookbook
          #{cookbook_name}'s + library
          file: #{filename}")
          Kernel.load(filename) ❶
          @events.library_file_loaded(filename)
        rescue Exception => e
          @events.library_file_load_failed(filename, e)
          raise
        end
      end
    end

    ...

    end
  end
end
```

❶ Amidst the various utility method calls inside the load_libraries_from_cook
    book method, we're calling Ruby's built-in Kernel.load method to load each
    library file into memory.

 For a fun code spelunking exercise, why not continue to trace Chef's
execution from the do_run method of the Chef::Client class that we
looked at in "The Chef::Client Class do_run Method" on page 86, and
see if you can find the code path that leads to this method?

As we can see in this code listing, Chef uses Ruby's built-in Kernel.load method to load
each library file it has located into memory. More accurately, the Kernel.load method
actually *loads and executes* the Ruby code contained in the file passed to it, which means
that any modules or classes contained in that file are available to Chef. The end result
is similar to the functionality of the require method that we learned about in "Using
Other Classes and Modules" on page 41. We've now made Chef aware of any modules,
classes, or methods defined in our library file, and they can now be used in recipes and
other cookbook components.

We've learned how Chef loads libraries and makes them available to our other cookbook
components, but what are they actually used for in the real world? Libraries in Chef
have several typical use cases:

Creating mixins or classes to use in recipe code
    Probably the most popular use of libraries in Chef is to create modules containing
    methods to use in our recipe code, which are then included as mixins, just as we
    saw in "Modules as Mixins" on page 39. We'll learn how to do this in "Library
    Example 1: Modules and Mixins" on page 181 and "Library Example 2: Methods in a

Custom Namespace" on page 184. Libraries can also be used to define or extend Ruby classes that will be accessible by Chef, as in the following two use cases.

Extending Chef classes

A more advanced use of libraries in Chef is to extend Chef's core classes or override their methods. For example, if you want to add an extra method to the `Chef::Node` class that can be used on the node object in your recipe code, you can define this in a library. We'll look at an example of extending Chef's core classes in "Library Example 3: Extending Core Chef Classes" on page 186.

Implementing heavyweight resources and providers

One of the most common uses for libraries in Chef is to facilitate the implementation of heavyweight resources and providers. We won't cover this use case any further in this chapter, as it is weighty enough to have a chapter all to itself later in the book (Chapter 9).

Now that we've examined some of the theory behind libraries and how they are typically used, let's put this theory into practice and look at some practical examples.

Library Example 1: Modules and Mixins

The first type of library we're going to learn to create is one that defines functions inside a module, and is then included in our recipes as a *mixin*. As we saw in "Modules as Mixins" on page 39, *mixing* a module into our Ruby classes is done by including the module namespace in our code using the `include` keyword, which then makes any functions defined inside that module available as if they had been declared locally. When we need to include mixins in our Chef cookbook code, however, there are a couple of additional details we have to consider, which we'll learn about here.

Let's not get too far ahead of ourselves yet, though. We'll start off by creating a library that defines a module containing a function we'd like to use in our recipe code. Paste the code in Example 7-8 into */tmp/part3_examples/cookbooks/testcookbook/libraries/ useful_functions.rb*.

Example 7-8. /tmp/part3_examples/cookbooks/testcookbook/libraries/useful_meth-ods.rb

```
module UsefulMethods ❶
  def stop_file_exists? ❷
    ::File.exists?("/tmp/stop_chef")
  end
end
```

❶ Here, we declare the namespace of our module as `UsefulMethods`.

❷ Inside our module, we define a simple function that returns `true` or `false` depending on whether or not the specified file exists.

Now that we've created our library, we also need to create a recipe that will include that library. Paste the code in Example 7-9 into */tmp/part3_examples/cookbooks/testcookbook/recipes/library_test.rb*.

Example 7-9. /tmp/part3_examples/cookbooks/testcookbook/recipes/library_test.rb

```
::Chef::Recipe.send(:include, UsefulMethods) ❶

if stop_file_exists? ❷
  Chef::Log.fatal("Stop file exists!")
  exit 1
else
  Chef::Log.warn("No stop file. Carrying on as normal.")
end
```

❶   Here, we include our `UsefulMethods` mixin in our recipe code (see the sidebar "Using Mixins Inside Chef Recipes" for an explanation of why we didn't just use the `include` keyword).

❷   Here, we use the `stop_file_exists?` function we defined inside our library.

Using Mixins Inside Chef Recipes

In Example 7-10, you may have noticed that we used a slightly odd syntax for including our module—instead of simply using `include UsefulMethods`, as we did in "Modules as Mixins" on page 39, this time we used the syntax `::Chef::Recipe.send(:include, UsefulMethods)`. But why was this necessary?

The reason is due to the fact that Chef actually has two phases of execution when it comes to our recipes:

The compile phase
> The compile phase happens when Chef loads the recipe files contained in our cookbooks during the "Load Cookbook Data" stage of the run (see "Load Cookbook Data" on page 68). At this point in the Chef run, any native Ruby code in our recipes is executed, and any resource blocks that are defined in our recipe code are added to the resource collection.

The execution phase
> The execution phase happens during the next stage of the run (see "Converge Node" on page 69). This is when Chef steps through the resource collection and executes our recipe resources on the node—under the hood, this means that Chef finds a provider that implements each resource, and executes it.

This behavior means that if we use the `include UsefulMethods` syntax we've used before in our recipe code, during the execution phase Chef would try to locate a provider for this `include` resource that we seem to have used in our recipe—which of course would not exist, causing an error. What we actually want is to use our function during the

---

compile phase of the Chef run, because we want it to be treated as native Ruby code instead of a Chef resource block.

The syntax we used in our recipe here, `::Chef::Recipe.send(:include, UsefulMe thods)`, uses the `send` method that all Ruby objects inherit from the Ruby `Object` class to make a method call to `include` *inside* the `Chef::Recipe` class. This is the class under which Chef evaluates our recipes—basically, the class in which Chef will look for the `stop_file_exists?` method if we use it in a recipe.

Essentially, we're using a Ruby trick to force Chef to include our `UsefulMethods` module in the `Chef::Recipe` class during its compile phase, instead of during the execution phase. This trick is useful to remember, as it's widely used when mixing library modules into recipes in Chef.

Now let's try kicking off a Chef run of our `testcookbook::library_test` cookbook and see how it behaves:

```
$> chef-client --once --why-run --local-mode \
  --config /tmp/part3_examples/client.rb \
  --override-runlist testcookbook::library_test
Starting Chef Client, version 11.10.4
[Tue, 20 May 2014 12:29:41 +0000] WARN: Run List override has been provided.
[Tue, 20 May 2014 12:29:41 +0000] WARN: Original Run List: []
[Tue, 20 May 2014 12:29:41 +0000] WARN: Overridden Run List:
  [recipe[testcookbook::library_test]]
resolving cookbooks for run list: ["testcookbook::library_test"]
Synchronizing Cookbooks:
  - testcookbook
Compiling Cookbooks...
[Tue, 20 May 2014 12:29:41 +0000] WARN: No stop file. Carrying on as normal.
Converging 0 resources
[Tue, 20 May 2014 12:29:41 +0000] WARN: Skipping final node save
  because override_runlist was given

Running handlers:
Running handlers complete

Chef Client finished, 0/0 resources would have been updated
```

As we can see in this output, during the compile stage of our run, Chef executes our `stop_file_exists?` method and prints the appropriate log message. We've just created our first library!

What we've done in this example is mix methods into the `Chef::Resource` namespace. This means that any methods we define in our module will be available inside our Chef recipes after the module has been included. But what if we want to organize our method namespace a little more? We don't want mixed-in method names clashing, so next we're going to look at how to use more complex namespaces in our library modules.

Library Example 2: Methods in a Custom Namespace

In the previous section, we looked at an example of mixing methods from a module into our recipe code through the use of a library, which we then included in our recipe code. This method works perfectly well for simple use cases, but using mixins has the side effect of making methods available to our class as if they'd been defined in that class, and it's sometimes not very clear what specific set of functionality a particular method relates to.

If we were implementing mixins to allow our recipe code to interface with different database systems, for example, we would want to be able to distinguish between a connect method that talked to MySQL and a connect method that talked to MSSQL.

In this example, we're going to look at how we can use Ruby's object-oriented nature to define new namespaces under Chef's existing classes to help us give more structure and clarity to our library methods. We're going to use the same stop_file_exists? method that we created in "Library Example 1: Modules and Mixins" on page 181, but this time we want it to live under a more informative namespace. To get started, paste the code in Example 7-10 into a new library file, */tmp/part3_examples/cookbooks/testcookbook/libraries/stop_file.rb*.

Example 7-10. /tmp/part3_examples/cookbooks/testcookbook/libraries/stop_file.rb

```
class Chef::Recipe::StopFile ❶
  def self.stop_file_exists? ❷
      ::File.exists?("/tmp/stop_chef")
  end
end
```

❶ This time, instead of defining our own module name, we're creating a new namespace under the Chef::Recipe class called Chef::Recipe:StopFile. Essentially, we're extending a built-in Chef class with a new namespace to hold our method. It's important to note here that the namespace we add our class under must already exist, or Ruby will raise an exception.

❷ We're using Ruby's self keyword here to specify that our method is a class method, not a class *instance* method. This allows us to call the method by using Chef::Recipe::StopFile.stop_file_exists? instead of first having to create an instance of the Chef::Recipe::StopFile class.

Now let's modify our recipe code to use our newly namespaced method. Paste the code in Example 7-11 into */tmp/part3_examples/cookbooks/testcookbook/recipes/library_test.rb*.

Example 7-11. /tmp/part3_examples/cookbooks/testcookbook/recipes/library_test.rb

```
if StopFile.stop_file_exists?
  Chef::Log.fatal("Stop file exists!")
```

```
  exit 1
else
  Chef::Log.warn("No stop file. Carrying on as normal.")
end
```

Note that unlike in Example 7-10 in the previous section, we haven't specifically mixed in our module using `include` this time. The reason for this is that when our library file is evaluated during the Chef run's compile phase, the fact that it lives under the `Chef::Recipe` namespace means that it automatically becomes available to anything else in that namespace. This includes our Chef recipes, which, as we saw earlier, are evaluated in the `Chef::Recipe` context.

What this means in practical terms is that we don't have to manually include libraries that define namespaces under `Chef::Recipe`, and that when we call our method we only need to specify the part of its namespace that comes after `Chef::Recipe`—in this case, `StopFile.stop_file_exists?`.

Now that we've created our new namespaced library and modified our recipe code accordingly, let's kick off another Chef run on our `testcookbook::library_test` recipe and make sure that everything still works as it should:

```
$> chef-client --once --why-run --local-mode \
  --config /tmp/part3_examples/client.rb \
  --override-runlist testcookbook::library_test
Starting Chef Client, version 11.10.4
[Tue, 20 May 2014 13:41:22 +0000] WARN: Run List override has been provided.
[Tue, 20 May 2014 13:41:22 +0000] WARN: Original Run List: []
[Tue, 20 May 2014 13:41:22 +0000] WARN: Overridden Run List:
  [recipe[testcookbook::library_test]]
resolving cookbooks for run list: ["testcookbook::library_test"]
Synchronizing Cookbooks:
  - testcookbook
Compiling Cookbooks...
[Tue, 20 May 2014 13:41:22 +0000] WARN: No stop file. Carrying on as normal.
Converging 0 resources
[Tue, 20 May 2014 13:41:22 +0000] WARN: Skipping final node save
  because override_runlist was given

Running handlers:
Running handlers complete

Chef Client finished, 0/0 resources would have been updated
```

As we see in the above output, our Chef run behaved exactly the same as it did when we manually mixed in our module in our first example, with the added benefit that we've now sensibly namespaced our modules.

As you come to develop more advanced libraries, the need for this degree of namespace separation will become just as clear as the need for multiple objects in more complex Ruby code. Imagine if the Chef classes we've examined thus far in the book had all been implemented under one class! It would be much harder to make sense of what's going on, and the same principle applies to libraries and their namespaces.

In our final example of the chapter, we're going to learn how to create libraries that extend Chef's core object classes to add additional functionality that we can use in our recipe code.

Library Example 3: Extending Core Chef Classes

One of the most powerful use cases for libraries in Chef is to modify Chef's core object classes so that we can add or change the functionality of these classes on the fly. Let's take a look at another problem that our friends at AwesomeInc have been working on.

The team at AwesomeInc are creating a cookbook that is going to generate the configuration file for an application they are deploying. This configuration file requires several network interfaces to be specified, which are available for the application to use. AwesomeInc's plan is to have Chef detect the status of all the network interfaces on the node running this recipe, and produce a list of any currently enabled interfaces that can then be added to the configuration file.

To start with, the team considers parsing the Ohai attributes for the node, which of course contain all of the relevant network interface data. But this ends up producing rather messy cookbook code, as the *state* attribute of each interface is nested inside the Ohai `interfaces` attribute hash. They consider creating an Ohai plugin to store this information on the node in a friendlier format, but dismiss this idea as it essentially means storing duplicate information on the node, but in a different format.

In this example, we're going to learn how AwesomeInc can create a library that extends the node object with an `interface_statuses` method, which will extract the name and status of each interface from the Ohai data and return it for use in recipe code.

We're going to extend an existing Chef class, but before we can do so we need to actually identify the class in question. As we learned in Chapter 3, the node object that is accessible to us in our recipe code is actually an instance of the `Chef::Node` class, which lives at *lib/chef/node.rb* (*http://bit.ly/gh-noderb*).

Now that we've identified the class to extend, we're ready to create a library that adds our new `interface_statuses` method. Paste the code in Example 7-12 into */tmp/part3_examples/cookbooks/testcookbook/libraries/node_interface_methods.rb*:

Example 7-12. /tmp/part3_examples/cookbooks/testcookbook/libraries/node_interface_methods.rb

```
class Chef
  class Node
    def interface_statuses(&block)
      node[:network][:interfaces].each do |name, info|
```

```
            block.call(name, info["state"])
          end
        end
      end
    end
```

Note that we're defining the Chef::Node class directly here, not inheriting from it or mixing in methods with a module. Ruby allows us to essentially *reopen* an already existing class definition to add new methods, and this is exactly what we're doing here: we're not overwriting the existing definition of Chef::Node provided by Chef, but rather opening it up and adding a new method.

Next, we define our interface_statuses method. Note that we're passing it a slightly odd-looking parameter, &block. & is a special construct in Ruby that, when used in front of a parameter in a method definition, allows us to capture a block of code—that is, the code between do and end--as a single parameter.

Our method then iterates over the node[:network][:interfaces] Ohai attribute hash and calls the same block that we passed into the method, giving it the name and in fo["state"] elements of the relevant interfaces that Ohai attributes as its parameters.

This code might seem a little hard to understand at this stage, so let's examine how we can use our new method in a recipe. Paste the code in Example 7-13 into */tmp/ part3_examples/cookbooks/testcookbook/recipes/node_library_test.rb*.

Example 7-13. /tmp/part3_examples/cookbooks/testcookbook/recipes/ node_library_test.rb

```
node.interface_statuses do |if_name, status|
  Chef::Log.warn("The status of interface #{if_name} is #{status}")
end
```

This recipe code is extremely simple, but its interaction with our interface_sta tuses method bears a little more explanation. In our recipe, we call the node.inter face_statuses method, and then define a block containing the code we want to run on the results of this method. Remember that &block parameter we passed to our interface_statuses method in our library code? In this example, that block is the Chef::Log.warn line we added to our recipe code.

When we run our method, it iterates over each element of node[:network][:inter faces] and extracts the key and value of the Ohai attribute hash for each interface, assigning the key the name name and the value the name info. It then executes its block parameter (in this case, the Chef::Log.warn line) for each result.

When we call block, we're passing it two parameters: the name of the interface, and the "state" element of the info hash. These are made available to our cookbook as the if_name and status variables when we use our new method in our recipe code.

Now let's kick off a Chef run on our `testcookbook::node_library_test` recipe and see what this code does in practice:

```
$> chef-client --once --why-run --local-mode \
  --config /tmp/part3_examples/client.rb \
  --override-runlist testcookbook::node_library_test
Starting Chef Client, version 11.10.4
[Tue, 20 May 2014 14:45:10 +0000] WARN: Run List override has been provided.
[Tue, 20 May 2014 14:45:10 +0000] WARN: Original Run List: []
[Tue, 20 May 2014 14:45:10 +0000] WARN: Overridden Run List:
  [recipe[testcookbook::node_library_test]]
resolving cookbooks for run list: ["testcookbook::node_library_test"]
Synchronizing Cookbooks:
  - testcookbook
Compiling Cookbooks...
[Tue, 20 May 2014 14:45:10 +0000] WARN: The status of interface lo is unknown
[Tue, 20 May 2014 14:45:10 +0000] WARN: The status of interface eth0 is up
Converging 0 resources
[Tue, 20 May 2014 14:45:10 +0000] WARN: Skipping final node save
  because override_runlist was given

Running handlers:
Running handlers complete

Chef Client finished, 0/0 resources would have been updated
```

As this output shows, during the compile phase of the Chef run, our `node.inter face_statuses` method is called. It iterates over each interface it finds in the node attributes, producing a `Chef::Log.warn` line for each interface that tells us its name and status.

In this example, with just a nine-line library and a three-line recipe, we were able to add an entirely new method to Chef's built-in `Chef::Node` class and use it in our recipe code to help produce a simpler, more readable cookbook for our friends at AwesomeInc.

Summary and Further Reading

In this part of the chapter, we've barely scratched the surface of the possibilities that exist for using libraries in your Chef cookbooks—quite simply because trying to document every possible library would be like trying to document every possible cookbook or every possible use of Ruby.

What I've tried to do instead here is to give you a flavor of the different ways libraries are most commonly used and the typical sorts of functionality that each pattern is most commonly used for. We've also looked at an example of each pattern to learn how it works in practice. As I mentioned in the introduction to this part of the chapter, the one use case for libraries that hasn't been covered at all in this chapter is *heavyweight* resources and providers. That's a topic weighty enough to require its own chapter (Chapter 9 of this book).

Readers interested in diving deeper into libraries and what members of the Chef community have used them for might also want to have a look at the following cookbooks:

chef-whitelist

The chef-whitelist (*http://bit.ly/chef-wl*) cookbook, written by Daniel Schauenberg at Etsy, is used to help manage infrastructure upgrades by defining pattern-based whitelists that can easily be checked in recipe code with the node.is_in_whitelist? method this library adds. You can read more about chef-whitelist on Etsy's *Code as Craft (http://bit.ly/codeascraft)* blog.

whitelist-node-attrs

The whitelist-node-attrs (*http://bit.ly/gh-wl-node*) cookbook, written by Chef, Inc., was created in response to an issue one of Chef's largest customers was having with the amount of data Ohai was saving back to the server for each node. Chef, Inc.'s solution was to create a library that overrides the .save method of the Chef::Node class to only save whitelisted attributes back to the Chef server.

In the next chapter, we're going to start learning about how we can create our own bespoke resources and the providers that power them.

## CHAPTER 8

Lightweight Resources and Providers

Chef ships with a number of useful resources and associated providers that we can use in our recipe code to implement a great deal of functionality, such as interacting with package managers, copying files onto nodes, managing system users, and working with source code management systems such as Git. However, as you might expect, these built-in resources do not provide every single piece of functionality we might want to incorporate into our infrastructure code.

As we touched on in "Think Critically" on page 7, the people at Chef, Inc. are smart folks. They know there's no way they can provide resources to cater for every possible task people might want to perform with Chef—there are just too many possibilities—so they don't try. What they have done instead is to make it as easy as possible for us to create our own resources and providers that cater to our specific requirements—making a new provider to make the `package` resource work with a new package management system, for example, or creating an entirely new resource and provider to configure a high-availability database cluster.

In the last chapter, we looked at *definitions*, which are recipe macros that allow us to wrap one or more other resources into a reusable chunk. Definitions go some way toward allowing us to implement our own resource types but as we saw, suffer from a number of limitations—namely, that they cannot define multiple actions and cannot be notified.

In this chapter and the next, we're going to dive deeper into Chef's resource model and learn how to create fully fledged resources and their supporting providers, which are not subject to the limitations of definitions. We're going to learn:

- How resources and providers work under the hood
- The different types of bespoke resources and providers supported by Chef

- The pros and cons of each methodology, and when you might choose them

As with previous chapters, we'll also work through a number of examples to build up our own resources and see them in action.

Introduction to Resources and Providers

At some point or another, we've all used Chef's built-in resource types in our infra-structure code. Each resource is specified in our recipes as a block of code that contains the parameters needed by the resource, the action for the resource to take, and optionally other resources to subscribe to and notify. Let's look at a typical example we might see in a recipe, using Chef's built-in `package` resource:

```
package "httpd" do
  version "2.2.15-15"
  action :install
end
```

The resource block we have used here is very simple. It has the name `httpd` and specifies the parameter `version` and the action `:install` to tell Chef that version 2.2.15–15 of the `httpd` package should be installed. But what if we need to install this package on multiple operating systems? As many Chef users know, the built-in `package` resource knows how to interface with a variety of package management systems on different operating systems. But how does it know how to do that? How does Chef pack all of this functionality into the four lines of code shown here?

Under the hood, cookbook resources in Chef are actually composed of two distinct but complementary components:

Resources

Resources in Chef define the *characteristics* of the new recipe functionality being implemented—specifically, the *actions* that recipe block can take, and the *attributes* it supports. In the case of the `package` resource, the resource definition might say, for example, that it supports the `:install`, `:uninstall`, and `:upgrade` actions and the attributes `name` and `version`. (In reality, the `package` resource supports many more actions and attributes than this, but you get the idea.) The crucial thing to note here is that the resource does not actually define how any of its supported actions should be implemented; it just defines which actions are available. The functionality required to implement the actions defined in a resource is supplied by its providers.

Providers

Providers in Chef complement resources, and implement the behavior that drives the actions specified by each resource. To do this, providers are able to make use of existing cookbook resources such as `package` or `file` in addition to native Ruby code. A resource can be backed by one or more providers. Usually, if we want to choose between multiple providers, we have to specify a specific provider in the resource block, like this:

```
service "httpd" do
  action [:enable, :start]
  provider Chef::Provider::Service::Upstart
end
```

In this code, we're forcing the service resource to use the Service::Upstart provider.

Automatically Choosing Providers

One of the most powerful features of Chef's resource and provider model is that resources are able to have many providers. Most of Chef's built-in cookbook resources make use of a special technique to allow Chef to automatically pick out of several possible providers the one that implements the necessary functionality for the specific platform running Chef. For example, on a Redhat–based Linux operating system, the package resource would make use of a provider designed to interface with yum, while on Debian a provider would be chosen to interface with apt, and so on for each of the supported operating systems.

This automatic provider selection is controlled by the Chef::Platform class, which lives at *lib/chef/platform/provider_mapping.rb* (*http://bit.ly/provider-map*). This class defines mappings for each supported platform to specify the default provider for each resource type that platform should use. Example 8-1 shows the mapping for CentOS.

Example 8-1. Excerpt of lib/chef/platform/provider_mapping.rb

```
:centos   => {
  :default => {
    :service => Chef::Provider::Service::Redhat,
    :cron => Chef::Provider::Cron,
    :package => Chef::Provider::Package::Yum,
    :mdadm => Chef::Provider::Mdadm,
    :ifconfig => Chef::Provider::Ifconfig::Redhat
  }
},
```

As we see here, this mapping tells Chef that when a package resource is being executed on CentOS, the Chef::Provider::Package::Yum class should be used. To help visualize this interaction between Chef's built-in resources and providers, have a look at Figure 8-1.

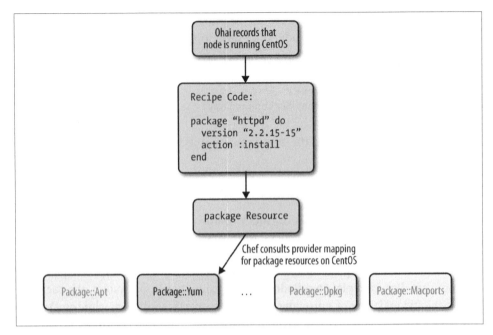

Figure 8-1. Package resource and providers

This powerful and flexible behavior is usually invisible to the people writing Chef cookbooks, too (unless they manually specify a provider), and makes it very easy to write platform-agnostic cookbooks. When creating our own providers, we're able to tap into this provider mapping to create entirely new mappings for our own resource types to enable us to automatically support multiple platforms, or to modify the mappings for built-in resources if we're adding new providers to built-in resources. We'll learn how to do this in "Advanced HWRP Tricks" on page 240.

Resources and Providers—Lightweight Versus Heavyweight

The customizability and flexibility offered by Chef's resources and providers is of course extremely useful, but it is of limited utility to us unless we can create our own resources and providers to implement functionality not supported by Chef out of the box. Fortunately for us, Chef, Inc. has made it extremely easy for us to do just this. Chef actually supports two different "styles" of custom resources and providers:

Lightweight resources and providers

Lightweight resources and providers (LWRPs) in Chef are written using a special domain-specific language (DSL) to abstract away much of the more complex underlying Ruby code needed to implement resources and providers. Chef, Inc. has designed LWRPs to make it as easy as possible to create your own resources and providers, allowing you to focus on their actual behavior rather than worrying about class structure and syntax. In the remainder of this chapter, we'll learn how to create our own LWRPs.

The trade-off with LWRPs is that there may sometimes be situations where the DSL doesn't quite do everything you want it to, and you need to dive deeper into the underlying code. In that case, there's an alternative.

Heavyweight resources and providers
Heavyweight resources and providers (HWRPs) in Chef are written in pure Ruby instead of a DSL and, unlike LWRPs, do not make use of an abstraction layer. Whereas LWRPs are designed to be simple and easy to create, HWRPs leverage the full power offered by Chef's resource and provider model at the expense of being more complex and long-winded to write. We'll extend the LWRP knowledge we gain in this chapter to learn how to write HWRPs in Chapter 9, and examine when HWRPs may be a better choice than LWRPs (and vice versa).

Now that we've examined how resources and providers combine to drive the functionality that powers our infrastructure code, let's dive in to how to actually create them!

Introduction to LWRPs

LWRPs in Chef make use of a special Ruby DSL to allow Chef users to implement their own resources and providers. The DSL used by LWRPs abstracts away much of the underlying code needed to create resources and providers and integrate them with Chef's class structure. This allows the end user to focus on the behavior of their resources rather than having to worry about class inheritance, method names, and so on.

LWRPs can make use of existing cookbook resources in the same way as the definitions we examined in Chapter 7, with the added benefit that LWRPs are used to create fully fledged resources that can be notified and that can define multiple supported actions. For situations where combining existing cookbook resources just doesn't cut it, LWRPs also support using native Ruby code to implement totally customized behavior.

Throughout the remainder of this chapter, we're going to explore Chef's LWRP DSL and use it to create a number of resources and providers. As with other chapters in this book, we'll start with the minimum skeleton needed to define an LWRP, and then gradually extend it with more complex behaviors as we level up our understanding of the LWRP DSL and how it integrates with Chef.

We're going to start off by working through another problem with our friends at AwesomeInc. In Chapter 7, we helped them create a cookbook definition called `awesomea tor_prepare` to set up the working environment for an internal tool they were going to install. During this process, we learned that definitions cannot be notified by other resources and cannot define more than one action to perform.

As creation of their `awesomeator` tool and supporting cookbook progresses, the folks at AwesomeInc realize that they'd actually like to be able to clean up the tool's working environment when the tool is uninstalled, and would like installation or removal of the tool to automatically trigger the preparation or cleanup of its working environment. We're going to help them convert the `awesomeator_prepare` definition into an LWRP that will support both installation/preparation and cleanup of the working environment, and be configurable via parameters specified in the recipe code.

LWRP Example 1: Getting Started with LWRPs

We're going to start off our LWRP by defining a skeleton resource and associated provider to outline the actions and parameters that it will support. We'll create the resource component of our LWRP and examine the code it contains first, before going on to create a minimal provider to complement it. We'll then use our new LWRP in a recipe to explore how its behavior differs from the definitions we created in Chapter 7.

 Before working through the examples in this chapter, please make sure you've followed the steps in "Creating a Test Environment" on page 167 to create your test environment.

Example 1: Creating a Resource

The first stage in the construction of an LWRP is to define the resource it will implement. As we saw earlier in this chapter, the resource definition does not itself contain any implementation code to power the resource, but rather serves to define the actions and attributes that the resource supports.

Because we're going to be converting the definition we constructed in Chapter 7 to an LWRP, we already know the attributes that we need to support:

name
> The name parameter contains the value specified in our recipe after the name of the resource itself. For instance, in our earlier example of package "httpd", the name would be httpd. Unlike definitions, it is mandatory for full resources to be given a name.

working_dir
> We'll need a working_dir parameter to specify the working directory to be used by the awesomeator tool.

config_file
> We'll also need a config_file parameter to specify the path where the awesomea tor config file will be stored.

As we discussed earlier, however, our LWRP is going to be able to clean up the `aweso
meator` working environment as well as create it. To support both of these behaviors,
our LWRP needs to support multiple actions:

`:prepare`

> When our LWRP is called with the `:prepare` action, it creates the working envi-
> ronment for the `awesomeator` tool.

`:cleanup`

> When our LWRP is called with the `:cleanup` action, it removes the working envi-
> ronment.

Now that we've designated the actions and parameters that our resource will define, we
can go ahead and create the resource definition file. We're going to be using several
methods defined by the LWRP DSL in this example—we'll be looking at the LWRP DSL
in much more detail in "The LWRP Domain-Specific Language" on page 200, so don't
worry if the methods we're using are a little confusing for now.

As we saw in "Cookbook Structure Revisited" on page 166, resources live in the cookbook's *resources* directory, so we're going to paste the code in Example 8-2 into */tmp/
part3_examples/cookbooks/testcookbook/resources/awesomeator.rb*.

Example 8-2. /tmp/part3_examples/cookbooks/testcookbook/resources/awesomeator.rb

```
actions :prepare, :cleanup ❶
default_action :prepare ❷

attribute :name, :kind_of => String, :name_attribute => true ❸
attribute :working_dir, :kind_of => String, :default => "/tmp/awesomeator" ❹
attribute :config_file, :kind_of => String, :default => "/etc/awesomeator.conf" ❺
```

❶   We begin by calling the `actions` method of the DSL, and passing each action
        we want to support as a *symbol* to that method. As we see here, the only thing
        we specify in the resource definition is the name of each action.

❷   Next, we call the `default_action` method of the DSL and specify that the `de
        fault_action` of our resource will be `:prepare`. This means that if we don't
        explicitly specify an action when we use the resource in our recipes, it defaults
        to performing the `:prepare` action.

❸   Here, we call the `attribute` method of the DSL to configure our `name` attribute.
        We're stating that it's a `String`, and using the `:name_attribute` parameter to
        specify that this attribute should be used as the name of our resource.

❹ ❺   Finally, we define our `working_dir` and `config_dir` attributes with calls to the
        `attribute` method of the DSL. We're stating that each is a `String`, and we're
        also assigning a default value to each, which will be used if one is not specified
        in recipes using this resource.

Resource Naming

As you might have noticed, we haven't specified what our resource will actually be called when we use it in our recipes. Chef actually dynamically constructs the name of each LWRP resource from the cookbook that contains the resource and the name of the file in the *resources* directory.

In this case, because the resource lives in the `testcookbook` cookbook and is defined in a file called *awesomeator.rb* in the *resources* directory of that cookbook, Chef combines this information to make the resource name `testcookbook_awesomeator`. This is used in our recipes like this:

```
testcookbook_awesomeator "foo" do
  ...
end
```

The one exception to this rule is when the resource definition lives in */resources/default.rb*. In this case, Chef names the resource solely after the cookbook in which it lives.

It's also worth noting that any hyphens in the name of the cookbook that contains the LWRP will be converted to underscores. For example, if we had a cookbook named `awesome-cookbook` containing a resource in a file called *foo.rb*, we would use the name `awesome_cookbook_foo` in our recipe code to make use of this resource.

The resource definition we've created here is now in the final form we'll use to help the team at AwesomeInc create their LWRP. Resource definitions contain very little code—in this case, we're simply defining that our resource will support two actions and three parameters. The meat of the LWRP is contained in its associated provider, which we're going to start creating next.

Example 1: Creating a Provider

Now that we have defined the actions and attributes our resource will support, we need to create a *provider* to actually implement these actions. As this is our first provider example, we're not going to implement the full provider here, but we will define enough of its structure to allow us to use our LWRP in a recipe. We'll add more behavior to our provider later in this chapter.

As we saw in "Cookbook Structure Revisited" on page 166, providers live in the cookbook's */providers* directory. In the case of LWRPs, the provider component needs to have the same filename as the resource component (*awesomeator.rb*), so we'll paste the code in Example 8-3 into */tmp/part3_examples/cookbooks/testcookbook/providers/awesomeator.rb*.

Example 8-3. /tmp/part3_examples/cookbooks/testcookbook/providers/awesomeator.rb

```
def whyrun_supported? ❶
  true
end

action :prepare do ❷
end

action :cleanup do ❸
end
```

❶ As we're going to be using why-run mode to test our cookbook, we need to add a special `whyrun_supported?` method to our provider to let Chef know that it will work correctly in this mode. We'll look at this method in more detail in "The LWRP Domain-Specific Language" on page 200.

❷ Here we're defining an `action` block called `:prepare` to define what code will be executed when our LWRP is used with the `:prepare` action.

❸ Here we're defining an `action` block called `:cleanup` to define what code will be executed when our LWRP is used with the `:cleanup` action.

As this example demonstrates, we can actually implement our provider in very little code—the minimum code we really need in a provider is an `action` block for each of the actions our LWRP will support. These blocks are empty for now, but as we'll see next, our provider can still be used in a recipe.

Example 1: Using Our LWRP in a Recipe

Now that we've created the resource and provider components of our custom LWRP, let's try using it in a recipe to see what happens. We're going to create a new recipe under our `testcookbook` cookbook called `awesomeator_lwrp` to try out our new resource, so paste the line of code in Example 8-4 into */tmp/part3_examples/cookbooks/testcookbook/recipes/awesomeator_lwrp.rb*.

Example 8-4. /tmp/part3_examples/cookbooks/testcookbook/recipes/awesomeator_lwrp.rb

```
testcookbook_awesomeator "production" ❶
```

❶ As we saw in "Resource Naming" on page 198, the name of our custom resource is `testcookbook_awesomeator`, constructed from the name of the cookbook that contains the resource and the name of the resource definition in its *resources* directory. We're passing our resource the name `production`.

In this example, we're going to use the default parameter values we configured in our resource definition, so we don't need to configure any parameters in our recipe. Let's try a Chef run with our new `testcookbook::awesomeator_lwrp` recipe and see what happens:

```
$> chef-client --once --why-run --local-mode \
  --config /tmp/part3_examples/client.rb \
  --override-runlist testcookbook::awesomeator_lwrp
Starting Chef Client, version 11.10.4
[Sat, 03 May 2014 13:24:24 +0000] WARN: Run List override has been provided.
[Sat, 03 May 2014 13:24:24 +0000] WARN: Original Run List: []
[Sat, 03 May 2014 13:24:24 +0000] WARN: Overridden Run List:
  [recipe[testcookbook::awesomeator_lwrp]]
resolving cookbooks for run list: ["testcookbook::awesomeator_lwrp"]
Synchronizing Cookbooks:
  - testcookbook
Compiling Cookbooks...
Converging 1 resources
Recipe: testcookbook::awesomeator_lwrp
  * testcookbook_awesomeator[production] action prepare (up to date)
[Sat, 03 May 2014 13:24:24 +0000] WARN: Skipping final node save
  because override_runlist was given

Running handlers:
Running handlers complete

Chef Client finished, 0/1 resources would have been updated
```

As we can see here, when Chef encounters our `testcookbook::awesomeator_lwrp` recipe, it executes the `:prepare` action of our `testcookbook_awesomeator` resource. Because that action doesn't contain any code in our provider, it informs us that nothing needs to be done for that resource:

```
testcookbook_awesomeator[production] action prepare (up to date)
```

We've now created an LWRP! We created the resource definition, created a provider to implement the actions it defines, and used it in a recipe. Before we dive into adding more code to our provider to implement the functionality our LRWP needs, we're going to take a more detailed look at the methods we've already been using from the LWRP DSL and the other methods it exposes to enable us to easily create our LWRPs.

The LWRP Domain-Specific Language

In order for us to add any more behavior to our LWRP, it's important that we have a good understanding of the LWRP domain-specific language so that we are aware of the various features and capabilities it can provide us with. The LWRP DSL is actually split into two subcomponents: one for resources, and one for providers. As we discussed briefly in the introduction to this chapter, the LWRP DSL is an abstraction layer on top of the native classes used by Chef to power resources and providers.

It may therefore not come as much of a surprise to learn that the LWRP DSLs for resources and providers are implemented behind the scenes as special subclasses of Chef's native resource and provider classes—we'll meet these native classes in much greater detail in Chapter 9 when we look at heavyweight resources and providers.

In this section of the chapter, we're going to look at the DSLs defined for both lightweight resources and lightweight providers, and the methods and attributes they expose to power our LWRPs.

Resource DSL

The resource component of the LWRP DSL is defined in the `Chef::Re source::LWRPBase` class that lives at *lib/chef/resource/lwrp_base* (*http://bit.ly/lwrp-baserb*). Because the LRWP DSL is actually an abstraction layer over the built-in Chef classes for creating resources and providers, `Chef::Resource::LWRPBase` is a subclass of `Chef::Resource`, the superclass from which all resources in Chef inherit, which lives at *lib/chef/resource.rb* (*http://bit.ly/gh-resourcerb*).

We won't be looking at the `Chef::Resource` superclass directly in this chapter—although we will be looking at it more closely when we create HWRPs in Chapter 9. In this section, we're going to focus specifically on the methods `Chef::Re source::LWRPBase` defines to provide the *resource* portion of the LWRP DSL:

actions

> The `actions` method, which we used in "Example 1: Creating a Resource" on page 196, takes a comma-delimited list of symbols and defines the list of actions the resource will support.

default_action

> The `default_action` method, which we also used in "Example 1: Creating a Resource" on page 196, is used to specify the default action to be used by a lightweight resource when none is specified in the recipe. It takes a symbol containing the default action to be used as a parameter.

state_attrs

> The `state_attrs` method is used to specify the system state attributes that will be tracked by the reporting feature of Enterprise Chef. These parameters are specified as a comma-separated list of symbols. Because only Enterprise Chef supports this feature, we won't be making further use of it in this book, but interested readers can find out more about this method on the Chef Documents (*http://docs.opscode.com/ reporting.html#state-attrs-recipe-dsl-method*) site.

attribute

> The `attribute` method, which we also used when creating our resource, is used to define an attribute that will belong to the resource. It's common to have multiple

calls to this method in a resource definition—we had three in Example 8-2, specifying the characteristics of each resource being defined.

Attribute Validation Options

The `attribute` method of the resource DSL supports a number of validation options that can be used in addition to the name of the resource to ensure that the types and values passed to that parameter are exactly as we expect:

`:callbacks`

> The `:callbacks` option allows us to specify a hash of key/value pairs to validate our attribute value against. The value of each element will be a block of Ruby code that, for the validation check to succeed, must evaluate to `true`. In practical terms, this option allows us to call out to other methods and Ruby code to validate our attribute values when other attribute validation options don't allow the required functionality. You can see an example of using callbacks to validate an attribute on the Chef Documents (*http://docs.opscode.com/lwrp_custom_resource.html#call backs*) site.

`:default`

> The `:default` option, which we used in "Example 1: Creating a Resource" on page 196, allows you to specify a value to use for this attribute when none is specified in the recipe. Note that if you're also using the `:kind_of` option, the default value must be of the same type.

`:equal_to`

> The `:equal_to` option allows you to specify one or more possible values that the supplied attribute value must equal. For example, `:equal_to =>` `[:true, :false]`. The equality test used here is `==`.

`:kind_of`

> The `:kind_of` option allows you to specify the desired type of the attribute as a Ruby class. We used this option in Example 8-2 to ensure that our attributes were of type `String`. If also using the `:default_value` option, you should make sure that the value supplied is of the class required by this option.

`:name_attribute`

> The `:name_attribute` option allows us to designate a particular attribute as representing the name of the resource, as specified in recipe code. In Example 8-2, this was the `name` attribute.

`:regex`

> The `:regex` option allows you to specify a regular expression that the supplied attribute value must match.

:required
> The :required option allows you to mark a particular attribute as mandatory. If this attribute is not supplied when the resource is used in a recipe (and no default value has been given), an exception is thrown and the Chef run fails.

:respond_to
> The :respond_to option allows you to specify that a particular attribute must have a particular method. This allows us to, for example, permit an attribute to be of any class that implements a to_s method, without the need to restrict our attribute to a specific list of class types.

These validation options are used as parameters to the attribute method in the same fashion we saw in Example 8-2:

```
attribute :working_dir, :kind_of => String, :default => "/tmp/awesomeator"
```

The use of attribute validation options allows us a great deal of control over the attributes that we permit to be given to our LWRP. This control frees us from having to implement attribute validation in our providers because the attribute validation options used in the resource should do this for us.

Although not strictly part of the LWRP resource DSL, I'm also going to include in this list a built-in Ruby method that is frequently used in resource definitions:

attr_accessor
> Unlike the other methods listed in this section, the attr_accessor method (which we met in "Getter and Setter Methods" on page 31) is actually defined by Ruby itself, but is frequently used in LWRPSs for situations where the provider might need to write to an attribute as well as read from it. Think of calls to the attribute method as defining a read-only parameter to be passed to the provider, while calls to attr_accessor define an attribute on the resource that can be both read and written to by the provider.

Now that we've explored the methods and validation options the LWRP DSL provides to create resource definitions that describe the actions and attributes our resources support, let's move on to look at the methods the DSL supplies for our providers.

Provider DSL

Just as the resource portion of the LWRP DSL is defined as a special type of resource, the provider component is defined in the Chef::Provider::LWRPBase class, which lives at *lib/chef/provider/lwrp_base.rb* (*http://bit.ly/gh-lwrpbase*). In the same way as we saw with resources in the last section, to provide the abstraction layer of the LRWP DSL Chef::Provider::LWRPBase is actually a subclass of Chef::Provider, the superclass from which all providers in Chef inherit, which lives at *lib/chef/provider.rb* (*http://bit.ly/ gh-provider*).

We won't be looking at the `Chef::Provider` superclass directly in this chapter, although we will look at it more closely when we create HWRPs in Chapter 9. In this section, we're going to focus specifically on the methods `Chef::Provider::LWRPBase` defines for the *provider* portion of the LWRP DSL:

action

> The `action` method is used to declare a code block that specifies the steps to be performed for a specific action of the resource. One `action` block needs to be defined for each object supported by the LWRP, as we saw in "Example 1: Creating a Resource" on page 196. The code contained inside the `action` block powers the behavior that occurs when that action is triggered during a chef-client run.

use_inline_resources

> The `use_inline_resources` method is used to ensure that any LWRPs containing other cookbook resources are treated as standalone resource collections—this enables Chef to make sure that any notifications generated by resources inside the LWRP are shown as being generated by the LWRP itself. The history behind (and exact behavior of) this method is somewhat lengthy and complex, so for the purposes of this book it's sufficient to remember that you should *always* call this method if you're going to be using cookbook resources in your provider—this is in fact likely to become default behavior in a future version of chef-client. Readers interested in more information on exactly what this method does can find a detailed explanation of the behavior of `use_inline_resources` on the Chef Documents (*http://bit.ly/ use-inline*) site.

whyrun_supported?

> The `whyrun_supported?` method is used to indicate whether or not a provider will function correctly when chef-client is executed in why-run mode. If this method is not included or if the return value from the method is `false`, then Chef will skip over the resource block that makes use of this provider when running in why-run mode. Note that if we define this method as returning `true` and are creating a provider that uses native code or other LWRPs in addition to built-in Chef resources, there are some steps we must take in our code to ensure that our code actually does work nicely in why-run mode. We'll examine these steps in "Provider Internals" on page 209.

In addition to these methods, the provider DSL also defines three methods that enable us to help Chef identify whether or not our LWRP is up-to-date. In Chef, a resource being up-to-date means that it is fully converged on the node—i.e., that the state described in the resource reflects the current state of the node. To use a simple example, in the case of the `package` resource, the resource being up-to-date means that the correct version of the relevant package was installed. I've listed these methods here for completeness, but don't worry too much about them for now—we're going to dive into them in much greater detail in "Provider Internals" on page 209:

load_current_resource

> The load_current_resource method is used to tell chef-client how to detect the *current* state of our resource—that is, the state that the resource defined in our recipe has at the start of the Chef run.

current_resource

> The current_resource method is used to represent the resource described in the load_current_resources method. Chef allows us to access this object elsewhere in our provider so that we're able to easily compare the *current* and *desired* states of our resource in our provider code.

new_resource

> The new_resource method represents the *desired* state of the resource, as described in our recipe. The object returned by this method also allows our provider to automatically access attributes defined by that resource.

At this point, you might be feeling somewhat confused by the complexity of some of the DSL methods we've seen here—but don't worry! Throughout the rest of the chapter, we'll work our way through a number of LWRP examples that gradually introduce these methods into our resource and provider code. On that note, let's dive into another example and extend our provider from the previous section with the code needed to power its action methods.

LWRP Example 2: Extending the Provider

In "LWRP Example 1: Getting Started with LWRPs" on page 196, we created a resource definition for our testcookbook_awesomeator LWRP, and a blank provider that defined empty action blocks for each of its supported actions. In this example, we're going to extend our provider to carry out the tasks needed to prepare and clean up the working environment for the awesomeator tool.

The steps needed to prepare the working environment are exactly the same as they were in Chapter 7:

1. The working directory needs to be created.
2. The specified configuration file must be created and populated with the chosen working directory.

In addition to this, of course, we also need to define the actions to take when we want to clean up our working environment:

1. The specified configuration file should be deleted.

2. The working directory needs to be deleted.

Armed with this information and the knowledge we've gained on Chef's LWRP DSL, we're now in a good position to start adding code to our provider class. As we touched on briefly in "Introduction to Resources and Providers" on page 192, providers in Chef are able to make use of cookbook resources as well as native Ruby code. This means that any cookbook resource we can use in a recipe can also be used inside a provider if we wish.

This handy fact means that we can use Chef's built-in `directory` and `template` resources to power our provider, just as we did with the definition we created in Chapter 7. Paste the code in Example 8-5 into the same provider file as we used before, */tmp/ part3_examples/cookbooks/testcookbook/providers/awesomeator.rb*.

Example 8-5. /tmp/part3_examples/cookbooks/testcookbook/providers/awesomeator.rb

```
def whyrun_supported?
  true
end

action :prepare do
  directory new_resource.working_dir do ❶
    action :create
    recursive true
  end

  template new_resource.config_file do ❷
    source 'awesomeator.conf.erb'
    variables({
      :working_dir => new_resource.working_dir
    })
  end
  new_resource.updated_by_last_action(true) ❸
end

action :cleanup do
  file new_resource.config_file do ❹
    action :delete
  end

  directory new_resource.working_dir do
    action :delete
    recursive true
  end
  new_resource.updated_by_last_action(true)
end
```

❶ Here we're using Chef's built-in `directory` resource to create the specified working directory. We're using the `new_resource` method of the provider DSL to allow us to access the resource we define in our recipe code. Attributes passed to that resource are exposed as methods of the `new_resource` object, so here we're calling `new_resource.working_dir` to access the `working_dir` attribute.

❷ Here we're using Chef's built-in `template` resource to create the specified configuration, populated with the working directory. Note again that we're using method calls to the `new_resource` object to allow us to access the attributes of our resource.

❸ Next, we call the `updated_by_last_action` of the `new_resource` object to let Chef know that our LWRP was not already up-to-date, and that actions were carried out to converge the resource.

❹ Here we use a `file` resource with `action :delete` to remove the configuration file, and follow this with a `directory` resource with `action :delete`. As with the `:create` action, we're using the `new_resource` method to allow us to access attribute values passed to our resource.

As we can see in this code, the `new_resource` method of the provider DSL allows us to access the resource block defined in our recipe by returning an object representing the resource block we defined in our recipe code. Any attributes we define in our resource (in our case, `name`, `working_dir` and `config_file`) will be made available as methods of this object.

It's also worth pausing to note our use of the `new_resource.updated_by_last_ac tion` method call, in step 3. As we'll examine in more detail in "Provider Internals" on page 209, because our provider can contain native Ruby code as well as cookbook resources, it's not safe for Chef to make any assumptions in the provider code about whether or not a resource should be considered as updated. In the case of this example, if we didn't add this `new_resource.updated_by_last_action` method call, Chef would default to assuming that our `testcookbook_awesomeator` resource was up-to-date, even if the resources we used in our `action` blocks were actually updated.

Now let's try running our `testcookbook::awesomeator_lwrp` recipe again and see how the output of the run changes:

```
$> chef-client --once --why-run --local-mode \
  --config /tmp/part3_examples/client.rb \
  --override-runlist testcookbook::awesomeator_lwrp
Starting Chef Client, version 11.10.4
[Mon, 05 May 2014 10:52:14 +0000] WARN: Run List override has been provided.
[Mon, 05 May 2014 10:52:14 +0000] WARN: Original Run List: []
[Mon, 05 May 2014 10:52:14 +0000] WARN: Overridden Run List:
  [recipe[testcookbook::awesomeator_lwrp]]
resolving cookbooks for run list: ["testcookbook::awesomeator_lwrp"]
```

```
Synchronizing Cookbooks:
 - testcookbook
Compiling Cookbooks...
Converging 1 resources
Recipe: testcookbook::awesomeator_lwrp
 * testcookbook_awesomeator[production] action prepare

Recipe: <Dynamically Defined Resource>
 * directory[/var/awesomeator] action create
   - Would create new directory /var/awesomeator

 * template[/etc/awesomeator.conf] action create
   - Would create new file /etc/awesomeator.conf

[Mon, 05 May 2014 10:52:15 +0000] WARN: Skipping final node save
 because override_runlist was given

Running handlers:
Running handlers complete

Chef Client finished, 3/3 resources would have been updated
```

This time, when Chef runs our `testcookbook_awesomeator` resource with ac
tion `:prepare`, the resources we defined inside the `action :prepare` block of our
provider are executed. Let's try using the `:cleanup` action of our resource now and verify
that it also works as we'd expect. Paste the code in Example 8-6 into */tmp/part3_exam-
ples/cookbooks/testcookbook/recipes/awesomeator_lwrp.rb.*

*Example 8-6. /tmp/part3_examples/cookbooks/testcookbook/recipes/awesomea-
tor_lwrp.rb*

```
testcookbook_awesomeator "production" do
  action :cleanup
end
```

Note that the only thing we changed here from the previous recipe is that we now
explicitly state that `action :cleanup` should be triggered instead of the default ac
tion `:prepare` that was used before. Now let's try running our recipe again:

```
$> chef-client --once --why-run --local-mode \
  --config /tmp/part3_examples/client.rb \
  --override-runlist testcookbook::awesomeator_lwrp
Starting Chef Client, version 11.10.4
[Mon, 05 May 2014 11:07:38 +0000] WARN: Run List override has been provided.
[Mon, 05 May 2014 11:07:38 +0000] WARN: Original Run List: []
[Mon, 05 May 2014 11:07:38 +0000] WARN: Overridden Run List:
  [recipe[testcookbook::awesomeator_lwrp]]
resolving cookbooks for run list: ["testcookbook::awesomeator_lwrp"]
Synchronizing Cookbooks:
  - testcookbook
Compiling Cookbooks...
```

```
Converging 1 resources
Recipe: testcookbook::awesomeator_lwrp
  * testcookbook_awesomeator[production] action cleanup

Recipe: <Dynamically Defined Resource>
  * file[/etc/awesomeator.conf] action delete (up to date)
  * directory[/tmp/awesomeator] action delete (up to date)
[Mon, 05 May 2014 11:07:38 +0000] WARN: Skipping final node save
  because override_runlist was given

Running handlers:
Running handlers complete

Chef Client finished, 1/3 resources would have been updated
```

This time, we see that the `:cleanup` action of our LWRP was triggered. As we ran our provider's `:prepare` action in why-run mode, though we never actually created the relevant directory and file on disk, so the `:cleanup` action has nothing to do here.

Over the last two examples, we've created a custom LWRP comprising a resource that defines the actions and attributes supported, and a provider to define the meat of implementing those actions. Our LWRP supports multiple actions, allowing us to vary its functionality from our recipe code by simply changing the action we choose. Our provider made use of existing cookbook resources to provide the functionality we needed, and we also learned how to let Chef know that our LWRP was updated during the course of the Chef run.

However, the fact that up to this point we've only made use of Chef's built-in cookbook resources in our providers also means that many of the core provider behaviors and features that make LWRPs such a flexible and powerful tool have been abstracted away from us inside those resources. When we start to create providers using native Ruby code, this is no longer the case. In the next section, we're going to dive deeper into the internal workings of native providers and how they integrate with Chef.

Provider Internals

Thus far in our recipe customizations, we've used Chef's built-in cookbook resources to power both our definitions in Chapter 7, and our LWRPs in this chapter. As we touched on briefly in "Introduction to Resources and Providers" on page 192, however, it's also possible to implement providers using native Ruby code.

Say, for example, you wanted to create a provider to interact with a third-party API. Although you may be able to implement part of this using cookbook resources, it's more than likely that you'll also need to use some custom Ruby code, and it would drastically reduce the usefulness of LWRPs if this were not possible.

When we implement native lightweight providers, we have to take into account some behaviors that have up to this point been hidden away inside the providers for the cookbook resources we have been using. In "Anatomy of a Chef Run" on page 62, we saw that two key components of Chef are that Chef runs should be *convergent* and *idempotent*. Let's revisit these terms in the context of resources and providers:

Idempotence
> When implementing providers, we have to ensure that our provider is idempotent; that is, that it carries out any necessary actions on only the first Chef run where those action are needed, and does not repeat them unnecessarily on additional runs.

Convergence
> When implementing providers, convergence means that we have to be sure the provider is bringing our node *closer* to the state defined in our recipe code, rather than further away.

On the face of it, these two concepts seem fairly straightforward. We have to make sure that our providers bring our node toward the state in our recipes, and don't repeat unnecessary actions. Sounds simple, right? If we're using built-in cookbook resources, this *is* in fact simple, because Chef, Inc. has already done the hard work for us. We've seen this in action when resources show as "up-to-date" in the output of our Chef runs. When we want to implement providers using native Ruby code, however, all of a sudden we become responsible for implementing this behavior.

For us to be able to implement this functionality ourselves, we have to be able to compare the state of the resource at the start of the run against the state defined in our recipe. If those states differ, we must carry out the actions necessary to bring the *current* state of our resource in line with the state defined in our recipe code—this is the idea of *convergence*. We also need to make sure that any behaviors implemented in our provider are executed only if the past and current resource states differ, and do nothing if the states are the same (again, idempotence). Finally, we need to ensure that if we do make any changes, we let Chef know that our resource has been updated.

In this section, we're going to dive deeper into providers and look at the following topics:

- How to identify and access the desired state of our resource
- How to identify and access the current state of our resource
- How to establish whether or not our resource has already converged
- How to tell Chef that our resource has been changed

Desired Resource State

The first component of native provider functionality we're going to examine is how we can identify the *desired* state of our resource. For example, consider the following package resource block:

```
package "httpd" do
  version "2.2.15-15.el6"
  action :install
end
```

This resource block tells us everything we need to know about the *desired* state of this resource. After the Chef run, we want version 2.2.15–15.el6 of the httpd package to be installed. This also applies to more complex resources, which can even depend on third-party services. Consider the following example, which makes use of the dynect cook book (*http://bit.ly/gh-dynect*) from Chef, Inc. to create DNS records via the DynECT API (*http://bit.ly/dynect-api*):

```
dynect_rr "myhost" do
  record_type "A"
  rdata({ "address" => "1.2.3.4" })
  fqdn "myhost.mydomain.com"
  customer node["dynect"]["customer"]
  username node["dynect"]["username"]
  password node["dynect"]["password"]
  zone     node["dynect"]["zone"]
  action :update
end
```

This resource block communicates with a third-party API (in this case, the DynECT DNS API) to create an A record for our host. But regardless of the complexity of the underlying resource or the steps needed to carry out this behavior, the desired state of the resource is once again right there in the recipe code: after the Chef run, we want a DNS A record to have been created, pointing myhost.mydomain.com to 1.2.3.4.

This is all very useful, but how do we access the resource defined in our recipe code from inside its provider? As we touched on briefly in "Provider DSL" on page 203, the LWPR DSL already provides us with a method to do exactly this—the new_resource method.

The new_resource method is defined in the Chef::Provider class from which Chef::Provider::LWRPBase inherits (Chef::Provider::LWRPBase is the class that supplies the provider component of the LWRP DSL we met in "Provider DSL" on page 203). The new_resource method returns an object of type Chef::Resource::*<Resour ceName>*, which is the instantiated object created from the resource definition underlying the resource block in our recipe code.

To use the example of our earlier `testcookbook_awesomeator` LWRP, the `new_re source` method in the provider returns a `Chef::Resource::TestcookbookAwesomea tor` resource representing the resource block we defined in our recipe code. All attributes of our resource are accessible as methods of this object—Chef creates them dynamically when it creates the object.

In our `testcookbook_awesomeator` resource, we defined three resources: `name`, `work ing_dir`, and `config_dir`. Table 8-1 illustrates how these attributes map to methods of `new_resource`.

Table 8-1. Mappings of attributes to new_resource methods

Attribute name	new_resource method
:name	new_resource.name
:working_dir	new_resource.working_dir
:config_file	new_resource.config_file

Through the `new_resource` method exposed to our provider through its superclass `Chef::Provider::LWRPBase`, the *desired* state of our resource is easy to access—but this is only half of the puzzle. We also need to be able to introspect into the *current* state of our resource.

Current Resource State

The next piece of information we need to ensure that our providers are both convergent and idempotent is a way to access the current state of our resource—that is, the state of the resource described in our recipe at the beginning of the Chef run, before any recipe code has been executed. This resource could be anything from a file on the node to an object defined by a third-party API, and will typically be in one of three states:

- The resource defined in our recipe does not yet exist.
- The resource does exist, but its current state differs from the desired state defined in our recipe.
- The resource does exist, and its current state is identical to the desired state defined in our recipe.

Whereas the desired state of our resource can be extracted directly from our recipe, calculating the current state of the resource can require a little more work. To illustrate this, let's look again at the `package` resource we saw earlier:

```
package "httpd" do
  version "2.2.15-15.el6"
  action :install
end
```

The desired state of this resource is plain to see in the recipe: we want Chef to install version 2.2.15–15.el6 of the `httpd` package. Chef doesn't need to know *how* to perform this action at this point, just what the action and attributes we desire are. Calculating the current state of this resource is a little harder, though. Chef has to interact with the relevant packaging system to check if `httpd` is already installed, and if so, what version.

As I'm sure you can imagine, it would be impossible for Chef to implement behavior that let it automatically detect the current state of every possible LWRP, and the people at Chef, Inc. of course recognize this, too. What they have done instead is provide us with a way to incorporate this behavior into our providers, through the use of another method we met briefly in "Provider DSL" on page 203: `load_current_resource`.

The `load_current_resource` method is actually defined in the `Chef::Provider` class, but for the purposes of this chapter we're going to use the overridden version of this method defined in the `Chef::Provider::LWRPBase` class, which lives at *lib/chef/provider/lwrp_base.rb* (*http://bit.ly/gh-lwrpbase*). We'll examine the version of this method defined in the `Chef::Provider` class in Chapter 9.

As we can see in Example 8-7, `Chef::Provider::LWRPBase` defines this as an empty method so that we can override it in native providers, but still allow providers using cookbook resources to function correctly without having to define this method.

Example 8-7. Excerpt of lib/chef/provider/lwrp_base.rb

```
def load_current_resource
end
```

What Chef has done here is define a method that is designed to be overridden, with the specific implementation details of the method left up to us. This method is common to all providers and can be called during the Chef run when the current state of a resource needs to be calculated.

The simplest and most common pattern to use when implementing the `load_cur rent_resource` method is to use it to instantiate and populate the object exposed by the provider DSL's `current_resource` method, which we met in "Provider DSL" on page 203.

 As with many of the customization types we've looked at so far, there is no canonically correct method of implementing the `load_cur rent_resource` method for your provider, and Chef places no restrictions on how you use this method other than its name. For readers interesting in exploring other patterns for implementing the `load_current_resource` method, I'll link to several cookbooks in "Summary and Further Reading" on page 225 that demonstrate alternative patterns in their providers.

To demonstrate this pattern in action, let's look at an example and break it down step by step:

```
def load_current_resource

    # Instantiate a new instance of our resource type and assign
    # it to the class-instance variable @current_resource.
    @current_resource = Chef::Resource::MycookbookResourcename.new(
                            new_resource.name)

    # Set the "foo" attribute of current_resource
    current_resource.foo("Bar")

    #Return the @current_resource object
    @current_resource
end
```

The first step we perform in this method definition is to instantiate an instance of the resource type we're describing (in this case, the fictional MycookbookResourcename) and assign it to the @current_resource class instance variable. The single parameter we're passing to the .new method is the name we want to give to the resource we're creating. Note that we're setting this parameter to the name attribute of the new_resource object —this means that our current_resource object will have the same name as the resource defined in our recipes.

 The @current_resource class instance variable is defined in the Chef::Provider class, which lives at lib/chef/provider.rb (*http://bit.ly/ gh-provider*) and is the superclass for Chef::Provider::LWRPBase.

Giving the current_resource object the same name parameter as the new_resource object is technically not a requirement, but doing so makes a lot of sense given that both objects represent different states of the same resource. This convention can also come in particularly useful when the name of a resource actually plays a part in its functionality, as in file "/tmp/foo", where the name of the resource block is actually key to the functionality of the resource rather than just a label.

After we instantiate the @current_resource variable, we can access it using the current_resource method of the provider DSL, and that's exactly what we do next when we're setting the value of current_resource.foo. Just as we saw with the new_resource object in "Desired Resource State" on page 211, Chef automatically defines a method for each attribute of a resource specified in the resource definition, allowing us to set values using current_resource.<attribute_name>.

A good rule of thumb to bear in mind when implementing the load_current_resource method is that the method should *only* contain code needed to instantiate the current_resource object. If you find yourself adding other code to this method, you might want to move it to the provider's action methods.

The final step of our load_current_resource method is to return the created @current_resource class instance variable—the return value of this method isn't actually used by anything, but it's a Ruby convention to always have your methods return an explicit value.

Identifying and Executing Changes

Now that we've identified the current and desired states of our resource, we need to turn that into actionable information to identify changes that our provider needs to make to move our resource toward convergence and how to carry out those actions in an idempotent manner. This process will usually occur inside the action blocks of your provider. The exact implementation of the logic in the action methods of your provider will depend very much on its purpose, but there are some best practices that can help fulfill the criteria we talked about in "Criteria for Customization" on page 10.

Keep it simple, keep it relevant

Don't overcomplicate the logic you're using in your provider, and don't try to cram logic for multiple use cases inside a single action when it might make sense to implement several actions. Consider, for example, a resource that needs to delete a file.

To ensure idempotence, the resource should make sure that the file currently exists before trying to delete it so that we don't waste time trying to delete a nonexistent file. We might implement this by checking that the filename listed in the current_resource.file_name attribute actually exists, like this:

```
action :delete_file do
  if ::File.exists?(current_resource.file_name)
    converge_by("Delete file #{current_resource}") do
      ::File.delete(current_file.file_name)
      new_resource.updated_by_last_action(true)
    end
  end
end
```

Note that in this example, we've also wrapped the ::File.delete line that actually changes the node inside a converge_by block. This method is defined by the Chef::Provider class, and is designed to make changes to the node interact nicely with why-run mode. In why-run mode, the comment passed to the converge_by block is displayed instead of the code inside the block being executed. We'll see this behavior in action later in the chapter.

In this example, we've kept the scope of our action limited and the code inside the `action` block simple and relevant to the task being carried out by the action. This may seem like a basic step to consider, but when coding complex providers it's common to find yourself trying to cram too much functionality into one `action` block when perhaps two should be used. Making time to pause and consider whether an `action` block is both simple and relevant is a useful step in avoiding this sort of "feature creep."

Pick your state object sensibly

As we've seen thus far in this section, there are no hard-and-fast guidelines dictating when you should use attributes of `new_resource` to control your provider logic, and when you should use attributes of `current_resource`. With our `:delete_file` action, for example, we could have checked whether or not the `file_name` attribute of the `new_resource` object already exists. In this specific case, they're describing exactly the same file—the difference between our resource states is whether or not it has been deleted, not its name.

However, intuitively it makes more sense to check whether the current state of the file resource is that it exists—i.e., if `current_resource.file_name` currently exists. Making intuitive distinctions like this when our two resource state objects might contain the same attribute values is quite common when writing LWRPs, especially when dealing with resources that represent artifacts such as packages and files that exist on the node.

Remember the criteria

As a general rule of thumb, when writing the logic to control the behavior of your provider, try to be mindful of the criteria we learned about in "Criteria for Customization" on page 10—think a year down the line to when a new junior employee is getting to grips with Chef and starts trying to understand your provider. Will the way you're checking attributes of `current_resource` make sense to the newcomer, or will he be found wondering why you're creating a file without using the `name` attribute passed to `new_resource` in the recipe?

Because providers are so specific to the task at hand and so flexible in the ways they can be written, especially when it comes to comparing the current and desired state of resources, I argue that these customization criteria are even more important here than when creating Ohai plugins, for example, which have a much more rigidly defined structure. Don't settle for simply writing a provider that works. If you put in the time and effort to write a modular, understandable provider that will make as much sense to you in six months as it does now, that effort will pay itself off many times over in the future.

Informing Chef About Updates

So far, we've learned how to identify and load the current and desired states of our resource and examined how to turn those states into actionable information to guide the steps our provider needs to take to converge the resource. The final piece of the puzzle is actually telling Chef that our resource has been updated—that is, when we've made a change or changes have occurred to converge our resource into its desired state.

This part of the process is actually very simple—we've already used it in "LWRP Example 2: Extending the Provider" on page 205. The object returned by `new_resource` (of type `Chef::Resource::<CookbooknameResourcename>`) defines a method called `upda ted_by_last_action`, to which we pass the parameter `true` like this:

```
new_resource.updated_by_last_action(true)
```

Making this method call when our provider has made changes lets Chef know that our resource required changes to bring it into convergence with its desired state, and that, as the method name suggests, it was updated by the last action.

 When we use a `converge_by` block to make our provider compatible with why-run mode, it's not strictly necessary to call `new_re source.updated_by_last_action`—the `converge_by` block does this for us automatically. I've included the explicit method call in these examples for clarity.

In this section, we've covered a number of concepts and techniques to level up our providers. We've learned how to identify the current and desired state of our resources and access this information in our provider code. We then looked at how to turn this state information into actionable guidance for implementing idempotent and convergent actions in our provider, finishing off with how to let Chef know when our resource has been updated.

Now let's put our newfound knowledge into practice. In the next section, we're going to implement a convergent, idempotent native provider using the techniques and methods we've covered in this section.

LWRP Example 3: Native Provider

Now that we've learned why knowing the current and desired resource states are so important for ensuring idempotent and convergent Chef runs and how we can make use of this information, let's look at how to put these ideas into practice by creating a native LWRP to help our friends at AwesomeInc with another issue they're trying to solve.

Example 3: Preparing the Resource and Provider

The team at AwesomeInc have identified the need to create an LRWP that will allow them to manage backups of the configuration file used by their `awesomeator` tool. They want the new LWRP to be able to perform two tasks:

- Create a compressed backup of the configuration file if one that is less than 24 hours old does not already exist.
- Extract a previously compressed backup to the specified location.

Let's start off by creating the resource definition for our new LWRP. Paste the contents of Example 8-8 into */tmp/part3_examples/cookbooks/testcookbook/resources/backup.rb.*

Example 8-8. /tmp/part3_examples/cookbooks/testcookbook/resources/backup.rb

```
actions :compress, :extract
default_action :compress

attribute :name, :kind_of => String, :name_attribute => true
attribute :backup_file, :kind_of => String

attr_accessor :exists
```

As we see here, our resource definition defines two actions, `:compress` and `:extract`, and three attributes, `name`, `source_dir`, and `destination_dir`. Because we've already identified the actions that our resource will contain, we can also define a provider skeleton to support it. Paste the code in Example 8-9 into */tmp/part3_examples/cookbooks/testcookbook/providers/backup.rb.*

Example 8-9. /tmp/part3_examples/cookbooks/testcookbook/providers/backup.rb

```
def whyrun_supported? ❶
  true
end

action :compress do
end

action :extract do
end
```

❶   As we're going to need to run our provider in why-run mode, we're defining the `whyrun_supported` method we met in "Provider DSL" on page 203 to let Chef know that our provider is compatible with why-run.

In our previous example, when we created a provider using cookbook resources, at this point we were able to go ahead and add code to the `action` methods of our provider to populate it with code. Because this provider is going to contain native Ruby code, however, we first need to write its `load_current_resource` method to let Chef know how to determine the current state of our resource, as we saw in "Current Resource State" on page 212.

Example 3: The load_current_resource Method

As we saw earlier, when we want to create a provider containing native Ruby code, we can't depend on built-in cookbook resources to announce whether or not they've been updated—we have to determine this ourselves. The first step in this process is to create a `load_current_resource` method for our provider that represents the current state of the resource defined by our recipe code.

Remember, this method will not actually contain any logic to control the *behavior* of the provider. As we saw in "Current Resource State" on page 212, the `new_resource` method defined by the LWRP DSL returns an object of type `Chef::Resource::Test cookbookBackup` with attributes set to the values defined in our recipe code. All we want the `load_current_resource` method to do here is to create another `Chef::Re source::TestcookbookBackup` object that represents the current state of our resource.

In this case, our resource definition defines two attributes—`name` and `backup_file`—so correspondingly, our `load_current_resource` method needs to instantiate our resource object and set those attributes. In this case, the `name` and `backup_file` attributes will have identical values for both the `current_resource` and `new_resource` objects, as both describe the same files. Note that none of our attributes give any indication as to whether or not the files described by these attributes actually exist—that comes later, in our `action` methods.

Let's define a `load_current_resource` method for our provider now. Paste the contents of Example 8-10 into */tmp/part3_examples/cookbooks/testcookbook/providers/back-up.rb*.

Example 8-10. /tmp/part3_examples/cookbooks/testcookbook/providers/backup.rb

```
def whyrun_supported?
  true
end

def load_current_resource
  # Instantiate and populate our @current_resource object
  @current_resource = Chef::Resource::TestcookbookBackup.new(new_resource.name) ❶
  @current_resource.backup_file(new_resource.backup_file) ❷
end

action :compress do
end
```

```
action :extract do
end
```

❶ We begin by instantiating our `Chef::Resource::TestcookbookBackup` class, passing it `new_resource.name` as its parameter and assigning it to `@current_re` `source`. The parameter passed to this object becomes its `.name` attribute so we don't need to manually set this attribute ourselves.

❷ Next, we call the `backup_file` method of `@current_resource` and assign it the value of `new_resource.backup_file`. This pattern of assigning attribute values of `@current_resource` the same values as those in `new_resource` is particularly common when dealing with resources describing single objects such as packages, files, or users where there are no attributes of the resource to determine whether or not the objects exist, and so on.

Now that we've defined our resource and provider skeletons and constructed a `load_current_data` method to describe the state of our resource, we're ready to actually make use of these resource states and add some code to our provider's `action` methods.

Example 3: Coding the Actions

Before we can write the code to power the `action` methods of our provider, we need to define exactly what it's going to do. The people at AwesomeInc want their tool to behave in the following ways:

- When the `:compress` action is used, a backup file will be created using *gzip* at *<backup_file>* that contains the file specified by *<name>*.

- When the `:extract` action is used, a backup file at *<backup_file>* will be extracted to *<name>*, again using *gzip*.

With this behavior defined, we're ready to start coding. Paste the code in Example 8-11 into */tmp/part3_examples/cookbooks/testcookbook/providers/backup.rb*.

Example 8-11. /tmp/part3_examples/cookbooks/testcookbook/providers/backup.rb

```
require 'zlib'

def whyrun_supported?
  true
end

def load_current_resource ❶
  # Instantiate and populate our @current_resource object
  @current_resource = Chef::Resource::TestcookbookBackup.new(new_resource.name)
  @current_resource.backup_file(new_resource.backup_file)
end
```

```
action :compress do
  # Check if the file to back up already exists
  if ::File.exists?(current_resource.name) ❷

    # If the backup file exists, calculate its age
    if ::File.exists?(current_resource.backup_file) ❸
      backup_file_age_hours = (Time.now -
        ::File.mtime(current_resource.backup_file))/60/60
    end

    # if the backup file doesn't exist or is over 24 hours old
    if !::File.exists?(current_resource.backup_file) || backup_file_age_hours > 24 ❹
      # Wrap changing logic in converge_by so it works in why-run mode
      converge_by("Create backup file #{ new_resource.backup_file }") do ❺
        # Compress the specified file with the specified name
        Chef::Log.info("Compressing #{new_resource.name}...")
        Zlib::GzipWriter.open(new_resource.backup_file) do |gz|
          gz.write IO.binread(new_resource.name)
        end
      end

      # Indicate to chef that we updated new_resource because we changed the node
      new_resource.updated_by_last_action(true) ❻
    else
      Chef::Log.warn("Backup file #{new_resource.backup_file} is only " +
        " #{backup_file_age_hours.round(2)} hours old. (Action will be skipped).")
    end
  else
    Chef::Log.warn("Can't find #{new_resource.name} to back up. " +
      " (Action will be skipped).")
  end
end

action :extract do
  # If the backup file we asked for exists
  if ::File.exists?(current_resource.backup_file)

    # Unless the destination file already exists
    unless ::File.exists?(current_resource.name)

      # Wrap changing logic in converge_by so it works in why-run mode
      converge_by("Extract backup file #{ new_resource.backup_file }") do
        # Extract the backup file to the specified file
        Chef::Log.info("Extracting #{new_resource.backup_file}...")
        ::File.open(current_resource.backup_file) do |f|
          gz = Zlib::GzipReader.new(f)
          ::File.open(current_resource.name, 'w') { |file| file.write(gz.read) }
          gz.close
        end
      end

      # Indicate to chef that we updated new_resource because we changed the node
```

```
        new_resource.updated_by_last_action(true) ❼
    else
        Chef::Log.warn("Destination file #{new_resource.name} " +
            "already exists. (Action will be skipped).")
    end
  else
   Chef::Log.warn("Can't find backup file #{new_resource.backup_file} " +
     "to extract. (Action will be skipped).")
  end
end
```

❶   Here we're instantiating a new instance of our resource and populating it with data to represent the current state of the node. Notice that because we're dealing with filenames, we're able to use the attributes defined in the recipe (accessed here through new_resource) to populate the current resource.

❷ ❸   Here we see several examples of using attributes of current_resource to guide
❹   the behavior of our resource ("If the file described by current_resource.name exists, do this…").

❺   Here we're wrapping our *changing* actions inside a converge_by block so that when run in why-run mode they tell us what they *would* do.

❻ ❼   Finally, we call the updated_by_last_action method of the new_resource object to let Chef know that our provider considers the resource to have been updated during this run—in our case, this means that we created a backup file.

::File Versus File

In Example 8-11, observant readers may have noticed that all of a sudden I've started to prefix method calls to Ruby's built-in File class with :: (i.e., ::File.open instead of the File.open syntax we've used elsewhere).

This is necessary due to Ruby's class namespacing rules. As we'll explore in greater detail in Chapter 9, LWRP providers actually exist under the Chef::Provider namespace. This means that any method calls we make look first in the Chef::Provider namespace our class lives in before moving on to other Ruby methods found in the standard library.

In the case of the method calls to File that we're making here, this means that Ruby will start by trying to call the Chef::Provider::File class before it ever gets to the File class in the standard library that we actually want to use. In this specific case, the Chef::Provider::File class actually exists—it's the provider for Chef's built-in file resource and is totally unrelated to Ruby's built-in File class!

The :: prefix we're using in front of the File class here is known as the *scope resolution operator* and indicates that we want to look for the File class in the *global* scope—

---

essentially, we skip looking for that class in our current namespace of Chef::Provid er first.

Next, let's add a new recipe to allow us to test out our new native LWRP in isolation. Paste the code in Example 8-12 into */tmp/part3_examples/cookbooks/testcookbook/ recipes/awesomeator_backup.rb*.

Example 8-12. /tmp/part3_examples/cookbooks/testcookbook/recipes/awesomeator_backup.rb

```
testcookbook_backup "/etc/awesomeator.conf" do
  backup_file "/tmp/awesomeator.gz"
  action :compress
end
```

Now we're ready to try a Chef run to try out our new LWRP!

```
$> chef-client --once --why-run --local-mode \
   --config /tmp/part3_examples/client.rb \
   --override-runlist testcookbook::awesomeator_backup
Starting Chef Client, version 11.10.4
[Thu, 08 May 2014 09:22:13 +0000] WARN: Run List override has been provided.
[Thu, 08 May 2014 09:22:13 +0000] WARN: Original Run List: []
[Thu, 08 May 2014 09:22:13 +0000] WARN: Overridden Run List:
   [recipe[testcookbook::awesomeator_backup]]
resolving cookbooks for run list: ["testcookbook::awesomeator_backup"]
Synchronizing Cookbooks:
   - testcookbook
Compiling Cookbooks...
Converging 1 resources
Recipe: testcookbook::awesomeator_backup
   * testcookbook_backup[/etc/awesomeator.conf] action compress
[Thu, 08 May 2014 09:22:14 +0000] WARN: Can't find
   /etc/awesomeator.conf to back up.  (Action will be skipped).
 (up to date)
[Thu, 08 May 2014 09:22:14 +0000] WARN: Skipping final node save
because override_runlist was given

Running handlers:
Running handlers complete

Chef Client finished, 0/1 resources would have been updated
```

As we can see in this output, when the :compress action of our LWRP is executed, our provider code checks to see if the requested file, */etc/awesomeator.conf*, exists. When the file is found to be missing, our provider prints a warning log message, and our resource is shown as up-to-date in the output of the Chef run. Now let's try creating the missing file and see how the output of our resource changes. Run the following command (this may require sudo):

```
$> echo "Chef is Awesome" > /etc/awesomeator.conf
```

Now that the file that our resource requires is present, let's run the same Chef run again and observe how the output changes:

```
$> chef-client --once --why-run --local-mode \
  --config /tmp/part3_examples/client.rb \
  --override-runlist testcookbook::awesomeator_backup
Starting Chef Client, version 11.10.4
[Thu, 08 May 2014 10:00:39 +0000] WARN: Run List override has been provided.
[Thu, 08 May 2014 10:00:39 +0000] WARN: Original Run List: []
[Thu, 08 May 2014 10:00:39 +0000] WARN: Overridden Run List:
  [recipe[testcookbook::awesomeator_backup]]
resolving cookbooks for run list: ["testcookbook::awesomeator_backup"]
Synchronizing Cookbooks:
  - testcookbook
Compiling Cookbooks...
Converging 1 resources
Recipe: testcookbook::awesomeator_backup
  * testcookbook_backup[/etc/awesomeator.conf] action compress
    - Would Create backup file /tmp/awesomeator_backup.gz

[Thu, 08 May 2014 10:00:39 +0000] WARN: Skipping final node save
  because override_runlist was given

Running handlers:
Running handlers complete

Chef Client finished, 1/1 resources would have been updated
```

This time, we see that when the :compress action of our resource is executed, the file is present: our compressed backup file is created, and the resource is shown as *updated* in the run output.

In this example, we've seen how to create a native provider without the use of any built-in cookbook resource types. We've made our provider aware of the current state of our resource using the load_current_resource method, and how to use this information to implement an idempotent and convergent resource. We've also seen how to make our provider why-run compatible using the converge_by method so that it can be tested without changing the underlying node.

 If you find yourself writing LWRPs that consist mainly of native Ruby code, you may wish to consider writing a heavyweight provider instead. We'll examine when you might want to choose an HWRP over an LWRP in the next chapter (see "Why Write HWRPs?" on page 228).

Summary and Further Reading

In this chapter, we've learned about a number of different aspects of creating our own lightweight resources and providers. We started off by reviewing the structure of cookbooks and how resources and providers fit in, before moving on to examine how Chef uses providers to implement multiplatform functionality.

We then created a simple LWRP skeleton of our own and ran it in a recipe, before diving deeper into the resource and provider DSLs that power LWRPs in Chef. We used this knowledge to extend our provider skeleton to provide a solution to one of AwesomeInc's problems. After a deep dive into the factors we have to consider when implementing idempotence and convergence in native providers, we used this knowledge to create a native provider of our own.

Readers interested in looking further into LWRPs, and especially those interested in exploring different implementation patterns for the load_current_resource method, may wish to explore the following cookbooks:

dynect
> The dynect cookbook (*http://bit.ly/gh-dynect*) is used to configure the various DNS services supported by the Dyn platform. It implements an LWRP to allow DNS operations such as adding A or CNAME records to be included as resource blocks in recipes.

rbenv
> Fletcher Nichol's rbenv cookbook (*http://bit.ly/chef-rbenv*) is used to manage the *rbenv* Ruby version management tool. It defines a number of LWRPs to support a variety of operations, such as installing new Ruby versions and installing plugins.

chef_handler
> The chef_handler cookbook (*http://bit.ly/chef-handler*), which we already touched on in "Handlers: Summary and Further Reading" on page 136, defines an LWRP to allow report and exception handlers to be enabled in recipe code rather than by manually editing *client.rb*.

homebrew
> The homebrew cookbook (*http://bit.ly/homebrew-ckbk*) is used to add support to Chef for the homebrew package management system. It defines LWRPs to support a number of homebrew operations, such as installing "tap" repositories and the Cask software manager.

hostsfile
> The hostsfile cookbook (*http://bit.ly/gh-hostsfile*) is used to manage your */etc/hosts* file (or Windows equivalent) through Chef. It defines an LWRP to support adding hostsfile entries in a number of different configurations.

In the next chapter, we're going to dive deeper into the world of heavyweight resources and providers, which do not use the abstraction layer provided by the LWRP DSL but rather make use of native Ruby classes to leverage the full power of Chef's resource and provider model at the expense of the simplicity afforded by LWRPs.

## CHAPTER 9

Heavyweight Resources and Providers

In Chapter 8, we learned how lightweight resources and providers give us an easy and flexible way to create our own resources and providers, using a DSL to abstract away much of the complexity involved in interacting with Chef's resource and provider classes. In this chapter, we're going to learn about heavyweight resources and providers, which trade the convenience and ease of use afforded by the LWRP abstraction layer for being able to leverage the full power of Chef's resource and provider classes.

Heavyweight resources and providers are written in native Ruby, and are particularly useful when the behavior of the LWRP DSL doesn't quite fit your needs, or when you want to extend one of Chef's built-in resource types. In this chapter, we'll learn:

- How the structure of an HWRP differs from that of an LWRP
- What the components of an HWRP are
- How to create your own HWRPs
- How to extend existing Chef resource types
- How to make use of Chef's provider mapping to have Chef automatically use your provider

As with previous chapters, we'll also augment our learning by working through a series of code examples to help our friends at AwesomeInc with some of the issues they have been experiencing.

Because LWRPs and HWRPs share some underlying commonalities, I recommend that, if you haven't already done so, you read through Chapter 8 before starting this chapter. Much of the material in the earlier sections of Chapter 8 is equally applicable to both LWRPs and HWRPs, and we will be extending some of the examples we created in that chapter here. Reading through Chapter 8 along with this chapter will help to give you a deeper understanding of LWRPs, HWRPs, and how they integrate with Chef.

Introduction to HWRPs

HWRPs in Chef are native Ruby classes that are used to implement resources and providers in Chef. The *heavyweight* part of their name comes from the fact that they do not use a DSL to abstract away any of the structure and code needed to do so in the way that LWRPs do, but rather interact directly with Chef's resource and provider classes. This means that HWRPs are a little more time-consuming and complex to write than LWRPs, but this must be balanced against the increased power and functionality that HWRPs afford.

Why Write HWRPs?

Given that we've already said that HWRPs are a little harder to write than LWRPs, why would we ever really want to create them? Couldn't we just get by with LWRPs and live without that extra power and functionality we mentioned? While this is certainly possible for many use cases, there are two scenarios in particular where writing an HWRP is either necessary, or a better option:

Extending built-in resources
> One of the most common uses for HWRPs is to add additional providers to Chef's built-in resources. Let's say, for example, we want to add support to Chef's pack age resource for a new package management system. If we used the LWRP DSL, there would be no way to tell Chef that our provider should belong to the pack age resource instead of a resource in the *resources* directory of the same cookbook —the LWRP DSL simply doesn't allow us to do this.

> If we write a heavyweight provider using native Ruby, however, adding our provider to the package resource is as simple as inheriting from a particular superclass. We'll learn exactly how this is done in "HWRP Example 2: Extending the package Resource" on page 251.

Writing native providers
> The other common use case for creating HWRPs instead of LWRPS is when we are writing providers that use native code instead of cookbook resource blocks. If our provider makes use of cookbook resource blocks, the convenience afforded by the

LWRP DSL allows us to create compact and easily understandable providers that leverage the wide range of functionality provided by these resources. When we use native Ruby code in our providers, however, things can become more confusing. As we saw in the last chapter, it is entirely possible to build LWRPs using native Ruby code, but the end result is a somewhat confusing mix of methods and blocks defined by the LWRP DSL interacting with methods and blocks defined by the underlying `Chef::Provider` superclass interacting with the native code we've added ourselves.

If our provider is written in the heavyweight style using purely native Ruby, however, the class structure is much more obvious—everything looks like the standard Ruby classes we're used to, and we eliminate potentially confusing interactions between our code, the LWRP DSL, and the superclasses from which it inherits. A good rule of thumb when writing providers is the more native Ruby code in your provider, the more you should give consideration to writing an HWRP instead of an LWRP.

HWRPs in Cookbooks

The LWRPs we met in Chapter 8 locate their resources and providers in the *resources* and *providers* directories of cookbooks, respectively. During a chef-client run, Chef will parse the contents of these directories and convert our LWRPs to their respective native Ruby classes behind the scenes before executing the code they contain. Because our HWRP is already going to be defining native Ruby classes, we don't want Chef trying to use its LWRP parsing magic on our HWRP classes.

For this reason, the components of our HWRP (both resource and provider) live in the *libraries* directory of our cookbooks. As you'll recall from "Load Cookbook Data" on page 68, library classes—i.e., anything defined in a cookbook's *libraries* directory—are loaded right at the beginning of this stage of the Chef run process, before attributes, resources, providers, or definitions.

When Chef loads files from the *libraries* directory, it uses Ruby's built in `Kernel.load` method (as we saw in "What Is a Library?" on page 179) to load the class definition file into memory. This makes it available for any other Ruby class to use, and is central to how HWRPs work in Chef.

Now that we've looked at the potential use cases for HWRPs and when these might be a good option to choose, let's dive right in and learn how to create them.

HWRP Example 1: Getting Started with HWRPs

In "LWRP Example 3: Native Provider" on page 217, we created the `awesomeator_back up` LWRP for our friends at AwesomeInc, and they're quite happy with it—the native provider we created satisfied the original requirements they gave, and has been working well up to this point. However, the team at AwesomeInc wants to make some changes to the provider to add some more complex behavior so that the resource can:

- Create a compressed backup of a configuration file if one does not already exist that is under 24 hours old.
- Keep a configurable number of previous backups in addition to the most current.
- Extract a previously compressed backup to the specified location.
- Optionally clean up old backups after extraction.

In addition to the :compress and :extract actions and the name and backup_file attributes we defined in Example 8-8, this new behavior requires the addition of two new attributes, num_backups and cleanup.

 If you haven't already done so, I recommend skimming through the LWRP examples listed in Chapter 8 to familiarize yourself with the behavior of the existing resources and providers we will convert to HWRPs before continuing with this chapter.

The folks at AwesomeInc are finding the mix of native code and the LWRP DSL a little hard to work with when adding this new functionality, so they have decided to convert their LWRP to an HWRP, which they've decided to call awesome_backup. In this example, we're going to start off the process of creating a new HWRP by creating the skeleton resource and provider that will power this new HWRP.

 Before working through the examples in this chapter, please make sure you've followed the steps in "Creating a Test Environment" on page 167 to create your test environment.

Example 1: Creating a Resource

Let's start off by creating our skeleton resource definition. Since heavyweight resources and providers both live under the cookbook's *libraries* directory, I prefer to give the filename a suffix indicating which is which. To that end, paste the code in Example 9-1 into */tmp/part3_examples/cookbooks/testcookbook/libraries/ awesome_backup_resource.rb*.

Example 9-1. /tmp/part3_examples/cookbooks/testcookbook/libraries/awesome_back-up_resource.rb

```
class Chef
  class Resource ❶
```

```
class AwesomeBackup < Chef::Resource ❷

  provides :awesome_backup, :on_platforms => :all ❸

  def initialize(name, run_context=nil)
    super ❹
    @resource_name = :awesome_backup ❺
    @allowed_actions = [:compress, :extract] ❻
    @action = :compress

    # Now we need to set up any resource defaults ❼
    @name = name
    @backup_file = nil
    @cleanup = false
    @num_backups = 3

  end

  # Create methods to get and set our attribute values ❽
  def name(arg=nil)
    set_or_return(:name, arg, :kind_of => String)
  end

  def backup_file(arg=nil)
    set_or_return(:backup_file, arg, :kind_of => String)
  end

  def cleanup(arg=nil)
    set_or_return(:cleanup, arg, :kind_of => [TrueClass, FalseClass])
  end

  def num_backups(arg=nil)
    set_or_return(:num_backups, arg, :kind_of => Fixnum)
  end
end
  end
end
```

❶   Here we're specifying that our class will live inside the Chef::Resource class—this is known as class *nesting*. In Ruby, we nest classes in this way to indicate that our class will only ever represent a subclass of the class it is nested inside (in this case, Chef::Resource). Defining our class in this way means that we can only ever refer to it as Chef::Resource::AwesomeBackup and never just as AwesomeBackup. Functionally, this works in the same way as the module namespaces we learned about in "Modules as Namespaces" on page 38. This namespacing is necessary so that our *resource* class called AwesomeBackup does not clash with our *provider* class called AwesomeBackup, which we will be creating next.

❷ Our AwesomeBackup class inherits from the Chef::Resource superclass, which lives at *lib/chef/resource.rb* (*http://bit.ly/gh-resourcerb*). This is the superclass from which all resources in Chef inherit, and it's also the superclass of the LWRP resource DSL we met in the last chapter. Inheriting from Chef::Resource is what marks our class as a *heavyweight resource.*

❸ Here we're calling the provides method of the Chef::Resource class to tell Chef that our resource provides the awesome_backup resource on all supported platforms. We can optionally pass specific platforms in the :on_platforms parameter of this method to indicate that our resource only works on specific operating systems, such as linux or windows—the default behavior is for no such constraint to be set.

❹ In the initialize method of our resource, we're first calling the built-in Ruby method super. This method executes the equivalently named method (in this case, initialize) of our superclass, Chef::Resource, before continuing.

❺ Here we're setting the @resource_name class instance variable (defined in Chef::Resource) to let Chef know the name of the resource we're providing that will be used in cookbooks.

❻ Next, we set the @allowed_actions class instance variable to specify the actions our resource will permit, and the @action class instance variable to specify the default action.

❼ Here, we initialize the default values for all of our resource attributes. Assigning @name = name is equivalent to the :name_attribute => true parameter assignment we used in our LWRP examples. All other attributes are given default values, or nil if no default value is desired.

❽ Finally, we define a method for each of our attributes. These methods function in much the same way as a Ruby attr_accessor method, but they make use of the powerful set_or_return method defined by Chef::Resource, which augments standard get/set behavior to allow us to specify the same attribute validation parameters we used in our LWRP (see "Resource DSL" on page 201) in addition to just setting or returning the value of the attribute.

Note that in our resource definition here we called the class AwesomeBackup, rather than the name of TestcookbookAwesomebackup it would have been given if we used an LWRP. The names we give our classes when writing HWRPs are left entirely up to us—the automatic naming of classes in LWRPs is a convenience to avoid the need to create full class definitions.

Now that we've created our resource definition, we're going to need a skeleton provider to go along with it before we can try out our new HWRP in a Chef run.

Example 1: Creating a Provider

As with our LWRP examples in Chapter 8, we're only going to create the skeleton of our provider here; we'll add code to power its `action` methods later in the chapter.

Much in the same way that Chef automatically locates a matching provider to go with resources when creating LWRPs, when we create HWRPs Chef knows to look for a provider with a matching class name to the resource being used. Because HWRPs are Ruby classes, however, the actual name of the file doesn't have to match (in fact, it can't, because both live in the *libraries* directory).

 It's actually possible to override this automatic provider selection behavior—we'll learn how to do this in "Advanced HWRP Tricks" on page 240, along with how to tap into the Chef provider mapping we learned about in "Automatically Choosing Providers" on page 193.

Sticking with the sensible naming convention we used for our heavyweight resource, paste the code for our provider skeleton, shown in Example 9-2, into */tmp/part3_examples/cookbooks/testcookbook/libraries/awesome_backup_provider.rb*.

Example 9-2. /tmp/part3_examples/cookbooks/testcookbook/libraries/awesome_backup_provider.rb

```
class Chef
  class Provider ❶
    class AwesomeBackup < Chef::Provider ❷

      def whyrun_supported? ❸
        true
      end

      def load_current_resource ❹
        @current_resource = Chef::Resource::AwesomeBackup.new(new_resource.name)
        @current_resource.backup_file(new_resource.backup_file)
        @current_resource.cleanup(new_resource.cleanup)
        @current_resource.num_backups(new_resource.num_backups)
      end

      # Define methods for our actions ❺
      def action_compress

      end

      def action_extract

      end

    end
```

```
    end
end
```

❶ Here we state that our class will live inside the `Chef::Provider` class, in the same way that we did with our resource and the `Chef::Resource` class in Example 9-1.

❷ Our `AwesomeBackup` class inherits from the `Chef::Provider` superclass, which lives at *lib/chef/provider.rb* (*http://bit.ly/gh-provider*). This is the superclass from which all providers in Chef inherit, and it's also the superclass of the LWRP provider DSL we met in the last chapter. Inheriting from `Chef::Provider` is what marks our class as a heavyweight provider.

❸ Just as we did with our LWRP examples, we're defining the `whyrun_supported` method here to let Chef know that our provider class will act correctly when Chef is run in why-run mode.

❹ Here we're creating the `load_current_resource` method for our provider, just as we did for our native LWRP in "LWRP Example 3: Native Provider" on page 217. The method is actually identical to the method we defined in our LWRP example, aside from the addition of two extra attributes here. Note that when creating a heavyweight provider, the `load_current_resource` method is mandatory, and must be defined—the LWRP DSL overrides this method to make it optional, but heavyweight providers inherit the method directly from `Chef::Provider`, which will raise an exception if `load_current_resource` is not overridden.

❺ Finally, we define empty method bodies for our actions. These are very similar to the `action :foo` blocks we used in our LWRP provider, except in heavyweight providers the block becomes a full method named `action_foo`.

We've only created a skeleton provider with empty `action` methods so far, but this gives us a complete enough HWRP to be able to add it to a recipe, as we'll see next.

Example 1: Using Our HWRP in a Recipe

Now that we have our heavyweight resource definition and provider skeleton, we can try it out in a Chef run and make sure that it works properly. We're going to create a new recipe under our `testcookbook` cookbook called `awesomeator_backup_hwrp` to try out our new resource. Paste the contents of Example 9-3 into */tmp/part3_examples/ cookbooks/testcookbook/recipes/awesomeator_backup_hwrp.rb*.

Example 9-3. /tmp/part3_examples/cookbooks/testcookbook/recipes/awesomea-tor_backup_hwrp.rb

```
awesome_backup "/etc/awesomeator.conf" do
  backup_file "/tmp/awesomeator.gz"
end
```

Now let's kick off a Chef run with our new recipe and see what happens:

```
$> chef-client --once --why-run --local-mode \
  --config /tmp/part3_examples/client.rb \
  --override-runlist testcookbook::awesomeator_backup_hwrp

Starting Chef Client, version 11.10.4
[Tue, 13 May 2014 14:13:48 +0000] WARN: Run List override has been provided.
[Tue, 13 May 2014 14:13:48 +0000] WARN: Original Run List: []
[Tue, 13 May 2014 14:13:48 +0000] WARN: Overridden Run List:
  [recipe[testcookbook::awesomeator_backup_hwrp]]
resolving cookbooks for run list: ["testcookbook::awesomeator_backup_hwrp"]
Synchronizing Cookbooks:
  - testcookbook
Compiling Cookbooks...
Converging 1 resources
Recipe: testcookbook::awesomeator_backup_hwrp
  * awesome_backup[/etc/awesomeator.conf] action compress (up to date)
[Tue, 13 May 2014 14:13:48 +0000] WARN: Skipping final node save
  because override_runlist was given

Running handlers:
Running handlers complete

Chef Client finished, 0/1 resources would have been updated
```

As we can see here, when our recipe was executed, Chef called the :compress action of our awesome_backup resource, which reported that it was already up-to-date because its action methods contained no code to indicate otherwise. Now that we've verified that our skeleton HWRP works as we expect in a Chef run, we're ready to extend it by adding the code to our action methods to provide the functionality the people at AwesomeInc is looking for.

Example 1: Extending the Provider

With our resource definition and skeleton provider defined and tested in a Chef run, we're ready to add code to the action methods of our provider class to provide the functionality AwesomeInc are looking for.

In this example, we utilize the same code that we used in the action methods of our native provider in "Example 3: Coding the Actions" on page 220, but extend it to meet AwesomeInc's new requirements. Novice or inexperienced Ruby coders may find it helpful to make sure they understand the code in Example 8-11 before proceeding with this example.

Let's recap what each action will do based on the requirements we identified in "HWRP Example 1: Getting Started with HWRPs" on page 229:

`:compress`

The `:compress` action of our provider should carry out the following steps:

- If an existing backup file (named in the `backup_file` attribute) exists and was created more than 24 hours ago, rotate it to *<backup_file>-1*.
    - *<backup_file>-1* should be moved to to *<backup_file>-2*, and so on, up to a maximum of the value specified by the `num_backups` parameter.
    - The file specified by the `name` attribute should then be compressed to *<back up_file>*.

- If no existing file is found, or the existing file was created within the last 24 hours, no further action will be taken.

`:extract`

The `:extract` action of our provider should carry out the following steps:

- If a backup file named according to the `backup_file` attribute exists, extract its contents to the file indicated by the `name` attribute.

- If the `cleanup` attribute has a value of `true`, remove the backup file after extraction.

Now that we've defined the behavior we want our `action` methods to implement, let's get coding! Paste the code in Example 9-4 into */tmp/part3_examples/cookbooks/test-cookbook/libraries/awesome_backup_provider.rb*:

Example 9-4. /tmp/part3_examples/cookbooks/testcookbook/libraries/awesome_back-up_provider.rb

```
require 'fileutils'

class Chef
  class Provider
    class AwesomeBackup < Chef::Provider

      def whyrun_supported?
        true
      end

      def load_current_resource
        @current_resource = Chef::Resource::AwesomeBackup.new(new_resource.name)
        @current_resource.backup_file(new_resource.backup_file)
        @current_resource.cleanup(new_resource.cleanup)
        @current_resource.num_backups(new_resource.num_backups)
      end

      # Define methods for our actions
      def action_compress
```

```ruby
# Check if the file to back up already exists
if ::File.exists?(current_resource.name) ❶

   # If the backup file exists, calculate its age
   if ::File.exists?(current_resource.backup_file)
     backup_file_age_hours = (Time.now -
        ::File.mtime(current_resource.backup_file))/60/60
   end

  # If the backup file is over 24 hours old (which also means
  # that it exists)
  if !::File.exists?(current_resource.backup_file) ||
    backup_file_age_hours > 24

    # Check if the number of backups we want to keep is > 0
    # before trying to rotate
    if @current_resource.num_backups < 0
      # Wrap changing logic in converge_by so it works in why-run mode
      converge_by("Rotate backup files "+
        "(retaining maximum #{@current_resource.num_backups})") do ❷
        # Rotate existing backup files
        (@current_resource.num_backups - 1).downto(1).each do |f|
          if ::File.exists?("#{current_resource.backup_file}-#{f}")
            ::FileUtils.mv("#{current_resource.backup_file}-#{f}",
              "#{current_resource.backup_file}-#{f+1}")
          end
          if ::File.exists?(current_resource.backup_file)
            # Rotate current backup file
            ::FileUtils.mv(current_resource.backup_file,
              "#{current_resource.backup_file}-1")
          end
        end
      end
    end

    # Wrap changing logic in converge_by so it works in why-run mode
    converge_by("Create backup file #{ new_resource.backup_file }") do
      # Compress the specified file with the specified name
      Chef::Log.info("Compressing #{new_resource.name}...")
      Zlib::GzipWriter.open(new_resource.backup_file) do |gz|
        gz.write IO.binread(new_resource.name)
      end
    end

    # Indicate to Chef that we updated new_resource because we
    # changed the node
    new_resource.updated_by_last_action(true) ❸
  else
    Chef::Log.warn("Backup file #{new_resource.backup_file} is only " +
      " #{backup_file_age_hours.round(2)} hours old. " +
      "(Action will be skipped).")
  end
```

```ruby
      else
        Chef::Log.warn("Can't find #{new_resource.name} to back up. " +
          " (Action will be skipped).")
      end
    end

    def action_extract
      # If the backup file we asked for exists
      if ::File.exists?(current_resource.backup_file)
        # Unless the destination file already exists
        unless ::File.exists?(current_resource.name)
          # Wrap changing logic in converge_by so it works in why-run mode
          converge_by("Extract backup file #{ new_resource.backup_file }") do
            # Extract the backup file to the specified file
            Chef::Log.info("Extracting #{new_resource.backup_file}...")
            ::File.open(current_resource.backup_file) do |f|
              gz = Zlib::GzipReader.new(f)
              ::File.open(current_resource.name,
                'w') do |file|
                file.write(gz.read)
              end
            end
          end

          # If the current_resource.cleanup attribute is true
          if current_resource.cleanup
            # Wrap changing logic in converge_by so it works in why-run mode
            converge_by("Delete backup file #{ new_resource.backup_file }") do
              # Delete the backup file
              ::File.delete(new_resource.backup_file)
            end
          end

          # Indicate to Chef that we updated new_resource because we
          # changed the node
          new_resource.updated_by_last_action(true)

        else
          Chef::Log.warn("Destination file #{new_resource.name} " +
            "already exists.  (Action will be skipped).")
        end
      else
        Chef::Log.warn("Can't find backup file #{new_resource.backup_file} " +
          "to extract.  (Action will be skipped).")
      end
    end
  end
end
```

❶ Here we see several examples of using attributes of current_resource to guide the behavior of our resource ("If the file described by current_resource.name exists, do this…").

❷ Here we're wrapping our *changing* actions inside a converge_by block so that when run in why-run mode they tell us what they *would* do.

❸ Finally, we call the updated_by_last_action method of the new_resource object to let Chef know that our provider considers the resource to have been updated during this run—in our case, this means that we created a backup file.

With our new code in place, it's time to try out our expanded provider and see it in action. Before we do that, however, let's create the */tmp/awesomeator.conf* file that our resource uses as its name attribute—otherwise, we'll get a message saying that the file we were trying to compress didn't exist. Run the following command to create this file (may require sudo):

```
$> echo "Chef is Awesome" > /tmp/awesomeator.conf
```

Now let's try another Chef run on our testcookbook::awesomeator_backup_hwrp recipe and see what the output looks like:

```
$> chef-client --once --why-run --local-mode \
  --config /tmp/part3_examples/client.rb \
  --override-runlist testcookbook::awesomeator_backup_hwrp
Starting Chef Client, version 11.10.4
[Tue, 13 May 2014 17:08:46 +0000] WARN: Run List override has been provided.
[Tue, 13 May 2014 17:08:46 +0000] WARN: Original Run List: []
[Tue, 13 May 2014 17:08:46 +0000] WARN: Overridden Run List:
  [recipe[testcookbook::awesomeator_backup_hwrp]]
resolving cookbooks for run list: ["testcookbook::awesomeator_backup_hwrp"]
Synchronizing Cookbooks:
  - testcookbook
Compiling Cookbooks...
Converging 1 resources
Recipe: testcookbook::awesomeator_backup_hwrp
  * awesome_backup[/tmp/awesomeator.conf] action compress
    - Would Rotate backup files (retaining maximum 3)
    - Would Create backup file /tmp/awesomeator.gz

[Tue, 13 May 2014 17:08:46 +0000] WARN: Skipping final node save
  because override_runlist was given

Running handlers:
Running handlers complete

Chef Client finished, 1/1 resources would have been updated
```

As we can see in this output, this time when the `:compress` action of our resource is executed during the Chef run, why-run mode tells us that any existing backup file is rotated, and a new backup file is created.

 If you have a test node available, why not try running the recipe we just created without why-run mode and see how it behaves when you use different combinations of parameters or the `:extract` action? Please don't run any code on a production server, though!

Thus far in this chapter, we've learned how to translate our LWRP example from the previous chapter into an HWRP by way of an introduction to the classes and syntax required for implementing resources and providers in native Ruby—but this is only part of the powerful functionality offered by HWRPs. After all, if all that HWRPs were good for was turning LWRPs into native Ruby code, that wouldn't be much incentive to write them! Before diving into another code example, in the next section we're going to examine some advanced tips and tricks to level up our HWRP knowledge.

Advanced HWRP Tricks

The example HWRP we've looked at so far in this chapter has been what you might call a very "standard" HWRP—that is, we created a heavyweight resource and a corresponding heavyweight provider to implement a self-contained resource to use in our recipe code. Although useful, this is only part of the full range of functionality and flexibility that we can access when writing HWRPs in Chef. In this section, we're going to examine a number of more advanced topics to level up our HWRP writing and knowledge of Chef's resource and provider ecosystem. We're going to learn about:

- Mixing LWRPs and HWRPs
- Overriding Chef's provider resolution mechanism
- Implementing new providers for Chef's built-in resources
- Accessing Chef's multiplatform provider map

Mixing HWRPs and LWRPs

Thus far, when creating LWRPs and HWRPs we have always created both the resource and the provider in the same style: lightweight resource with lightweight provider and heavyweight resource with heavyweight provider. This makes teaching the creation of LWRPs and HWRPs easier, but is not actually strictly necessary.

In reality, it's entirely possible to mix lightweight resources with heavyweight providers and vice versa without any issue—just because you decide to convert your provider to heavyweight syntax doesn't mean that the resource has to be heavyweight, too. But, I hear you ask, how is such a thing possible?

The answer to this question lies in the way that Chef actually implements the LWRP DSL. Remember, as we discussed in Chapter 8, the LWRP DSL is an abstraction layer over Chef's native resource and provider classes. When a Chef run is initiated, Chef parses any LWRPs that we have created and turns them back into their equivalent heavyweight classes.

We already saw a hint of this when we looked at creating the `load_current_resource` method in "Example 3: The load_current_resource Method" on page 219. Here, we referred to our LWRP resource as an object of the type `Chef::Resource::Testcook bookBackup`—note that this is a very similar class name to the heavyweight `Chef::Re source::AwesomeBackup` class we created earlier on in this chapter.

By the time it comes to execute the code defined in our custom resources and providers, Chef doesn't care whether the classes it is dealing with were originally lightweight or heavyweight, because they will all now be instances of `Chef::Resource::<Resource name>` or `Chef::Provider::<Providername>`. This brings us to the one caveat of mixing LWRPs and HWPRs, which is class naming.

As we saw in the sidebar "Resource Naming" on page 198, Chef will automatically name each of our LWRP classes based on the name of the cookbook and the filename in the cookbook's *resources* or *providers* directory. When mixing LWRPs and HWRPs, this means that we have to name our heavyweight components in a way that will match the naming of any lightweight components. Let's see this in action with a quick example—we're going to create a lightweight resource and combine this with a heavyweight provider. The provider will only contain skeleton code, but it will demonstrate LWRP and HWRP mixing in action.

First, let's create a very simple lightweight resource. Paste the code in Example 9-5 into */tmp/part3_examples/cookbooks/testcookbook/resources/mixerate.rb*.

Example 9-5. /tmp/part3_examples/cookbooks/testcookbook/resources/mixerate.rb

```
actions :magic
default_action :magic

attribute :name,  :kind_of => String, :name_attribute => true
```

Based on the LWRP class naming we learned about in the previous chapter, we know that this resource will become the `Chef::Resource::TestcookbookMixerate` class. This gives us the information we need to create a heavyweight provider to power our resource. Paste the code in Example 9-6 into */tmp/part3_examples/cookbooks/testcookbook/libraries/mixerate.rb*.

Example 9-6. /tmp/part3_examples/cookbooks/testcookbook/libraries/mixerate.rb

```
class Chef
  class Provider
    class TestcookbookMixerate < Chef::Provider ❶

      def whyrun_supported?
        true
      end

      def load_current_resource
        @current_resource = Chef::Resource::TestcookbookMixerate.new(
          new_resource.name) ❷
      end

      def action_magic
        Chef::Log.warn("Magic has happened!")
      end
    end
  end
end
```

❶   Here we're naming our heavyweight provider class with the same name that it
    would automatically receive from Chef if it were a lightweight provider—this is
    the provider name our lightweight resource expects to find.

❷   Here we're referring to the full class name of our lightweight resource to
    construct our load_current_resource method. Remember, because this is a
    heavyweight provider, it is mandatory to define that method.

Now that we've created a lightweight resource and a heavyweight provider, let's quickly
make a recipe that will use this resource so that we can test it out. As our resource is
lightweight, it will be automatically named by Chef—this means that we need to use the
name testcookbook_mixerate in our recipe. Paste the code line in Example 9-7 into /
tmp/part3_examples/cookbooks/testcookbook/recipes/mixerate.rb.

Example 9-7. /tmp/part3_examples/cookbooks/testcookbook/recipes/mixerate.rb

```
testcookbook_mixerate "magical LWRP and HWRP mixing"
```

Now, let's kick off a Chef run of our new testcookbook::mixerate recipe and see what
happens:

```
$> chef-client --once --why-run --local-mode \
--config /tmp/part3_examples/client.rb \
--override-runlist testcookbook::mixerate
Starting Chef Client, version 11.10.4
[Thu, 15 May 2014 10:27:49 +0000] WARN: Run List override has been provided.
[Thu, 15 May 2014 10:27:49 +0000] WARN: Original Run List: []
[Thu, 15 May 2014 10:27:49 +0000] WARN: Overridden Run List:
  [recipe[testcookbook::mixerate]]
```

```
resolving cookbooks for run list: ["testcookbook::mixerate"]
Synchronizing Cookbooks:
  - testcookbook
Compiling Cookbooks...
Converging 1 resources
Recipe: testcookbook::mixerate
  * testcookbook_mixerate[magical LWRP and HWRP mixing] action magic
    [Thu, 15 May 2014 10:27:49 +0000] WARN: Magic has happened!
 (up to date)
[Thu, 15 May 2014 10:27:49 +0000] WARN: Skipping final node save because
override_runlist was given

Running handlers:
Running handlers complete

Chef Client finished, 0/1 resources would have been updated
```

As we see in the output here, when Chef executes the `:magic` action of our `testcook` `book_mixerate` resource, the message we defined in the `action_magic` method of our provider is displayed on the screen. We've just mixed a lightweight resource and a heavyweight provider!

It's also entirely possible to mix a heavyweight resource with a lightweight provider, should you choose to do so, although this is much less common—mainly because the provider is usually where most of the logic lives! If you mix things this way, Chef's automatic LWRP naming needs to be taken into account. You can name your heavyweight resource whatever you want, but the class name of the lightweight provider will be translated to `Chef::Provider::<Cookbookname><Providerfilename>`. By default, this means that to automatically use the provider, your heavyweight resource class needs to be called `Chef::Resource::<Cookbookname><Providerfilename>` too.

Chef's automatic provider resolution mechanism, which we've seen in action throughout the last two chapters, is extremely useful, but in cases like this one it can occasionally be a little annoying, too. Next, we're going to look at how to override this mechanism to allow us to manually specify the provider class to be used by our resource.

Overriding Automatic Provider Resolution

As we have seen in both our LWRP examples in Chapter 8 and our HWRP examples in this chapter, Chef's automatic provider resolution mechanism will look for a subclass of `Chef::Provider` with a name matching the resource class that we are using. In the majority of cases, this automatic provider resolution works well, but there are certain use cases where we might wish to override this behavior and specify a provider ourselves. Consider the following scenarios:

- You want to create a more simplistic resource to install packages that will leverage Chef's built-in `package` resource behind the scenes.

- You want to mix a heavyweight resource with a lightweight provider, but don't want to name the resource Chef::Resource::<Cookbookname><Providerfilename>.

In both of these cases, we need to tell Chef that we want our resource to use a specific provider class instead of the class that Chef would automatically look for. Luckily, the way that Chef implements provider resolution allows us to do exactly this.

As we've already seen, resources in Chef inherit from the Chef::Resource superclass, which lives at *lib/chef/resource.rb* (*http://bit.ly/gh-resourcerb*). This class defines a class instance variable called @resource (and an associated attr_accessor method) that stores the provider to be used by the class. Example 9-8 illustrates how this resource is used in conjunction with the automatic provider resolution mechanism in the provider_for_action method of the Chef::Resource class (comments added).

Example 9-8. provider_for_action method of Chef::Resource class

```
def provider_for_action(action)
    # If this instance of the class has a provider specified
    if self.provider
      # Then use it for this action
      provider = self.provider.new(self, self.run_context)
      provider.action = action
      provider
    else
      # Otherwise, automatically look for a provider
      Chef::Platform.provider_for_resource(self, action)
    end
  end
```

As we can see in this code, before initiating its automatic provider resolution behavior, Chef checks to see if the current instance of the Chef::Resource class has a value specified in its provider attribute. If so, it uses that value as the provider instead. What this means in practical terms is that by setting this attribute in our resource class, we can tell Chef exactly what provider we wish to use.

Let's look at an example of this manual provider specification in action. To keep the example simple, we're going to create a *heavyweight* resource definition but back it with a *lightweight* provider. Instead of sticking with the LWRP naming convention, however, we're going to give our resource and provider different names, manually instructing the resource which provider to use.

First, let's create our heavyweight resource definition. I've used the *_resource* file naming convention here, as we did in previous examples, so paste the code shown in Example 9-9 into */tmp/part3_examples/cookbooks/testcookbook/libraries/wizardry_resource.rb*.

Example 9-9. /tmp/part3_examples/cookbooks/testcookbook/libraries/wizar-dry_resource.rb

```
class Chef
  class Resource
    class Wizardry < Chef::Resource

      provides :wizardry, :on_platforms => :all

      def initialize(name, run_context=nil)
        super
        @resource_name = :awesome_backup
        @allowed_actions = [:magic]
        @action = :magic
        @provider = Chef::Provider::TestcookbookHogwarts
        @name = name
      end

      def name(arg=nil)
        set_or_return(:name, arg, :kind_of => String)
      end
    end
  end
end
```

In this code, we set the `@provider` class instance variable to instruct our `Chef::Re
source::Wizardry` resource to use the `Chef::Provider::TestcookbookHogwarts` pro-
vider—if we didn't do this, Chef would have tried to locate a provider called `Chef::Pro
vider::Wizardry`.

Now that our heavyweight resource is in place, let's create a lightweight provider to go
along with it. Paste the code in Example 9-10 into */tmp/part3_examples/cookbooks/
testcookbook/providers/hogwarts.rb*.

Example 9-10. /tmp/part3_examples/cookbooks/testcookbook/providers/hogwarts.rb

```
def whyrun_supported?
  true
end

action :magic do
  Chef::Log.warn("You're a wizard, Harry!")
end
```

Finally, let's create a recipe to try out our new resource. Paste the line in Example 9-11
into */tmp/part3_examples/cookbooks/testcookbook/recipes/provider_override.rb*.

Example 9-11. /tmp/part3_examples/cookbooks/testcookbook/recipes/provider_over-ride.rb

```
wizardry "Where's that owl"
```

Now we're ready to try running our `testcookbook::provider_override` recipe and see for ourselves whether the manually-specified provider in our `wizardry` resource is executed correctly:

```
$> chef-client --once --why-run --local-mode \
  --config /tmp/part3_examples/client.rb \
  --override-runlist testcookbook::provider_override
Starting Chef Client, version 11.10.4
[Thu, 15 May 2014 12:59:01 +0000] WARN: Run List override has been provided.
[Thu, 15 May 2014 12:59:01 +0000] WARN: Original Run List: []
[Thu, 15 May 2014 12:59:01 +0000] WARN: Overridden Run List:
  [recipe[testcookbook::provider_override]]
resolving cookbooks for run list: ["testcookbook::provider_override"]
Synchronizing Cookbooks:
  - testcookbook
Compiling Cookbooks...
Converging 1 resources
Recipe: testcookbook::provider_override
  * awesome_backup[Where's that owl] action magic
    [Thu, 15 May 2014 12:59:01 +0000] WARN: You're a wizard, Harry!
 (up to date)
[Thu, 15 May 2014 12:59:01 +0000] WARN: Skipping final node save because
  override_runlist was given

Running handlers:
Running handlers complete

Chef Client finished, 0/1 resources would have been updated
```

As this output demonstrates, we successfully overrode Chef's provider resolution mechanism to force our heavyweight `Chef::Resource::Wizardry` resource to use the `Chef::Provider::TestcookbookHogwarts` lightweight provider.

The example we've just worked through is, of course, somewhat contrived for the sake of simplicity, but let's consider the other scenario mentioned at the beginning of this section. Say for example that we want to create a custom resource that will use specific package installation defaults to install packages on our nodes.

Rather than creating an entirely new provider, it would make sense to have our resource wrap Chef's existing package provider and pass through our custom default options. Using the technique we just saw here, this is extremely easy to do—all we need to do is set the `@provider` class instance variable in our resource to the relevant provider class, such as `Chef::Provider::Package::Yum`. As long as the actions and resources specified by our resource are compatible with those the provider supports, our custom resource can now tap into Chef's built-in provider.

The next advanced HWRP technique we're going to learn about is how we can extend Chef's built-in resources with additional providers to build in support for additional software and systems.

Implementing Multi-Provider Resources

As we've seen throughout this book, Chef ships with support for a relatively wide variety of operating systems and associated software. Many of its built-in resources, such as package and service, are in reality backed by multiple providers, one of which is automatically chosen at runtime by Chef (as we saw in "Automatically Choosing Providers" on page 193). But how does this behavior actually work?

All of Chef's built-in resources and providers are implemented as HWRPs, which means that they are written as native Ruby classes and do not make use of the LWRP DSL. You can find them in the *lib/chef/resource* (*http://bit.ly/gh-resources*) and *lib/chef/provider* (*http://bit.ly/gh-chef-prov*) directories of the Chef repository.

Some of these built-in provider classes (such as that defined in *directory.rb*, which, as you might have guessed, implements the directory resource) are extremely similar to the HWRP classes we have already written in this chapter. The directory provider implements a single class that makes use of Ruby's standard libraries to handle its underlying directory creation, deletion, and modification tasks. This enables a single provider class to support multiple platforms because Ruby's standard libraries handle the platform-specific differences.

When it comes to implementing resources such as package, however, things are not quite so straightforward. There are no Ruby libraries to enable someone to say "install this package" and have it automatically work for any package management system on any platform. Consequently, Chef, Inc. had to come up with a way to enable a single resource to be backed by multiple providers, all of which support different package management systems while still implementing the same top-level actions and attributes, such as :install and version.

To solve this problem, the people at Chef, Inc. were able to make use of the object-oriented nature of Ruby. To explore exactly how this solution works, let's dive into the code of the Chef::Provider::Package class, which lives at *lib/chef/provider/package.rb* (*http://bit.ly/gh-packagerb*).

 As we have learned in this chapter, Chef::Provider::Package is the provider class Chef will look for by default to power the package resource defined in the Chef::Resource::Package class, which lives at *lib/chef/resource/package.rb* (*http://bit.ly/gh-package*).

On the face of things, the Chef::Provider::Package class is just the same as any other HWRP—it defines methods such as load_current_resource and whyrun_supported, just as we would expect, and it defines methods for each of its supported actions, such as action_install and action_remove (again, just as we would expect). But let's take a closer look at the contents of these methods. In Example 9-12, we're focusing on the `action_remove` method.

Example 9-12. Excerpt of lib/chef/provider/package.rb

```ruby
class Chef
  class Provider
    class Package < Chef::Provider

      ...

      def action_remove
        if removing_package?
          description = @new_resource.version ?
            "version #{@new_resource.version} of " :
          converge_by("remove #{description}
          package #{@current_resource.package_name}") do
            remove_package(@current_resource.package_name, @new_resource.version)
            Chef::Log.info("#{@new_resource} removed")
          end
        else
          Chef::Log.debug("#{@new_resource} package does not exist - nothing to do")
        end
      end

      ...

      def remove_package(name, version)
        raise Chef::Exceptions::UnsupportedAction,
          "#{self.to_s} does not support :remove"
      end
    end
  end
end
```

As we can see in this excerpt from the `Chef::Package::Provider` class, the `action_remove` method eventually ends up calling the `remove_package` method, to which it passes the name and version of the package to remove. This is entirely in line with what we've seen in our own HWRP examples so far. When we look at the contents of the `remove_package` method, however, we see that it simply raises an exception.

This is because the `Chef::Provider` class is designed only to provide the structure for the `package` resource and generic methods to perform simple checks like whether or not the `current_resource` object has a `version` attribute set (i.e., whether or not the package currently exists)—it leaves the implementation of any package manager–specific behavior to subclasses of `Chef::Provider::Package` for us to implement however we wish.

You can find the source code for the Chef::Provider::Package subclasses provided by default with Chef in the *lib/chef/provider/package* (*http://bit.ly/prov-pack*). Each of these classes implements the methods left "blank" by the Chef::Provider::Package superclass according to the package manager it supports.

Chef chooses between these subclasses of Chef::Provider::Package by using the provider mapping we learned about in "Automatically Choosing Providers" on page 193.

To see an example of this provider subclassing in action, let's take a look at how two of the provider subclasses override the remove_package method we saw defined in Chef::Provider::Package. First, let's look at the Chef::Provider:Package::Rpm class, which lives at *lib/chef/provider/package/rpm.rb* (*http://bit.ly/gh-rpmrb*). This class interfaces with the RPM package management system on Red Hat Linux and its derivatives. It defines the remove_package method as shown in Example 9-13.

Example 9-13. Excerpt of lib/chef/provider/package/rpm.rb

```
class Chef
  class Provider
    class Package
      class Rpm < Chef::Provider::Package

        ...

      def remove_package(name, version)
        if version
          run_command_with_systems_locale(
            :command => "rpm #{@new_resource.options} -e #{name}-#{version}"
          )
        else
          run_command_with_systems_locale(
            :command => "rpm #{@new_resource.options} -e #{name}"
          )
        end
      end

        ...

      end
    end
  end
end
```

Next, let's look at the Chef::Provider:Package::Apt class, which lives at *lib/chef/provider/package/apt.rb* (*http://bit.ly/gh-aptrb*). This class interfaces with the APT package management system on Debian Linux and its derivatives. It defines the remove_pack age method, as seen in Example 9-14.

Example 9-14. Excerpt of lib/chef/provider/package/apt.rb

```ruby
class Chef
  class Provider
    class Package
      class Apt < Chef::Provider::Package

        ...

        def remove_package(name, version)
          package_name = "#{name}"
          run_noninteractive("apt-get -q -y#{expand_options(@new_resource.options)}
            remove #{package_name}")
        end

        ...

      end
    end
  end
end
```

As we see here, these provider subclasses define completely different remove_package resources. But as far as Chef is concerned, this doesn't matter. What Chef wants to be able to do is call the action_remove method of the Chef::Provider::Package class and have that provider do whatever is needed to remove the specified package on whatever operating system Chef is running on.

Of course, under the hood, that provider class is either selecting an appropriate provider class from the provider mapping, as we saw in "Automatically Choosing Providers" on page 193, or making use of the provider manually specified in recipe code. As long as the Chef::Provider::Package class is able to call the remove_package method and have the chosen subclass override this method as necessary, it doesn't need to care about the exact implementation details of what that provider subclass does.

This pattern of defining a superclass that defines several methods left blank for subclasses to implement is commonly used in Chef for resources such as package and provider that have to support multiple platforms under the hood and cannot simply use Ruby's standard libraries to do so.

But how exactly do we implement our own subclass of Chef::Provider::Package to allow Chef to support additional package managers? How do we tap into Chef's provider mapping to allow us to specify that our new provider should be the default package provider on CentOS, for example? Next we're going to work through one final example in which we'll do exactly this.

HWRP Example 2: Extending the package Resource

To finish off the chapter, we're going to put the HWRP knowledge we've gained thus far to use and learn how to implement our own subclass provider for the built-in `pack age` resource and set it to be used by default on the platform of our choice.

To ensure that this example code is not platform-specific and can be run without the need for network access, the fictional `awesomeator` package management system we're going to interface with in this example will in reality be a simple text file. Installing a package will result in a line being added to the text file containing the name of the package and the version installed, and removing the package will remove this line from the text file.

Our fictional `awesomeator` package manager will only support the `:install` and `:re move` actions of the `package` resource—for simplicity, we're not going to implement actions such as `:upgrade` and `:purge` that would normally be supported.

Example 2: Creating a Provider

The first stage in implementing our own subclass provider for the `package` resource is, of course, to create our provider class. Because we need to use Ruby's object-oriented behavior here, we're going to implement a heavyweight provider class that correspond-ingly needs to live in the cookbook's *libraries* directory. Paste the code in Example 9-15 into */tmp/part3_examples/cookbooks/testcookbook/libraries/awesomeator_package.rb*.

Example 9-15. /tmp/part3_examples/cookbooks/testcookbook/libraries/awesomea-tor_package.rb

```
class Chef
  class Provider
    class Package
      class Awesomeator < Chef::Provider::Package ❶

        def load_current_resource ❷
          @current_resource = Chef::Resource::Package.new(@new_resource.name)
          current_resource.package_name(@new_resource.package_name)
          installed_version = get_installed_version
          if installed_version
            current_resource.version(installed_version.last.chomp)
          else
            current_resource.version(nil)
          end
        end

        def install_package(name, version) ❸
          if ::File.exists?("/tmp/awesome_repo")
            packages = ::File.readlines("/tmp/awesome_repo")
          else
```

```
      packages = []
    end
    exists = !packages.select{|s|s.include?(name)}.empty?
    if exists
      packages = packages.map do |p|
        p.include?(name) ? "#{name}-#{version}\n" : p
      end
    else
      packages << "#{name}-#{version}\n"
    end
    write_to_package_db(packages)
  end

  def remove_package(name, version) ❹
    packages = ::File.readlines("/tmp/awesome_repo")
    packages = packages.map{|p|p.include?(name) ? nil : p}
    write_to_package_db(packages)
  end

  private ❺

  def get_installed_version
    repo_file = "/tmp/awesome_repo"
    if ::File.exists? repo_file
      packages = ::File.readlines(repo_file)
      results = packages.select do |p|
        p.include?(new_resource.package_name) ? p : nil
      end
      results.empty? ? nil : results.first.split("-")
    else
      return nil
    end
  end

  def write_to_package_db(package_data)
    ::File.open("/tmp/awesome_repo", 'w') do |file|
      file.write(package_data.join("\n"))
    end
  end
      end
    end
  end
end
```

❶ Here we're defining our Chef::Provider::Package::Awesomeator class as a subclass of Chef::Provider::Package. Note that we're subclassing the Chef::Provider::Package class itself, not just the Chef::Provider class, as we did in our previous HWRP examples. This allows us to access the methods and attributes defined by the Chef::Provider::Package superclass so that we are able to implement only those methods relating to the specific package manager our class is designed to integrate with.

❷ Although we're subclassing an existing provider, we still need to implement the load_current_resource method in our subclass because how we populate attributes such as version will depend on the specific package manager the provider interfaces with.

❸ Here, we override the install_package method from our Chef::Provid er::Package superclass to install packages as required by our fictional aweso meator package manager. In this case, we're writing a line to our "package repository" file.

❹ Then we override the remove_package method from the Chef::Provider::Pack age superclass we saw in "Implementing Multi-Provider Resources" on page 247 to remove packages as required by our fictional awesomeator package manager. In this case, we're removing any lines mentioning our package from our package repository file and then writing the file back to disk.

❺ Lastly, we define several methods needed by our class under the private keyword. private methods can only be called by the class that contains those methods, not by any other class.

Example 2: Using Our Provider in a Recipe

Now that we've defined our subclass provider, let's create a new recipe to try adding and removing some packages using our new provider. Paste the code in Example 9-16 into */tmp/part3_examples/cookbooks/testcookbook/recipes/package_test.rb*.

Example 9-16. /tmp/part3_examples/cookbooks/testcookbook/recipes/package_test.rb

```
package "sriracha" do ❶
  version "1.2.3"
  provider Chef::Provider::Package::Awesomeator
  action :remove
end

package "cholula" do ❷
  version "1.2.4"
  provider Chef::Provider::Package::Awesomeator
end
```

❶ Here we're using the `package` resource to say that we want to `:remove` version 1.2.3 of the package `sriracha`, and that we want to use `Chef::Provider::Pack age::Awesomeator` to do so.

❷ Next, we use the `package` resource to say that we want to `:install` version 1.2.4 of the package `cholula`, and that we again want to use `Chef::Provider::Pack age::Awesomeator` to do so. Note that `:install` is the default action of the package resource, which is used here because we didn't specify another action.

With our provider class and recipe created, let's try kicking off a Chef run of our `test cookbook::package_test` recipe:

```
$> chef-client --once --why-run --local-mode \
  --config /tmp/part3_examples/client.rb \
  --override-runlist testcookbook::package_test
Starting Chef Client, version 11.10.4
[Sun, 18 May 2014 13:48:23 +0000] WARN: Run List override has been provided.
[Sun, 18 May 2014 13:48:23 +0000] WARN: Original Run List: []
[Sun, 18 May 2014 13:48:23 +0000] WARN: Overridden Run List:
  [recipe[testcookbook::package_test]]
resolving cookbooks for run list: ["testcookbook::package_test"]
Synchronizing Cookbooks:
  - testcookbook
Compiling Cookbooks...
Converging 2 resources
Recipe: testcookbook::package_test
  * package[sriracha] action remove (up to date)
  * package[cholula] action install
    - Would install version 1.2.4 of package cholula

[Sun, 18 May 2014 13:48:23 +0000] WARN: Skipping final node save
  because override_runlist was given

Running handlers:
Running handlers complete

Chef Client finished, 1/2 resources would have been updated
```

In this output, we see that when our provider was instructed to remove the `sriracha` package, it reported that it was already up-to-date because this package did not exist in our repository data file. When we came to install the `cholula` package, this did not exist in our repository data file either, so why-run mode reported that this package would be installed.

Although in reality our `Chef::Provider::Package::Awesomeator` class is only adding and removing lines to and from a text file, as far as Chef is concerned we have now implemented a subclass provider of the `package` resource. It can be used in recipes, is compatible with why-run mode (thanks to the methods inherited from its `Chef::Pro vider::Package` superclass), and is both idempotent and convergent. Implementing such a class for a real package management system would of course likely involve a little more code, but the techniques are just the same—we only have to implement the methods specific to the package manager we need to interface with.

 We'll look at some more examples of implementing subclasses of built-in Chef providers in "Summary and Further Reading" on page 258 to see how the techniques we learned about here are being used in the real world.

But wait—we still have to manually specify in the recipe that we want to use our new provider class. How do we make it the default? Fear not, dear reader, and read on!

Example 2: Tapping into Chef's Provider Mapping

In "Automatically Choosing Providers" on page 193, we saw how Chef uses a provider map to select the appropriate provider from a range of possible candidates for the platform on which Chef is being run. This provider mapping is controlled by the Chef::Platform class, which lives at *lib/chef/platform/provider_mapping.rb* (*http://bit.ly/provider-map*). This class contains the @platforms class instance variable (a Hash), which allows the default provider for each resource type to be specified at three different levels of granularity:

Default

The default key of the provider map specifies the provider to be used for each resource type when a more specific mapping is not available. Here's a small sample of the default mapping key:

```
:default  => {
  :file => Chef::Provider::File,
  :directory => Chef::Provider::Directory,
  :link => Chef::Provider::Link
  ....
```

Platform default

The provider mapping also contains a key for each of the platforms supported by Chef. This key is the same value that is stored in the node.platform attribute. It in turn contains a default key that specifies the provider to be used on that platform for resources such as package and service that support multiple platforms. Here's the provider mapping for CentOS Linux:

```
:centos   => {
  :default => {
    :service => Chef::Provider::Service::Redhat,
    :cron => Chef::Provider::Cron,
    :package => Chef::Provider::Package::Yum,
    :mdadm => Chef::Provider::Mdadm,
```

```
        :ifconfig => Chef::Provider::Ifconfig::Redhat
      }
    },
```

Platform version-specific

When platform-specific granularity is not sufficient, it is also possible to specify a key under each platform that defines a version constraint. This version constraint, which is evaluated against the `node.platform_version` attribute, allows a more fine-grained selection of providers for various versions of each platform. Here's the provider mapping for Ubuntu Linux, which makes use of this feature:

```
:ubuntu   => {
  :default => {
    :package => Chef::Provider::Package::Apt,
    :service => Chef::Provider::Service::Debian,
    :cron => Chef::Provider::Cron,
    :mdadm => Chef::Provider::Mdadm
  },
  ">= 11.10" => {
    :ifconfig => Chef::Provider::Ifconfig::Debian
  }
}
```

By default, of course, this mapping only contains mappings for resources and providers shipped with Chef. However, the `Chef::Platform` class also defines a `set` method that allows us to change any of the default mappings, and even define mappings for our own custom resources.

The `set` method takes as its parameter a `Hash` that defines the mapping to be set or overwritten. This `Hash` can contain the following keys:

`:platform`

This optional key specifies a platform to define the mapping for (e.g., `:centos`). If omitted, the mapping is added to the `default` key.

`:version`

This optional key specifies a platform version constraint to define the mapping for. If included, the `:platform` key must also be defined.

`:resource`

This mandatory key specifies the resource for which we're going to specify a provider (e.g., `:package`).

`:provider`

This mandatory key specifies the provider that we're assigning to the resource, as in `Chef::Provider::Package::Yum`.

Let's extend our provider to use the `set` method of the `Chef::Platform` class to modify Chef's provider mapping. Add the following line to the *end* of */tmp/part3_examples/*

---

cookbooks/testcookbook/libraries/awesomeator_package.rb (substituting `centos` with the name of the platform you're using to run this example code):

```
Chef::Platform.set :platform => :centos, :resource => :package,
  :provider => Chef::Provider::Package::Awesomeator
```

 Modifications to Chef's provider mapping of the sort seen here are not permanent, and are applied when the code in your provider is executed. If the cookbook containing the provider that modifies this mapping is not in the run list of your node (or is later removed from the run list), then the provider mapping will use its default values when Chef is next run on the node.

Now let's modify our `testcookbook::package_test` recipe to use the default provider for `package`. Paste the code in Example 9-17 into */tmp/part3_examples/cookbooks/test-cookbook/recipes/package_test.rb*.

Example 9-17. /tmp/part3_examples/cookbooks/testcookbook/recipes/package_test.rb

```
package "sriracha" do ❶
  version "1.2.3"
  action :remove
end

package "cholula" do ❷
  version "1.2.4"
end
```

❶ ❷ Note that in both of our package resources here, we've removed the explicit provider specification we previously used—this means that the default `pack age` provider for our platform specified in the provider mapping will be used.

Now that we've modified Chef's provider mapping in our provider class and amended our recipe to let Chef's automatic provider detection choose our provider for us, let's kick off a Chef run of our `testcookbook::package_test` recipe again and see what happens:

```
$> chef-client --once --why-run --local-mode \
  --config /tmp/part3_examples/client.rb \
  --override-runlist testcookbook::package_test
Starting Chef Client, version 11.10.4
[Sun, 18 May 2014 15:35:35 +0000] WARN: Run List override has been provided.
[Sun, 18 May 2014 15:35:35 +0000] WARN: Original Run List: []
[Sun, 18 May 2014 15:35:35 +0000] WARN: Overridden Run List:
  [recipe[testcookbook::package_test]]
resolving cookbooks for run list: ["testcookbook::package_test"]
Synchronizing Cookbooks:
  - testcookbook
```

```
Compiling Cookbooks...
Converging 2 resources
Recipe: testcookbook::package_test
  * package[sriracha] action remove (up to date)
  * package[cholula] action install
    - Would install version 1.2.4 of package cholula

[Sun, 18 May 2014 15:35:35 +0000] WARN: Skipping final node save
  because override_runlist was given

Running handlers:
Running handlers complete

Chef Client finished, 1/2 resources would have been updated
```

As we can see here, our Chef run behaved identically to when we manually specified a provider in our recipe code—except that this time our `Chef::Provider::Awesomea tor` class was automatically chosen as the default provider class for `CentOS` when Chef consulted its provider mapping, which had been modified by our provider.

Summary and Further Reading

In this chapter, we've augmented our knowledge about Chef's resource and provider model to learn how to create *heavyweight* resources and providers that utilize the full power and control afforded by Ruby's object-oriented behavior (at the expense of the simplicity and ease of use offered by LWRPs).

We started off by examining the differences between lightweight and heavyweight resources and providers and why we might choose one over the other before looking at how to create the skeleton needed for a functioning HWRP. We then learned how to extend the provider of our HWRP to implement the `action` methods that drive its behavior.

We explored a number of more advanced aspects of HWRPs, including how they can coexist with LWRPs, how we can override Chef's built-in provider selection mechanism, and how Chef implements cross-platform resources that are backed by multiple providers. We finished off the chapter by looking at an example of creating a new provider to extend Chef's built-in `package` resource, and learned how to modify Chef's built-in provider mapping to alter the default provider classes chosen by resources on various platforms.

Readers interested in learning more about HWRPs and the different ways in which they are used may wish to explore the following cookbooks:

homebrew

> The homebrew cookbook (*http://bit.ly/homebrew-ckbk*), now maintained by Chef, Inc., adds support for the homebrew package management system to Chef. It uses

an HWRP to add Homebrew support to Chef's `package` resource, and sets its provider as the default class for nodes running Mac OS X and Mac OS X Server.

logstash

The `logstash` cookbook (*http://bit.ly/chef-logstash*), written by Miah Johnson to allow the creation and management of `logstash` (*http://logstash.net/*) environments, makes extensive use of heavyweight resources and providers.

jenkins

The `jenkins` cookbook (*http://bit.ly/gh-jenkins*), written and maintained by Chef, Inc., allows the creation and configuration of master and slave nodes for the Jenkins CI (*http://jenkins-ci.org/*) system and makes extensive use of HWRPs.

swap

The `swap` cookbook (*http://bit.ly/gh-swap*), written by Seth Vargo, allows the creation of swap files and demonstrates a lightweight resource coexisting with a heavyweight provider, as we learned about in "Mixing HWRPs and LWRPs" on page 240.

In Part IV, we're going to leave the Chef run and our cookbook code behind, and learn about other types of customization supported by Chef, from plugins to extend `knife`, through how to leverage the power of the Chef server API, to advanced customizations that change the default behavior of core Chef objects.

## PART IV

Other Customizations

In Part IV of this book, we're going to leave Chef runs and recipes behind and look at the different types of customizations we can make to extend other parts of our Chef infrastructure. We'll examine:

- How to create and extend Knife plugins
- How to interact with the Chef API to write scripts and reports
- How to contribute our customizations back to the community

## CHAPTER 10

Customizing Knife

In previous chapters, we mainly focused on customizations to the Chef run itself, and creating providers and resources for use in our recipes. In this chapter, we're going to move outside of the Chef run and look at how we can customize Knife. As we saw in "Chef Client Tools" on page 59, Knife is the primary command-line tool for interacting with Chef servers and is installed by default as part of the Chef installation process. Out of the box, Knife ships with a number of default plugins that support a variety of common tasks, such as:

- Uploading cookbooks to the Chef server
- Bootstrapping nodes to install and run chef-client
- Creating, modifying, and deleting user and client objects
- Setting run lists on nodes

You can find a full listing of the commands supported by Knife out of the box on the Chef Documents (*http://bit.ly/get-knife*) site.

As with many of the features and tools that Chef ships with, however, Knife is not limited to only those commands provided by Chef, Inc. Under the hood, every command supported by Knife is driven by its extensible and flexible plugin interface, which we can also use to implement our own Knife commands.

In this chapter, we'll learn about:

- How to obtain and navigate around the Knife source code

- The common framework shared by all Knife plugins
- The anatomy of executing a Knife command
- How to create and run our own Knife plugins
- How Knife plugins work under the hood
- How to ensure that our Knife plugins provide a standardized user experience
- The objects and functionality that Chef provides to support Knife plugins

We'll then finish off by using the concepts learned throughout this chapter to revisit the last of the three problems AwesomeInc has been experiencing that we explored in "Criteria for Customization" on page 10.

The Knife Source Code

The source code for Knife (particularly its plugins) will be a useful aid when working through the material in this chapter. Knife and its default plugins are shipped as part of the main Chef repository, so to grab your own copy, please follow the instructions in "Getting the Chef Source Code" on page 74.

Let's take a moment to look at where the different components of Knife live inside the Chef repository—we'll be examining a number of these classes throughout this chapter, and it's useful to have a mental picture of the lay of the land. Source files related to Knife can be found in several different directories under the main Chef repository, as shown here:

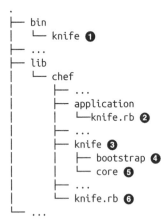

```
.
├── bin
│   └── knife ❶
├── ...
├── lib
│   └── chef
│       ├── ...
│       ├── application
│       │   └── knife.rb ❷
│       ├── ...
│       ├── knife ❸
│       │   ├── bootstrap ❹
│       │   └── core ❺
│       ├── ...
│       └── knife.rb ❻
└── ...
```

❶   *bin/knife* is the executable wrapper that is run when `knife foo` commands are executed in the terminal.

❷ *lib/application/knife.rb* is called by the *bin/knife* wrapper script and serves to validate and parse command-line options, before initializing the `Chef::Knife` class we see in step 6.

❸ The *lib/chef/knife* directory contains a large number of class definition files that implement the out-of-the-box plugins shipped with Knife. Each default Knife command has a corresponding class definition file in this directory. These default plugin class definitions can serve as an excellent reference guide when implementing custom plugin classes.

❹ The *lib/chef/knife/bootstrap* directory contains ERB templates for a number of different operating systems to be used by the `knife bootstrap` command.

❺ The *lib/chef/knife/core* directory contains a number of supporting classes used by many knife plugins. We'll look at these classes in more detail later in this chapter.

❻ *lib/chef/knife.rb* is the class definition file for the `Chef::Knife` class that implements much of the logic involved in running Knife commands, similarly to how the `Chef::Client` class at *lib/chef/client.rb* (see "The Chef::Application::Client Class" on page 80) implements much of the logic involved in a chef-client run. This class is also the superclass from which all Knife plugins inherit.

Now that we've looked at how the Knife source code is structured, let's take a closer look at what a Knife plugin actually looks like.

Introduction to Knife Plugins

As with many of the customizations we've looked at in this book so far, all Knife plugins share the same common structure. Understanding the features that all Knife plugins share (and, more importantly, why these commonalities exist) is crucially important when implementing your own plugin classes, so before we go on to look at how Knife commands are executed, we're going to examine this skeleton plugin framework.

Regardless of their complexity, all Knife plugins are based on a common framework that looks like this:

```
class Awesome < Chef::Knife ❶

  deps do ❷
    # Dependencies
    require 'useful/class'
  end

  def run ❸
    puts "Ohai chefs!"
```

```
    end
  end
```

❶   All Knife plugins inherit from the Chef::Knife superclass, which lives at *lib/chef/knife.rb* (*http://bit.ly/knife-rb*). The name of the class is used to determine the corresponding Knife command implemented by the plugin.

❷   The deps block is used by Knife to allow plugin classes to *lazily load* dependencies. We'll examine what the lazy loading of dependencies means and how it differs from simply using a require statement (as we've done in previous examples) in more detail in the next section, as this concept is directly related to the way Knife loads and executes plugins.

❸   The run method is the main entry point into a plugin class. Knife calls it to tell a plugin to carry out its programmed behavior, in the same way that Ohai calls the collect_data method of its plugins (as we saw in "Ohai Example 1: Plugin Skeleton" on page 97).

Knife Plugin Class Naming

Unlike the formatter classes we looked at in "Creating Formatters" on page 142, which use the cli_name attribute to tell Chef how to refer to them, Knife uses the name of each plugin class (provided that it inherits from the Chef::Knife superclass) to determine which Knife command the plugin implements. Each uppercased word in the class name corresponds to a word in the Knife command that will execute this plugin.

For example, the knife node list command is implemented by a class named NodeList and the knife data bag from file command is implemented by a class called DataBagFromFile. For this reason, the names that we choose for our Knife plugin classes are extremely important.

So now we know what a bare-bones Knife plugin class actually looks like—but how does Knife get from the user running a command like knife node list to the run method of the NodeList class actually being called?

Anatomy of a Knife Command

Because Knife is typically used to execute single, discrete commands, it treats its plugins somewhat differently than other Chef tools, such as Ohai (which we learned about in Chapter 4). Whereas Ohai uses its plugins to augment its collection of attributes and thus executes all of the plugins it knows about each time it is run, Knife only wants to execute the specific plugin that implements the command executed by the user.

This means that each time Knife is executed, it must identify the command being executed and then locate and load the plugin class that implements that command. And Knife can't simply look at its default plugins; it also has to be aware of any customized plugins we've installed. An understanding of how this process works is invaluable when creating our own Knife plugins, so before looking at how to create our own plugin classes we're going to take a minute to learn a little more about the underlying structure and behavior of Knife.

Let's examine what actually happens under the hood when we execute a Knife command such as `knife node list`. Every time we execute a Knife command it performs a number of distinct steps to enable it to identify, load, and execute the correct plugin. These steps are illustrated in Figure 10-1.

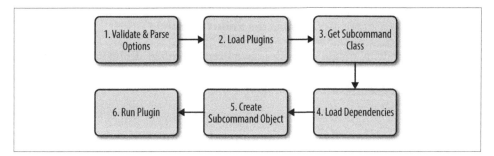

Figure 10-1. Knife command anatomy

Let's examine these steps in a little more detail.

Step 1: Validate and Parse Options

The first step performed when a Knife command is run is for Knife to validate and parse the subcommands (e.g., `cookbook upload`) and options (e.g., `--freeze`) that have been passed along with the command. If invalid subcommands or options have been passed, Knife displays a *usage guide* showing a list of all valid commands and options and quit. If a partially invalid subcommand has been specified (e.g., `cookbook splat`), Knife displays a usage guide for that subcommand only, and quit.

> The only options Knife knows about (and hence validates) at this point are the default options common to all Knife commands. These are specified in the `Chef::Application::Knife` class, which lives at *lib/chef/application/knife.rb* (*http://bit.ly/kniferb-app*).

If all subcommands and options are valid, Knife proceeds to the next step.

Step 2: Load Plugins

After a list of subcommands and options has been successfully parsed, Knife next needs to search for all of the available Knife plugins. It looks for plugin class definition files in the following locations:

- First, it looks in the *~/.chef/plugin_manifest.json* file—this is an optional JSON file containing the definitive list of all plugin files to be loaded.
- If no *plugin_manifest.json* file is present, Knife looks in the *lib/chef/knife* directories (if one exists) of all gems installed via RubyGems.
- Knife also explicitly looks in the *lib/chef* directory of the chef gem—this is where the default Knife plugin classes are located.
- Finally, Knife looks in the *~/.chef/plugins/knife/* directory (if it exists) under the home directory of the user running the Knife command.

When all the available plugin class files have been identified, Knife loads them into memory so that it can access the actual Class objects defined by these files. Any non-lazily loaded dependencies are also required at this stage.

"Lazy" Dependency Loading

When Knife loads plugin classes into memory during this step, it does so using the load method of Ruby's built-in Kernel module. This loading process results in any defined require statements being executed. Because Knife does not yet know which plugin class it will need, it can't make any decisions about which dependencies need to be loaded. As a result, *all* dependencies defined in *any* plugin class are loaded during this step, regardless of which Knife command has actually been executed.

When complex Knife plugins are installed that require a number of dependencies, this global dependency loading can result in the execution time of even the simplest Knife commands increasing significantly. To mitigate this problem, Chef allows plugins to declare dependencies using a strategy called *lazy loading*.

We'll examine lazy loading in more detail when we look at the implementation of our own plugin classes, but essentially the process involves a plugin class declaring its require statements inside a special deps block like this:

```
deps do
  require 'useful/thing'
end
```

As this block is not evaluated when the plugin class is loaded into memory during this step, this avoids dependencies being loaded into memory until later in the process, when

---

Knife has identified the plugin class it actually needs. Dependency loading occurs in step 4.

These Class objects are then assembled into a plugin list so that Knife can locate and instantiate the correct class for the command being executed later in the process. This list is stored as a Hash, where each *key* is a "snake-cased" representation of the class name and each *value* is a Class object representing the class itself.

 "Snake casing" a string means changing all the words to use lower-case letters and separating them with the underscore character instead of a space—effectively turning the string into a continual *snake* of characters. For example, the snake-cased representation of Custom izing Chef is cool would be customizing_chef_is_cool.

For example, the Chef::Knife::NodeList class (which lives at *lib/chef/knife/node_list.rb* (*http://bit.ly/gh-nodelist*) would be represented in the hash as follows:

```
"node_list" => Chef::Knife::NodeList
```

Step 3: Get Subcommand Class

The next step of the process is for Knife to evaluate the subcommands and options it was passed on the command line and construct the name of the class it needs to instantiate. During this step, Knife takes all arguments passed to the knife command that do not contain the - character and joins them into a snake-cased string, lowercasing all the words, and separating them with _ characters.

To use our knife node list -v example again, during this stage of the process Knife will perform the following steps:

1. Extract the node list component of the Knife command and turn this into the snake-cased string node_list

2. Look up the node_list key of the plugins Hash assembled in the previous step. As we saw earlier, the value of this key is the class named Chef::Knife::NodeList.

3. The Chef::Knife::NodeList class is then returned as the result of this step.

Step 4: Load Dependencies

Having identified the exact class that implements the command we specified, Knife now evaluates the optional deps block defined in the code of that plugin class to load any dependencies that the plugin requires. This loading of dependencies only when we are sure they are needed is the second part of Knife's lazy loading strategy, described in the earlier sidebar.

Step 5: Create Subcommand Object

Now that all of its dependencies have been loaded, Knife instantiates our plugin class object using its .new method, as we saw in "Classes" on page 30. In the case of our knife node list example, this equates to running:

```
Chef::Knife::NodeList.new
```

Because our plugin class has only just been instantiated, during this step Knife also populates it with the settings loaded from the *knife.rb* configuration file. This ensures that the plugin uses the same configuration settings as the parent Knife process.

Step 6: Run Plugin

The final step in the process is to actually run the plugin itself. Before doing this, however, Knife uses the settings loaded from the *knife.rb* configuration file to connect to the configured Chef server and authenticate using the client key specified in *knife.rb*.

At this point, if we passed the --local-mode option to our Knife command, the Chef server settings defined in *knife.rb* are overridden and a local chef-zero instance is started. Knife then runs in local mode, sending all server commands to chef-zero instead of the Chef server configured in *knife.rb*.

After server connectivity has been configured, Knife calls the run method of the object we created in the previous step, thereby handing the execution process over to the plugin object. When the plugin has finished carrying out its tasks, it exits and the process of running a Knife command is complete.

Creating a Test Environment

The final thing we need to do before starting to implement our own knife plugins is to create a test environment in which to safely run our example code. As with the test environments we've created in previous chapters, our test environment uses chef-zero to run Knife in local mode, which creates a safe sandbox for testing out customizations.

 Although running the examples from this chapter in the test environment we create here is very much recommended, it is not strictly necessary—if you already have an existing Knife configuration set up, you can use this, although you will likely see different output from the example commands. As always, please do not run example code against your production Chef server.

Like the chef-client test environment we created in "Preparing a Test Environment" on page 114, Knife supports the --local-mode option to start up a local chef-zero server, which causes Knife to run in local mode. Before we can do that, however, we need to complete a couple of preparatory steps. After these steps have been completed, your test environment will allow you to run all of the examples in this chapter on your local machine—no network access is needed.

Prerequisites and Preparation

The assumptions stated in "Assumptions" on page 23 still apply to this section with regard to the development environment I'm assuming you are working with.

You also need to have the ssh-keygen command installed on your development machine. For Red Hat and CentOS systems, this is provided by the openssh package, and on Debian/Ubuntu systems by the openssh-client package. On Mac OS X, this command is installed by default.

The first step in preparing our test environment is to create the */tmp/part4_examples* directory for our test files to live in:

```
$> mkdir /tmp/part4_examples
```

Next, we create a dummy key for Knife to use when authenticating to our chef-zero server. Unlike when communicating with a real Chef server, which requires the client key to be generated on the Chef server itself, chef-zero accepts any key in a valid format. To create our dummy key, run the following command and hit Enter for each input prompt shown:

```
$> ssh-keygen -f /tmp/part4_examples/customizing_chef.pem

Generating public/private rsa key pair.
Enter passphrase (empty for no passphrase):
Enter same passphrase again:
Your identification has been saved in /tmp/part4_examples/customizing_chef.pem.
Your public key has been saved in /tmp/part4_examples/customizing_chef.pem.pub.
The key fingerprint is:
d6:b2:09:f0:f8:2f:04:31:24:ef:58:19:8c:1b:8a:35 jcowie@mydomain.com
The key's randomart image is:
+--[ RSA 2048]----+
|   .+o           |
|   Eo+o          |
|.o +=o           |
|o .+.+   .        |
|  . o.o S .      |
|     ..o +       |
|     .. o        |
```

```
|      ..      |
|      ..      |
+-----------------+
```

You should see output from this command similar to that shown here. Now that we have our dummy client key, we need to create a *knife.rb* configuration file to tell Knife how to talk to our test environment. Paste the contents of Example 10-1 into */tmp/part4_examples/knife.rb*.

Example 10-1. /tmp/part4_examples/knife.rb

```
chef_server_url   'http://127.0.0.1:8889'
node_name         'cctest'
client_key        '/tmp/part4_examples/customizing_chef.pem'
cache_options( :path => '/tmp/part4_examples/checksums' )
chef_repo_path    '/tmp/part4_examples/chef-zero/playground'
```

Our final preparatory step is to grab a copy of the chef-zero code: this contains a ready-made "playground" directory containing cookbooks, node objects, roles, and environments and is ideal for testing example code as we'll be doing here. To download the chef-zero code, run the following commands:

```
$> cd /tmp/part4_examples
$> git clone https://github.com/opscode/chef-zero.git
```

Verifying That the Test Environment Works Correctly

The final step in the preparation of our test environment is verifying that it works correctly. To do this, we're going to run `knife` using the following command:

```
$> knife node list --config /tmp/part4_examples/knife.rb --local-mode
```

In this command, I've passed the following options to `knife`:

`--config /tmp/part4_examples/knife.rb`
This option tells Knife to use the configuration file */tmp/part4_examples/knife.rb*, which we prepared in the preceding section.

`--local-mode`
This option tells Knife to run in local mode, starting up a local chef-zero instance to communicate with instead of the server. chef-zero will also use the `chef_re po_path` configuration parameter we set in *knife.rb* to use the */tmp/part4_examples/ chef-zero/playground* directory as its data store—this parameter determines the data chef-zero serves us when we request data such as nodes or cookbooks.

Here's what happens when we actually run this command:

```
$> knife node list --config /tmp/part4_examples/knife.rb --local-mode

desktop
dns
```

```
lb
ldap
www
```

If all of the instructions in the previous steps were completed successfully, you should see similar output to that shown here, which lists all of the nodes stored in our chef-zero test environment.

Now that we have a working test environment to run our plugin examples under, let's finally start creating some Knife plugins! Alongside each of the plugin examples we look at in this chapter, we'll examine the various helper classes both Knife and Chef provide us with and how we can use them in our own custom plugin classes.

Knife Example 1: Wrapping an Existing Plugin

One of the simplest and most common use cases for Knife plugins is augmenting the functionality provided by an existing plugin. In this example, we're going to create a plugin that makes use of the built-in Chef::Knife::Search plugin, which provides the knife search command and lives at *lib/chef/knife/search.rb* (*http://bit.ly/gh-searchrb*).

The scenario here is that we have a commonly used search query to locate nodes within our infrastructure whose names match a particular pattern and that are in the _default environment. Instead of repeatedly running the command knife search node "name:*foo* AND chef_environment:_default", we're going to create a *wrapper* plugin that takes the name of the node we want to search for, and then constructs the search query for us and runs the Chef::Knife::Search plugin to execute it.

Because Knife only loads plugins from the specific locations listed in "Step 2: Load Plugins" on page 268, we need to store our example code in one of those locations—we'll use the *~/.chef/plugins/knife* directory. While logged in as the user you'll be running Knife commands as, run the following command to create this directory:

```
$> mkdir -p ~/.chef/plugins/knife
```

> On Linux and other Unix-based operating systems, the tilde symbol (~) is an abbreviation for the home directory of the currently logged in user. This abbreviation is *not* supported on Windows—if you're running these example Knife plugins on Windows you'll need to replace the tilde symbol in directory paths with the full path to your user's home directory.

Now that we've created the directory for our example plugins to live in, let's paste the code in Example 10-2 into *~/.chef/plugins/knife/awesome_search.rb*.

Example 10-2. ~/.chef/plugins/knife/awesome_search.rb

```
module Awesome
  class AwesomeSearch < Chef::Knife ❶

    deps do
      require 'chef/knife/search' ❷
    end

    def run ❸

      # Assign the first command-line argument
      # after the plugin name to the variable "query"
      query = "name:*#{name_args.first}* AND chef_environment:_default" ❹

      knife_search = Chef::Knife::Search.new ❺
      knife_search.name_args = ['node', query] ❻
      knife_search.run ❼
    end
  end
end
```

❶   Our AwesomeSearch plugin inherits from the Chef::Knife superclass, which lives at *lib/chef/knife.rb* (*http://bit.ly/knife-rb*). This is the class from which all Knife plugins inherit.

❷   Here we're specifying a require statement inside the deps block, ensuring that our dependency chef/knife/search is lazily loaded, as we saw in ""Lazy" Dependency Loading" on page 268.

❸   The run method of our class is the method Knife calls to execute our plugin.

❹   The name_args method is a built-in method provided by Ruby that allows us to access the parameters passed to the program being executed as an array. Here we want the first element after the actual Knife command, which in this case is the name of the node we'll be searching for.

❺   Here we're creating a new instance of the Chef::Knife::Search class, just as Knife would if we executed the knife search command directly.

❻   Next, we call the name_args method of our Chef::Knife::Search object to pass it the parameters that it needs. If we were running the knife search command manually, these would be passed on the command line as the name_args method we used in step 4, but because we're calling this plugin ourselves, we need to pass these options through to the plugin class manually.

❼ Finally, we call the `run` method of the `Chef::Knife::Search` object we created in step 5. Note that our `AwesomeSearch` plugin class does not directly output any data itself; the output is produced by the `Chef::Knife::Search` plugin we're wrapping, just as if we ran the `knife search` command manually from a terminal.

Now let's try running our plugin. As we called our plugin class `AwesomeSearch`, this means that Knife knows that the command to execute it will be `knife awesome search`, as we saw in the sidebar "Knife Plugin Class Naming" on page 266. We'll also pass Knife the `--config` and `--local-mode` parameters to ensure that it loads the configuration we created in "Creating a Test Environment" on page 270 and runs in local mode:

```
$> knife awesome search ldap --config /tmp/part4_examples/knife.rb --local-mode
1 items found

Node Name:   ldap
Environment: _default
FQDN:
IP:
Run List:
Roles:
Recipes:
Platform:
Tags:
```

As we see here, when our plugin is executed, Knife parses the options passed and uses the `awesome search` portion of the command to identify that our `AwesomeSearch` plugin class should be executed, passing it the remaining word, `ldap`, as a parameter. Knife also knows that the `--config` and `--local-mode` options we specified are global rather than plugin-specific. The result of the search query shown here was generated by the `Chef::Knife::Search` plugin when it was executed by our `AwesomeSearch` plugin.

The plugin example we looked at here is extremely simplified and does not contain any error handling or input validation, but it does serve to demonstrate how we can create our own custom Knife plugin classes and interact with other Knife plugins.

In our next example, we'll use the same scenario, but this time instead of wrapping an existing plugin we implement the search query and display of search results ourselves. As we'll handle outputting the results of this plugin ourselves rather than leaving it to another plugin, before we can implement this plugin we need to examine the classes Knife provides for formatting and displaying output. We're going to examine two class types:

Presenter classes
Presenter classes are used by Knife to format structured data such as `Chef::Node` objects so that it can be output to the user. We'll look at these in the next section.

The UI class

Knife provides a special UI class to handle interacting with the user and displaying output, allowing us to ensure a consistent user experience across all Knife plugins. We'll meet the UI class in "The UI Class" on page 279.

Presenting Presenters!

The first category of helper class provided by Knife that we'll examine here is *presenter* classes. Much of the data stored in the Chef server about our nodes, roles, cookbooks, and other items is complex structured data with multiple levels of nested attributes—this sort of data is extremely easy for computers to work with, but not so easy for us to display nicely to the end user.

To help solve this problem, Knife ships with presenter classes that handle parsing this data and converting it into more convenient formats to output from our Knife plugin classes. In this section, we'll meet the presenter classes shipped with Knife, and examine the methods and formats they support.

Chef::Knife::Core::GenericPresenter

The base presenter class provided by Knife is `Chef::Knife::Core::GenericPresent er`, which lives at *lib/chef/knife/core/generic_presenter.rb* (*http://bit.ly/generic-pre*). Unlike the more abstract base classes we've seen so far in this book, the `Chef::Knife::Core::GenericPresenter` class does not merely define empty method bodies for its subclasses to inherit, but rather provides a comprehensive set of methods capable of formatting and outputting the majority of the structured data likely to be encountered when writing Knife plugins.

The `Chef::Knife::Core::GenericPresenter` class is used as the default presenter by Knife unless another presenter has been specified—we'll learn how to do this when we meet the UI class in the next section. This presenter class supports a number of different formats to display structured data, which Knife users can request by passing the `-F` option to Knife (which then passes it through to the plugin class being executed).

Supported Output Formats

The `Chef::Knife::Core::GenericPresenter` class supports outputting the following formats. Each format is named according to the value that is passed to Knife's `-F` option to request it, and the examples here show a `Chef::Environment` object being output in that particular format:

json

The `json` format produces the JSON (*http://bit.ly/json-syntax*) representation of the structured data, an example of which can be seen here:

```
{
  "name": "production",
  "description": "This is just production",
  "cookbook_versions": {
  },
  "json_class": "Chef::Environment",
  "chef_type": "environment",
  "default_attributes": {
  },
  "override_attributes": {
  }
}
```

yaml

The yaml format produces the YAML (*http://bit.ly/yaml-spec*) representation of the structured data, an example of which can be seen here:

```
--- !ruby/object:Chef::Environment
cookbook_versions: {}

default_attributes: {}

description: This is just production
name: production
override_attributes: {}
```

text

The text format produces a textual summary of the structured data, formatted to be easily readable when output to a terminal. An example of this format can be seen here:

```
chef_type:          environment
cookbook_versions:
  apache: >= 1.0.0
default_attributes:
description:         This is just production
json_class:          Chef::Environment
name:                production
override_attributes:
```

pp

The pp format is used to print a string representation of the underlying Ruby object representing the structured data. An example of this format can be seen here:

```
production
```

summary

The summary format is used by default if no other format is specified; this currently generates the same output as the text format.

Although the `Chef::Knife::Core::GenericPresenter` class defines a number of methods, we're only going to look at those methods most commonly used directly in Knife plugins here. A full method listing can be found in the source code of this class, located at *lib/chef/knife/core/generic_presenter.rb* (*http://bit.ly/generic-pre*). The most commonly used methods are:

`format`
> The `format` method is the main entry point into the `Chef::Knife::Core::Gener icPresenter` class. This method takes structured data such as `Chef::Node` objects and returns it in the format requested by the user. If no format is specified, the default `summary` format mentioned in the previous sidebar will be used.

`format_for_display`
> The `format_for_display` method performs preliminary formatting on structured data to prepare it for outputting to the user, such as extracting subsets of the data when only part of it is to be output. An example of when this method would be used is when the `-i` option is passed to the `knife search` command to return only the IDs of matching objects rather than the entire objects.

Chef::Knife::Core::NodePresenter

Knife currently ships with only one additional presenter, the `Chef::Knife::Core::No dePresenter` class, which lives at *lib/chef/knife/core/node_presenter.rb* (*http://bit.ly/ node-present*).

This class is a subclass of `Chef::Knife::Core::GenericPresenter`, and overrides the `format` method from its superclass to nicely format `Chef::Node` objects when they are being output by Knife plugins. `Chef::Node` objects often contain a large number of deeply nested data structures to represent all their saved attributes, and require some extra formatting prior to display.

You can see an example of this presenter in action in the output of "Knife Example 1: Wrapping an Existing Plugin" on page 273—the `Chef::Knife::Search` plugin, which we wrap in that example, contains logic to use `Chef::Knife::Core::NodePresenter` if the type of object being searched for is a node, and `Chef::Knife::Core::GenericPre senter` when we're searching for any other type of object.

Between `Chef::Knife::Core::GenericPresenter` and `Chef::Knife::Core::Node Presenter`, it is possible to format all of the structured data Chef produces that you might want to display in your Knife plugins. For this reason, although it would certainly be possible to define additional presenter classes, we're not going to do so here.

Now that we've examined the classes that Chef provides us for formatting data for output, let's meet the second of the helper classes we're going to need for our second example, which allows us to interact with the user and terminal.

The UI Class

To standardize the user experience of interacting with Knife across all plugins, Chef ships with a special class that integrates with Knife and provides a number of methods for interacting with both the user and the terminal.

The `Chef::Knife::UI` class lives at *lib/chef/knife/core/ui.rb* (*http://bit.ly/gh-uirb*) and is available to all Knife plugins as the `ui` object, which is defined in the `Chef::Knife` superclass from which all Knife plugins inherit. The `Chef::Knife::UI` class defines a number of methods, documented here by category.

User Interaction Methods

The `Chef::Knife::UI` class provides two handy methods for asking questions of Knife users and collecting the responses:

ask_question
> The `ask_question` method allows you to ask the user a question and collect a free-text response. This method also accepts a default answer to use if none is given—this will be shown to the user when the question is asked.

confirm
> The `confirm` method is specifically designed for asking Knife users questions to which a `Yes` or `No` response is expected. If the user responds with `No`, Knife will immediately exit with status code 3.

Message Output Methods

The `Chef::Knife::UI` class also provides a number of handy methods for displaying output messages on screen at different levels of severity to indicate informational events, error messages, and so on. Where the user's terminal supports colored output, some severity levels use a colored prefix such as `WARNING` in yellow, `ERROR` in red, etc. to provide a further visual indication of the severity of the message:

msg
> The `msg` method prints output to the terminal at a standard *informational* severity level. This level essentially produces the same output that you would see if `puts` were used.

info
> The `info` method prints output to the terminal at a standard *informational* severity level, but prefixed with a white (if color is supported) `INFO`.

warn

The `warning` method prints output to the terminal at a *warning* severity level, prefixed with a yellow (if color is supported) `WARNING`.

error

The `error` method prints output to the terminal at an *error* severity level, prefixed with a red (if color is supported) `ERROR`.

fatal

The `fatal` method prints output to the terminal at a *fatal* severity level, prefixed with a red (if color is supported) `CRITICAL`.

color

The `color` method allows a message to be printed in a specific color—for example, `color("ERROR:", :red)` or `color("WARNING:", :yellow)`—if the output terminal supports colored output.

There is no *functional* difference between these output methods; the only difference is the prefix attached to the output message. Which severity level should be used when displaying messages to the user is left to the discretion of plugin creators.

Other Output Methods

The `Chef::Knife::UI` class provides several useful methods to allow plugin authors to output structured data (such as `Chef::Node` objects) to the user, and to query Knife about the format in which structured data should be presented and what features are supported by the current output environment:

color?

The `color?` method allows a plugin author to query whether or not colored output is supported by the user's environment. This is typically used to avoid calling methods such as `color` unless colored output would actually be visible to the user. Currently, colored output is supported by Knife when the output device is a `tty` terminal, and the Knife command is not being run on a Windows machine.

output

The `output` method is used to display structured data to the user in the desired format—although a default format can be used, it is also possible to specify a particular format by passing the `-F` option to Knife. Under the hood, this method calls the `format` method of the configured presenter to format the data before outputting it. A list of output formats and methods supported by Knife's presenter classes can be seen in "Presenting Presenters!" on page 276.

interchange?

> The `interchange` method is used to query whether or not the user has requested output in a data interchange format such as JSON or YAML. This method is typically used to control whether or not output should be printed with explanatory text, etc., or simply output in the requested format. An example of this technique can be seen in the `Chef::Knife::Search` plugin source code (*http://bit.ly/chef-search*).

use_presenter

> The `use_presenter` method allows a Knife plugin author to specify that a specific presenter class should be used to handle output from the plugin, for example using the `Chef::Knife::Core::NodePresenter` class when node objects are displayed.

Object Editing Methods

The `Chef::Knife::UI` class defines two methods that allow objects stored on the Chef server to be easily edited:

edit_data

> The `edit_data` method allows the user to use the editor configured via the system's `$EDITOR` environment variable to edit Chef objects via temporary files. This method is primarily used by the `edit_object` method (described next), but can also be used to edit objects that have previously been loaded elsewhere in the plugin. We'll look at examples of editing objects using this method in "Editing and Saving Objects Interactively" on page 292.

edit_object

> The `edit_object` method allows the user to load and edit objects on the Chef server (such as roles, nodes, and environments) using a text editor of choice. This method is used by various Knife commands, such as `knife role edit` and `knife node edit`, to allow the JSON representation of objects stored on the Chef server to be edited by users—under the hood, the object is downloaded to the user's machine, output to a temporary file, edited using the `edit_data` method, and then reuploaded to the server. We'll examine how to edit objects in this way in "Editing and Saving Objects Interactively" on page 292.

HighLine Methods

Knife makes use of the third-party HighLine (*http://bit.ly/gh-highline*) library to provide some of its user interaction functionality. The `Chef::Knife::UI` class defines several methods that allow the methods of the same name from the HighLine library to be called without the need to instantiate a new `HighLine` object. These include:

`highline`

> The `highline` method returns the `HighLine` object used by many of the methods of `Chef::Knife::UI`, allowing it to be accessed directly if desired.

`ask`

> The `ask` method calls the corresponding `ask` method of the HighLine library, which is documented in the HighLine Documentation (*http://bit.ly/ruby-hl*).

`ui.list`

> The `list` method calls the corresponding `list` method of the HighLine library, which is documented in the HighLine Documentation (*http://bit.ly/ruby-hl*).

Examples of using the various methods of the `Chef::Knife::UI` class can be seen later in this chapter, and on the Chef Documents site (*http://bit.ly/usr-interact*).

Knife Example 2: Search Plugin

In this example, we'll use the same scenario that we did in "Knife Example 1: Wrapping an Existing Plugin" on page 273 wherein we want to locate nodes within our infrastructure whose names match a particular pattern, and that are in the `_default` environment. This time, however, we're going to display a warning to the user that the node we're searching for has been found in this environment—in our hypothetical scenario, we don't want nodes to be in this environment.

To do this, we're going to have to implement the search query and format the results ourselves, as the output will be different from that displayed by the `Chef::Knife::Search` plugin. Paste the code in Example 10-3 into the same file that we used for "Knife Example 1: Wrapping an Existing Plugin" on page 273, *~/.chef/ plugins/knife/awesome_search.rb*.

Example 10-3. ~/.chef/plugins/knife/awesome_search.rb

```
module AwesomeInc
  class AwesomeSearch < Chef::Knife

    deps do
      require 'chef/search/query'
      require 'chef/knife/core/node_presenter' ❶
    end

    banner "knife awesome search QUERY" ❷

    def run
      ui.use_presenter Chef::Knife::Core::NodePresenter ❸
      search_object = Chef::Search::Query.new ❹
      query = "name:*#{name_args.first}*"

      result_items = []
```

```
    result_count = 0

    # Call the method of our Chef::Search::Query
    # object and add each item to our results array; also
    # increment our results counter
    search_object.search('node', query) do |item| ❺
      result_items << item
      result_count += 1
    end

    # Display the number of results we have as a "Warning"
    ui.warn "#{result_count} Nodes found in the _default environment:" ❻
    ui.warn("\n")

    # Loop over our results
    # and output them
    result_items.each do |item|
      output(item) ❼
      unless config[:id_only]
        ui.msg("\n")
      end
    end
  end
 end
end
```

❶ Here we're requiring as a dependency the Chef::Knife::Core::NodePresent
er class we met in "Presenting Presenters!" on page 276.

❷ The banner method we're calling here determines the output Knife shows when
we run this command with incorrect or missing parameters. It's entirely optional,
but can make it easier to use your plugin classes as it displays a more user-
friendly guide to the options and parameters to use.

❸ Here we're telling the ui object to use Chef::Knife::Core::NodePresenter as
its presenter—because we know our search query should only return node
objects, we're able to benefit from the additional formatting this class provides
us over Chef::Knife::Core::GenericPresenter.

❹ Here we're creating a new Chef::Search::Query object, which lives at *lib/chef/
search/query.rb* (*http://bit.ly/gh-queryrb*). This class allows us to run search
queries against the Chef API and is also used by the Chef::Knife::Search class
we wrapped in "Knife Example 1: Wrapping an Existing Plugin" on page 273.
The query on the next line is in exactly the same format as the one we used in
"Knife Example 1: Wrapping an Existing Plugin" on page 273.

❺ Next, we call the `search` method of our `Chef::Search::Query` class, passing it the index that we want to search in (`node`) and the query we want to use. Remember, as we saw in "Chef Server" on page 60, Chef defines separate indexes for the various types of objects it stores, so we need to specify which index our query will be run against.

❻ We're using the `warn` method of the `ui` object here to display the number of search results we found, formatted as a `WARNING`.

❼ Finally, we use the `output` method of the `ui` object to print our search results to screen.

Now let's try running our new example plugin:

```
$> knife awesome search ldap --config /tmp/part4_examples/knife.rb --local-mode
WARNING: 1 Nodes found in the _default environment:
WARNING:
Node Name:   ldap
Environment: _default
FQDN:
IP:
Run List:
Roles:
Recipes:
Platform:
Tags:
```

As you can see, the output displayed by our plugin here is similar to that shown when we wrapped the `Chef::Knife::Search` plugin class in our first example—but this time, we're displaying a `WARNING` before our search results.

The decision of whether to wrap an existing plugin or implement the desired behavior yourself, as we did here, is one you will likely have to make yourself when implementing custom Knife plugins that perform similar functions to one or more of the default Knife plugins. My advice would be to wrap existing plugins as we did in "Knife Example 1: Wrapping an Existing Plugin" on page 273 where possible, unless you're implementing functionality not provided by the existing plugin, or that cannot be easily added by wrapping.

So far in this chapter, we've looked at how to wrap existing Knife plugins, how to run search queries, and the classes that Knife provides to interact with the user and display output from our plugins. More often than not, however, when creating Knife plugins we're going to want to work with the actual data stored on the Chef server. So, before we dive into our next example, let's take a look at the helper classes Knife provides us with to implement this behavior in our plugins.

Working with Chef Objects

One of the most common tasks performed by Knife plugins is the manipulation of data stored on the Chef server. For example, if you're creating a plugin to create nodes on a particular cloud system, such as EC2, you're probably going to want to create a client on the Chef server for that node to authenticate against. If you're creating a workflow plugin to automate common Knife commands, you might want to create or update existing node, cookbook, or environment objects on the Chef server.

In this section, we're going to meet the class definitions that represent Chef's core object types, such as nodes, roles, and environments, before learning about the helper classes that Chef provides to allow us to load and manipulate objects, then save them back to the server.

Chef, Inc. defines a number of useful classes in the Chef repository—which of course Knife also lives under—that represent the different types of objects stored on the Chef server. These class definitions allow us to interact with the Chef server's API without having to worry about authenticating, constructing API requests, and so on. Chef defines one class for each of the core object types stored on the server:

Clients

Client objects are represented by the `Chef::ApiClient` class, which lives at *lib/chef/api_client.rb* (*http://bit.ly/gh-apiclient*).

Cookbooks

Cookbook objects are represented by the `Chef::CookbookVersion` class, which lives at *lib/chef/api_client.rb* (*http://bit.ly/gh-ckbkvrb*). Because the Chef server treats each version of each cookbook separately, there is no single object for, say, the `apache` cookbook, but rather an individual `Chef::CookbookVersion` object for each version of the `apache` cookbook that was uploaded.

Data bags

Data bag objects are represented by the `Chef::DataBag` class, which lives at *lib/chef/data_bag.rb* (*http://bit.ly/gh-databag*).

Data bag items

Data bag item objects are represented by the `Chef::DataBagItem` class, which lives at *lib/chef/data_bag_item.rb* (*http://bit.ly/data-bag-item*). Note that Chef defines separate objects for both the data bag itself and the items it holds—this allows us to choose whether to access an entire data bag, or specific items that it contains.

Encrypted data bag items

Encrypted data bag item objects are represented by the `Chef::EncryptedDataBa gItem` class, which lives at *lib/chef/encrypted_data_bag_item.rb* (*http://bit.ly/e-databag*). As with standard data bag items, encrypted data bag items are defined by objects separate from the data bag that holds them. This class implements additional functionality on top of the `Chef::DataBagItem` class to provide the encryption behavior necessary to support encrypted data bag items.

Environments
> Environment objects are represented by the `Chef::Environment` class, which lives at *lib/chef/environment.rb* (*http://bit.ly/gh-enviro*).

Nodes
> Node objects are represented by the `Chef::Node` class, which lives at *lib/chef/node.rb* (*http://bit.ly/gh-noderb*).

Roles
> Role objects are represented by the `Chef::Role` class, which lives at *lib/chef/role.rb* (*http://bit.ly/gh-rolerb*).

Users
> User objects are represented by the `Chef::User` class, which lives at *lib/chef/user.rb* (*http://bit.ly/gh-userrb*). *Users* in Chef are distinct from *clients*—a user object is typically created to allow access to your Chef server's web UI if using the open source Chef server, or to grant certain permissions to if using hosted Enterprise Chef.

All of these classes, although they do not share a common superclass, allow us to use the same techniques and method names to access, manipulate, and save the objects to the server. We'll first examine the two principal ways of loading objects from the server, before looking at how to manipulate and save them.

Loading Objects: Searching

The first way that Knife provides us with to access objects from the server is via the results of search queries—we actually already used this method in "Knife Example 2: Search Plugin" on page 282. Consider the snippet of the code we used in that example, reproduced here in Example 10-4.

Example 10-4. Excerpt of ~/.chef/plugins/knife/awesome_search.rb

```
search_object = Chef::Search::Query.new
query = "name:*#{name_args.first}*"

search_object.search('node', query) do |item|
  # Do stuff with results
end
```

When we run a search query and iterate the results like this, each result in the collection is an instance of one of the classes we defined in "Working with Chef Objects" on page 285. In this snippet, for instance, because we specified that we want to search in the node index, all results returned by the search query are Chef::Node objects. Let's observe this in action with a quick demonstration (Example 10-5), which we'll paste into *~/.chef/plugins/knife/awesome_object_demo.rb*.

Example 10-5. ~/.chef/plugins/knife/awesome_object_demo.rb

```
module AwesomeInc
  class AwesomeObjectDemo < Chef::Knife

    deps do
      require 'chef/search/query'
    end

    def run
        search_object = Chef::Search::Query.new
        query = "name:*#{name_args.first}*"
        search_object.search('node', query) do |item|
          ui.msg "#{item.name}: #{item.class}" ❶
        end
    end
  end
end
```

❶ For each result of the search query, instead of formatting it for output as we did in "Knife Example 2: Search Plugin" on page 282 we simply output a ui.msg message containing the name and class.

When we run our demo plugin using our Knife test environment, we see the following output:

```
$> knife awesome object demo ldap \
--config /tmp/part4_examples/knife.rb --local-mode
ldap: Chef::Node
```

As we see here, Chef is outputting the name and class of each result returned by the search query—our method call to item.class shows us that the object returned in the search results on this occasion is indeed a Chef::Node object.

For cases where we want to fetch all objects matching a specified criterion (such as name:ldap in our example here), using a Chef search is the recommended technique. However, Chef search queries do not allow us to access *all* of the data types stored on the Chef server. As we learned in "Chef Server" on page 60, Chef provides the following search indexes, which we can specify in calls to the Chef::Search::Query object we used in the previous example:

- client
- *<data_bag_name>* (Chef defines a separate search index for each data bag)
- environment

- node

- role

But what do we do if we want to access a single, specific object without the overhead of searching an entire index, or we want to access data such as Chef::CookbookVersion objects for which Chef does not define a search index? Well, luckily for us, there's a way to do that, too.

Loading Objects: Direct Loading

To allow us to load Chef objects directly instead of having to run a search query to find them, each of the class definitions listed in "Working with Chef Objects" on page 285 defines a load method. This method will take either one or several parameters that give Chef the name of the object to be loaded, and any other information that might be needed (such as, in the case of a data bag item, the name of the data bag that contains it). I've listed a quick summary of the parameters taken by the load method of each object type here (with the body of each load method removed for brevity):

Clients—Chef::ApiClient

```
def self.load(name)
  # Takes the name of the client as its parameter
end
```

Cookbooks—Chef::CookbookVersion

```
def self.load(name, version="_latest")
  # Takes the name of the cookbook and the
  # desired version as parameters. version
  # defaults to "_latest" if not supplied.
end
```

Data bags—Chef::DataBag

```
def self.load(name)
  # Takes the name of the data bag as its parameter
end
```

Data bag items—Chef::DataBagItem

```
def self.load(data_bag, name)
  # Takes the name of the data bag as its first parameter
  # and the name of the item in that data bag as its second
end
```

Encrypted data bag items—Chef::EncryptedDataBagItem

```
def self.load(data_bag, name, secret = nil)
  # Takes the name of the data bag as its first parameter,
  # the name of the item in that data bag as its second,
  # and the decryption secret as its third; this defaults to nil
end
```

Environments—`Chef::Environment`

```
def self.load(name)
  # Takes the name of the environment as its parameter
end
```

Nodes—`Chef::Node`

```
def self.load(name)
  # Takes the name of the node as its parameter
end
```

Roles—`Chef::Role`

```
def self.load(name)
  # Takes the name of the role as its parameter
end
```

Users—`Chef::User`

```
def self.load(name)
  # Takes the name of the user as its parameter
end
```

To view the full class definitions that define these methods, please see the source files listed for each object type in "Working with Chef Objects" on page 285.

Now that we've examined the `load` methods defined by each class, we're ready to try using them in another example. This time, we'll load a node object directly using the `load` method of the `Chef::Node` class. Paste the code in Example 10-6 into the same file that we used for the earlier example in this section, *~/.chef/plugins/knife/ awesome_object_demo.rb*.

Example 10-6. ~/.chef/plugins/knife/awesome_object_demo.rb

```
module AwesomeInc
  class AwesomeObjectDemo < Chef::Knife

    deps do
      require 'chef/node'  ❶
    end

    def run
      node_object = Chef::Node.load(name_args.first)  ❷
      ui.msg "#{node_object.name}: #{node_object.class}"  ❸
    end
  end
end
```

❶ Because we're going to be calling a method of the `Chef::Node` class, we need to require it—note that the `require` statement is in the `deps` block to ensure that the dependency is lazily loaded, as we examined in ""Lazy" Dependency Loading" on page 268.

❷ Here we're calling the `load` method of the `Chef::Node` class with the node name we passed to the plugin as its parameter, and assigning it to the `node_object` variable.

❸ Finally we're using a `ui.msg` method call to output the `name` and `class` of `node_object`.

Let's run our example plugin code, this time using `www` as the node we want to load instead of `ldap`:

```
$> knife awesome object demo www \
--config /tmp/part4_examples/knife.rb --local-mode
www: Chef::Node
```

As we see here, when we run our plugin example, we again see that we've got a `Chef::Node` object—but this time we loaded it directly from the Chef server instead of getting it from the results of a search query.

We've now explored the two ways in which Knife plugins are able to load objects from the Chef server, but what happens when we want to then *modify* our object and save it back to the server? Chef provides us with two ways to do this, too, depending on how we want to edit the object: we can edit objects interactively, where we allow the user to specify the desired changes in an editor, or noninteractively, where we simply change the object behind the scenes.

Editing and Saving Objects Noninteractively

The first and most straightforward method of editing and saving objects that we'll examine here is the noninteractive method—this means that the plugin edits the object behind the scenes and saves it back to the Chef server with no input from the user other than parameters passed to the Knife plugin.

Essentially, this method involves utilizing "setter" methods provided by Chef's core object classes to allow us to alter the attributes of an object. It's important to note that this method does not allow totally free-form editing of the objects; we're only able to alter attributes of our objects for which they define corresponding setter methods.

A comprehensive list of methods supported by the objects we've looked at can be found in the class files listed in "Working with Chef Objects" on page 285, but as a general rule of thumb most of these objects define methods for each of their "top-level" attributes.

For example, the `Chef::Node` object defines `chef_environment`, `run_list`, `normal_attrs`, `override_attrs`, etc.

As with the other classes we've looked at in this book, I recommend having a browse through the class files to explore the various methods and attributes each class provides.

Let's look at an example of amending the `chef_environment` attribute of a `Chef::Node` object. As before, we'll paste this code (Example 10-7) into *~/.chef/plugins/knife/awesome_object_demo.rb*.

Example 10-7. ~/.chef/plugins/knife/awesome_object_demo.rb

```
module AwesomeInc
  class AwesomeObjectDemo < Chef::Knife

    deps do
      require 'chef/node'  ❶
    end

    def run
      node_object = Chef::Node.load(name_args.first)  ❷
      # Print our node's chef_environment before we change it
      ui.msg "chef_environment is currently #{node_object.chef_environment}"
      node_object.chef_environment = name_args.last  ❸
      # Print our node's chef_environment again after we change it
      ui.msg "chef_environment is currently #{node_object.chef_environment}"
      node_object.save  ❹
    end
  end
end
```

❶ As in our previous example, the only dependency our plugin has is the `Chef::Node` object, as we'll only be loading node objects here.

❷ Here we're loading our node object just as we did in our previous example, by calling the `load` method of `Chef::Node` and passing in the first parameter we gave on the command line.

❸ Next, we call the `chef_environment` method of our node object and set it to the last parameter we gave on the command line. This changes the value in our local copy of the `Chef::Node` object, but it has not yet been saved back to the server.

❹   Finally, we call the `save` method on our `Chef::Node` object. This method saves our local modified copy of the node back to the Chef server. It's important to note that only during this final step is the data stored on the Chef server altered.

Let's try running our new example code:

```
$> knife awesome object demo www production \
   --config /tmp/part4_examples/knife.rb --local-mode
chef_environment is currently _default
chef_environment is currently production
```

This output shows that the `chef_environment` attribute on the www node has now been changed from `_default` to `production`. To verify that our change has indeed been saved to the Chef server, let's use the `knife node show` command to output the www node object saved on our test Chef server:

```
$> knife node show www --config /tmp/part4_examples/knife.rb --local-mode
Node Name:   www
Environment: production
FQDN:
IP:
Run List:
Roles:
Recipes:
Platform:
Tags:
```

As we can see, the copy of our www node object saved on the Chef server reflects the change we made locally.

Editing and Saving Objects Interactively

The second method of editing and saving objects is via Knife plugins such as `knife node edit` and `knife data bag edit`, which allow the user to edit an object stored on the Chef server via the configured text editor to quickly and easily test modifications.

Under the hood, when we edit objects in this way the object is first loaded, then downloaded from the server as JSON to a temporary file, at which point the user edits the JSON file directly via the configured text editor. When editing is complete, the object is saved back to the server. In this section, we're going to look at some different methods of combining the object loading and saving techniques we've already learned in this chapter with the methods provided by the `ui` object to implement this behavior.

The first and most simple pattern for editing objects we're going to look at is the `Chef::UI` class's `edit_object` method. This method provides a convenient wrapper to download an object from the server, edit the object, then save it back to the server if any changes have been made. The `edit_object` method takes two parameters: the class of the object to edit, and the name of the object to edit. Let's make use of this method by adding the code in Example 10-8 to *~/.chef/plugins/knife/awesome_object_demo.rb*.

Example 10-8. ~/.chef/plugins/knife/awesome_object_demo.rb

```
module AwesomeInc
 class AwesomeObjectDemo < Chef::Knife
   def run
       ui.edit_object(Chef::Node, name_args.first)
   end
 end
end
```

Our plugin class is extremely simple this time around, and our `run` method consists of a single call to the `edit_object` method of the `ui` object. We're passing `Chef::Node` as the first parameter to tell it the type of object we want to edit, and `name_args.first` as the second parameter to let it know the name of the object. When we try running our plugin and pass in the `www` node as our parameter, we should see a JSON representation of this node open up in the text editor specified by the `EDITOR` environment variable (simulated here):

```
$> knife awesome object demo www \
  --config /tmp/part4_examples/knife.rb --local-mode

Opens in editor:

{
  "name": "www",
  "chef_environment": "production",
  "json_class": "Chef::Node",
  "automatic": {
  },
  "normal": {
  },
  "chef_type": "node",
  "default": {
  },
  "override": {
  },
  "run_list": [

  ]
}
```

While still in the editor, let's try adding an attribute to the `normal` attribute hash of our node object, so that this section of the file now looks like this:

```
"normal": {
  "awesome_level" : 100
},
```

Next, save the file and exit the editor. At this point, we should see the following output:

```
Saved node[www]
```

This output lets us know that our changes to the www node have now been saved back to the server. Let's use the knife node show command to show us the JSON representation of our www node and check this for ourselves:

```
$> knife node show www --config /tmp/part4_examples/knife.rb --local-mode -f json
{
  "name": "www",
  "chef_environment": "production",
  "run_list": [

  ],
  "normal": {
    "awesome_level": 100
  }
}
```

When the www node is loaded from the server and output to the terminal, we see that the awesome_level attribute we added is still present in the object's JSON. For many of the circumstances in which you might want to interactively edit an object in your Knife plugins, the edit_object method of the ui object will provide the functionality you need while keeping your code as simple as possible.

However, this method does restrict what we can do with the object editing workflow—we can only load, edit, and save the object, and are not able to modify the process in any way. So what do we do if we want to introduce some slightly more advanced behavior? What if, for example, we want to make a noninteractive change to our object and then allow users to interactively edit the object to confirm our change and add further changes if they wish to?

If we look at the source code of the UI class (Example 10-9), we see that the edit_ob ject method is really just a wrapper around the loading and saving techniques we've already seen in previous examples along with a call to the edit_data method of the ui object.

Example 10-9. Excerpt of lib/chef/knife/core/ui.rb

```
class Chef
  class Knife
    class UI

      # Other methods and comments removed

      def edit_object(klass, name)
          object = klass.load(name) ❶

          output = edit_data(object) ❷
```

```
      # Generate the JSON representations of original and edited objects,
      # then check if the object has actually been modified, and only
      # save if it has.
      object_parsed_again = Chef::JSONCompat.from_json(
        Chef::JSONCompat.to_json(object),:create_additions => false)
      output_parsed_again = Chef::JSONCompat.from_json(
        Chef::JSONCompat.to_json(output), :create_additions => false)
      if object_parsed_again != output_parsed_again
        output.save ❸
        self.msg("Saved #{output}")
      else
        self.msg("Object unchanged, not saving")
      end
      output(format_for_display(object)) if config[:print_after] ❹
    end
   end
  end
end
```

❶   Here we're calling the `load` method of the class passed in as the `klass` parameter (this will be a class like `Chef::Node` or `Chef::Role`) to load the object, just as we did in the earlier examples in this chapter. `klass` is a commonly used naming convention in Ruby to indicate a variable that will hold a `Class` object.

❷   Next, we call the `edit_data` method to allow us to edit the object we just loaded. As we examined earlier in this section, behind the scenes this opens a temporary file containing the JSON representation of the loaded object, which we can then edit in our configured text editor. Note that because the `edit_object` method is in the `Chef::UI` class, just as the `edit_data` method is, we don't need to add any prefix to our method call.

❸   Finally, if the object has changed (i.e., if the JSON representation of the object returned from `edit_data` is not identical to the JSON representation of the object passed in), then we call the `save` method of our edited object to save the object back to the Chef server.

❹   We can then optionally display the modified object to the user if the `:print_af ter` configuration option has been set.

Because the `edit_object` method seen here uses relatively simple method calls, if we want to customize this process we can easily replicate the behavior in this method and modify it as required. Let's test this out in our example plugin by implementing the example we talked about earlier—we're going to combine noninteractive and interactive object editing by adding the code in Example 10-10 to *~/.chef/plugins/knife/ awesome_object_demo.rb*.

Example 10-10. ~/.chef/plugins/knife/awesome_object_demo.rb

```
module AwesomeInc
 class AwesomeObjectDemo < Chef::Knife

    deps do
      require 'chef/node' ❶
    end

    def run
        node_object = Chef::Node.load(name_args.first) ❷
        ui.msg "Setting chef_environment of #{name_args.first}" +
          " to #{name_args.last}"
        node_object.chef_environment(name_args.last) ❸
        output = ui.edit_data(node_object) ❹
        ui.msg "Saving #{output}"
        output.save ❺
    end
 end
end
```

❶   Because once again we're going to be editing a Chef::Node object, we need to
      require the chef/node class. As in previous examples, this is done in the deps
      block to ensure that we lazily load our plugin's dependencies.

❷   Just as we did in previous examples, we call the load method of the Chef::Ob
      ject class next, passing in name_args.first, to load our node object from the
      server.

❸   Here, we call the chef_environment method of our loaded node object and pass
      in name_args.last to set the node's chef_environment attribute, just as we did
      in "Editing and Saving Objects Noninteractively" on page 290.

❹   Next, we call the edit_data method of the ui object and pass in the object we
      loaded and edited in steps 2 and 3 to allow the user to interactively edit our
      object. We assign the result of this method call to the output variable.

❺   Finally, we save the output object back to the server by calling its save method.
      Note that to keep things simple, we're calling the save method without checking
      whether or not the object has been modified.

Now let's try running our example plugin and compare its results to those we saw earlier,
when using the edit_object method (again the editor section is simulated here). We'll
pass the parameters www and _default to our plugin:

```
$> knife awesome object demo www _default
--config /tmp/part4_examples/knife.rb --local-mode -f json
Setting chef_environment of www to _default

Opens in editor:
```

```
{
  "name": "www",
  "chef_environment": "_default",
  "json_class": "Chef::Node",
  "automatic": {
  },
  "normal": {
  },
  "chef_type": "node",
  "default": {
  },
  "override": {
  },
  "run_list": [

  ]
}
```

Save the file and exit the editor. At this point, we should see the following output:

```
Saved node[www]
```

This time when we run our plugin, after the node object is loaded the chef_environ
ment attribute is changed to _default noninteractively before the object is opened in
our configured text editor, allowing us to confirm the change that has been made and
add any other changes we might want to make. Note that because we are not explicitly
checking whether the object has been altered before saving it, when we exit our text
editor the object is saved regardless of whether or not we make further changes.

Advanced Node Editing

Readers interested in looking at slightly more advanced object editing behavior might
wish to take a look at the Chef::Knife::NodeEditor class, which lives at *lib/chef/knife/
core/node_editor.rb* (*http://bit.ly/gh-node-edit*).

This class augments the techniques and methods we've examined throughout this section with error handling and checks geared specifically to editing node objects, such as:

- Ensuring that no invalid attributes are added to node objects
- Warning about the creation of new node objects when a node is renamed while
  being edited
- Ensuring that a properly configured editor has been specified

We won't be using the Chef::Knife::NodeEditor class in this chapter, but you can see
it in action in the Chef::Knife::NodeEdit class, which lives at *lib/chef/knife/
node_edit.rb* (*http://bit.ly/node-edit-rb*) and implements the knife node edit command.

As our examples in this chapter have shown, nodes can be edited just the same as any of Chef's other core object types by using methods of the ui object like edit_data and edit_object. However, it's still worth being aware of the Chef::Knife::NodeEditor class and the additional safeguards it gives when node objects are being edited.

So far in this section, we've looked at how to load core objects from the server, edit them both interactively and noninteractively, and save them back to the server. The final aspect of working with objects in our Knife plugins that we're going to examine is how to create and update objects from JSON or Ruby files.

Creating and Updating Objects from Files

The final tool we're going to add to our toolbox for working with Chef objects in our Knife plugin classes is the ability to create and update objects from local JSON or Ruby files. A number of default Knife plugins implement this behavior, such as knife node from file and knife role from file, and the underlying techniques are extremely useful for those occasions when we need to interact with files contained in our Chef repository and upload them to the Chef server.

To implement this behavior, we're going to use the final Knife helper class we'll meet in this chapter: the Chef::Knife::Core::ObjectLoader class, which lives at *lib/chef/knife/core/object_loader.rb* (*http://bit.ly/gh-objectload*). Unlike the other helper classes we've met so far in this chapter, such as the Chef::Knife::UI class, the object loader is relatively simple.

The method of the Chef::Knife::Core::ObjectLoader class that we will primarily use here is the load_from method. Just as the load method defined by Chef's core object classes lets us load an object from the Chef server, the load_from method of the Chef::Knife::Core::ObjectLoader class lets us do the same thing from a local file.

Other Chef::Knife::Core::ObjectLoader Methods

The Chef::Knife::Core::ObjectLoader class defines a number of other methods to assist with locating and verifying files to upload to the Chef server. These can be found in the class definition file at *lib/chef/knife/core/object_loader.rb* (*http://bit.ly/gh-objectload*) and include:

find_file
: This method searches for the specified file either in the directory from which the command was executed, or under the cookbook_path defined in *knife.rb*.

find_all_objects
: This method locates all JSON and Ruby files under the specified path—essentially, a list of valid file types from which to potentially load objects.

`find_all_object_dirs`
  This method returns a list of all directories under the specified path in which to search for objects.

`file_exists_and_is_readable?`
  As the name suggests, this method verifies that the specified file actually exists and can be read by Knife.

Let's dive straight into another example and look at how to use this method in practice by writing a plugin to upload a new environment to the server from a JSON file. Add the code in Example 10-11 to the *~/.chef/plugins/knife/awesome_object_demo.rb* file.

Example 10-11. ~/.chef/plugins/knife/awesome_object_demo.rb

```
module AwesomeInc
 class AwesomeObjectDemo < Chef::Knife

   deps do
    require 'chef/knife/core/object_loader' ❶
   end

   def run
      loader = Chef::Knife::Core::ObjectLoader.new(Chef::Environment, ui) ❷
      ui.msg "Loading #{name_args.first}"
      environment_object = loader.load_from('environments', @name_args.first) ❸
      ui.msg "Saving environment #{name_args.first}"
      environment_object.save ❹
   end
 end
end
```

❶ First, we lazily load our dependency, the `Chef::Knife::Core::ObjectLoader` class.

❷ Next, we need to instantiate the `Chef::Knife::Core::ObjectLoader` class by calling its new method. This method takes two parameters: the type of object that will be loaded (`Chef::Environment`, in this case) and the `Chef::Knife::UI` object to use (`ui`, in this case).

❸ Now we call the `load_from` method of our `Chef::Knife::Core::ObjectLoad` er object. This method also takes two parameters: the subdirectory of the cook book_path configured in *knife.rb* to look for files in if they cannot be found in the current directory, and the name of the file to load.

❹ Finally, we call the `save` method of our `environment_object` to save it to the server. If the object being uploaded is new, as in this case, it is created. If it already exists on the server, it is updated.

Before we can run our example plugin, we're going to need to create a file to upload. As we've seen, the load_from method of the Chef::Knife::Core::ObjectLoader class will look for files to load in the directory from which the Knife command is being run, as well as the configured cookbook_path directory. So, let's paste the JSON in Example 10-12 into */tmp/part4_examples/awesome.json*.

Example 10-12. /tmp/part4_examples/awesome.json

```
{
  "name": "awesome",
  "description": "",
  "json_class": "Chef::Environment",
  "chef_type": "environment",
  "default_attributes": {
    "awesome_level": 100
  },
  "override_attributes": {}
}
```

Now that we have our plugin class and the file for it to load, we can go ahead and run it:

```
$> cd /tmp/part4_examples
$> knife awesome object demo awesome.json \
   --config /tmp/part4_examples/knife.rb --local-mode
Loading awesome.json
Saving environment awesome.json
```

As we see in the output here, the *awesome.json* file that we just created is first loaded, then saved. Let's list the environments on our test Chef server now with the knife environment list command to verify that our new environment has in fact been saved on the server:

```
$> knife environment list --local-mode \
   --config /tmp/part4_examples/knife.rb
awesome
production
staging
```

As we see here, the awesome environment we described in *awesome.json* has now been uploaded to the server, and it can be used alongside the existing production and stag ing environments.

In this section, we've examined a variety of techniques and classes for working with Chef objects in our Knife plugins. We've looked at how to load objects both from Knife searches and directly, how to edit objects interactively and noninteractively and save them back to the server, and how to create and update objects from local files. Now, to tie these techniques together with the topics covered throughout the rest of the chapter, we're going to look at a final, slightly more advanced example.

Knife Example 3: Tying It All Together

To round off the technical portion of the chapter, we're going to look at one final Knife plugin example. Here, we'll tie together the topics we've looked at so far in this chapter with a couple of new plugin code techniques to create a plugin that will allow us to load a node object and set its environment to the specified value, and *optionally* allowing the node object to be edited interactively before it is saved back to the server. Unlike in our previous plugin examples, in this example we'll include full input validation and error handling to more accurately represent the sort of plugin we might create in real life.

Paste the code in Example 10-13 into ~/.chef/plugins/knife/awesome_setup.rb.

Example 10-13. ~/.chef/plugins/knife/awesome_setup.rb

```
module AwesomeInc
  class AwesomeSetup < Chef::Knife

    # Lazily load our dependencies
    deps do
      require 'chef/node'
      require 'chef/knife/core/object_loader'
    end

    # Specify the banner to show when options are not specified
    banner "knife awesome setup NODE ENVIRONMENT (options)"

    option :interactive_edit, ❶
      :short => "-i",
      :long => "--interactive-edit",
      :description => "Allows node to be edited interactively"

    def run

      # Assign our parameters to variables for convenience
      node_name = name_args.first
      environment_name = name_args.last

      # Verify that our required options have been specified
      if node_name.nil? or environment_name.nil?
        show_usage ❷
        ui.fatal("You must specify a node name and an environment")
        exit 1
      end

      # Load the node object
      ui.msg "Loading node #{node_name}"
      node_object = Chef::Node.load(node_name)

      # Set the chef_environment of the node object to the
      # specified environment
      ui.msg "Setting environment of #{node_object} to #{environment_name}"
```

```
      node_object.chef_environment = environment_name

      # If the -i option was specified...
      if config[:interactive_edit] ❸
        # Then let the user edit the object interactively
        ui.info "Interactive edit requested, opening" +
          "#{node_name} in configured editor:"
        edited_object = ui.edit_data(node_object)
      end

      # Finally, save the object
      final_object = edited_object || node_object ❹
      ui.info "Saving #{final_object}"
      final_object.save
    end
  end
end
```

❶ The option method we're calling here makes use of Chef, Inc.'s mixlib-cli
   (*http://bit.ly/gh-mixlib*) gem, which provides methods for parsing command-
   line options in applications such as Knife. mixlib-cli is included in the Knife
   source code as a mixin, and the options it supports are documented on the Chef
   Documents site (*http://bit.ly/knife-options*). Options specified in this way are
   added to the config object so that we can access them elsewhere in our plugin
   code.

❷ The show_usage method is inherited from our plugin's superclass, Chef::Knife,
   and prints out a nicely formatted list of the options supported by our plugin
   combined with global options supported by all Knife plugins. The show_usage
   method is typically called when our plugin has not been passed the correct
   options, or an invalid option is used.

❸ Here we're checking if the :interactive_edit key of the config hash has been
   set (i.e., if the -i option was passed to our plugin). As we saw in step 2, options
   specified with calls to the option method are added to the config object so that
   we can access them in this way.

❹ The "double pipe" operator we're using here is the built-in Ruby "OR" operator,
   which in this case lets us say, "Assign the value of edited_object to final_ob
   ject if it is not nil OR, if final_object is nil, the value of node_object should
   be used instead."

Now let's try running our plugin class with some different combinations of options to
see how the logic we've incorporated into the class works. First, we're going to run the
plugin with none of the required options specified:

```
$> knife awesome setup --config /tmp/part4_examples/knife.rb --local-mode
USAGE: knife awesome setup NODE ENVIRONMENT (options)
```

```
    -s, --server-url URL                 Chef Server URL
        --chef-zero-port PORT            Port to start chef-zero on
    -k, --key KEY                        API Client Key
        --[no-]color                     Use colored output, defaults to false on
                                             Windows, true otherwise
    -c, --config CONFIG                  The configuration file to use
        --defaults                       Accept default values for all questions
    -d, --disable-editing                Do not open EDITOR, just accept the data
                                             as is
    -e, --editor EDITOR                  Set the editor to use for interactive
                                             commands
    -E, --environment ENVIRONMENT        Set the Chef environment
    -F, --format FORMAT                  Which format to use for output
    -i, --interactive-edit               Allows node to be edited interactively
    -z, --local-mode                     Point knife commands at local repository
                                             instead of server
    -u, --user USER                      API Client Username
        --print-after                    Show the data after a destructive operation
    -V, --verbose                        More verbose output. Use twice for max
                                             verbosity
    -v, --version                        Show chef version
    -y, --yes                            Say yes to all prompts for confirmation
    -h, --help                           Show this message
FATAL: You must specify a node name and an environment
```

In this output, we see our banner being combined with the output of the show_usage method to display a nicely formatted list of options supported by our plugin, and instructions for the format in which it expects its parameters. Next, let's try passing our plugin the correct options and having it edit our node object noninteractively:

```
$> knife awesome setup www awesome
--config /tmp/part4_examples/knife.rb --local-mode
Loading node www
Setting environment of node[www] to awesome
Saving node[www]
```

This time, we see our plugin class loading the www node, setting its environment to awesome, and then saving it back to the server. Finally, let's try passing the -i option to our plugin to specify that we want to interactively edit the node object after the environment is set (editor section simulated):

```
$> knife awesome setup www production
--config /tmp/part4_examples/knife.rb --local-mode -i
Loading node www
Setting environment of node[www] to production
Interactive edit requested, opening www in configured editor:

Opens in editor:

{
  "name": "www",
  "chef_environment": "production",
```

```
        "json_class": "Chef::Node",
        "automatic": {
        },
        "normal": {
        },
        "chef_type": "node",
        "default": {
        },
        "override": {
        },
        "run_list": [

        ]
      }
```

Save the file and exit the editor. At this point, we should see the following output:

```
Saved node[www]
```

This time, we see that passing the `-i` option to our plugin class lets us interactively edit the `www` node object after the plugin has noninteractively set its environment.

We've looked at a number of different techniques and examples for writing Knife plugins in this chapter, but most of the plugins we've looked at thus far have been (intentionally) relatively trivial. In the real world, what sort of Knife plugins might we want to create, and how useful really are the techniques we've covered in this chapter? We'll see a number of real-world example of Knife plugins in "Summary and Further Reading" on page 306, but before that we're going to revisit our friends at AwesomeInc and see how Knife plugins might help them solve the final problem we learned about in "Criteria for Customization" on page 10.

Revisiting AwesomeInc—Plugin Best Practices

As we saw in Chapter 1, the folks at AwesomeInc are already using Knife's built-in commands to drive their Chef workflow, but they've been finding that as both the team and the infrastructure being managed grow, the corresponding increase in the frequency and complexity of Chef changes is making it increasingly hard to keep track of what has been changed by whom and when. The team has also been finding that it is increasingly overwriting changes made by other team members when working simultaneously on the same cookbook, role, or environment.

So, given what we've learned in this chapter about writing Knife plugins, what advice can we offer AwesomeInc to answer the question, "How do we stop our developers and ops staff treading all over each other's changes?" Here are a few suggestions:

Wrap existing plugins where possible.
> As we've already seen in this chapter, Knife ships with a number of default plugins for accomplishing common tasks. Where possible, I recommend that AwesomeInc

---

create wrapper classes around existing plugins to add functionality allowing them to send notifications of Chef changes to their internal monitoring and chat systems. Just as in general software development, it usually doesn't pay to reinvent the wheel — the folks at AwesomeInc should make use of the functionality and classes supplied with Chef to minimize the amount of functionality they have to code in their customizations.

Make use of helper classes.

Where wrapping an existing Chef plugin is not possible—for example if the team wanted to alter the workflow of a particular Chef task, as we did in "Editing and Saving Objects Interactively" on page 292—AwesomeInc should make use of the Chef helper classes we've learned about in this chapter. Much of the functionality provided by Knife's default plugins is underpinned by these classes, and using them helps to ensure a unified user experience across all Knife plugins. Classes such as `Chef::Knife::ObjectLoader` and the `UI` class also provide methods that can be utilized to implement more complex Knife plugins, while still minimizing the amount of "reinventing the wheel" that has to be done.

Make plugins configurable.

To make their plugin classes as flexible as possible, I recommend that AwesomeInc make the most of Knife's built-in capability to handle command-line options and parameters to add configurable behavior to their plugin classes as we did in the previous section. Creating plugins that implement a core subset of functionality while also allowing users to tweak and control the specific options used means that a wide number of use cases and user preferences can be catered for in a much smaller number of plugin classes, than if all options were mandatory.

Let the community help.

When looking at creating Knife plugins to help solve problems, I recommend that AwesomeInc investigate community resources such as the "Community Plugins" page (*http://bit.ly/comm-knife*) provided by Chef, Inc. to see if anyone else in the Chef community has already solved those specific problems first. It is often the case that other Chef users will have experienced the same issues and may have open sourced their solutions. Even if community solutions don't exactly fit AwesomeInc's needs, they can often provide a good starting point.

In the case of the specific problem AwesomeInc is trying to solve here, the desire to solve issues uncovered when scaling Chef and the teams that work with it were the motivation for the development of many of the Chef workflow tools we looked at in "Workflow Tooling" on page 14. knife-spork (*http://bit.ly/knife-spork*), in particular, was originally developed at Etsy to solve exactly the sorts of problems that AwesomeInc is experiencing—as our infrastructure and the number of users making Chef changes grew, it became harder to keep track of changes and avoid overwriting other people's changes, and the flexibility and power of Knife plugins helped us solve these problems.

Summary and Further Reading

In this chapter, we covered a number of different aspects of Knife plugin development. We learned about the common skeleton shared by all Knife plugins, before looking at the anatomy of a Knife command's execution. We then looked at how to wrap existing Chef plugins and run search queries against Chef, creating a test environment in which to run our example plugins along the way. We met the various helper classes that are provided with the Chef source code to help us interact with users and format and display the output of our plugins. Finally, we learned how to work with the various object types that are stored on the Chef server, before revisiting AwesomeInc to look at how Knife plugins might be utilized to solve one of the problems they're experiencing.

Hopefully the material we've covered in this chapter will help you in the implementation of your own Knife plugins and give you some ideas for plugins to create, but as with many of the customization types we've looked at in this book, there are simply too many possibilities for us to cover everything that could possibly be implemented in a Knife plugin.

Readers interested in diving deeper into Knife plugin development may wish to check out the source code of the Knife plugins we looked at in Chapter 1, in "Workflow Tooling" on page 14 and "Knife Plugins" on page 15. Chef, Inc. also maintains a list of community-contributed Knife plugins on the Chef Documents site (*http://bit.ly/comm-knife*): you'll find a mix of plugins that add extra functionality to existing Knife commands, plugins that make use of Chef core objects to perform a variety of tasks, and plugins that integrate with third-party systems such as cloud provider APIs.

In the next chapter, we're going to examine the Chef API in much more extensive detail, looking at the methods and data it exposes and how we can use these to create reports and visualizations of our Chef infrastructure.

## CHAPTER 11

The Chef API

In Chapter 10, we met several core Chef objects, such as `Chef::Node` and `Chef::Envi ronment` that provide us with an abstraction layer around the underlying API used to communicate with the Chef server. In this chapter, we're going to look at the API itself and how and why you might want to use it. We'll learn about:

- What the Chef API is and why it's provided
- The requirements for communicating with Chef's API
- How to authenticate to the API
- How to call API methods
- The endpoints supported by the API and the data they return
- The helper classes Chef provides for communicating with the API

We'll also look at a number of examples of using the Chef API as we work through the chapter.

Introduction to the Chef API

If you take another look at the Chef architecture diagram in "Chef Architecture" on page 58, you'll see the *Erchef* component, which provides the core API that enables both Chef's client tools and the outside world to communicate with Chef server. To use the technical definition, this is an HTTP-based RESTful API that accepts and returns JSON data to allow us to read from and write to a Chef server.

Entire books have been written about exactly what the term REST means, but for the purposes of this book we're going to use the definition "structured to make it easy for our code to talk to the API efficiently while still allowing us mere mortals to understand the information that is being exchanged."

What this means in practical terms is that to communicate with the Chef API, we send HTTP requests to specific Chef server URLs known as endpoints, and provided the server identifies us an authorized client, it then process our requests and sends us back JSON data with the results. A request could involve reading data from the server, writing data to the server, or even asking the server to delete data.

The fact that Chef's API is HTTP-based actually helps with the implementation of this functionality, because the HTTP protocol supports different *verbs* (such as GET, PUT, and DELETE) that are designed to tell the server we're communicating with the action that should be performed with the request data we send it. For example, if we send the Chef Server API a DELETE request, this indicates that we want the server to delete the object we specify in the URL.

Correspondingly, the Chef API carries out different actions depending on the verbs sent to its endpoints. For example, a properly authenticated GET request to */roles/foo* returns that role, whereas a DELETE request to */roles/foo* causes the server to delete it.

The full list of endpoints and verbs supported by the Chef API is documented in Appendix A.

So Why Use the Chef API?

Many of the examples we've looked at so far in this book have communicated with the Chef API under the hood, but the various helper classes and methods provided with Chef have abstracted this away from us. After all, to use the roles scenario we discussed in the last section, Knife already provides us with a plugin for deleting roles, and the Chef::Role class already provides us with the .load method to fetch a role from the server. So why on earth would we want to talk to the Chef Server API manually if all of these handy helper classes are already provided for us? Let's look at some of the reasons:

Not everybody uses Ruby.

Although it's the only programming language we've looked at in this book thus far, Ruby is far from the only programming language in use today. As Chef, Inc. currently only provides Ruby helper classes, users of other programming languages who want to communicate with the Chef API must talk to it directly, or implement their own helper classes that do so in those languages. We'll look at some of the helper classes provided for other languages later on in the chapter.

Helper classes and methods don't do everything.

The helper classes and methods we've seen so far in this book that use the API, such as the `load` and `save` methods of the core object classes, are primarily used within Chef itself to fulfill specific functions, and as a result they usually only use specific portions of the API. If you find yourself trying to perform tasks not directly supported by an existing class or method, or find yourself combining tasks in a way that would requires multiple helper objects at once, it might prove more convenient to access the Chef API directly.

Lightweight code.

Although Chef provides a number of useful helper classes, as we've seen, the Chef code is often somewhat heavyweight, as many helper classes implement API wrapper methods alongside a variety of other functionality. If all we want our code to do is talk to the Chef API, implementing the API communication directly rather than including multiple Chef classes and using a method or two from each can make our code significantly more lightweight and performant.

Because the people at Chef, Inc. want to make our lives as easy as possible, the Chef repository actually includes helper classes specifically designed solely for communicating with the Chef API when using Ruby. Because we're going to be using Ruby for our code examples, we'll meet these helper classes later in this chapter; but before we do, we're going to dive deeper into exactly how the Chef API fits together.

As has been the case with many of the other areas of Chef we've looked at in this book, a good understanding of what exactly a helper class is abstracting away from you will not only help you debug issues, but help you gain a clearer understanding of how that class fits into the wider Chef ecosystem—so let's dive in!

Authenticating to the Chef API

As you might imagine, authenticating to the Chef API is the first step in making an API request to the Chef server. We've actually already looked at a number of code examples that authenticate against the Chef API behind the scenes, in "Authenticate/Register" on page 64 when we examined the anatomy of Chef runs, and in "Anatomy of a Knife Command" on page 266 when we examined how Knife plugins authenticate against the Chef server before running.

In these sections, however, the details of this authentication process were abstracted away so that we didn't have to worry about anything other than specifying the correct client key to use. When communicating directly with the API, in contrast, we need to properly authenticate our API requests ourselves.

Because the Chef API is HTTP-based, we pass our authentication information as *headers* in the requests we make to the server. Let's remind ourselves how headers fit into the structure of HTTP requests with a quick look at what happens when we request the Google UK home page (Figure 11-1).

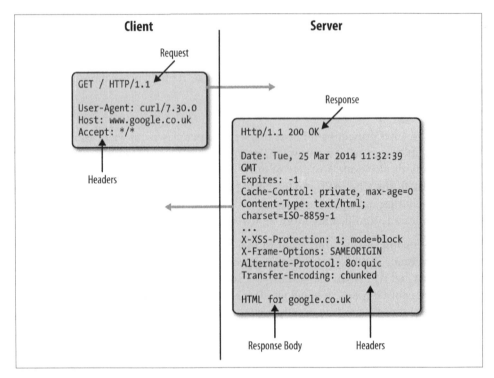

Figure 11-1. HTTP request/response

As we see in this diagram, each request to the server comprises the request itself, and an arbitrary number of headers. In this case, the headers tell the server the `User-Agent` string of the software making the request, the `Host` the request is being made against, and finally (in the `Accept` header) what response types the client can accept.

The server then returns its response, which contains headers specifying various details such as how the response should be cached and whether or not it is encoded or compressed, followed by the actual response body—in this case, the source code for the Google UK home page.

Like all HTTP-based services, the Chef API follows this same pattern of communication. We submit HTTP requests to the server with the correct authentication headers, then the server either carries out the requested action if we were authorized to make that request, or returns an error if we were not authorized. We're going to examine the authentication headers required by the Chef server by looking at an example API request. In Example 11-1, we simulate asking the Chef API for a list of environments.

Example 11-1. Example Chef API request with headers

```
GET /environments HTTP/1.1
  Host: chef.mycompany.com:443
  Accept: application/json
  X-Chef-Version: 11.10.0
  X-Ops-Sign: algorithm=sha1;version=1.0;
  X-Ops-Userid: myuser
  X-Ops-Timestamp: 2014-03-26T13:37:00Z
  X-Ops-Content-Hash: 2jmj7l5rfasfgSw0ygaVb/vlWAghYkK/YBwk=
  X-Ops-Authorization-1: BE3NnHeh5yFTiT3ifuwLSPCCYasdfXaRN5oZb4c6hbW0aefI
  X-Ops-Authorization-2: sL4j1qtEZzi/2WeF67UuytdsdfgbOc5CjgECQwqrym9gCUON
  X-Ops-Authorization-3: yf0p7PrLRCNasdfaHhQ2LWoE/+kTcu0dkasdfvaTghfCDC57
  X-Ops-Authorization-4: 155i+Zlthfasfhbfrtukusb IUGBKUYFjhbvcds3k0i0gqs+V
  X-Ops-Authorization-5: /sLcR7JjQky7sdafIHNEEBQrISktNCDGfFI9o6hbFIayFBx3
  X-Ops-Authorization-6: nodilAGMb166@haC/fttwlWQ2N1LasdqqGomRedtyhSqXA==
```

That's quite a lot of headers! Let's break them down and examine each one in detail:

Host

The Host header is a standard header used in all HTTP requests to tell the destination server which hostname is being requested. As most HTTP servers are capable of serving multiple hostnames, this allows the server to properly route the requests. In this case, because we're communicating with the server over HTTPS, we specify :443 to indicate the SSL port should be used.

Accept

As we saw in our earlier example, the Accept header is used to tell the HTTP server what types of responses our HTTP client can handle. Including this header is technically optional here as Chef will only ever return JSON, but we're including it for clarity.

X-Chef-Version

The X-Chef-Version header is used to tell the chef server which Chef-client version has been used to make the request. This ensures that responses are returned in the correct format for the client, since multiple chef-client versions might be communicating with the server. When we're talking to the API manually, as we will be in this chapter, this header should be set to the installed chef-client version for the sake of simplicity.

X-Ops-Sign

The X-Ops-Sign header is used to let the Chef server know what algorithm has been used to hash the data included with our request. At the time of writing, this header should always be set to algorithm=sha1;version=1.0;, as shown in this example.

X-Ops-Userid

The X-Ops-Userid header tells the server which client is making the request—this allows the server to validate that the headers have been signed using the correct client key.

X-Ops-Timestamp

The X-Ops-Timestamp header contains a timestamp of when the request to the server was made. This timestamp should always be in the format YYYY-MM-DDTHH:MM:SSZ. Note that the time portion of this timestamp is prefixed with a T and suffixed with a Z. For the interested reader, this timestamp is in ISO 8601-compliant format (*http://bit.ly/iso-8601*).

X-Ops-Content-Hash

The X-Ops-Content-Hash header contains the body of the request (if we're sending data to the server) hashed using the SHA1 algorithm, and then encoded as Base64. If you're not familiar with these terms, don't worry; we'll look at this in more detail in our code examples later in the chapter.

X-Ops-Authorization-n

Finally, we come to the X-Ops-Authorization-n headers. These headers (six of them in the above example) contain a specially formatted Base64-encoded string that has been signed with the private key of the client making the request. This string, which is composed of a number of items of data about the request, is then broken into 60-character-long lines, with each resulting line being added to the next X-Ops-Authorization-n header. This header is used by the Chef server to ensure that the request has been correctly authenticated, and that the authentication headers from a previous request have not been copied and reused.

To see these headers in action, we're going to dive into a code example to look at how we can construct the headers ourselves and send properly authenticated requests to the Chef API. But first, as in previous chapters, we need to prepare a test environment to run our example code in.

Creating a Test Environment

The final thing we need to do before starting to implement our own code to send requests to the Chef API is to create a test environment in which to safely run our examples. As in previous chapters, we ideally don't want to send requests to a production Chef server while we're learning about how the Chef API works, so we're going to need to use a "mock" Chef server. Luckily for us, chef-zero (which we've been using to power the running of chef-client and Knife in local mode in previous chapters) is in fact a lightweight Chef server that supports an identical API to full Chef servers and should be ideal for our purposes.

We're going to reuse the test environment we created in "Creating a Test Environment" on page 270 here, so if you haven't already done so you should complete the steps listed in that section. In that test environment, we created a client key to authenticate to the server, and we downloaded the chef-zero source code so that we could make use of the "playground" directory it provides to give us test data to use with our chef-zero server.

 As chef-zero provides a mock Chef server, it will accept any authentication key it is given. Open source and hosted Enterprise Chef servers require valid authentication keys tied to a client before API requests will be permitted.

When we used this test environment to run Knife commands we were using the --local-mode option of the knife command to start up chef-zero for us. To run our API examples, however, we're going to need to start up chef-zero manually (as we won't be running it as part of a knife or chef-client command) and load the "playground" data into it so that we have some data to work with.

I've created a quick bash script that performs these tasks for us, so to get started, paste the code in Example 11-2 into */tmp/part4_examples/test_environment*.

Example 11-2. /tmp/part4_examples/test_environment

```
#!/usr/bin/env bash

if [ $# -ne 1 ]
then
  echo "Usage: 'test_environment start|stop'"
  exit $E_BADARGS
fi


case "$1" in

start) echo "Starting Chef-Zero"
    chef-zero &
    echo "Loading playground data"
    cd /tmp/part4_examples/chef-zero/playground
    knife upload . -c /tmp/part4_examples/knife.rb
    echo "Test environment ready to rock!"
    ;;
stop) echo  "Stopping Chef-Zero"
    ps -ef | grep /usr/bin/chef-zero | grep -v grep | \
      awk '{print $2}' | xargs kill -9
    ;;
esac
```

Next we need to make the script executable. To do this run the following command:

```
$> chmod 755 /tmp/part4_examples/test_environment
```

After that's done, you can run the script from inside the */tmp/part4_examples* directory with the start or stop parameters to, respectively, start and stop your chef-zero test environment. Here is an example of the output you should see from each command:

```
$> ./test_environment start

Starting Chef-Zero
Loading playground data
>> Starting Chef Zero (v1.7.2)...
>> Puma (v1.6.3) is listening at http://127.0.0.1:8889
>> Press CTRL+C to stop
Created environments/awesome.json
Created nodes/desktop.json
Created nodes/dns.json
Created nodes/www.json
Created nodes/ldap.json
Created nodes/lb.json
Created data_bags/dns
Created data_bags/passwords
Created environments/production.json
Created environments/staging.json
Created data_bags/users
Created cookbooks/apache2
Created data_bags/passwords/github.json
Created data_bags/passwords/twitter.json
Created data_bags/dns/services.json
Created data_bags/users/sethvargo.json
Created data_bags/users/jkeiser.json
Created data_bags/users/schisamo.json
Created cookbooks/php
Test environment ready to rock!

$> ./test_environment stop

Stopping Chef-Zero
```

We now have a working test server to make API requests against. Before moving on, you should make sure that your test environment is running (execute ./test_environ ment start from inside */tmp/part4_examples*). Now let's dive into some code!

API Example 1: Authenticating and Making a GET Request

Now that we've examined the authentication headers required by the Chef API and created a test environment in which to run our example code. let's look at a code example that constructs the required authentication headers and then makes a call to the API to request a list of environments from the server. Paste the code in Example 11-3 into */tmp/part4_examples/api_manual_get.rb*.

 Example 11-3 contains some fairly advanced Ruby code to interface directly with the Chef API. Later in the chapter, we'll cover helper objects provided by Chef to abstract away this functionality, so readers less comfortable with Ruby may optionally wish to move straight to "The Chef::Rest Class" on page 318. However, I'd recommend at least skimming the comments in the code listed here.

Example 11-3. /tmp/part4_examples/api_manual_get.rb

```ruby
#!/usr/bin/env ruby

# Require our dependencies (all in Ruby standard library)
require "base64"
require 'digest/sha1'
require "net/http"
require "uri"

# Print an error if no command-line argument given
if ARGV.empty?
  puts "ERROR: You must supply a path to request from the API"
  exit 1
end

# Our client key, client name, and Chef server URL
client_key = "/tmp/part4_examples/customizing_chef.pem"
client_name = "cctest"
chef_server = "http://127.0.0.1:8889"
# The path to call will be our first command-line parameter
path = ARGV[0]
# We're going to do a GET request, so the request body
# will be empty
body = ""

# Base64 encode the path and body of our request
hashed_path = Base64.encode64(Digest::SHA1.digest(path)).chomp
hashed_body = Base64.encode64(Digest::SHA1.digest(body)).chomp

# Generate timestamp
timestamp = Time.now.strftime("%Y-%m-%dT%H:%M:%SZ").to_s

# Construct our first set of headers, some of which will be used
# to construct the X-Ops-Authorization headers next

headers = {'X-Ops-Timestamp' => timestamp,
           'X-Ops-Userid' => client_name,
           'X-Chef-Version' => '11.10.0',
           'Accept' => 'application/json',
```

```
            'X-Ops-Content-Hash' => hashed_body,
            'X-Ops-Sign' => 'version=1.0'
        }

# Construct the specially formatted string needed to generate
# X-Ops-Authorization headers. This string must always be in the
# format and order shown here and contain the headers shown.
canonical_request="Method:GET\\n" +
                "Hashed Path:#{hashed_path}\\n" +
                "X-Ops-Content-Hash:#{hashed_body}\\n" +
                "X-Ops-Timestamp:#{timestamp}\\n" +
                "X-Ops-UserId:#{client_name}"

# Sign our canonical_request string with the specified client key
command = `printf \"#{canonical_request}\" |
  openssl rsautl -sign -inkey #{client_key}`

signed_hash = `#{command}`

# Then encode it as Base64 and split the encoded hash into 60-char-long lines
encoded_hash = Base64.encode64(signed_hash).gsub("\n","").scan(/.{1,60}/m)

# Split up our newly constructed X-Ops-Authorization headers
# and add them to the headers hash
encoded_hash.each_with_index do |text,index|
  headers["X-Ops-Authorization-#{index+1}"] = text
end

# Then output our final headers to screen
puts "Request Headers:"
headers.each{|key,value|puts "#{key}:#{value}"}

# Construct the full path we're going to request from the API
full_path = "#{chef_server}#{path}"
puts ""
puts "Making GET request to #{full_path}"

# Parse the full_path into a URI object
uri = URI.parse(full_path)

# Initialize our Net::HTTP object
http = Net::HTTP.new(uri.host, uri.port)
# Use SSL if our Chef server URL contained https://
if uri.scheme == "https"
  http.use_ssl = true
  # Ignore self-signed SSL cert errors
  # DO NOT DO THIS IN PRODUCTION CODE!!!
  http.verify_mode = OpenSSL::SSL::VERIFY_NONE
end

# Create a new Net::HTTP::Get object, which we populate with
# our headers
```

```
request = Net::HTTP::Get.new(uri.request_uri,headers)

# Finally, send the request to the API
resp = http.request(request)

# Print the response code and body of our request
puts "Response Code: #{resp.code}"
puts "Response Body: #{resp.body}"
```

Now let's try running our example code. We're going to request a list of environments, so we pass the /environments endpoint as our parameter:

```
$> ruby api_manual_get.rb /environments
Request Headers:
X-Ops-Timestamp:2014-03-27T14:07:18Z
X-Ops-Userid:cctest
X-Chef-Version:11.10.0
Accept:application/json
X-Ops-Content-Hash:2jmj7l5rSw0yVb/vlWAYkK/YBwk=
X-Ops-Sign:version=1.0
X-Ops-Authorization-1:THKX0SwaJdTsiQVa4gHPXQk5ZpeAe9O2qeWBggYfwC5C5EoUuKoetcJTGR/
X-Ops-Authorization-2:/Lbn7TNqwrZJdqxQKeQRXA2wKrc+6XVgOC5iOhtacub1UsgKwBxQNo3mISd
X-Ops-Authorization-3:2cV1baxL5vr4vVqC5RzcNVBBgua5rxmwh0ku1x7ZA20HyvowrQG+Eav/oyA
X-Ops-Authorization-4:6kYdopiRHHqTojayvbk+lNALkS6XDKHmqQ8mOZFWnEP8hLtc4TWP4qQeIcO
X-Ops-Authorization-5:7kYSG4tWXrmK50SqfoCRsS1DCf3J/wCvv5QrkIQlPqGDv8Pwg76BXFpuJ+5
X-Ops-Authorization-6:hLlc+lVSGJi2moOFXFWpuh8Tvp9MU2t6CCeaO6wSjg==

Making GET request to http://127.0.0.1:8889/environments
Response Code: 200
Response Body: {
  "_default": "http://127.0.0.1:8889/environments/_default",
  "awesome": "http://127.0.0.1:8889/environments/awesome",
  "production": "http://127.0.0.1:8889/environments/production",
  "staging": "http://127.0.0.1:8889/environments/staging"
}
```

In this output, we see that our code first constructs the headers needed to authenticate to the Chef API before going on to make a GET request to the /environments API endpoint. The chef-zero server then authenticates our request and when it has determined that we're authorized to issue that request, returns the list of environments to us as JSON.

A detailed understanding of how the Chef API works under the hood is extremely useful and can be invaluable when trying to debug issues or communicate with Chef from programming languages other than Ruby—but having to create all that header-generation code and run it every time we want to make an API request is somewhat tiresome.

I'm a firm believer in the importance of understanding the fine details of how Chef works under the hood, but I'm also a believer in using helper classes to abstract away complex code where possible. Fortunately, to allow us to make API requests from our Ruby code without having write authentication code ourselves or pick and choose from among all of Chef's core object classes, Chef, Inc. has provided us with another helper class designed specifically for making API requests to the Chef server, which we're going to meet next.

 Chef API libraries have also been created for a number of other popular programming languages, including Python (*http://bit.ly/pychef-023*), Go (*http://bit.ly/chef-golang*), and Node.js (*http://bit.ly/gh-chefnode*). If you want to implement the Chef API in a language without an existing client library, hopefully the preceding code example will give you a good starting point!

The Chef::Rest Class

To abstract away the need to manually construct authentication headers to include with our API requests to the Chef server, Chef provides the `Chef::Rest` class, which lives at */lib/chef/rest.rb* (*http://bit.ly/gh-restrb*) and defines a number of methods to allow us to use different HTTP verbs to make requests to the Chef API. First, let's take a look at how to instantiate the class.

The `initialize` method of the `Chef::Rest` class takes three parameters: the URL of the Chef server, the name of the client to authenticate API requests against, and the path to the private key to use when generating the authentication headers. The following code shows examples of each:

```
chef_server_url = "http://127.0.0.1:8889"
client_name = "cctest"
signing_key_filename="/tmp/part4_examples/customizing_chef.pem"

rest = Chef::REST.new(chef_server_url, client_name, signing_key_filename)
```

The `Chef::Rest` class also defines methods to allow you to make API calls to the Chef API using specific HTTP verbs. To avoid the need for users of this class to manually parse the JSON they send to and from the API, Chef processes the data fed into these methods to convert it into JSON objects, and converts the data returned from API calls into native Chef objects such as `Chef::Environment` and `Chef::Node` wherever possible. The following verb methods are defined:

get_rest
> The `get_rest` method allows you to make a GET request to the API. It takes one mandatory parameter: the API endpoint to send the request to. It also allows you to optionally specify whether you want to return raw JSON data rather than a Chef object, and a list of extra headers to send to the server.

delete_rest

The `delete_rest` method allows you to send a DELETE request to the API. It takes one mandatory parameter: the API endpoint to send the request to. It also allows you to optionally specify a list of extra headers to send to the server.

post_rest

The `post_rest` method allows you to send a POST request to the API. It takes two mandatory parameters: the API endpoint to send the request to and the JSON data to be sent to the server. It also allows you to optionally specify a list of extra headers to send to the server.

put_rest

The `put_rest` method allows you to send a PUT request to the API. It takes two mandatory parameters: the API endpoint to send the request to and the JSON data to be sent to the server. It also allows you to optionally specify a list of extra headers to send to the server.

POST Versus PUT?

As we see in the list of methods defined by the `Chef::Rest` class, there are actually two HTTP verbs that can be used to send data to the server: POST and PUT. So which should you use? Put simply, the HTTP specification recommends that POST should be used when an object is to be *created*, and PUT when an object is to be *updated*.

The HTTP specification also states that PUT requests should be idempotent—just as with idempotence in Chef, this means that five identical PUT requests should have exactly the same effect as one PUT request, and that actions will only be carried out when necessary.

We can see this distinction in action in the `save` method of the `Chef::Role` class, shown in Example 11-4 (comments added), where the code first tries to update a role using the `put_rest` method; then, if a `404` error is encountered (i.e., the role does not exist on the server), it is created using the `post_rest` method instead.

Example 11-4. Excerpt of lib/chef/role.rb

```
# Save this role via the REST API
  def save
    begin
      # Try updating the role using the put_rest method
      chef_server_rest.put_rest("roles/#{@name}", self)
    rescue Net::HTTPServerException => e
      raise e unless e.response.code == "404"
      # If we got a 404 error, try creating it using post_rest instead
      chef_server_rest.post_rest("roles", self)
    end
```

```
        self
    end
```

Now that we've examined the methods provided by the `Chef::Rest` class, let's replicate the code example we created in "API Example 1: Authenticating and Making a GET Request" on page 314, but this time use the `Chef::Rest` class to demonstrate exactly how much code is abstracted away inside this helper class. Paste the code in Example 11-5 into */tmp/part4_examples/api_helper_get.rb*.

Example 11-5. /tmp/part4_examples/api_helper_get.rb

```ruby
#!/usr/bin/env ruby

require 'chef'

# Print an error if no command-line argument given
if ARGV.empty?
  puts "ERROR: You must supply a path to request from the API"
  exit 1
end

chef_server_url = "http://127.0.0.1:8889"
client_name = "cctest"
signing_key_filename="/tmp/part4_examples/customizing_chef.pem"
path = ARGV[0]

rest = Chef::REST.new(chef_server_url, client_name, signing_key_filename)

returned_data = rest.get_rest(path)

puts returned_data
```

Now let's try running our example code, passing it the same `/environments` endpoint as we did in our manual example:

```
$> ruby api_helper_get.rb /environments
{"_default"=>"http://127.0.0.1:8889/environments/_default",
 "awesome"=>"http://127.0.0.1:8889/environments/awesome",
 "production"=>"http://127.0.0.1:8889/environments/production",
 "staging"=>"http://127.0.0.1:8889/environments/staging"}
```

As this output shows, we've just authenticated to the server and made exactly the same request as in the example code in the previous section, with the server once again returning us a list of environments. This time, however, we did it in much fewer lines of code. When writing code to talk to the Chef API in Ruby, the `Chef::Rest` class will nearly always be the best option, and we'll be using this class for the remainder of the examples in this chapter.

In our next example, we're going to look at how to make use of the input and output conversion that the Chef::Rest class applies to our API calls to combine multiple API calls to several endpoints—this pattern is often used to retrieve a list of object names and URLs from the server before making a GET request to each object.

API Example 2: Combining Multiple API Requests

As we saw in the last section, the Chef::Rest helper class makes it extremely easy for us to make API requests directly against the Chef API. So far, however, we've only looked at making a single GET request to the /environments endpoint. In this example, we're going to look at a slightly more complex example involving making multiple requests to the Chef API, which will also demonstrate Chef's input/output conversion in action.

First, we're going to GET a list of environments from the server, then GET each environment in that initial list, update the description fields of those environments for which that field is currently empty, and finally PUT the modified environments back to the server. Paste the code in Example 11-6 into /tmp/part4_examples/api_example_2.rb.

Example 11-6. /tmp/part4_examples/api_example_2.rb

```ruby
#!/usr/bin/env ruby

require 'chef'

chef_server_url = "http://127.0.0.1:8889"
client_name = "cctest"
signing_key_filename="/tmp/part4_examples/customizing_chef.pem"

rest = Chef::REST.new(chef_server_url, client_name, signing_key_filename)

# GET a list of environments by calling the /environments endpoint
environment_list = rest.get_rest("/environments")

# Iterate over our environments list
environment_list.each do |env|
  env_name = env.first ❶
  puts "Checking environment #{env_name}"

  # For each environment we got back, GET that environment
  # by calling the /environments/NAME endpoint
  env_object = rest.get_rest(env.last) ❷

  # Check if the environment has an empty description attribute
  if env_object.description.empty? ❸
    puts "Description empty, updating..."
    env_object.description("This is the #{env_object.name} environment")
    # Save the environment back to the server by making a
    # PUT request to the /environments/NAME endpoint
    puts "Saving #{env_object.name} environment to the server"
```

```
      rest.put_rest("/environments/#{env_object}",env_object)
  else
    puts "Description OK"
  end
end
```

❶ As we saw in "API Example 1: Authenticating and Making a GET Request" on page 314, the /environments endpoint returns a name and a URL for each environment. Because we only care about the name of the environment here, we're using the first element of that array only.

❷ Here we're making use of the last element of the array for each environment to give us the URL to get that environment directly because the API already gives us this, there's no need for us to manually construct the URL!

❸ The Chef::Rest class has automatically converted the environment downloaded from the server from JSON into a Chef::Environment object. This means we can now access the methods and attributes of the environment without having to parse the returned JSON ourselves.

 The results shown for this example and the following Knife command depends on you having created the awesome.json file used in "Creating and Updating Objects from Files" on page 298 so that your test environment loads the awesome environment. The example code will work just fine without this environment, but if you haven't worked through that section yet you will see different output than that shown here.

Let's try running our example now:

```
$> ruby api_example_2.rb
Checking environment _default
Description OK
Checking environment awesome
Description empty, updating...
Saving awesome environment to the server
Checking environment production
Description OK
Checking environment staging
Description OK
```

As this output shows, our code iterates over the list of environments retrieved from the server, getting and checking the description in this case of each one. The only environment found to have an empty description was the awesome environment, so its description was updated and then the modified environment object was saved back to the Chef server. We can verify that this worked correctly by using Knife to inspect the awesome environment with this command:

```
$> knife environment show awesome -c /tmp/part4_examples/knife.rb
chef_type:          environment
cookbook_versions:
default_attributes:
  awesome_level: 100
description:        This is the awesome environment
json_class:         Chef::Environment
name:               awesome
override_attributes:
```

Now that we've created a slightly more complex example, let's level up our Chef API skills a little further and look at the sorts of errors returned by API calls and how to handle them in our code.

Error Handling

When working with an API like that provided by the Chef server, in addition to knowing how to send requests, it's also extremely important to be aware of the possible responses the server might send back—especially when an error has occurred. Helper classes like Chef::Rest make things easier for us, of course, but mistakes ranging from using the incorrect Knife key to mistyping an API endpoint name can result in a range of errors being returned instead of the data we expect.

As this is an HTTP-based API, all responses (whether errors or not) sent by the server have a *response code* in addition to any data that is returned. The full HTTP specification defines a large range of possible codes for both successful and failed responses, but the number of these you're likely to encounter when talking to the Chef API is much smaller. The most common response codes are listed in Table 11-1, with a short explanation of each.

Table 11-1. Chef API response codes

Response code	Description
200	OK. The request was successful.
201	Created. The object was created.
401	Unauthorized. The user could not authenticate to the Chef server.
403	Forbidden. The user who made the request authenticated, but is not authorized to perform the requested action.
404	Not Found. The requested object does not exist.
409	Conflict. The object already exists.
412	Precondition Failed. Usually means that a required cookbook, cookbook version, or cookbook dependency is missing.
413	Request Entity Too Large. A request may not be larger than 1,000,000 bytes.

Interested readers can find a detailed list of the response codes that can be returned by each of the Chef API endpoints on the Chef Documents (*http://bit.ly/chef-server-api*) site. The full list of response codes defined by the HTTP 1.1 specification is available at the W3C site (*http://bit.ly/stat-codes*).

When Chef::Rest encounters an error—that is, when the response code is *not* 200 or 201—it raises an exception to alert us to that fact. Because Chef::Client can't predict exactly what we did to trigger the error, it can't decide by itself how to fix the error or if we expected it, so it alerts us by throwing an exception and lets us take things from there.

All exceptions thrown by the Chef::Rest object are of the type Net::HTTPServerEx ception. This same exception type is also thrown by Ruby's built-in Net::HTTP libraries when errors occur. The simple fact that we know any HTTP errors returned by the Chef API are always of this particular class means that we can only rescue exceptions of that type, as we saw in "Handling Exceptions" on page 46, while ensuring that any other types of exceptions are not accidentally caught.

Let's look at a simple example program that will GET the environment passed in on the command line and rescue any 404 (not found) responses, so that we can nicely handle our users accidentally asking for nonexistent environments. Paste the code in Example 11-7 into */tmp/part4_examples/api_error_handling.rb*.

Example 11-7. /tmp/part4_examples/api_error_handling.rb

```ruby
#!/usr/bin/env ruby

require 'chef'

chef_server_url = "http://127.0.0.1:8889"
client_name = "cctest"
signing_key_filename="/tmp/part4_examples/customizing_chef.pem"
env = ARGV[0]

# Our API calls will be inside a begin..rescue block this time
begin
  rest = Chef::REST.new(chef_server_url, client_name, signing_key_filename)

  # Make a GET call to /environments/NAME with the environment
  # name passed in on the command line
  returned_data = rest.get_rest("/environments/#{env}")

  puts returned_data

# Only catch exceptions of type Net::HTTPServerException
rescue Net::HTTPServerException => e
  # If the response code was 404...
```

```
  if e.response.code == "404"
    # Print our nice error message and exit with exit code 1
    puts "The environment #{env} does not exist."
    exit 1
  else
    # Reraise the exception
    raise e
  end
end
```

If we run this command with an environment we know exists passed as the parameter, then we should see the following output:

```
$> ruby api_error_handling.rb production
production
```

If, however, we then try running our command with a nonexistent environment passed as the parameter, we should see our nicely formatted error message:

```
$> ruby api_error_handling.rb foo
The environment foo does not exist.
```

Of course, we've only captured a single category of error in a very simple example, but the same techniques can be used to capture other categories of error, such as trying to authenticate to the Chef server with an invalid client key or trying to add invalid cookbooks to an environment. If you wanted to write a rescue block to cater for several different error response codes at once, you might do something like this:

```
  rescue Net::HTTPServerException => e
    case e.response.code
    when "404"
      ...
    when "403"
      ...
    when "401"
      ...
    else
      # Reraise the exception
      raise e
    end
  end
```

In the above snippet, we're still only rescuing the single exception class Net::HTTPSer verException, but because we know all Chef API errors will be raised as this class, we're able to respond to multiple error conditions with a tightly scoped rescue block that won't inadvertently trap other exception types in its net.

So far in this chapter, we've looked at how to authenticate to the Chef API, make requests, and handle errors. However, there are other Chef helper classes that implement much of the functionality we've covered thus far. We explored some of the reasons why you might wish to talk to the Chef API directly instead of picking and choosing between multiple helper classes in "So Why Use the Chef API?" on page 308, but is it always the case that you can find a helper class to remove the need to directly talk to the API?

In the next section, we're going to look at some endpoints exposed by the Chef API that are not wrapped by any Chef helper classes and can only be accessed by making direct requests to the API itself.

Secrets of the Chef API

As we saw in "So Why Use the Chef API?" on page 308, although much of the Chef API is abstracted away by Chef's wrapper classes, there are often considerations such as performance or language choice that mean that you might want to talk to the Chef API directly. Furthermore, in this section we're going to meet two functions of the Chef API that are *only* accessible by communicating directly with the Chef API—at the time of writing, there are currently no Chef classes that wrap the functionality of these API calls.

The /_status Endpoint

As we saw in the Chef architecture diagram in Figure 3-1, Erchef—the component of Chef server that provides the API we've been communicating with—in turn communicates with several backend components, namely SOLR for search indexes and PostgreSQL for the backing database. When debugging issues with Chef, or simply when checking the status of components in our monitoring systems, it's desirable to be able to ensure that Erchef is communicating properly with those other components.

To allow us to do this, the Chef API exposes the /_status endpoint. This endpoint simply takes a GET request and returns the status of Erchef's communication with the Chef server's backend services. chef-zero, which we've been using for our test environment, does not provide this endpoint as it is a single process running entirely in memory to mock a Chef server. This means that we're unable to test the output of the /_status endpoint in our test environment, but I've included the necessary code to run it against your production Chef server in Example 11-8, should you choose to do so.

Example 11-8. Code to query the Chef API's /_status endpoint

```ruby
#!/usr/bin/env ruby

require 'chef'

chef_server_url = "" # Your Chef server
client_name = "" # Your client name
signing_key_filename="" # Your client key

rest = Chef::REST.new(chef_server_url, client_name, signing_key_filename)

returned_data = rest.get_rest("/_status")
```

```
puts returned_data
```

For those of you unable (or unwilling) to query the /_status endpoint of a production Chef server, I've included the output returned by this endpoint for both functional and broken Erchef communication here.

If everything is working correctly and Erchef can talk to all of its backend services, a GET request to the /_status endpoint will return the following output:

```
{ "status":"pong",
  "upstreams":{
    "chef_solr":"pong",
    "chef_sql":"pong"
  }
}
```

If, however, there is a fault and Erchef cannot talk to all of its backend services, a GET request to the /_status endpoint will return this output instead, indicating where the problem is:

```
{ "status":"fail",
  "upstreams":{
    "chef_solr":"fail",
    "chef_sql":"pong"
  }
}
```

Here, for example, we can see that chef_solr is experiencing an issue—this also changes the top-level status attribute to fail.

The /_status endpoint is useful for quick status checks on your Chef servers, but it can also be extremely useful when hooking your Chef server up to monitoring systems. In addition to checking that the required processes for chef-solr, PostgreSQL, and Erchef are running, this endpoint also allows you to verify the state of affairs from Erchef's point of view—that is, if the processes are running but communication isn't working, you're able to identify and remedy the issue.

Partial Search

The second API feature that we're going to look at in this section is known as "partial search." Before diving into that, however, let's quickly refresh our memories on how "standard" Chef search works. Most search queries are sent to the Chef server from one of the following sources:

- A recipe using the search method
- Knife plugins or other classes using the Chef::Search::Query object

- A script communicating with the API directly

In all three cases, behind the scenes a GET request will be sent to the Chef API's /search endpoint. When this happens, Chef will return the entirety of every object that matches the search query. In most cases (unless an API call is made manually, without using the Chef::Rest object), each object returned in the results will then be converted automatically by Chef into the relevant native object type, such as Chef::Node or Chef::Role.

Let's see this in action with a code example, which will search for nodes with a name matching the parameter we pass in on the command line. Paste the contents of Example 11-9 into /tmp/part4_examples/api_search.rb.

Example 11-9. /tmp/part4_examples/api_search.rb

```ruby
#!/usr/bin/env ruby

require 'chef'
require 'uri'

chef_server_url = "http://127.0.0.1:8889"
client_name = "cctest"
signing_key_filename="/tmp/part4_examples/customizing_chef.pem"

index = "node"  ❶
name = ARGV[0]

rest = Chef::REST.new(chef_server_url, client_name, signing_key_filename)

returned_data = rest.get_rest("search/#{index}?q=#{URI.escape("name:#{name}")}")  ❷

puts returned_data
```

❶ Here we're specifying that we want to search the node index. As we saw in "Chef Server" on page 60, Chef defines separate indexes for the various object types we can search for.

❷ Next, we send a GET request to the /search/INDEX endpoint with our search query passed as a query string parameter, as documented on the Chef Documents (*http://bit.ly/searchindex*) site. Note that we're also wrapping our query string with URI.escape to ensure we don't have any invalid characters in the URL we send to the Chef API.

Now let's try running our example code, passing the node name ldap as the parameter:

```
$> ruby api_search.rb ldap
{"rows"=>[node[ldap]], "start"=>0, "total"=>1}
```

As we see in this output, the results of our search query are contained in the rows key of the returned JSON. Inside this key, we see an array containing a single Chef::Node object—node[ldap] is the string representation of this object, as we're using puts to output our results to the screen.

Typically, the results of a Chef search query will be a collection of nodes, roles, environments, etc. If you're really only interested in a couple of fields from each result, you have to iterate over the collection and extract the relevant attributes. This isn't especially difficult—we did this very thing in "Loading Objects: Searching" on page 286—but it does mean that you've just downloaded an entire collection of objects, only to throw most of the data away.

Searches that might return hundreds or even thousands of results can cause significant bandwidth and memory usage as the data is downloaded onto the node and then processed. This especially applies to node searches, where returned node objects can contain a large number of attributes. Wouldn't it be nice if we were able to tell the Chef server to only return the specific fields of matching objects that we're actually interested in? Well, it turns out that the Chef API actually supports this very behavior, although you'll only find it documented on the Chef Documents (*http://bit.ly/chef-server-api*) site— none of the existing Chef classes that implement search currently implement this feature, which, as you may have already guessed, is known as "partial search."

Provided that you're happy communicating directly with the Chef API, which hopefully at this stage in the chapter you are, making use of partial search is actually very easy: you simply change your GET request to the /search endpoint into a POST request, and supply it a list of keys defining the attributes of the results that you want to return as the request body.

Let's modify our earlier code example to still search the node index, but this time only return the name and chef_environment attributes of the matching Chef::Node objects. Paste the code in Example 11-10 into the file we used before, */tmp/part4_examples/ api_search.rb*.

Example 11-10. /tmp/part4_examples/api_search.rb

```ruby
#!/usr/bin/env ruby

require 'chef'
require 'uri'

chef_server_url = "http://127.0.0.1:8889"
client_name = "cctest"
signing_key_filename="/tmp/part4_examples/customizing_chef.pem"

type = "node"
name = ARGV[0]
keys = { ❶
        name: [ 'name' ],
```

```
        environment: [ 'chef_environment' ]
    }

rest = Chef::REST.new(chef_server_url, client_name, signing_key_filename)

returned_data = rest.post_rest("search/#{type}?q=" +
  "#{URI.escape("name:#{name}")}", keys) ❷

puts returned_data
```

❶ Here we're defining a Hash containing the list of attributes we want to be returned
    from our search query. Each element in this Hash consists of a name and an array
    of the object attributes to be grouped under that name in the results. For example,
    here we've defined our keys Hash as name: [*name*] to indicate that the "name"
    element of each result will contain just the name attribute of the matching object.

❷ Here we call the post_rest method of our Chef::Rest object instead of the
    get_rest method we used earlier, and pass it the keys Hash we defined in step
    1 as a parameter. The input/output processing carried out by the Chef::Rest
    class will automatically convert this Hash into valid JSON data to be sent to the
    Chef API.

Now let's try running our partial search example and see how the results of the search
query change:

```
$> ruby api_search.rb ldap
{"rows"=>[{"url"=>"http://127.0.0.1:8889/nodes/ldap", "data"=>
  {"name"=>"ldap", "environment"=>"_default"}}], "start"=>0, "total"=>1}
```

This time, in our output we see that instead of a Chef::Node object, each row consists
of an array of hashes for the given node that contains the URL to the node object and a
data hash containing each of the keys we requested.

It's important to remember that using partial search is not a free optimization—it moves
the processing cost of extracting fields from search results to the Chef server from the
individual node. It does, however, save network bandwidth because each object is processed locally on the server.

Partial search is not currently supported by any native Chef classes; however, if you want
to make use of it in cookbooks, Chef, Inc. provides the Partial Search cookbook (*http://
bit.ly/partial-search*), which defines the partial_search method that can be used in
recipes in the same way as the existing search method. At the time of writing, Chef,
Inc. plans to include support for partial search in native classes in Chef 11.14.0.

Summary and Further Reading

In this chapter, we've learned about a number of different aspects of the Chef API. We started off by looking at why we might want to communicate directly with the Chef API, and created a test environment to allow us to send API requests to a mock chef-zero server. We then examined the structure of HTTP requests, before looking at how to construct and format the specific authentication headers needed to sign our API requests.

We then looked at a code example illustrating how to construct and send GET requests to the Chef API, before meeting the `Chef::Rest` helper class provided to abstract away a lot of the heavy lifting involved in this process. We then learned how to utilize the I/O formatting provided by `Chef::Rest` to combine multiple API requests, using the objects returned by each request to construct the next. We also examined how to respond to errors returned by our API requests, before diving into some API endpoints not implemented by other Chef classes.

Readers interested in learning more about the Chef API may find the following resources useful:

- Appendix A provides a handy quick reference of the various endpoints supported by the Chef API, and the HTTP verbs supported by each endpoint.
- The Chef Documents (*http://bit.ly/chefdocs-endp*) site provides much more comprehensive documentation on each endpoint, along with the specific error codes and data each endpoint might return.
- Readers interested in interfacing with the Chef API from other programming languages may find the Chef API clients written for Python (*http://bit.ly/pychef-023*), Go (*http://bit.ly/chef-golang*), and Node.js (*http://bit.ly/gh-chefnode*) useful.

Now that we've covered the various customizations supported by Chef, in the next chapter we're going to look at some best practices, guidelines, and advice around open sourcing your customizations and contributing them to the community.

## CHAPTER 12

Contributing Your Customizations

Thus far in our journey through customizing Chef, we have focused on the different types of customization supported and how to create and use them. In this chapter, we're going to jump forward a little to the point when you have created the customizations you need to make Chef work for your business requirements, and are perhaps starting to think about sharing your customizations with the wider Chef community—this is, after all, one of the main strengths of the Chef community, and I've referred to a number of community-created customizations in various chapters of this book. We'll learn about:

- Being a good open source citizen
- Following open source best practices
- Packaging and releasing Chef-specific customizations

So, you've worked through the material in this book to learn how to create Chef customizations, and you've used the "Criteria for Customization" on page 10 to craft the customized plugins, handlers, formatters, or recipes to make Chef fit the requirements of your business. If you're anything like me, you've probably also benefited from the Chef community along the way—advice, guidance, or maybe even code—and finally you're done. Your customizations are complete, your coworkers are much happier with your Chef setup and infrastructure code, and your Chef pain points have been eliminated.

It's at this point that you may well consider open sourcing your customizations, so that others can benefit and avoid having to replicate the work you did if they experience the same problems. A large part of Chef's strength comes from its community, after all!

The minimum requirement for open sourcing code is to find somewhere to host it, and then upload it. There are a number of free open source code hosting websites, such as GitHub (*https://www.github.com*), GitLab (*https://www.gitlab.com*), Bitbucket (*https://*

www.bitbucket.org), and SourceForge (*http://www.sourceforge.net*), which make it extremely quick and easy to share your code with the world. However, unless you simply want to upload your code and forget about it, there's a little more to think about when it comes to open sourcing your customizations. The first portion of this chapter is designed to share the experiences of both myself and other open source maintainers and what we've learned about how to be a good citizen of the open source community.

Most of the lessons and recommendations in this chapter are, of course, not hard-and-fast requirements that you must fulfill before you're allowed to open source code, but rather things to consider that will help both you and the wider Chef community make the best use possible of your contributions.

Documentation

One of the first and most important things to consider when open sourcing code is how it's documented. As the author of your customization, you're an expert on how it works, how to install and configure it, and any peculiarities or bugs it may exhibit. If you're introducing new users inside your business to the tool, you can ensure you're on hand to help them out and walk them through any issues, but this is not the case when a new user happens across your code on a source code hosting site.

When other members of the Chef community encounter your code, the first thing they're going to want to do is figure out whether or not it's what they're looking for, and how it's different from similar cookbooks or tools out there. They might be looking for a tool they can use to solve a specific problem, examples of how to implement particular functionality, or something entirely different, but the evaluation process remains the same.

As an open source author, the documentation you supply with your contribution is one of the most powerful tools you have to help your potential users with this process. Documentation might take the form of wiki articles, a README file, or simply comments in your code; regardless of the format, ensuring that your contribution is as comprehensively documented as possible is invaluable to your users.

It's often useful to write the README for your customization before you've even started the code, as this helps to ensure that the purpose and functionality of your customization are clearly defined before you write any code—this documentation technique is known as *Readme-Driven Development*.

 Readers interested in diving a little deeper into Readme-Driven Development may wish to read Tom Preston-Warner's excellent blog post (*http://bit.ly/readme-dd*) on the subject.

It's a universal truth that very few of us enjoy writing documentation, but imagine being in the position of your new user and happening across a tool that *looks* like it might solve your problem, but only being able to tell for sure by reading the source code. Think of documenting your code well as a variety of "paying it forward"—if you've benefited in the past from comprehensively documented tools and code, strive to give your users the same experience.

Here are some aspects of your Chef customizations that it's often helpful to document:

Dependencies and requirements

The chances are good that your code will have been written to run under specific versions of software or on specific systems, or may have dependencies on third-party libraries, Ruby gems, APIs, and so on (and possibly all of the aforementioned). It's very helpful to document these dependencies and requirements thoroughly so users of your code are able to determine whether or not they are able to use your contribution, for example, under Windows, on an isolated network with no Internet access, or under Ruby 1.8.

If your code requires specific versions of its dependencies, this is also worth documenting. In the Ruby ecosystem particularly, changes in commonly used third-party libraries can often introduce changes that break other tools that use those libraries. Clarifying for your users exactly which versions of dependent tooling and software your code has been written for and tested under will make things a lot easier for them!

Installation and configuration

The next step in helping your users to get up and running with your open source contribution is to document how to install and configure it. Later in this chapter we'll cover a number of packaging formats for distributing your customizations, which can often automate installation and initial configuration. Despite these, it's helpful to document exactly what steps are needed to run the code and any configuration that's needed, especially if you're just distributing source code.

If your code supports optional configuration parameters, plugins, or other ways to augment or control its functionality, then these should also be documented as comprehensively as possible. Because we're dealing primarily with Chef customizations in this book, you could even create a cookbook to go along with your customization.

Usage instructions

After your users have installed and configured your customization, they're going to need to know how to use it. Do they run it from the command line? Should it run automatically when they kick off a Chef run? What options does it support? It's good practice (not to mention extremely helpful) to document usage instructions for your customization as thoroughly as possible. This is especially important when it comes to customizations such as Knife plugins, which can often implement a variety of new Knife commands and options, and interface with external systems other than Chef.

When it comes to documentation, even if you don't particularly enjoy writing it (I certainly don't), try to remember to pay it forward—write the documentation for your customizations (preferably before you start coding) that you would like other people to have written for you when you use their code.

Supporting Your Code

After you've documented your code, the next area to consider when open sourcing is what level of support you are prepared to provide. After all, when you open source a customization, you should expect that eventually Chef users will likely make use of it. When open sourcing code, it's important to consider whether you're willing to maintain the code going forward or if it's provided "as is." Computer software being what it is, there will invariably be bugs in the code or aspects of its behavior that don't work quite the way your users expect under certain circumstances.

Here are some aspects of supporting your code that it might be useful to consider:

Will you fix bugs?
> If your users submit bug reports, are you able/willing to spend time fixing these, or is the code provided "as is," with no intention of it being updated or fixed?

Will you accept external bugfixes?
> Are you willing or able to accept bugfixes from users outside of your organization into your customization? If you're publishing your customization under your organization's name, are they also happy for you to accept bugfixes from external users?

Are you willing to fix use cases that differ from yours?
> The chances are good that eventually somebody will use your customization for something you didn't expect or originally design for. As we've seen throughout this book, everybody's use case for Chef is different—are you willing to fix issues that occur when people use your customizations in ways you didn't expect?

What if your circumstances change?
> It may be the case that your circumstances change, and you find yourself unable to dedicate enough time to supporting your customization—say you get a new job or have a child, for example. In these situations, open source projects often take a backseat. It's worth considering how changes like these might change the support you offer for your code. Would you be willing to hand the project over to new maintainers if you were unable to maintain it, for example?

It's perfectly acceptable for the answers to all of these questions to be "no," of course, but if this is the case I recommend that you document specifically that your customization is provided as is and will not be supported by you—nothing is more frustrating for a user of open source software than filing a bug report and getting no response from the maintainer of the code. You can help manage your users' expectations by planning ahead of time, and stating clearly and concisely exactly what level of support they can expect from you or other maintainers of your customization.

Managing Contributions

In addition to how you support your customizations, it's important to consider how you will manage contributions submitted by members of the Chef community. As we've seen throughout the book, Chef is used differently in many organizations, and your users may wish to contribute new features or changes to your customizations that better fit their use cases.

In some cases, you will be able to accept these customizations without any issues—one of the great strengths of the Chef community, and indeed the wider open source community, is that you're able to benefit from the experience and skills of developers and operations engineers external to your organization to improve your customizations.

However, eventually you will likely encounter suggestions for contributions that may alter your customization in a way that makes it less useful for your specific use case, and it's useful to consider ahead of time how you will handle these situations. I'm the original author and maintainer of a Knife plugin called knife -spork (*http://bit.ly/knife-spork*) that was originally developed to help drive the Chef workflow at Etsy. Over the years, although knife-spork has benefited immensely from many community contributions —not least a plugin framework and major refactor from the prolific Seth Vargo—I've also had to reject contributions that don't fit with the way that Etsy uses the tool. In this case, Etsy is the primary user of knife-spork, and I have to bear that in mind when managing external contributions.

Your situation might be very similar to mine, or you might choose to maintain a separate internal version of the tool so you're able to accept any external contributions you like. Either way, it's useful to have a clear strategy in mind for how you will manage contributions to your customizations going forward.

Along with forming this strategy, it's equally important to inform your users of any specific requirements you have for contributions or the way they are written. There are two things to consider here:

Contribution guidelines
> Contribution guidelines set out any requirements you have for how your users should submit customizations. For example, a common requirement for many open source projects is that contributions must be submitted on a "feature branch" and must be documented in a ticket or issue on the project's bug tracking system. This ensures that the maintainer of the project can clearly see which particular bug or

feature request a contribution relates to and who submitted it, and provides a convenient forum for ongoing discussions around the issue or feature in question.

Clearly documenting requirements such as these gives your users a clear understanding of what is required from their contributions, and it also makes it much easier for you as the maintainer to keep track of submissions when everybody contributes in a consistent manner. Try to keep your contribution guidelines simple and concise, too; if your users have to create a doctoral thesis in order to submit a change, they might decide not to bother.

Coding standards

Many open source projects also define a set of coding standards that lay out any stylistic or functional requirements to which contributions must adhere. For example, the maintainer of a project might require that any contributions include tests that validate that the contributed code works correctly, or that any changes be submitted as plugins rather than altering the core functionality of the tool. There's no set formula for the coding standards your contribution should use, but these guidelines provide an excellent opportunity for you to keep your users informed of any requirements you have in this area. Automated testing tools such as Foodcritic (*http://bit.ly/food-critic*) and Travis CI (*http://travis-ci.org*) can help to enforce coding standards too, through automated testing—we'll look at these in more detail in the next section.

Testing Your Software

Alongside clear documentation and well-defined support and contribution guidelines for your open source code, another vital component that it would be remiss of me not to include here is automated software testing. Although often considered to be the preserve of QA teams and full-time software developers, software testing is a valuable discipline for any open source author to master.

In the context of this chapter, testing software doesn't just mean verifying that code or recipes work by trying them out for yourself; it means creating a suite of test scenarios and employing associated automated testing tools to verify that your code passes them. Simply put, the aim is to verify that your application or cookbook behaves in the expected manner. This not only aids you as the original author of your code, but is also extremely useful for contributors seeking to patch or add features; a comprehensive test suite allows contributors to quickly and easily verify that their changes to your code have not caused any breakages (insofar as the test suite can tell, of course).

The topic of software testing is far too broad to be covered in detail in this book, so this section focuses on providing you with tooling and resources specific to Chef and the wider Ruby ecosystem to allow you to dive into the subject yourself in greater detail.

Ruby and Infrastructure Testing Tools

This section lists some testing tools that are not specific to Chef itself, but are commonly used for the creation of test suites for Ruby code or more generalized infrastructure automation:

RSpec
> RSpec (*http://rspec.info/*) is one of the most popular testing frameworks in the Ruby world. It allows you to write tests in a DSL that resembles natural language to describe how your code should behave in certain scenarios, and provides tooling to allow you to quickly and easily run all of your tests at once, providing you with a report of passes or failures.

Cucumber
> Cucumber (*http://cukes.info/*) is another commonly used testing framework; it is often used in conjunction with RSpec to test more high-level aspects of functionality, such as user interactions, and provides tooling to run and report on the status of its tests.

Serverspec
> Serverspec (*http://serverspec.org/*) augments the functionality provided by RSpec to allow you to write scenarios that describe how your servers should be configured, rather than how your code behaves. This allows you, for example, to write tests that verify that OpenSSH has been configured correctly on a test VM after it has executed the OpenSSH cookbook. Serverspec is not Chef-specific and will work in conjunction with any configuration management tool and a wide variety of operating systems.

Continuous Integration Tools

Continuous integration (CI) is a methodology that advocates developers pushing their code into the main "master" branch of the repository frequently, and automatically testing it to ensure that nothing has broken since the last change. By merging and testing small changes continuously in this way, development teams—and even individual developers—are able to quickly and easily identify errors that have crept into the code. CI aims to make code quality assurance and testing a continually applied discipline, rather than something that happens in a single protracted step immediately prior to a release.

The quality of the tests applied to code in continuous integration is just as important as the frequency with which changes are made. For CI to work effectively, tests should verify that the most critical parts of the system work as expected to avoid the introduction of unexpected regressions or bugs. The greater the *code coverage* of your testing suite—literally, the more of your code for which you have written effective tests—the greater the confidence you will be able to have in your automated testing process.

When it comes to open source software, the use of continuous integration systems makes it extremely easy for the maintainers of projects and those contributing changes to quickly and easily verify that contributions have not broken any tests. This section lists two of the most popular continuous integration systems for open source projects:

Travis CI

> Travis CI (*http://travis-ci.org*) is one of the most popular hosted CI systems currently in use. It comes in both free and paid-for variants and supports a number of different programming languages and testing tools—including Ruby and RSpec— to allow open source authors to quickly and easily incorporate CI into their projects.

Jenkins

> Jenkins (*http://jenkins-ci.org/*) is another popularly used CI system, but rather than being hosted like Travis CI, it is typically deployed inside an organization. It supports a comprehensive range of programming languages and testing tools, and is easily extensible via a flexible plugin API.

Chef-Specific Tooling

Now that we've looked at some general testing and CI tools and frameworks, we're going to look at a number of tools that are specifically designed to work with Chef and to test various types of Chef customizations:

ChefSpec

> ChefSpec (*http://bit.ly/chefspec*), written by Seth Vargo, allows you to write RSpec tests for Chef recipes. ChefSpec allows recipe authors to write tests that verify that recipes have carried out the expected actions, and supports simulating test execution with different combinations of operating systems, node attributes, etc.

Test Kitchen

> Test Kitchen (*http://bit.ly/t-kitchen*), created by Fletcher Nichol, provides a framework and tooling to allow cookbook authors to quickly and easily create virtual machines to test their code on a variety of platforms, such as EC2, Rackspace, Vagrant, and Docker. Many cookbooks, including those for Chef server (*http://bit.ly/chefserver-ck*) and MySQL (*http://bit.ly/mysql-ckbk*), now ship with built-in support for Test Kitchen.

Leibniz

> Leibniz (*http://bit.ly/a-leibniz*), written by Stephen Nelson-Smith of Atalanta Systems, allows Test Kitchen runs to be incorporated into Cucumber tests so that real-world tests of recipe code can be treated as scenarios in your test suite.

Foodcritic

> Foodcritic (*http://bit.ly/food-critic*), written by Andrew Crump, is a tool that allows "lint" checks to be written for Chef cookbooks. Simply put, lint checks look for suspicious or undesirable behavior in code. In the Chef context, this might be

something like using the `execute` resource to run a command for which Chef provides a better built-in resource. Foodcritic can be integrated with CI systems such as Jenkins and Chef workflow tools such as knife-spork (*http://bit.ly/knife-spork*) to enforce style and behavioral guidelines in your cookbook code.

Further Reading

Readers interested in learning more about writing tests for their Ruby and cookbook code may find the following resources useful:

- *Test-Driven Infrastructure with Chef*, by Stephen Nelson-Smith, extensively covers the concept of test-driven infrastructure with Chef. The idea behind this book is that if we treat our infrastructure as code, we should also be testing it like code!

- *The RSpec Book* (Pragmatic Bookshelf), written by the lead developer of RSpec, David Chelimsky, explains in detail how to use both RSpec and Cucumber to incorporate testing into your code and workflows.

- Seth Vargo, the author of ChefSpec, has given a talk that you can watch online (*http://bit.ly/ckbk-testing-vid*) and has written blog posts to introduce Chef users to unit testing (*http://bit.ly/vargo-utc*) and ChefSpec (*http://bit.ly/unit-test-chef*).

Versioning Your Software

Fixing bugs in your software and accepting contributions to it of course means that your customization is unlikely to remain in its original form for very long—which brings us to the topic of versioning. If you've used RubyGems or installed any software on your computer, you'll doubtless have noticed that software is typically released with a specific version number attached to it, and any patches or additional features typically result in a new release of the software with a different version number.

On the face of things, versioning may seem just that simple—you change the version number and release your software—but there's a little more to it than that. Most pieces of software will, over their lifetimes, evolve from their original forms. Some releases of the software include critical bugfixes, some include only minor feature additions, and some include significant changes in functionality that are incompatible with older versions of the software. You might even find yourself supporting multiple versions of your software in parallel, and patching older versions alongside a newer version.

While clearly documenting a new release in a CHANGELOG file goes some way toward solving this problem, versioning your software in a standardized and predictable way can also be extremely helpful to your users. One of the most popular methodologies for software versioning, and the one that we will focus on in this section, is *semantic versioning*.

Semantic Versioning

The semantic versioning specification (*http://semver.org*) uses a three-component version numbering system. In a version number such as 1.0.0, the numbers should be read from left to right as *major* release number, *minor* release number, and *patch* release number. The semantic versioning specification aims to use version numbers to give you an idea about what has likely been modified between versions of the software, and lays out some simple rules for when each component of the version number should be incremented:

Major version increment

The major release number should be incremented when non-backward-compatible changes are introduced to the API of the software (that is, changes that affect the way in which people or systems interface with your software). An example of a major version change would be moving from 1.0.1 to 2.0.0—typically, when the major version number changes, the minor and patch version numbers reverts to 0, although this can vary.

Minor version increment

The minor release number should be incremented when you add new functionality to your software in a backward-compatible manner (i.e., changes do not affect the way in which people or systems interface with your software). An example of a minor version change would be moving from 1.0.1 to 1.1.0—typically, when the minor version number changes, the patch version number reverts to 0, although this can vary.

Patch version increment

The patch release number should be incremented when you have added backward-compatible bugfixes to your software. An example of a patch version change would be moving from 1.0.1 to 1.0.2.

To see semantic versioning in practice, let's look at some hypothetical examples:

- The author of the knife-foo Knife plugin needs to push out an urgent bugfix to resolve an unexpected exception that was introduced into her code in version 1.2.5. She knows that her fix for this issue will be backward-compatible with older versions, so she decides to release version 1.2.6, a patch release.

- The author of version 1.2.3 of a popular cookbook is going to release a new version that replaces LWRPs with HWRPs and gives the provided resource new names. As this resource name change will break existing usage of the cookbook in recipe code, he decides that this should be a major release and releases version 2.0.0.

- The authors of version 5.2.1 of an Ohai plugin have created a new version that adds some new node attributes. As the attributes created by the existing version have not changed in any way in the new version, they decide that this should be a minor release and release version 5.3.0.

Semantic Versioning and Cookbooks

The need for consistent and clear version numbers applies just as much to Chef cookbooks as to Knife or Ohai plugins, and the principles of semantic versioning can be applied in the same way. Two members of the Chef community, Nathen Harvey (*https://twitter.com/nathenharvey*) and Mike Fiedler (*https://twitter.com/mikefiedler*), have authored the Cookbook Versioning Policy (*http://bit.ly/ckbk-vp*) to more explicitly map the general principles documented in the semantic versioning specification to Chef cookbooks.

The Cookbook Versioning Policy examines changes to various components of cookbooks and whether they should be considered major-, minor-, or patch-level changes.

Thus far we've mainly considered aspects of being a good open source citizen that directly benefit your users, or you as a maintainer. The final area we're going to look at in this section is one that is both a little more complex and often ignored because the benefits are less immediate—licensing and copyright.

Licensing and Copyright

 When reading this section, please remember that I am not a lawyer. The information in this section is for general guidance on copyrights and software licensing and is not legal advice. If you need more details on your rights or legal advice, please contact a lawyer.

When open sourcing software, one of the most important areas to consider—but also one of the most complicated—is the question of which license your code is released under, and who owns the copyright to the code being released. Open source developers often bypass this step entirely and release software without specifying a particular license, but this can mean that Chef community members are unable to use those contributions inside their companies, as many companies are unwilling to use or modify software without a clearly specified license and copyright statement.

As I mentioned in the disclaimer at the beginning of this section, I'm not a lawyer, and I'm not going to give you legal advice on software licensing or copyright law—what I'm going to try to do is offer some general pointers and areas to consider when dealing with these areas when you open source a customization.

Copyright

Computer software, including open source code, is protected by copyright law. The exact specifics of copyright law vary from country to country, but as a general rule it grants the owner of a work certain rights, and makes it illegal for anybody who is *not* the owner of a work to present it as their own.

When open sourcing software, it's important to make sure that you understand whether you are the copyright holder of the code or not—in some countries, code written on company time can be owned by the company, rather than the employee. If you're unsure about who owns the copyright to the code you're planning to open source, you should consult the legal department of your company or a copyright lawyer.

It's also extremely important to state clearly in your source code who the copyright owner is, as this also determines who has the authority to decide how the software can be used, modified, distributed, etc.

Licensing Your Code

The license under which your customization is distributed is what defines the permissible usage, modification, and distribution of your code, and any other third-party code your customization may include. Although it's not technically necessary to specify a license when you open source a customization, it is something I very much recommend —as mentioned earlier in this section, many companies will not use open source projects that don't stipulate a license agreement, and it also ensures you retain control over what people are able to do with your source code, the circumstances under which they can reuse some or all of your code, and so on.

But how do you choose a license? What open source licenses are there to choose from? One of the best resources I've found for navigating the software licensing maze is GitHub's ChooseALicense (*http://choosealicense.com*). It breaks down the characteristics and terms of the many commonly used open source licenses to help you choose a license that fits your requirements.

Choosing a license to distribute your code under is only part of the story, though—the second component of software licensing is ensuring that you comply with the licensing terms of any code written by other authors that is included in your customization. Some open source licenses stipulate that a copy of the license and the original copyright notice from the code must be included with any product that makes use of that code. Other open source licenses state that if code is used in commercial products, a copy of that product's source code should be made freely available.

Although software licensing has a reputation for being somewhat complex and opaque, it's worth your while as an open source author to familiarize yourself with the basics of the most commonly used licenses, such as the GPL, MIT, and Apache licenses, to ensure that you're able to choose a license for your software that allows people to use your code in the way you want it to be used, and also to ensure that you comply with the licensing requirements of any dependencies your customization might have.

So, you've thoroughly documented and tested your customization, you've created contribution guidelines and coding standards, you've chosen a license for your code and made sure it's released with accurate copyright information, and you're finally ready to release your code into the world. But what format should you choose? In the next part of the chapter, we're going to examine the most commonly used distribution formats for the various customization types we've covered in this book and how to use them.

Distributing Your Customizations

When it comes to actually choosing how to release, package, and distribute your Chef customizations, it might seem as though you're faced with a somewhat bewildering variety of options. In this section, we're going to take a whistle-stop tour through the various options available to us for distributing and versioning our Chef customizations, and which customization types each option is suited to.

Sharing the Source Code

As we saw earlier in the chapter, the distribution method that has the lowest barrier to entry is to upload the source code for your customization to a repository on any one of a number of code hosting sites. Many of these sites, such as GitHub (*https://www.github.com*), Bitbucket (*https://www.bitbucket.org*), and SourceForge (*http://www.sourceforge.net*), host your code for free (although many have commercial offerings, too) and provide a number of other useful services, such as issue tracking and usage statistics.

No special skills or knowledge are required to distribute your source code in this way, apart from familiarity with Git (*http://git-scm.com/*) or another version control system —we've already used Git in a number of places throughout the book, so I'm making the assumption that most of my readers are familiar with it.

Creating a New Repository on GitHub

GitHub (*https://github.com*) is one of the most popular open source code hosting websites in use today, and it hosts the source code for many of the projects we've seen in this book, such as Chef (*http://bit.ly/chef-gh*), Ohai (*http://bit.ly/gh-ohai*), Test Kitchen (*http://bit.ly/t-kitchen*), and Berkshelf (*http://bit.ly/berkshelf*).

Once you've signed up for an account with GitHub and logged in for the first time, you'll see a button for creating a new repository that looks like this:

Clicking this button takes you to a page with a number of options for configuring your new Git repository:

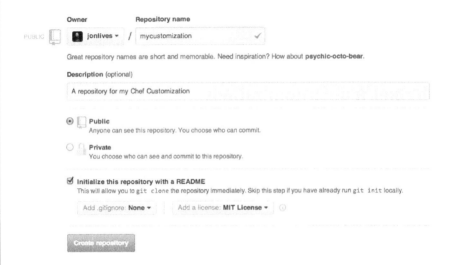

As you can see in this screenshot, there are a number of fields to fill in:

Repository name
> The *repository name* field is where you indicate what your open source project will be called. This field forms the last part of the GitHub URL (i.e., *chef* in *https:// github.com/opscode/chef*). The green checkmark indicates that you don't already have a repository with the specified name.

Description
> The *description* field is optional, and is fairly self-explanatory. It gives you a space to describe what your project is and briefly explain what it does.

Public/Private
> The *public/private* field allows you to specify whether your repository will be accessible only to specific GitHub users you approve, or to anybody using GitHub. If you want the wider Chef community to be able to view your code, you likely want to choose the *public* option here.

Initialize this repository with a README
> Checking this box adds a README file to your repository so that you can simply clone it straight away and start using it. Leaving this option unselected will necessitate a few more configuration steps before your repository can be used, so I recommend that readers new to GitHub select this option.

Add .gitignore

A *.gitignore* file allows you to specify certain files or folders in your repository that Git should ignore. GitHub allows you to add one automatically to your repository by choosing this option.

Add a license

GitHub allows you to automatically add a premade LICENSE file to your repository, populated from a choice of possible licenses. Here we've chosen the MIT license—see "Licensing and Copyright" on page 343 for more information on the importance of properly licensing your customization.

After you've filled in the fields in this form, click the "Create repository" button. Your public Git repository is now ready to use!

There are a number of pros and cons to choosing to share your source code on a site such as GitHub as your primary distribution mechanism. Table 12-1 lists some things to consider.

Table 12-1. Pros and cons of distribution via code hosting sites

Pros	Cons
Extremely simple and quick process	Installing and configuring your customization falls to the user
No packaging system or tooling to worry about, aside from source control software	No premade installation package, so installation is a manual process
Low maintenance overhead	Sometimes not clear whether the latest code is stable
Supports all customization types	
Easy for people to modify and contribute	

As you can see, there are a number of upsides to distributing your customization source code on a code hosting site—not least that it's extremely quick and simple to do, and all customization types are supported. However, there are also some downsides—notably, this method results in your users having to install and configure the customization themselves, which, depending on the complexity, can result in mistakes, misconfiguration, and other issues.

 When distributing the source code for your customization on a code hosting site, please take extra care to ensure you haven't accidentally included sensitive keys or passwords in your repository. Even if you remove them later, they might still be visible in your repository history.

The main weakness with simply providing your code in a Git repository, however, is that it is often unclear to your users exactly what state the code they are downloading is in. As you add to your customization and it gains in popularity, you may well find yourself using multiple "branches" to develop new features, or committing code to your "master" branch, which isn't quite ready for prime time yet. In short, how do your users tell whether the code they just cloned from GitHub is the latest stable release, or experimental code?

The solution to this problem is to provide *version artifacts* for your customization. In essence, a version artifact is a snapshot of your code that allows you to state, "this snapshot represents version 1.0.0." It gives your users the confidence that they're downloading a specific release that won't change—any new bugfixes or features would go into the next version number.

Distributing version artifacts for your customization means that your users no longer need to assume that the master branch of your source code repository is stable—in fact, it's good practice when dealing with any source code repository (whether yours or somebody else's) to remember the mantra, "master is always unstable."

In the remainder of this section, we're going to examine some of the version artifact types commonly used to distribute Chef customizations, and which customization types each option is best suited to.

Community Cookbooks

As the basic building block of any Chef infrastructure, cookbooks are one of the most commonly shared customization types. Historically, Chef, Inc. provided the Community Cookbooks site to allow Chef users to share and distribute versions of their cookbooks. Recently, they announced the Chef Supermarket (*http://bit.ly/chef-super*), a brand-new community site designed from the ground up to make it much easier for Chef community members to contribute and share code.

Chef cookbooks support versioning out of the box—this is what allows us to set version constraints in our Chef environments, and what allows workflow tools such as knife-spork (*https://github.com/jonlives/knife-spork*) to function. However, there's nothing to stop cookbook authors from making changes to the code of their cookbooks without incrementing the version number and pushing the changes to GitHub. This is where the concept of version artifacts we learned about in the last section comes into play

Chef Supermarket allows cookbook authors to upload "snapshots" of their cookbooks to the site, which are then downloadable as compressed archives. A cookbook author isn't able to upload the same version of a cookbook twice, which means that anybody who downloads version 1.0.0 of the Apache cookbook, for example, knows that this file will not change and will always represent the same snapshot of that cookbook's code.

Creating and uploading these cookbook snapshots is extremely easy. Here are two of the most commonly used tools for doing just this:

```
knife cookbook site share
```
Knife ships by default with the `cookbook site share` plugin, which allows Chef users to quickly and easily upload their cookbooks to Chef Supermarket (*http:// bit.ly/chef-super*) with a single command.

After the configuration instructions found in the `knife` cookbook site documentation (*http://bit.ly/knife-share*) have been followed, Chef users can upload their cookbook to the community site with the command `knife cookbook site share <cookbook_name> <category>`. This will automatically create a compressed archive of the current version of the cookbook, upload it to Chef Supermarket, add it to the specified category, and make it available for download.

As it is a Knife plugin, `knife cookbook site share` requires a correctly configured *knife.rb* configuration file and looks for cookbooks by default in Chef's configured `cookbook_path`.

Stove

Stove (*http://bit.ly/gh-stove*) is a standalone tool developed by Seth Vargo to make it easier to manage and release Chef cookbook versions without the necessity to configure Knife or store all your cookbooks in the same repository. With the advent of workflow tools such as Berkshelf (*http://bit.ly/berkshelf*), Chef cookbooks are increasingly being treated as individual artifacts that often live in separate repositories, and Stove makes it easy for Chef users to share these cookbook artifacts with the wider community.

Like `knife cookbook site share`, Stove will create an archive of your cookbook and upload it to the Chef Supermarket. It also supports integration with other systems, such as GitHub and Jira, to allow cookbook version releases to be associated with support tickets, issue tracker tickets, and so on.

These tools neatly cover the packaging and sharing of Chef cookbooks, but as we've seen throughout this book, Chef supports many more customization types. How do we distribute those? Next, we're going to revisit a stalwart of packaging and distributing Ruby code, RubyGems.

RubyGems

Ruby gems are one of the most commonly used packaging formats in the Ruby ecosystem, providing Ruby users with the version artifact creation and sharing behavior we've discussed in this chapter. Unlike cookbooks, however, Ruby gems are not Chef-specific —any Ruby program that provides an executable binary or classes to be required in other Ruby code can be packaged and distributed as a Ruby gem, which is then distributed through the RubyGems (*https://rubygems.org/*) website. This then also makes it available to be installed via the `gem install` command, which is preconfigured to use RubyGems as its default package source.

Back in "RubyGems" on page 42, we saw that when a Ruby gem is installed through the `gem install` command, the classes packaged into that gem are installed under Ruby's `LOAD_PATH`, and any executable binaries specified by the gem are installed under the system `PATH`.

To translate this into the context of Chef customizations, packaging your customization as a Ruby gem is most useful when you will be loading the customization into Chef or other classes using a `require` statement, or supplying a separate executable Ruby script to run your customization. Table 12-2 provides a handy quick reference for the customization types we've covered in this book that fit this usage pattern.

Table 12-2. Customization types suited to gem packaging

Customization type	Packageable as a Ruby gem?	Notes
Ohai plugins	Not Recommended	As we saw in Chapter 4, Ohai loads plugins from a list of specific locations. As Ruby gems are versioned, each new plugin installation or version change means changing the paths in this list. For this reason, packaging Ohai plugins as Ruby gems is not recommended.
Handlers	Yes	As handlers are instantiated in *client.rb* or *solo.rb* in the same way as any other Ruby object, they can easily be packaged as Ruby gems and loaded using a `require` statement.
Formatters	Yes	The above notes for handlers also apply to formatters.
Event dispatcher subscribers	Yes	The above notes for handlers also apply to event dispatcher subscribers.
Cookbooks	No	As cookbooks are added to nodes via the run list and not loaded using `require` statements, they are not easily packaged as Ruby gems.
Knife plugins	Yes	As documented in "Step 2: Load Plugins" on page 268, Knife implements built-in behavior to automatically load plugin classes installed by Ruby gems. Knife plugins are ideally suited to being shared in this format.
API scripts	Yes	When Chef API scripts are shipped as executable binaries or classes to be included in other code, they can be packaged as Ruby gems.

Once you've identified that your customization is a good candidate for packaging as a Ruby gem, however, how do you actually make one? The "Creating Ruby Gems" on page 351 sidebar gives a quick introduction to the Gemspec file that underpins the creation of any Ruby gem, and resources that may be of interest to readers interested in creating Ruby gems of their own.

Creating Ruby Gems

The structure, dependencies, and metadata needed to construct a Ruby gem are contained in a special file known as the Gemspec, which lives at the root of your project's directory structure and is typically named *<projectname>.gemspec*. Example 12-1 shows a sample Gemspec file for a fictional Knife plugin called "knife-foo" that demonstrates the different fields it supports.

Example 12-1. knife-foo.gemspec

```
Gem::Specification.new do |s|
  s.name        = 'knife-foo'
  s.version     = '1.0.0'
  s.date        = '2014-06-24'
  s.summary     = "The knife-foo Knife plugin"
  s.description = "Knife-foo is a Knife plugin that does cool stuff with Chef."
  s.authors     = ["Jon Cowie"]
  s.email       = 'jcowie@etsy.com'
  s.files       = ["lib/chef/knife/foo.rb"] ❶
  s.homepage    = 'http://rubygems.org/gems/knife-foo'
  s.license     = 'MIT'
end
```

❶   As we saw in "Step 2: Load Plugins" on page 268, Knife automatically loads classes under the *lib/chef/knife* directory of any installed Ruby gem. It is for this reason that our *foo.rb* plugin file has been placed under this directory.

Once a Gemspec file has been created, a Ruby gem is created by using the built-in gem build command. This produces a *.gem* file (in our example, we'd get *knife-foo-1.0.0.gem*) that can then be uploaded to RubyGems (*https://rubygems.org/*) and easily installed by RubyGems users.

Covering in detail the many options and tools supported when building Ruby gems would be somewhat out of scope for this chapter, but readers interested in learning more about packaging and distributing their customizations as Ruby gems may wish to read through the "Make your own gem" (*http://bit.ly/make-gem*) guide supplied by Ruby-Gems.org. The excellent *Ruby Cookbook* by Lucas Carlson and Leonard Richardson also contains a section on creating and distributing Ruby gems.

Thus far in this section, we've examined the pros and cons of sharing our customizations as source code without versioned artifacts, and how to create community cookbooks and Ruby gems to package and share customizations. We're going to finish off the section by looking at how to make use of the power of cookbooks to distribute customization types that don't fit either of these formats.

Distribution via Cookbook

When customizing Chef, there will always be situations where packaging mechanisms such as Ruby Gems might not quite fit your use case. If you want to share Ohai plugins, for example, these are loaded from a list of paths given to your chef-client configuration, and installing them from Ruby Gems would necessitate altering this path each time a new plugin or plugin version was installed. Likewise, you may wish to be able to distribute handlers without needing to modify the *client.rb* file to make use of them.

The final customization distribution mechanism we're going to look at in this section takes us back once more to the fundamental building block of Chef—the cookbook.

In Part II of this book, we dealt with a number of customization types that integrate with different stages of the Chef run: Ohai plugins, handlers, formatters, and event dispatcher subscribers. Because these customization types integrate directly with the Chef run, we're able to leverage the power of Chef and Ruby to create cookbooks that can load, and enable these customization types during the Chef run.

Luckily for us, we don't need to create these cookbooks from scratch, either—the clever folks at Chef, Inc. have already created two cookbooks that do a lot of the necessary work:

ohai
> The ohai cookbook (*http://bit.ly/ckbk-ohai*) provides a quick and easy means of Cheffing out Ohai plugins to nodes and rerunning Ohai to ensure that attributes generated by the new plugins are made available in the same Chef run that installs them.

chef_handler
> The chef_handler cookbook (*http://bit.ly/chef-handler*), like the ohai cookbook, provides an LWRP to allow report and exception handlers to be Cheffed onto nodes and enabled during a Chef run, rather than by modifying *client.rb*.

These cookbooks can easily be extended or made dependencies of your own custom cookbooks to allow you to easily distribute your Chef run customizations. When a customization is being distributed as part of a cookbook, of course, you're able to benefit from the built-in support for cookbook versioning and tooling for sharing those cookbooks that we learned about in "Community Cookbooks" on page 348 to create version artifacts and share them with the world.

Summary

In this chapter, we learned about a number of different areas that we need to think about when sharing our customizations with the Chef community. We looked at the importance of documenting our code, and setting expectations of how it will be supported and maintained after it is released. We then examined the importance of sensibly and

---

predictably versioning our customizations before reminding ourselves of the importance of paying attention to the copyright and license under which our customizations are distributed. We finished off the chapter by taking a quick look at the various mechanisms available to us for distributing our customizations.

And with the end of this chapter, dear readers, comes the end of this book. I hope that you've found it useful, and that it's helped deepen your understanding of how Chef can be customized to make it work in the best way for your business. Happy customizing!

Chef API Endpoints and Verbs

Full documentation for the Chef Server API can be found at the Chef Documents (*http://bit.ly/chefdocs-endp*) site, but I've included a list of supported endpoints and verbs here for reference (Table A-1).

Table A-1. Chef server API quick reference

Endpoint	GET	PUT	POST	DELETE
/clients	√	X	√	X
/clients/NAME	√	√	X	√
/cookbooks	√	X	X	X
/cookbooks/NAME	√	X	X	X
/cookbooks/NAME/version	√	√	X	√
/data	√	X	√	X
/data/NAME	√	X	√	X
/data/NAME/ITEM	√	√	X	√
/environments	√	X	√	√
/environments/NAME	√	√	X	√
/environments/NAME/cookbooks/NAME	√	X	X	X
/environments/NAME/cookbook_versions	X	X	√	X
/environments/NAME/cookbooks	√	X	X	X
/environments/NAME/nodes	√	X	X	X
/environments/NAME/recipes	√	X	X	X
/environments/NAME/roles/NAME	√	X	X	X
/nodes	√	X	√	√
/nodes/NAME	√	√	X	√
/principals/NAME	√	X	X	X

Endpoint	GET	PUT	POST	DELETE
/roles	√	X	√	X
/roles/NAME	√	√	X	√
/roles/NAME/environments	√	X	X	X
/roles/NAME/environments/NAME	√	X	X	X
/sandboxes	√	X	X	X
/sandboxes/ID	X	√	X	X
/search	√	X	X	X
/search/INDEX	√	X	√	X
/_status	√	X	X	X
/users	√	√	√	√

Index

Symbols

We'd like to hear your suggestions for improving our indexes. Send email to index@oreilly.com.

About the Author

Jon Cowie is a senior operations engineer at Etsy, where he mixes his love of both coding and operations to try and solve interesting problems. He has created and open sourced a number of projects, including the Chef tools knife-spork and knife-preflight, and has spoken at several of O'Reilly's Velocity conferences.

Colophon

The animal on the cover of *Customizing Chef* is a ruffed grouse (*Bonasa umbellus*). The ruffed grouse is a non-migratory bird that ranges from the northeastern United States to northern Alaska and Canada. It is also the state bird of Pennsylvania.

Although the bird is sometimes identified incorrectly as a grey partridge, it does have a variety of nicknames, including the "prairie chicken," "drummer," or "thunderchicken." Ruffed grouses can be either grey or brown, and both sexes have the ruff on the side of the head for which the species is named. In fact, the sexes have similar markings and are the same size, which makes them difficult to tell apart, even at close range. Females and males alike display their fanned tail feathers when courting or frightened, which is often accompanied by the rapid beating of their wings that creates a low-frequency sound that travels for a quarter mile or more.

The ruffed grouse spends most of its time on the ground, and seems to have a particular affinity for thick brush, aspen stands, and the clover bushes along road beds. Grouse hunting is still common over much of the northern and western United States and in Canada, and is often done with shotguns or dogs. Despite this, the population remains healthy and follows a pattern of prosperity and decline that is still a mystery to scientists, who refer to it simply as "the grouse cycle."

Many of the animals on O'Reilly covers are endangered; all of them are important to the world. To learn more about how you can help, go to animals.oreilly.com.

The cover image is from Tenney's *Elements of Zoology*. The cover fonts are URW Typewriter and Guardian Sans. The text font is Adobe Minion Pro; the heading font is Adobe Myriad Condensed; and the code font is Dalton Maag's Ubuntu Mono.

Get even more for your money.

Join the O'Reilly Community, and register the O'Reilly books you own. It's free, and you'll get:

- $4.99 ebook upgrade offer
- 40% upgrade offer on O'Reilly print books
- Membership discounts on books and events
- Free lifetime updates to ebooks and videos
- Multiple ebook formats, DRM FREE
- Participation in the O'Reilly community
- Newsletters
- Account management
- 100% Satisfaction Guarantee

Signing up is easy:

1. Go to: oreilly.com/go/register
2. Create an O'Reilly login.
3. Provide your address.
4. Register your books.

Note: English-language books only

To order books online:
oreilly.com/store

For questions about products or an order:
orders@oreilly.com

To sign up to get topic-specific email announcements and/or news about upcoming books, conferences, special offers, and new technologies:
elists@oreilly.com

For technical questions about book content:
booktech@oreilly.com

To submit new book proposals to our editors:
proposals@oreilly.com

O'Reilly books are available in multiple DRM-free ebook formats. For more information:
oreilly.com/ebooks

O'REILLY®

Have it your way.

Lightning Source UK Ltd.
Milton Keynes UK
UKOW06f1934031114

240937UK00003B/13/P